FREE Study Skills Videos/DVD Offer

Dear Customer,

Thank you for your purchase from Mometrix! We consider it an honor and a privilege that you have purchased our product and we want to ensure your satisfaction.

As part of our ongoing effort to meet the needs of test takers, we have developed a set of Study Skills Videos that we would like to give you for <u>FREE</u>. These videos cover our *best practices* for getting ready for your exam, from how to use our study materials to how to best prepare for the day of the test.

All that we ask is that you email us with feedback that would describe your experience so far with our product. Good, bad, or indifferent, we want to know what you think!

To get your FREE Study Skills Videos, you can use the **QR code** below, or send us an **email** at studyvideos@mometrix.com with *FREE VIDEOS* in the subject line and the following information in the body of the email:

- The name of the product you purchased.
- Your product rating on a scale of 1-5, with 5 being the highest rating.
- Your feedback. It can be long, short, or anything in between. We just want to know your impressions and experience so far with our product. (Good feedback might include how our study material met your needs and ways we might be able to make it even better. You could highlight features that you found helpful or features that you think we should add.)

If you have any questions or concerns, please don't hesitate to contact me directly.

Thanks again!

Sincerely,

Jay Willis
Vice President
jay.willis@mometrix.com
1-800-673-8175

MFT

Study Guide

3 Full-Length Practice Tests

Secrets Review for the
Marriage and Family Therapy
National Licensing Exam

2nd Edition

Written and edited by the Mometrix Test Prep

Printed in the United States of America

This paper meets the requirements of ANSI/NISO Z39.48-1992 (Permanence of Paper).

Mometrix offers volume discount pricing to institutions. For more information or a price quote, please contact our sales department at sales@mometrix.com or 888-248-1219.

Mometrix Media LLC is not affiliated with or endorsed by any official testing organization. All organizational and test names are trademarks of their respective owners.

Paperback
ISBN 13: 978-1-5167-2365-2
ISBN 10: 1-5167-2365-1

DEAR FUTURE EXAM SUCCESS STORY

First of all, **THANK YOU** for purchasing Mometrix study materials!

Second, congratulations! You are one of the few determined test-takers who are committed to doing whatever it takes to excel on your exam. **You have come to the right place.** We developed these study materials with one goal in mind: to deliver you the information you need in a format that's concise and easy to use.

In addition to optimizing your guide for the content of the test, we've outlined our recommended steps for breaking down the preparation process into small, attainable goals so you can make sur you stay on track.

We've also analyzed the entire test-taking process, identifying the most common pitfalls and showing how you can overcome them and be ready for any curveball the test throws you.

Standardized testing is one of the biggest obstacles on your road to success, which only increases the importance of doing well in the high-pressure, high-stakes environment of test day. Your results on this test could have a significant impact on your future, and this guide provides the information and practical advice to help you achieve your full potential on test day.

Your success is our success

We would love to hear from you! If you would like to share the story of your exam success or if you have any questions or comments in regard to our products, please contact us at **800-673-8175** or **support@mometrix.com**.

Thanks again for your business and we wish you continued success!

Sincerely,
The Mometrix Test Preparation Team

Need more help? Check out our flashcards at:
http://mometrixflashcards.com/MFT

TABLE OF CONTENTS

Introduction

Thank you for purchasing this resource! You have made the choice to prepare yourself for a test that could have a huge impact on your future, and this guide is designed to help you be fully ready for test day. Obviously, it's important to have a solid understanding of the test material, but you also need to be prepared for the unique environment and stressors of the test, so that you can perform to the best of your abilities.

For this purpose, the first section that appears in this guide is the **Secret Keys**. We've devoted countless hours to meticulously researching what works and what doesn't, and we've boiled down our findings to the five most impactful steps you can take to improve your performance on the test. We start at the beginning with study planning and move through the preparation process, all the way to the testing strategies that will help you get the most out of what you know when you're finally sitting in front of the test.

We recommend that you start preparing for your test as far in advance as possible. However, if you've bought this guide as a last-minute study resource and only have a few days before your test, we recommend that you skip over the first two Secret Keys since they address a long-term study plan.

If you struggle with **test anxiety**, we strongly encourage you to check out our recommendations for how you can overcome it. Test anxiety is a formidable foe, but it can be beaten, and we want to make sure you have the tools you need to defeat it.

Secret Key #1 – Plan Big, Study Small

There's a lot riding on your performance. If you want to ace this test, you're going to need to keep your skills sharp and the material fresh in your mind. You need a plan that lets you review everything you need to know while still fitting in your schedule. We'll break this strategy down into three categories.

Information Organization

Start with the information you already have: the official test outline. From this, you can make a complete list of all the concepts you need to cover before the test. Organize these concepts into groups that can be studied together, and create a list of any related vocabulary you need to learn so you can brush up on any difficult terms. You'll want to keep this vocabulary list handy once you actually start studying since you may need to add to it along the way.

Time Management

Once you have your set of study concepts, decide how to spread them out over the time you have left before the test. Break your study plan into small, clear goals so you have a manageable task for each day and know exactly what you're doing. Then just focus on one small step at a time. When you manage your time this way, you don't need to spend hours at a time studying. Studying a small block of content for a short period each day helps you retain information better and avoid stressing over how much you have left to do. You can relax knowing that you have a plan to cover everything in time. In order for this strategy to be effective though, you have to start studying early and stick to your schedule. Avoid the exhaustion and futility that comes from last-minute cramming!

Study Environment

The environment you study in has a big impact on your learning. Studying in a coffee shop, while probably more enjoyable, is not likely to be as fruitful as studying in a quiet room. It's important to keep distractions to a minimum. You're only planning to study for a short block of time, so make the most of it. Don't pause to check your phone or get up to find a snack. It's also important to **avoid multitasking**. Research has consistently shown that multitasking will make your studying dramatically less effective. Your study area should also be comfortable and well-lit so you don't have the distraction of straining your eyes or sitting on an uncomfortable chair.

 The time of day you study is also important. You want to be rested and alert. Don't wait until just before bedtime. Study when you'll be most likely to comprehend and remember. Even better, if you know what time of day your test will be, set that time aside for study. That way your brain will be used to working on that subject at that specific time and you'll have a better chance of recalling information.

Finally, it can be helpful to team up with others who are studying for the same test. Your actual studying should be done in as isolated an environment as possible, but the work of organizing the information and setting up the study plan can be divided up. In between study sessions, you can discuss with your teammates the concepts that you're all studying and quiz each other on the details. Just be sure that your teammates are as serious about the test as you are. If you find that your study time is being replaced with social time, you might need to find a new team.

Secret Key #2 – Make Your Studying Count

You're devoting a lot of time and effort to preparing for this test, so you want to be absolutely certain it will pay off. This means doing more than just reading the content and hoping you can remember it on test day. It's important to make every minute of study count. There are two main areas you can focus on to make your studying count.

Retention

It doesn't matter how much time you study if you can't remember the material. You need to make sure you are retaining the concepts. To check your retention of the information you're learning, try recalling it at later times with minimal prompting. Try carrying around flashcards and glance at one or two from time to time or ask a friend who's also studying for the test to quiz you.

To enhance your retention, look for ways to put the information into practice so that you can apply it rather than simply recalling it. If you're using the information in practical ways, it will be much easier to remember. Similarly, it helps to solidify a concept in your mind if you're not only reading it to yourself but also explaining it to someone else. Ask a friend to let you teach them about a concept you're a little shaky on (or speak aloud to an imaginary audience if necessary). As you try to summarize, define, give examples, and answer your friend's questions, you'll understand the concepts better and they will stay with you longer. Finally, step back for a big picture view and ask yourself how each piece of information fits with the whole subject. When you link the different concepts together and see them working together as a whole, it's easier to remember the individual components.

Finally, practice showing your work on any multi-step problems, even if you're just studying. Writing out each step you take to solve a problem will help solidify the process in your mind, and you'll be more likely to remember it during the test.

Modality

Modality simply refers to the means or method by which you study. Choosing a study modality that fits your own individual learning style is crucial. No two people learn best in exactly the same way, so it's important to know your strengths and use them to your advantage.

For example, if you learn best by visualization, focus on visualizing a concept in your mind and draw an image or a diagram. Try color-coding your notes, illustrating them, or creating symbols that will trigger your mind to recall a learned concept. If you learn best by hearing or discussing information, find a study partner who learns the same way or read aloud to yourself. Think about how to put the information in your own words. Imagine that you are giving a lecture on the topic and record yourself so you can listen to it later.

For any learning style, flashcards can be helpful. Organize the information so you can take advantage of spare moments to review. Underline key words or phrases. Use different colors for different categories. Mnemonic devices (such as creating a short list in which every item starts with the same letter) can also help with retention. Find what works best for you and use it to store the information in your mind most effectively and easily.

Secret Key #3 – Practice the Right Way

Your success on test day depends not only on how many hours you put into preparing, but also on whether you prepared the right way. It's good to check along the way to see if your studying is paying off. One of the most effective ways to do this is by taking practice tests to evaluate your progress. Practice tests are useful because they show exactly where you need to improve. Every time you take a practice test, pay special attention to these three groups of questions:

- The questions you got wrong
- The questions you had to guess on, even if you guessed right
- The questions you found difficult or slow to work through

This will show you exactly what your weak areas are, and where you need to devote more study time. Ask yourself why each of these questions gave you trouble. Was it because you didn't understand the material? Was it because you didn't remember the vocabulary? Do you need more repetitions on this type of question to build speed and confidence? Dig into those questions and figure out how you can strengthen your weak areas as you go back to review the material.

 Additionally, many practice tests have a section explaining the answer choices. It can be tempting to read the explanation and think that you now have a good understanding of the concept. However, an explanation likely only covers part of the question's broader context. Even if the explanation makes perfect sense, **go back and investigate** every concept related to the question until you're positive you have a thorough understanding.

As you go along, keep in mind that the practice test is just that: practice. Memorizing these questions and answers will not be very helpful on the actual test because it is unlikely to have any of the same exact questions. If you only know the right answers to the sample questions, you won't be prepared for the real thing. **Study the concepts** until you understand them fully, and then you'll be able to answer any question that shows up on the test.

It's important to wait on the practice tests until you're ready. If you take a test on your first day of study, you may be overwhelmed by the amount of material covered and how much you need to learn. Work up to it gradually.

On test day, you'll need to be prepared for answering questions, managing your time, and using the test-taking strategies you've learned. It's a lot to balance, like a mental marathon that will have a big impact on your future. Like training for a marathon, you'll need to start slowly and work your way up. When test day arrives, you'll be ready.

Start with the strategies you've read in the first two Secret Keys—plan your course and study in the way that works best for you. If you have time, consider using multiple study resources to get different approaches to the same concepts. It can be helpful to see difficult concepts from more than one angle. Then find a good source for practice tests. Many times, the test website will suggest potential study resources or provide sample tests.

Practice Test Strategy

If you're able to find at least three practice tests, we recommend this strategy:

UNTIMED AND OPEN-BOOK PRACTICE

Take the first test with no time constraints and with your notes and study guide handy. Take your time and focus on applying the strategies you've learned.

TIMED AND OPEN-BOOK PRACTICE

Take the second practice test open-book as well, but set a timer and practice pacing yourself to finish in time.

TIMED AND CLOSED-BOOK PRACTICE

Take any other practice tests as if it were test day. Set a timer and put away your study materials. Sit at a table or desk in a quiet room, imagine yourself at the testing center, and answer questions as quickly and accurately as possible.

Keep repeating timed and closed-book tests on a regular basis until you run out of practice tests or it's time for the actual test. Your mind will be ready for the schedule and stress of test day, and you'll be able to focus on recalling the material you've learned.

Secret Key #4 – Pace Yourself

Once you're fully prepared for the material on the test, your biggest challenge on test day will be managing your time. Just knowing that the clock is ticking can make you panic even if you have plenty of time left. Work on pacing yourself so you can build confidence against the time constraints of the exam. Pacing is a difficult skill to master, especially in a high-pressure environment, so **practice is vital**.

Set time expectations for your pace based on how much time is available. For example, if a section has 60 questions and the time limit is 30 minutes, you know you have to average 30 seconds or less per question in order to answer them all. Although 30 seconds is the hard limit, set 25 seconds per question as your goal, so you reserve extra time to spend on harder questions. When you budget extra time for the harder questions, you no longer have any reason to stress when those questions take longer to answer.

Don't let this time expectation distract you from working through the test at a calm, steady pace, but keep it in mind so you don't spend too much time on any one question. Recognize that taking extra time on one question you don't understand may keep you from answering two that you do understand later in the test. If your time limit for a question is up and you're still not sure of the answer, mark it and move on, and come back to it later if the time and the test format allow. If the testing format doesn't allow you to return to earlier questions, just make an educated guess; then put it out of your mind and move on.

On the easier questions, be careful not to rush. It may seem wise to hurry through them so you have more time for the challenging ones, but it's not worth missing one if you know the concept and just didn't take the time to read the question fully. Work efficiently but make sure you understand the question and have looked at all of the answer choices, since more than one may seem right at first.

Even if you're paying attention to the time, you may find yourself a little behind at some point. You should speed up to get back on track, but do so wisely. Don't panic; just take a few seconds less on each question until you're caught up. Don't guess without thinking, but do look through the answer choices and eliminate any you know are wrong. If you can get down to two choices, it is often worthwhile to guess from those. Once you've chosen an answer, move on and don't dwell on any that you skipped or had to hurry through. If a question was taking too long, chances are it was one of the harder ones, so you weren't as likely to get it right anyway.

On the other hand, if you find yourself getting ahead of schedule, it may be beneficial to slow down a little. The more quickly you work, the more likely you are to make a careless mistake that will affect your score. You've budgeted time for each question, so don't be afraid to spend that time. Practice an efficient but careful pace to get the most out of the time you have.

6

Secret Key #5 – Have a Plan for Guessing

When you're taking the test, you may find yourself stuck on a question. Some of the answer choices seem better than others, but you don't see the one answer choice that is obviously correct. What do you do?

The scenario described above is very common, yet most test takers have not effectively prepared for it. Developing and practicing a plan for guessing may be one of the single most effective uses of your time as you get ready for the exam.

In developing your plan for guessing, there are three questions to address:

- When should you start the guessing process?
- How should you narrow down the choices?
- Which answer should you choose?

When to Start the Guessing Process

Unless your plan for guessing is to select C every time (which, despite its merits, is not what we recommend), you need to leave yourself enough time to apply your answer elimination strategies. Since you have a limited amount of time for each question, that means that if you're going to give yourself the best shot at guessing correctly, you have to decide quickly whether or not you will guess.

Of course, the best-case scenario is that you don't have to guess at all, so first, see if you can answer the question based on your knowledge of the subject and basic reasoning skills. Focus on the key words in the question and try to jog your memory of related topics. Give yourself a chance to bring the knowledge to mind, but once you realize that you don't have (or you can't access) the knowledge you need to answer the question, it's time to start the guessing process.

It's almost always better to start the guessing process too early than too late. It only takes a few seconds to remember something and answer the question from knowledge. Carefully eliminating wrong answer choices takes longer. Plus, going through the process of eliminating answer choices can actually help jog your memory.

Summary: Start the guessing process as soon as you decide that you can't answer the question based on your knowledge.

7

How to Narrow Down the Choices

The next chapter in this book (**Test-Taking Strategies**) includes a wide range of strategies for how to approach questions and how to look for answer choices to eliminate. You will definitely want to read those carefully, practice them, and figure out which ones work best for you. Here though, we're going to address a mindset rather than a particular strategy.

Your odds of guessing an answer correctly depend on how many options you are choosing from.

Number of options left	5	4	3	2	1
Odds of guessing correctly	20%	25%	33%	50%	100%

You can see from this chart just how valuable it is to be able to eliminate incorrect answers and make an educated guess, but there are two things that many test takers do that cause them to miss out on the benefits of guessing:

- Accidentally eliminating the correct answer
- Selecting an answer based on an impression

We'll look at the first one here, and the second one in the next section.

To avoid accidentally eliminating the correct answer, we recommend a thought exercise called **the $5 challenge**. In this challenge, you only eliminate an answer choice from contention if you are willing to bet $5 on it being wrong. Why $5? Five dollars is a small but not insignificant amount of money. It's an amount you could afford to lose but wouldn't want to throw away. And while losing

$5 once might not hurt too much, doing it twenty times will set you back $100. In the same way, each small decision you make—eliminating a choice here, guessing on a question there—won't by itself impact your score very much, but when you put them all together, they can make a big difference. By holding each answer choice elimination decision to a higher standard, you can reduce the risk of accidentally eliminating the correct answer.

The $5 challenge can also be applied in a positive sense: If you are willing to bet $5 that an answer choice *is* correct, go ahead and mark it as correct.

Summary: Only eliminate an answer choice if you are willing to bet $5 that it is wrong.

8

Which Answer to Choose

You're taking the test. You've run into a hard question and decided you'll have to guess. You've eliminated all the answer choices you're willing to bet $5 on. Now you have to pick an answer. Why do we even need to talk about this? Why can't you just pick whichever one you feel like when the time comes?

The answer to these questions is that if you don't come into the test with a plan, you'll rely on your impression to select an answer choice, and if you do that, you risk falling into a trap. The test writers know that everyone who takes their test will be guessing on some of the questions, so they intentionally write wrong answer choices to seem plausible. You still have to pick an answer though, and if the wrong answer choices are designed to look right, how can you ever be sure that you're not falling for their trap? The best solution we've found to this dilemma is to take the decision out of your hands entirely. Here is the process we recommend:

Once you've eliminated any choices that you are confident (willing to bet $5) are wrong, select the first remaining choice as your answer.

Whether you choose to select the first remaining choice, the second, or the last, the important thing is that you use some preselected standard. Using this approach guarantees that you will not be enticed into selecting an answer choice that looks right, because you are not basing your decision on how the answer choices look.

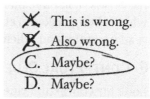

This is not meant to make you question your knowledge. Instead, it is to help you recognize the difference between your knowledge and your impressions. There's a huge difference between thinking an answer is right because of what you know, and thinking an answer is right because it looks or sounds like it should be right.

Summary: To ensure that your selection is appropriately random, make a predetermined selection from among all answer choices you have not eliminated.

9

Test-Taking Strategies

This section contains a list of test-taking strategies that you may find helpful as you work through the test. By taking what you know and applying logical thought, you can maximize your chances of answering any question correctly!

It is very important to realize that every question is different and every person is different: no single strategy will work on every question, and no single strategy will work for every person. That's why we've included all of them here, so you can try them out and determine which ones work best for different types of questions and which ones work best for you.

Question Strategies

⊘ READ CAREFULLY

Read the question and the answer choices carefully. Don't miss the question because you misread the terms. You have plenty of time to read each question thoroughly and make sure you understand what is being asked. Yet a happy medium must be attained, so don't waste too much time. You must read carefully and efficiently.

⊘ CONTEXTUAL CLUES

Look for contextual clues. If the question includes a word you are not familiar with, look at the immediate context for some indication of what the word might mean. Contextual clues can often give you all the information you need to decipher the meaning of an unfamiliar word. Even if you can't determine the meaning, you may be able to narrow down the possibilities enough to make a solid guess at the answer to the question.

⊘ PREFIXES

If you're having trouble with a word in the question or answer choices, try dissecting it. Take advantage of every clue that the word might include. Prefixes can be a huge help. Usually, they allow you to determine a basic meaning. *Pre-* means before, *post-* means after, *pro-* is positive, *de-* is negative. From prefixes, you can get an idea of the general meaning of the word and try to put it into context.

⊘ HEDGE WORDS

Watch out for critical hedge words, such as *likely, may, can, sometimes, often, almost, mostly, usually, generally, rarely,* and *sometimes.* Question writers insert these hedge phrases to cover every possibility. Often an answer choice will be wrong simply because it leaves no room for exception. Be on guard for answer choices that have definitive words such as *exactly* and *always.*

⊘ SWITCHBACK WORDS

Stay alert for *switchbacks*. These are the words and phrases frequently used to alert you to shifts in thought. The most common switchback words are *but, although,* and *however.* Others include *nevertheless, on the other hand, even though, while, in spite of, despite,* and *regardless of.* Switchback words are important to catch because they can change the direction of the question or an answer choice.

⊘ FACE VALUE

When in doubt, use common sense. Accept the situation in the problem at face value. Don't read too much into it. These problems will not require you to make wild assumptions. If you have to go beyond creativity and warp time or space in order to have an answer choice fit the question, then you should move on and consider the other answer choices. These are normal problems rooted in reality. The applicable relationship or explanation may not be readily apparent, but it is there for you to figure out. Use your common sense to interpret anything that isn't clear.

Answer Choice Strategies

⊘ ANSWER SELECTION

The most thorough way to pick an answer choice is to identify and eliminate wrong answers until only one is left, then confirm it is the correct answer. Sometimes an answer choice may immediately seem right, but be careful. The test writers will usually put more than one reasonable answer choice on each question, so take a second to read all of them and make sure that the other choices are not equally obvious. As long as you have time left, it is better to read every answer choice than to pick the first one that looks right without checking the others.

⊘ ANSWER CHOICE FAMILIES

An answer choice family consists of two (in rare cases, three) answer choices that are very similar in construction and cannot all be true at the same time. If you see two answer choices that are direct opposites or parallels, one of them is usually the correct answer. For instance, if one answer choice says that quantity x increases and another either says that quantity x decreases (opposite) or says that quantity y increases (parallel), then those answer choices would fall into the same family. An answer choice that doesn't match the construction of the answer choice family is more likely to be incorrect. Most questions will not have answer choice families, but when they do appear, you should be prepared to recognize them.

⊘ ELIMINATE ANSWERS

Eliminate answer choices as soon as you realize they are wrong, but make sure you consider all possibilities. If you are eliminating answer choices and realize that the last one you are left with is also wrong, don't panic. Start over and consider each choice again. There may be something you missed the first time that you will realize on the second pass.

⊘ AVOID FACT TRAPS

Don't be distracted by an answer choice that is factually true but doesn't answer the question. You are looking for the choice that answers the question. Stay focused on what the question is asking for so you don't accidentally pick an answer that is true but incorrect. Always go back to the question and make sure the answer choice you've selected actually answers the question and is not merely a true statement.

⊘ EXTREME STATEMENTS

In general, you should avoid answers that put forth extreme actions as standard practice or proclaim controversial ideas as established fact. An answer choice that states the "process should be used in certain situations, if..." is much more likely to be correct than one that states the "process should be discontinued completely." The first is a calm rational statement and doesn't even make a definitive, uncompromising stance, using a hedge word *if* to provide wiggle room, whereas the second choice is far more extreme.

☑ BENCHMARK

As you read through the answer choices and you come across one that seems to answer the question well, mentally select that answer choice. This is not your final answer, but it's the one that will help you evaluate the other answer choices. The one that you selected is your benchmark or standard for judging each of the other answer choices. Every other answer choice must be compared to your benchmark. That choice is correct until proven otherwise by another answer choice beating it. If you find a better answer, then that one becomes your new benchmark. Once you've decided that no other choice answers the question as well as your benchmark, you have your final answer.

☑ PREDICT THE ANSWER

Before you even start looking at the answer choices, it is often best to try to predict the answer. When you come up with the answer on your own, it is easier to avoid distractions and traps because you will know exactly what to look for. The right answer choice is unlikely to be word-for-word what you came up with, but it should be a close match. Even if you are confident that you have the right answer, you should still take the time to read each option before moving on.

General Strategies

☑ TOUGH QUESTIONS

If you are stumped on a problem or it appears too hard or too difficult, don't waste time. Move on! Remember though, if you can quickly check for obviously incorrect answer choices, your chances of guessing correctly are greatly improved. Before you completely give up, at least try to knock out a couple of possible answers. Eliminate what you can and then guess at the remaining answer choices before moving on.

☑ CHECK YOUR WORK

Since you will probably not know every term listed and the answer to every question, it is important that you get credit for the ones that you do know. Don't miss any questions through careless mistakes. If at all possible, try to take a second to look back over your answer selection and make sure you've selected the correct answer choice and haven't made a costly careless mistake (such as marking an answer choice that you didn't mean to mark). This quick double check should more than pay for itself in caught mistakes for the time it costs.

☑ PACE YOURSELF

It's easy to be overwhelmed when you're looking at a page full of questions; your mind is confused and full of random thoughts, and the clock is ticking down faster than you would like. Calm down and maintain the pace that you have set for yourself. Especially as you get down to the last few minutes of the test, don't let the small numbers on the clock make you panic. As long as you are on track by monitoring your pace, you are guaranteed to have time for each question.

☑ DON'T RUSH

It is very easy to make errors when you are in a hurry. Maintaining a fast pace in answering questions is pointless if it makes you miss questions that you would have gotten right otherwise. Test writers like to include distracting information and wrong answers that seem right. Taking a little extra time to avoid careless mistakes can make all the difference in your test score. Find a pace that allows you to be confident in the answers that you select.

12

⊘ KEEP MOVING

Panicking will not help you pass the test, so do your best to stay calm and keep moving. Taking deep breaths and going through the answer elimination steps you practiced can help to break through a stress barrier and keep your pace.

Final Notes

The combination of a solid foundation of content knowledge and the confidence that comes from practicing your plan for applying that knowledge is the key to maximizing your performance on test day. As your foundation of content knowledge is built up and strengthened, you'll find that the strategies included in this chapter become more and more effective in helping you quickly sift through the distractions and traps of the test to isolate the correct answer.

Now that you're preparing to move forward into the test content chapters of this book, be sure to keep your goal in mind. As you read, think about how you will be able to apply this information on the test. If you've already seen sample questions for the test and you have an idea of the question format and style, try to come up with questions of your own that you can answer based on what you're reading. This will give you valuable practice applying your knowledge in the same ways you can expect to on test day.

Good luck and good studying!

14

The Practice of Systemic Therapy

Systemic Theory and Clinical Practice

RESPECTING DIVERSITY AND JUSTICE WITHIN SYSTEMIC THERAPY TREATMENT

Systemic therapists respect **diversity** by acknowledging and appreciating each client's contextual factors, including sexual orientation, gender/gender identity, race/ethnicity, age, religion, abilities, and other identifying characteristics and intersectional frameworks.

Therapists promote **justice** through inclusion and the promotion of equity for all. Justice involves actively identifying and addressing the dynamic influence of systems of power and privilege on the client's presenting problem, contextual relationships, and the therapeutic relationship. Systemic therapists promote **social justice** by actively working to address and reduce the complex contributions of historical factors leading to marginalization, privilege, oppression, and discrimination. Social justice attempts to heal the harms done to others due to power differentials and disparities. The practice of social justice aims to restore and maintain fair and impartial access to opportunities and resources for all individuals within all social and cultural contexts.

CREATING A SAFE, NONJUDGMENTAL ATMOSPHERE WITHIN SYSTEMIC THERAPY

The marriage and family therapist (MFT) is ethically responsible for creating a therapeutic environment. The physical environment must facilitate confidentiality while fostering an environment conducive for trust building. Physical settings that are quiet, clean and clear of clutter, and include structures/systems to prevent interruptions are foundational to a therapeutic environment. Maintaining appropriate boundaries and providing personal space are necessary activities for fostering trust and engaging the client in treatment. Therapists must be cognizant of the influence of social and cultural factors on personal space and nonverbal interactions.

The therapist's ability to create a nonjudgmental atmosphere and therapeutic alliance is measured by the client–therapist bond, the collaborative nature of the relationship, and a mutual agreement on treatment goals. A trusting therapeutic relationship is associated with successful treatment outcomes. Trust and the belief that the therapist's methods are efficacious and pertinent are the foundations of ethical and responsible client care. Therapists must also aspire to build trust during the informed consent process, ensuring that it is transparent, straightforward, and delivered in language best understood by the client. Nonjudgmental attitudes are those in which clients feel validated, understood, and free to be their authentic selves. Therapists often reflect this by showing empathy, unconditional positive regard, and genuineness.

INTERACTIONAL PROCESS BETWEEN THE THERAPIST AND CLIENT

The therapeutic relationship is cultivated by trust, collaboration, and connection. Incorporating systemic theory and practice includes engaging with the client and the client's system in a respectful, caring, and flexible manner. The therapist must skillfully form multiple alliances within systems. The therapeutic bond can be measured by the extent to which all members feel supported and share in the purpose and goals of therapy. Therapists must be careful not to split alliances by engaging and connecting with some family members while avoiding or alienating others.

Therapists who obtain client feedback and possess appropriate competencies help instill clinical confidence and trust. It is also necessary to address roadblocks or factors that have the potential to cause a therapeutic rupture. Therapeutic ruptures may occur if a client feels unheard or unsupported. Repairing therapeutic ruptures enhances the working alliance and improves treatment outcomes. Critical components of the therapeutic relationship also include unconditional positive regard, empathy, authenticity, attunement to here-and-now emotional experiences, and remaining actively engaged and responsive.

Individual-Based Theory and Therapy Models

PERSON-CENTERED THERAPY AND GESTALT THERAPY

Carl Rogers is credited with developing person-centered therapy. Rogerian therapists take a nondirective approach to help clients achieve congruence between their self-image and ideal self (i.e., what they aspire to be). When this goal is reached, the client becomes a fully functioning person and is said to reach a state of self-actualization. Client-centered therapists help their clients reach self-actualization by expressing the following:

- **Genuineness:** Genuineness is the attitude conveyed when a counselor's internal processes are congruent with their external expressions.
- **Unconditional positive regard:** This involves counselors showing complete acceptance of the client as is—without judgment or disappointment.
- **Empathetic understanding:** Empathetic understanding is the counselor's ability to reflect the client's underlying feelings and view things from the client's perspective.

INDIVIDUAL-BASED THEORY AND THERAPY MODELS FOR GESTALT THERAPY

Developed by Fritz Perls, Gestalt therapy emphasizes personal responsibility, present-moment awareness, and successful integration of the smaller parts of a whole ("gestalts"). The main goal of Gestalt therapy is to help a client achieve maturity (self-responsibility) and integration (the ability to function as a systematic whole).

Gestalt techniques include all of the following:

- **Assuming responsibility:** Clients are asked to add the phrase "..., and I take responsibility for it" to the end of statements to increase personal responsibility for their thoughts, feelings, and actions.
- **Games of dialogue:** This is a psychodrama technique in which the therapist and client role-play bipolar personalities known as "top dog/bottom dog."
- **The "empty chair" technique:** This technique relies on projection to help clients build awareness, resolve interpersonal conflict, and process difficult emotions.

RATIONAL EMOTIVE BEHAVIOR THERAPY (REBT)

Albert Ellis is credited with developing rational emotive behavior therapy (REBT), which is based on the assumption that irrational or self-defeating beliefs serve as roadblocks to change by impeding progress and keeping the client "stuck." REBT emphasizes that irrational or self-defeating beliefs are created by engaging in "awfulizing" and "terriblizing." REBT therapists stress the importance of taking personal responsibility to defeat irrational beliefs. This is accomplished by helping clients transform "failure identities" into "success identities."

REBT uses the ABCDE model to challenge irrational thoughts. This is illustrated by having the client identify the following:

- A: Activating event
- B: Beliefs about the activating event
- C: Consequences of the beliefs
- D: Disputing the belief
- E: Effective behavior

STRENGTHS-BASED RESILIENCY (SBR)

Strengths-based resiliency (SBR) refers to the personal, environmental, social, and cognitive assets and resources a person possesses to successfully meet challenging life experiences. SBR is a dynamic process involving two conditions: (1) an adverse event or threat and (2) the ability to "bounce back" and recover from such difficulties. SBR is an individualized and interactive process that affirms a person's ability to grow and change through flexible thinking and improved self-efficacy. Therapists can help build SBR by identifying and accessing the client's intrapersonal and interpersonal strengths and resources within the client's system.

For children and adolescents, SBR involves a counterbalance between negative and positive environmental factors in a child's life. Positive factors include responsive relationships, financial resources, and skilled caregivers. Negative factors include abuse and neglect, poverty, mental illness, and a lack of educational success or support. SBR can be built by accessing positive resources in a child's system, which include supportive adults in the child's school, family, and community. Positive socioemotional contextual variables (i.e., assets and resources) are useful for developing SBR.

Theories of Human Development

HUMAN DEVELOPMENT THEORIES AS THEY RELATE TO ATTACHMENT

Human development is a complex process with multiple biopsychosocial domains of influence. In early childhood, attachment, or the infant–mother bond, can be viewed through the lens of various theorists, including the following:

- **Sigmund Freud** believed that attachment results from the mother's ability to meet the child's basic physiological needs (e.g., hunger) and oral stimulation. In Freud's oral stage of psychosocial development (ages 0–18 months), the infant's need for oral stimulation must be gratified in order to proceed to the next stage of development.
- **Erik Erikson** claimed that attachment is formed during the trust versus mistrust stage of psychosocial development (ages 0–18 months). Erikson believed that the primary caregiver instills trust in an infant by consistently responding to the infant's physical and psychological needs. A trusting parent–infant bond leads to safe and secure attachments later in life.
- **Harry Harlow** experimented with rhesus monkeys and found that monkeys preferred a cloth surrogate mother over a wire mesh mother who provided food, arguing that infants form attachments with primary caregivers who provide touch and tactile comfort.
- **John Bowlby's** attachment theory points to the infant–caregiver bond as the foundation of an individual's emotional, social, and psychological well-being throughout life. Bowlby proved that attachment develops as the result of a primary caregiver's ability to (1) serve as a secure base for the infant, allowing the infant to explore the surrounding environment safely and (2) actively engage in enjoyable interactions with the child.

MARY AINSWORTH'S THEORY OF ATTACHMENT

Mary Ainsworth expanded upon John Bowlby's theory of attachment using the "strange situation" experiment to identify three main attachment styles that shape adult behavior. Ainsworth's experiment measured infant responses and interactional behaviors at various intervals. Each interval involved a series of steps during which an infant, mother, and stranger are introduced, briefly separated, and then reunified.

The study begins with the infant and mother being left alone in a playroom. While the infant begins exploring the environment, a stranger enters and briefly talks with the mother. The mother then leaves the room quietly, leaving the infant with the stranger. The final step involves the mother returning to the room to be reunited with her child.

The experimental observations led to Ainsworth's classification of attachment styles as secure, insecure avoidant, and insecure resistant/ambivalent.

TYPES OF ATTACHMENT STYLES PUT FORTH BY MARY AINSWORTH

The three attachment styles that resulted from Mary Ainsworth's experiments include:

Secure attachment	Infants who displayed secure attachment expressed initial distress upon separation from their mothers. When the stranger attempted to console the infant, the infant resisted. Upon reunification with the mother, the infant returned to safely exploring the environment and became friendly with the stranger. Adults with secure attachments have the ability to form safe, trusting, and intimate relationships with others.
Insecure-avoidant attachment	Infants who displayed insecure-avoidant attachment showed no signs of distress when the mother left, interacted with the stranger during the mother's absence, and remained disinterested when the mother returned. Adults with insecure-avoidant attachment fear abandonment and approach intimate relationships with hesitancy.
Insecure resistant/ambivalent attachment	Infants who displayed insecure or ambivalent attachment responded with intense distress upon separation from their mothers. The infant reacted fearfully to the stranger and rejected the mother's attempt to provide comfort. Adults with insecure resistant/ambivalent attachment styles avoid intimate relationships and believe in self-sufficiency.

TYPE OF ATTACHMENT STYLE ADDED BY MARY MAIN AND JUDITH SOLOMON

Of note, researchers Mary Main and Judith Solomon later added **disorganized/disoriented** as an attachment style. Infants with this attachment style appear fearful and avoidant. Children with disorganized and disoriented attachment are often the victims of childhood abuse. They may appear dazed and confused as infants and are challenged in adulthood with establishing and maintaining personal and intimate relationships.

ERIK ERIKSON'S PSYCHOSOCIAL STAGES OF HUMAN DEVELOPMENT

Stage	Age	Developmental Task	Description
1	0–18 months	Trust vs. mistrust	Infants learn to trust caregivers when their needs for food, affection, comfort, and security are satisfied.
2	18 months to 3 years	Autonomy vs. shame/doubt	Caregivers help toddlers achieve autonomy through building self-efficacy and appropriately encouraging self-reliance.
3	3–6 years	Initiative vs. guilt	Children initiate social activities and learn interpersonal skills. Guilt occurs if a caregiver oversteps and responds with criticism when mistakes are made.
4	7–11 years	Industry vs. inferiority	Preteens take pride in social and academic achievements. Harsh criticism from adults or negative peer comparisons can lead to feelings of inferiority and a negative self-concept.
5	12–18 years	Identity vs. role confusion	Adolescents grapple with who they are and how they express themselves. Significant relationships help mold values, roles, beliefs, behaviors, and identity.
6	19–35 years	Intimacy vs. isolation	Young adults seek fulfillment through intimate relationships. Isolation and loneliness result from an inability to attain intimacy.

Stage	Age	Developmental Task	Description
7	35–64 years	Generativity vs. stagnation	Young adults and those in midlife focus on establishing a career, leaving a positive legacy, societal contributions, and family relationships. Stagnation is the absence of procreativity.
8	65+ years	Integrity vs. despair	Older adults assess their lives, contemplate accomplishments, and come to terms with death and acceptance. Despair occurs when a person believes that his or her life was void of meaning.

JEAN PIAGET'S STAGES OF COGNITIVE DEVELOPMENT

Jean Piaget developed the theory of cognitive development. The theory is based on the following four stages:

Age (years)	Stage	Description	Themes
0–2	Sensorimotor	Infants learn to explore and experience life through their senses. Object permanence is the understanding that a person or object still exists even though it is unseen. Schema (i.e., mental models) have not developed, causing separation anxiety and stranger anxiety as object permanence is developed.	Object permanence Stranger anxiety
2–7	Preoperational	Children develop language skills through words, images, and symbols. Logical or operational thinking begins as vocabulary and language skills rapidly develop. This stage is also marked by egocentric thinking, or the inability to consider that the viewpoints, needs, and concerns of others differ from their own.	Imaginary play (i.e., symbolic thought) Logical thought
7–11	Concrete operational	Children begin to comprehend mathematical operations and logical thinking. Conservation, which is the ability to understand that objects can change appearance yet remain the same, is developed.	Conservation Mathematical operations
12–adulthood	Formal operational	Individuals understand formal operations and engage in abstract thinking. Hypothetical and moral reasoning also develops.	Abstract logic Hypothetical and moral reasoning

PHYSICAL AND SEXUAL DOMAINS OF HUMAN DEVELOPMENT

Human development is **multidirectional** and **multidimensional**. Development is multidirectional, meaning the gains or losses in each domain may differ. For example, an adolescent who cannot think abstractly may be lacking a sense of self-identity. The multidirectional process of human development is viewed through a multidimensional lens—meaning **growth is measured across the physical, psychosocial, cognitive, and emotional domains.**

Within the context of human development, **physical development** includes measurements for height, weight, motor skills, the brain, sensory experiences, and a person's overall health and wellness. The domain of **sexual development** consists of sexual behaviors and age-related milestones, including childhood (e.g., self-stimulation, gender identity), adolescence (e.g., puberty), adulthood (e.g., possible sexual activity, pregnancy), and older adults (e.g., menopause, andropause).

PSYCHOSOCIAL AND EMOTIONAL DOMAINS OF HUMAN DEVELOPMENT

Erikson's stages of psychosocial development consider how family and social relationships influence emotional development. Albert Bandura, another cognitive constructionist, is known for social learning theory. Social learning theory is based on the premise that interactional factors—including the individual's environment, thoughts, and emotional responses—shape behavior.

Lev Vygotsky, a social constructivist, used the term "zone of emotional proximal development" to illustrate the range of learning and emotional development attained with the help of surrounding influences (i.e., the client system). This begins with parental reactions and emotional expressions. As children develop cognitively, ongoing parent–child discussions about emotions allow the child to understand the consequences of emotional expressions.

STAGES OF EMOTIONAL DEVELOPMENT

The stages of emotional development include the following:

Infancy:

- Emotional temperament (i.e., disposition, overall mood) develops.
- Emotional exchanges with caregivers are sought as infants seek independence and explore their surroundings.
- Socioemotional reciprocity is connected to social interactions and attachment.

Toddlerhood and early childhood:

- Feelings of frustration and defiance emerge as the toddler seeks autonomy.
- The ability to distinguish between a wide variety of emotions is refined.
- An understanding of situational determinants of emotion is developed.
- Emotional self-regulation is learned within social contexts and family systems.

Middle and late childhood:

- The capacity for emotional self-reflection emerges.
- An understanding of complex emotional experiences develops.
- The recognition that multiple aspects of events and behaviors are tied to emotional experiences is made.
- The ability to mask or suppress undesirable emotions in certain contexts is developed.

Adolescence:

- Less emotional dependence is placed on caregivers.
- Experiences of intense emotions occur.
- Peer groups serve as the context for emotional regulation.
- Complex and sometimes conflicting emotional experiences around dating, intimacy, and self-identity arise.

SPIRITUAL DOMAIN OF HUMAN DEVELOPMENT

Greenfield et al. (2009) define spirituality as "an individual's intrapsychic sense of connection with something transcendent (that which exists apart from and not limited by the material universe) and the subsequent feelings of awe, gratitude, compassion, and forgiveness." Spirituality is distinct from religious practice, which includes shared values, traditions, and beliefs. Religion and spirituality are both shown to contribute to improved health and psychological well-being.

Over 25% of US adults consider themselves to be "spiritual but not religious," a figure that has steadily increased over the past few decades. Meanwhile, studies have consistently shown that religion becomes increasingly important as one ages, with significantly higher percentages of adults over 65 reporting that they consider religion to be "very important" to them as compared to adults in the 18-40 age range. The benefits of religious practice among older adults include support with age-related challenges and opportunities for socialization.

Spiritual development can be understood using a framework that parallels Erikson's stages of cognitive development. In early childhood, children tend to rely on parental teachings. Around the ages of 7–12, children become less egocentric. During this time, they begin to discern moral situations and conform to societal norms. In adolescence, spiritual or religious beliefs are grounded in parental teachings but become challenged and shaped by peers. In adulthood, spiritual development parallels stage 7 (generativity vs. stagnation) as adults seek purpose and meaning in life, engage in self-reflection, and surrender to the unknown. The final stage of spiritual development is characterized by experiences of enlightenment, transcendence, or self-actualization.

Family Studies and Science

STEPFAMILIES/BLENDED FAMILIES AND REMARRIAGE

In 2022, the United States Census Bureau reported the following:

- 70% of children reside in two-parent households.
- For children with one parent, 21.4% live with their mother, compared to 4.4% who live with their father.
- 4% of children live with neither parent.
- >50% of children in out-of-home placements live with a grandparent.
- 1.7% of children live with at least one adoptive parent.
- 7% of children live with at least one stepparent.

Children in blended families or stepfamilies are likely to reencounter divorce because nearly 70% of those marriages also fail. Children in blended families who perceive their parents as having a secure emotional bond fare better than those who do not. Researchers have found that children between the ages of 10 and 14 have the most difficulty adjusting to blended families.

A child's adjustment to a blended family is also influenced by their relationship with the nonresidential parent. Frequent contact with the nonresidential parent improves outcomes. Research shows that visitation by nonresidential fathers who remarry decreases by 50% within the first year of remarriage.

OUT-OF-HOME PLACEMENT

Out-of-home placements for children include kinship care (i.e., placement with a relative), foster care, and institutions or group homes. According to the Adoption and Foster Care Analysis and Reporting System, in 2020, the reasons for children entering into foster care were highest for episodes of neglect (64%), parental substance use (35%), and the caregiver's poor coping skills (34%). Other reasons included parental incarceration, sexual abuse, and physical abuse. The negative impact of out-of-home placement is highest for children placed in institutions or group homes.

The **adverse effects** of out-of-home placement include the following:

- Substance misuse
- Suicidality
- Poor academic and job performance
- Premature death and increased mortality rates
- Higher arrest rates for violent crimes
- Higher rates of severe mental disorders
- Attachment issues, particularly for children <5 years old

SAME-SEX COUPLES

In 2015, the United States Supreme Court legalized same-sex marriage, stating that bans on same-sex marriage violate the Due Process and Equal Protection clauses outlined in the Fourteenth Amendment. Acceptance of same-sex marriage is on the rise. In 2019, the Pew Research Center found that 61% of Americans support same-sex marriage compared to 31% in 2004. However, in 2022, the Supreme Court overturned *Roe v. Wade*, ending a woman's constitutional right to have an abortion (although individual states and the voters in those states can still decide). This landmark decision was also paired with an opinion by a Supreme Court justice indicating that the same rationale could be used to challenge the legality of same-sex marriage and same-sex relations.

Fundamental knowledge of current legislation is necessary to assess and understand the unique challenges within the gay and lesbian clients' systems. Research suggests that policy changes and attitudes opposing same-sex marriage influence the overall health of gays and lesbians—including mortality rates. The impact of legislative changes can potentially increase experiences of discrimination, homophobia, stigma, and microaggressions—all of which have been linked to poorer physical and mental health outcomes and a decreased quality of life for the client and the client's system.

SAME-SEX COUPLES AND PARENTING

Social science research suggests that the overall health and well-being of children with same-sex parents do not differ from children with opposite-sex parents. This holds true in the areas of cognitive development, academic achievement, social adjustment, and self-esteem. Studies have also found that instances of substance misuse and early sexual activity are just as common for adolescents residing in homes with different-sex parents than with same-sex parents.

Research consistently shows that the well-being of all children is negatively impacted by socioeconomic factors and instability of the parental unit.

There are some studies that cite differences in outcomes for children in households with same-sex parents. Researchers challenging these claims cite that the following factors confound many studies:

- Accumulating longitudinal data is difficult due to the recent legalization of same-sex marriage.
- Many studies use cross-sectional data (i.e., a snapshot in time) to inform conclusions, which do not account for the influence of previous circumstances.
- Many studies do not include comparison groups of opposite-sex married parents or unmarried parents.

DIVERSE FAMILY PATTERNS OF MULTIPLE-PARTNER RELATIONSHIPS

Consensual nonmonogamy (CNM) refers to relationships in which all partners consensually engage in intimate and/or sexual relationships with other people. CNM is an umbrella term used to describe open, polyamorous, or swinging relationships. CNM is a relationship style in which each partner has full knowledge and consent, distinguishing it from infidelity. In the United States, an estimated 4–5% of the population engages in CNM.

Research indicates that individuals who identify as LGBTQIA+ (lesbian, gay, bisexual, transgender, questioning, queer, intersex, asexual, pansexual, and allies) are more apt to engage in CNM than their heterosexual counterparts. Individuals in consensual multipartner relationships report experiences of discrimination, marginalization, stigmatization, and moral condemnation. Individuals who disclose a CNM status may be faced with negative biases due to monogamous, couple-centric societal norms.

Individuals may be hesitant to disclose their multipartner status because of associated stereotypes. Empirically debunked stereotypes include beliefs that CNM individuals are harmful to children, create public health risks, only care about sex, and cannot make commitments. Additionally, people engaging in CNM report stigma from therapists and health-care professionals who adhere to stereotypes and discourage or condemn the behavior, leading to poorer health outcomes.

Marital Studies and Science

In 2019, the Pew Research Center found that the percentage of adults who have cohabitated is higher than those who have been married. Despite an uptick in societal acceptance of cohabitation, married couples reported higher measures of relationship satisfaction and mutual trust than those who cohabitated.

In the United States, the divorce rate for first-time marriages is approximately 40%, with the lowest rates among Hispanic and Asian couples. There is no difference in the percentage of divorced adults among non-Hispanic whites and African Americans. To date, approximately 11% of women and 8% of men are divorced.

The median age of married adults has increased over the past five decades, from age 23 for men in 1970 to age 30 in 2021. For women, the median age at first marriage in 1970 was 23, compared to age 28 in 2021. Divorce rates are higher among couples aged 15–34, with 24% of married couples in that age cohort ending in divorce. Indicators of early divorce include negative communication stances resulting in feelings of contempt, defensiveness, harsh criticism, and "shutting down" or stonewalling. Protective factors for couples include higher education and religious beliefs. Nearly 8 in 10 women with a college degree stay married for up to 20 years, compared to 1 in 4 women with a high school education.

Human Sexuality

HUMAN SEXUAL ANATOMY, PHYSIOLOGY, AND DEVELOPMENT

Sexual anatomy refers to male and female internal and external reproductive organs.

Internal female sexual anatomy includes all of following:

- Vagina
- Uterus
- Ovaries
- Fallopian tubes
- Cervix
- Bartholin's glands
- Skene's glands
- Hymen

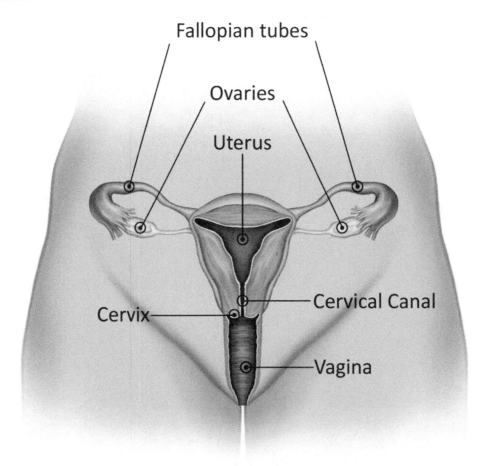

External female sexual anatomy (i.e., the vulva) includes the following:

- Labia majora
- Labia minora
- Prepuce
- Clitoris
- Vestibule
- Vestibular glands
- Mons pubis

Internal male sexual anatomy includes the following:

- Testicles
- Epididymis
- Vas deferens
- Seminal vesicle
- Prostate gland
- Cowper's gland
- Urethra

External male sexual anatomy (i.e., the penis and scrotum) includes the following:

- Glans
- Shaft
- Foreskin
- Frenulum

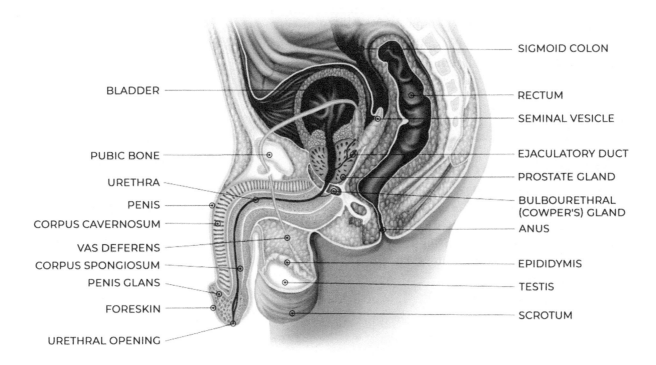

HUMAN SEXUAL DEVELOPMENT

Stage of Development	Common Sexual Behaviors
0–18 months	Self-stimulation publicly and privately Curiosity toward the genitalia and its functions Wants to take clothes off and remain naked publicly and privately
18 months–5 years	Self-soothing through masturbation publicly and privately Playful exploration of genitals with siblings or same-aged peers Mocks behaviors such as kissing or holding hands Curiosity around sexuality and reproduction Asks questions about bodily functions
5–8 years	Slang words developed for genitalia Pleasure seeking through masturbation Continued sexual play with same- or opposite-sex peers An understanding of gender roles and identities
9–12 years	Puberty begins for girls (aged 8–13) and boys (aged 9–14) Privacy and modesty around sexual development Information on adult sexuality is sought online or through other media outlets Masturbation in private Sexual attraction or interest begins
12–18 years	Growth of primary and secondary sex characteristics reaches completion Menarche (menstruation) in females and spermarche (ejaculation of semen) in males occur The possibility of sexual activity and pregnancy
19–30 years	The possibility of sexual activity and pregnancy Decisions made about partnerships, children, and career
31–45 years	Possibility of sexual activity Possibility of parenting responsibilities
46–64 years	Menopause or andropause Divorce or death of a partner
65+ years	Sexual response begins to slow Possibility of grandparenting Possibility of divorce or the death of a partner

SEXUAL RESPONSE CYCLE

Human sexual physiology is cyclical and involves physical and emotional responses. The sexual response cycle occurs during any sexually stimulating activity (e.g., masturbation, sexual intercourse). Males and females may differ in the timing of the phases, with females less likely to go through the stages in order. In addition, some individuals go through some phases and not others during different sexual encounters. The **phases of the sexual response cycle** are generally characterized by the following:

Phase I: Desire (libido)

- Increased heart rate.
- Skin becomes flushed.
- Nipples harden.
- Vaginal lubrication.
- Partial or complete penile erection.
- Women's clitoris and labia minora swell.
- Men's testicles swell, and the scrotum tightens.

Phase II: Arousal (plateau)

- Phase I changes intensify.
- The outer third of the vaginal walls (i.e., the orgasmic platform) tightens.
- The clitoris becomes more sensitive.
- Pre-seminal fluid may be released from the Cowper's gland.
- Myotonia (i.e., involuntary muscle spasms) in the face, hands, and feet.

Phase III: Orgasm

- Muscle contractions become involuntary.
- Muscles in feet spasm.
- Vaginal wall and/or uterus contracts.
- Penile ejaculation.
- Oxytocin is released, contributing to intimacy and emotional bonding.
- Flushed skin intensifies ("sex rash").

Phase IV: Resolution

- Genitalia gradually return to their prearousal shape and size.
- Muscles relax, which may be followed by fatigue.
- Overall well-being may be experienced.
- A quick return (i.e., multiple orgasms) to phase II is possible for women with continued stimulation.
- The refractory period, or when a male can return to orgasm, is individualized and varies with age.

Sexually Transmitted Infections

Routes of Transmission, Symptoms, and Complications

Sexually Transmitted Infection	Symptoms	Common Means of Transmission	Complications
HIV	Early symptoms (acute stage): Swollen glands, headache, sore throat, fever, upset stomach, body aches, and rash.	Vaginal, anal, and oral sex with an infected person. Sharing needles with an infected person. Mothers with HIV can spread the virus during pregnancy, birth, or breastfeeding.	If left untreated, HIV can lead to acquired immunodeficiency syndrome and death. Perinatal complications include stillbirth, low birth weight, and congenital deformities.
Syphilis	Primary stage: Chancres (sores) appear on or around the penis, vagina, anus, rectum, lips, or mouth. Secondary stage: Fever, fatigue, hair loss, sore throat, and body aches.	Vaginal, anal, and oral sex with an infected person. Pregnant mothers can transmit the infection to their unborn children. Syphilis can be spread during breastfeeding if there is an open sore(s) on the breast.	Tertiary (late-stage) syphilis symptoms include blindness, paralysis, tumors, and nervous system complications. Perinatal complications include miscarriage, premature birth, and slowed growth rate.
HSV	HSV-1: Oral blisters and mouth sores. HSV-2: Painful ulcers on the genitals and/or mouth, fever, muscle aches, and swollen lymph nodes (although HSV may be asymptomatic).	HSV-1: Oral transmission by an infected person. HSV-2: Vaginal, anal, and oral sex with an infected person; male-to-female sexual transmission is most common. Pregnant mothers can transmit the infection to their unborn children. HSV-2 can be spread during breastfeeding if there are active lesions on the breast.	HSV-1: Encephalitis and eye infection (both rare). HSV-2: Symptoms may recur with increased frequency and severity. There is an increased risk of contracting HIV and meningoencephalitis (rare). Perinatal complications include potentially fatal neonatal herpes, spontaneous abortion, and preterm labor.

Sexually Transmitted Infection	Symptoms	Common Means of Transmission	Complications
Chlamydia	Painful urination, pain during sex, rash, and vaginal or penile discharge. For women, bleeding after sex and pelvic pain. For men, testicular swelling.	Vaginal, anal, and oral sex with someone infected. Pregnant mothers can transmit the infection to their unborn children.	Pelvic inflammatory disease, infection near the testicles, infection in the prostate gland, infertility, ectopic pregnancy, and arthritis. Perinatal complications include preterm delivery, conjunctivitis, and pneumonia in newborns.
Gonorrhea	Rectal itching, sore throat, septic arthritis, eye pain, and swollen lymph nodes.	Vaginal, anal, and oral sex with an infected person (even if there is no contact with semen). Pregnant mothers can transmit the infection to their unborn children.	Pelvic inflammatory disease and/or infertility. The infection can spread to joints and other areas in the body. Gonorrhea increases the risk of HIV. Perinatal complications include low birth weight, premature delivery, and blindness in newborns.
Hepatitis B	Stomach pain, fatigue, loss of appetite, dark urine, vomiting, jaundice, and fever.	Vaginal, anal, and oral sex with an infected person. Sharing toothbrushes, needles, tattooing equipment, syringes, and razors with an infected person. Pregnant mothers can transmit the infection to their unborn children.	Cirrhosis of the liver, liver cancer, liver damage, and death. Perinatal complications include chronic, lifelong infections for 90% of infants infected.

Assessing, Hypothesizing, and Diagnosing

Therapeutic Alliance

THERAPEUTIC MILIEU

The **therapeutic milieu** is a stable environment provided by an organization to assist in a **treatment plan**. The main purposes of a milieu are to teach individuals certain social skills and to provide a **structured environment** that promotes interactions and personal growth along with attempting to control many types of deviant or destructive behaviors. There are **five main components** that the milieu should include in therapy. These components include containment, structure, support, involvement, and validation. Through the use of these components, the therapeutic milieu can help the individuals achieve their highest level of functioning.

CONTAINMENT COMPONENT

The **containment component** in a milieu involves the actual **physical safety** of the participants. It provides a **safe clean physical environment** as well as providing food and some medical care. The actual environment will often be very comfortable with colorful walls, pictures, and comfortable chairs and couches. Participants are allowed a certain freedom of movement throughout this environment. Many times, the participants will work to help maintain a clean and functioning environment. They may perform certain tasks or chores to help with the upkeep of the milieu. This containment will provide a feeling of safety and trust for the individual.

STRUCTURED COMPONENT

The **structured component** in the milieu lies hand in hand with **consistency**. The milieu provides a place with consistent staff members, consistent physical surroundings, and limits on behavior. This predictability allows the participants to feel safe and secure and to know what to expect. This environment also provides **structure** through providing an environment where the participants can interact with a purpose. These purposes can range from daily tasks and chores to the different roles they may assume within various meetings. Through acceptance of this consistent and structured environment, the individual can begin to achieve some level of self-responsibility and consequences for their actions.

SUPPORT COMPONENT

The **support component** in a milieu comes directly from the staff members involved in the milieu. Their goal is to help the participants have increased **self-esteem** through creating an environment of acceptance for all individuals. They provide a safe and comfortable atmosphere, therefore decreasing anxiety levels. Encouragement, empathy, nurturing, reassurance, and providing physical wellbeing for participants will help increase their feelings of self-worth. Consistency in attitudes and actions by all staff members are very important in the success of this setting. By providing this type of environment, the milieu will assist clients in their abilities to gain new healthy relationships and appropriate interactions with others.

INVOLVEMENT COMPONENT

The **involvement component** of the milieu is the development of a sense of **open involvement** for each client from the staff members. The staff should convey their desire to be personally involved with each client through both their actions and attitudes. They should encourage the clients to **communicate** with them openly about feelings and experiences. This sense of individual interest and involvement will help to increase the client's sense of self-worth and self-esteem. The staff members should encourage client involvement through encouraging client-lead group sessions and activities. By becoming involved, the clients have opportunities to practice new social skills, such as working together with others, learning to compromise, and dealing with conflict. The hope of involvement is to achieve the goal of appropriate social interactions for each client.

VALIDATION COMPONENT

The **validation component** of the milieu is the recognition of each client as an **individual**. The staff members should convey **respect and consideration** for each and every client. This respect and consideration should be shown through acts of kindness, empathy, nonjudgmental attitude, and acceptance of each individual for who they are. In a milieu, each client contributes through responsibilities and involvement in many decision-making processes. Through these actions, the clients should begin to feel some self-responsibility and with this new sense of responsibility comes validation for their individuality and humanity.

CHARACTERISTICS OF A SUCCESSFUL MILIEU

The characteristics of a **successful milieu** include:

- Successful communication between and among staff and clients
- Standards that provide consistency and security
- Client government using the democratic process
- Client responsibility for his or her own treatment
- Encouraging self-perception and change
- Acknowledging and positively dealing with destructive behavior and poor judgment

CONFLICT RESOLUTION

When attempting to **resolve conflict** between two or more individuals, the desired outcome is a feeling by each party of getting what they wanted out of the situation. Resolving conflict should include the following steps:

1. **Problem Identification**: The parties are each allowed their opportunity to discuss what they think is wrong. This portion of the resolution process may become emotional and involve angry outbursts.
2. **Ascertain Expectations**: Each party identifies exactly what they want. With the disclosure of these expectations, a sense of trust can begin to evolve. The mental health professional will need to remain objective and respectful to everyone involved during this phase.
3. **Identify Special Interest**: Determine if anyone has unspoken objectives or interests that could slow down the resolution progress. Everyone needs to be honest about what they want and need.
4. **Brainstorm Resolution Ideas**: Assist the parties with creating ideas to help resolve the conflict.
5. **Reach a Resolution**: Assist the parties in bringing together a situation where everyone can feel happy about the outcome.

CLIENT-PROVIDER RELATIONSHIP

INTRODUCTORY PHASE

The first thing the mental health care provider should do when meeting a client is to find out **why** they are there. This **initial phase** provides a time for the provider and client to get to know each other. There is no definite time frame and this phase can last for a few minutes to a few months. There are certain goals that should be accomplished during this time. The provider and client should develop a mutual sense of trust, acceptance, and understanding. They may enter into a contract with each other. They will need to determine expectations, goals, boundaries, and ending criteria for the contract. This initial phase often involves obtaining the client's history, his or her account of the problems, and developing a general understanding of the client.

WORKING PHASE

The second phase of the client-provider relationship is the **working phase**. During this time the client will identify and evaluate specific problems through the development of insight and learn ways to effectively **adapt their behaviors**. The provider will assist the client in working through feelings of fear and anxiety. They will also foster new levels of self-responsibility and coping mechanisms. The development of new and successful ways of approaching problems is the goal of this phase. The provider may often face resistance by the client to move through this phase, and by utilizing different communication techniques may help to assist the client in moving forward.

TERMINATION PHASE

The final stage of the client-provider relationship is the **termination or resolution phase**. This phase begins from the time the problems are actually solved to the actual **ending of the relationship**. This phase can be very difficult for both the client and the provider. The client must now focus on continuing without the guiding assistance of the therapy. The client will need to utilize their newfound approaches and behaviors. This time may be one of varying emotions for the client and they may be reluctant to end the relationship. They may experience anxiety, anger, or sadness. The provider may need to guide the client in utilizing their newfound strategies in dealing with their feelings about the termination of the relationship. Focus should be placed on the future.

CLIENT SAFETY ISSUES

PROFESSIONAL ASSAULT RESPONSE

A protocol for a **professional assault response** should be established at all mental health facilities because statistics show that 75% of mental health staff experience a **physical assault**. Most injuries are incurred by nursing staff caring for violent clients. Assaults may occur in both psychiatric units and emergency departments, where security staff may also be assaulted. Additionally, clients may be victims. Common injuries include fractures, lacerations, contusions, and unconsciousness from head injuries. Victims are at risk for psychological distress and post-traumatic stress syndrome, so a prompt response is critical. The assault response should include the following:

- Routine assessment of clients for violent or aggressive tendencies
- Protocol for managing violent or aggressive clients
- Physical assessment and medical treatment as needed for injuries
- Completion of an incident report by those who were involved or who observed the incident

Psychological intervention, including individual counseling sessions and critical incident stress management, require a response team that includes staff members who are trained to deal with crisis intervention (e.g., psychologists, psychiatrists, nurses, peer counselors, social workers).

Contraband and Unsafe Items

State regulations identify **contraband and unsafe items** that are prohibited from mental health and correctional facilities; however, each facility must develop site-specific restrictions and protocols for responding to contraband and unsafe items. **Contraband** may include the following:

- Alcohol or products (mouthwash) that contain alcohol
- Drugs, including prescription, over-the-counter, and illicit drugs
- Poisonous and toxic substances
- Pornographic or sexually explicit material
- Food (hoarded or excessive)

Depending on the type of facility or clients, a wide range of items may be considered **unsafe**. These often include the following:

- Knives, scissors, sharp instruments, and razor blades
- Flammable materials, such as lighter fluid and matches
- Breakable items, such as glass and mirrors
- Dangerous materials (which might be used for a suicide attempt), such as belts (over 2 in wide), large buckles, rope, electrical cords (i.e., over 6 feet in length), and wire
- Potential weapons, such as pens (except felt point), pencils, and plastic bags
- Electrical equipment, such as fans and recording devices

Therapeutic Communication

Verbal Communication

Verbal communication is achieved through spoken or written words. This form of communication represents a very small fraction of communication as a whole. Much information achieved verbally may be **factual** in nature. Communication occurs along a two-way path between the client and the provider. One limitation of verbal communication can be **different meanings of words** in different ethnic and cultural populations. The meanings may differ in denotative, actual meaning, and/or connotative, implied meaning, of the words. The use of words may differ depending upon personal experiences. The client may assume the provider understands their particular meaning of the word.

Empathy

Empathy is perhaps one of the most important concepts in establishing a therapeutic relationship with a client, and it is associated with **positive client outcomes**. It is the ability of one person to put themselves in the shoes of another. Empathy is more than just knowing what the other person means. The provider should seek to imagine the **feelings** associated with the other person's experience without having had this experience themselves and then communicate this understanding to the client. Empathy should not be confused with sympathy, which is feeling sorry for someone. The provider should also be aware of any social or cultural differences that could inhibit the conveyance of empathy.

Open-Ended Statements and Reflection

Broad **open-ended statements** allow the client the opportunity to expand on an idea or select a topic for discussion. This type of communication allows the client to feel like the provider is actually listening and interested in what they have to say. It also helps the client gain insight into his or her emotions or situations.

Reflection conveys interest and understanding to the client. It can also allow for a time of validation so the provider can show that they are actually listening and understanding the shared information. It involves some minimal repetition of ideas or summing up a situation. These ideas or summaries are directed back to the client often in the form of a question.

RESTATING AND CLARIFICATION

Restating and clarification are verbal communication techniques that the provider may use as part of therapeutic communication. **Restating** involves the repetition of the main points of what the client expressed. Many times, the provider will not restate everything but narrow the focus to the main point. This technique can achieve both clarification of a point and confirmation that what the client said was heard.

Clarification involves the provider attempting to understand and verbalize a vague situation. Many times, a client's emotional explanations can be difficult to clearly understand and the provider must try to narrow down what the client is trying to say.

SILENCE AND LISTENING

Silence and listening are very effective during verbal communication.

- **Silence** allows the client time to think and formulate ideas and responses. It is an intentional lull in the conversation to give the client time to reflect.
- **Listening** is more active in nature. When listening, the provider lends attention to what the client is communicating. There are two different types of listening.
  - **Passive listening** allows the client to speak without direction or guidance from the provider. This form of listening does not usually advance the client's therapy.
  - **Active listening** occurs when the provider focuses on what is said in order to respond and then encourage a response from the client.

RAPPORT AND VALIDATION

Communication between the mental health care provider and the client can be improved by establishing rapport and validating certain information. **Establishing rapport** with a client involves achieving a certain level of harmony between the provider and the client. This is often achieved through the establishment of trust through conveying respect, nonbiased views, and understanding. By establishing rapport, the provider helps the client feel more comfortable about sharing information.

Validation requires the provider to use the word "I" when talking with the client. It evaluates one's own thoughts or observations against another person's and often requires feedback in the form of confirmation.

USE OF THERAPEUTIC COMMUNICATION WITH GROUPS

A **group** is a gathering of interactive individuals who have commonalities. Interventions through **group sessions** can provide an effective treatment opportunity to allow for growth and self-development of the client. This setting allows the clients to interact with each other. This allows the clients to see the emotions of others, such as joy, sorrow, or anger, and to receive as well as participate in feedback from others in the group. The group can be very supportive and thrive in both inpatient and outpatient settings. The one thing the group cannot lack is definite **leadership and guidance** from the health care provider. The provider must guide the members of the group in facilitating therapeutic communications.

NON-THERAPEUTIC COMMUNICATION

Techniques that are detrimental to establishing a trusting therapeutic relationship include giving advice, challenging the client's communications, or indicating disapproval. **Giving advice** includes telling the client what they should do in a particular situation. This does not allow the client to develop the ability to solve their own problems and may not always be the right answer. **Challenging** occurs when the client's thoughts are disputed by the provider. This communication only serves to lower the client's self-esteem and create an environment of distrust between the client and the mental health care provider. **Disapproval** occurs when the provider negatively judges the client's beliefs or actions. This again serves to lower client self-esteem and does not foster their ability to solve their own problems or create new coping abilities.

NONVERBAL COMMUNICATION IN THE THERAPEUTIC RELATIONSHIP

Nonverbal communication occurs in the form of expressions, gestures, body positioning or movement, voice levels, and information gathered from the five senses. The **nonverbal message** is usually more accurate in conveying the client's feeling than the **verbal message**. Many clients will say something quite different than what their nonverbal communication indicates. Nonverbal communication may also vary by cultural influences. The mental health care provider must be aware of these cultural differences and respect their place within the therapy. The provider should utilize positive, respectful, non-threatening body language. A relaxed, slightly forward posture with uncrossed arms and legs may encourage communication.

VOCAL CUES, ACTION CUES, AND OBJECT CUES AS FORMS OF NONVERBAL BEHAVIORS

There are many different types of nonverbal behaviors. There are five main areas of **nonverbal communication**. They include vocal cues, action cues, object cues, space, and touch.

- **Vocal cues** can involve the qualities of speech, such as tone and rate. Laughing, groaning, or sounds of hesitation can also convey important communication.
- **Action cues** involve bodily movements. They can include things such as mannerisms, gestures, facial expressions, or any body movements. These types of movements can be good indicators of mood or emotion.
- **Object cues** include the use of objects. The client may not even be aware that they are moving these objects. Other times the client may choose a particular object to indicate a specific communication. This intentional use of an object can be less valuable than other forms of nonverbal communication.

Space and touch as nonverbal forms of communication can vary greatly depending upon social or cultural norms.

- **Space** can provide information about a relationship between the client and someone else. Most people living in the United States have four different areas of space. **Intimate space** is less than 1.5 feet, **personal space** is 1.5-4 feet, **social-consultative space** is 9-12 feet, and **public space** is 12 feet or more. Observations concerning space and the client's physical placement in a setting can give a great deal of insight into different interpersonal relationships.
- **Touch** includes personal or intimate space with an action involved. This fundamental form of communication can send very personal information and communicate feelings such as concern or caring.

39

VERBAL AND NONVERBAL COMMUNICATION CUES

It is critical that therapists carefully observe the client system's verbal and nonverbal cues to assist in forming a hypothesis about the nature of his or her relational interactions, including expressions of conflict, emotion, and love. Differences in verbal and nonverbal communication cues include the following:

Verbal Cues	Nonverbal Cues
Use of words, language, sounds, and phrases.	Body language, eye contact, and facial expressions.
Continuous and linear; includes the process of reflective thinking and articulation of thoughts.	Less intentional, involuntary, and unconscious reflection of underlying meaning and intent.
A less salient depiction of underlying emotions and mindset.	A more salient depiction of emotions and mindset; 60–65% of interpersonal communication is nonverbal.
Easier to understand and interpret due to one channel of expression (i.e., voice).	Harder to understand and interpret due to multiple channels of expression (e.g., body language, eye contact) and cultural differences in nonverbal expression.

POSITIVE RELATIONAL INTERACTIONS AND NEGATIVE RELATIONAL INTERACTIONS

Therapists using nonverbal cues to hypothesize the nature of the relational system must consider the context, situation, and environment. Cultural aspects of communication must also be recognized. For example, in some cultures (e.g., Asian), avoiding eye contact conveys respect, whereas in Western cultures, direct eye contact is a form of respect. Examples of **positive relational interactions** among family systems include adopting an open posture, respecting personal space, smiling, making eye contact, using an uplifting tone, nodding, and attending to one another.

Negative relational interactions may include finger-pointing, eye-rolling, turning away, aggressively staring, sitting far away, and using a negative tone of voice. The therapist is tasked with openly investigating inconsistencies and patterns in verbal and nonverbal communication through direct questioning and checking hypotheses with the client. The therapist must also rely on a global assessment and interpretation rather than basing conclusions on a single gesture or expression.

Assessment of the Client System

OBSERVING INTERACTIONAL PATTERNS WITHIN THE FAMILY SYSTEM

Therapists assess **interactional patterns** within the client system by identifying roles, norms, tasks, alliances, boundaries, and hierarchies. In family systems, each person is a part of the organizational structure. When one person in the organizational structure changes, the entire system changes. Each member of the system is mutually influenced and interdependent upon one another, and certain members may establish subsystems within the family.

Hierarchical subsystems have the power to organize the system and regulate boundaries. **Boundaries** are invisible lines that metaphorically separate family systems from the outside world. Hierarchies are composed of individuals within a system who have the power to make decisions, determine boundaries, monitor rules, and define interactional patterns. Hierarchies also determine each member's tasks, roles, and functions. In healthy systems, the boundaries are clear. In families with dysfunctional interactional patterns, boundaries are rigid or enmeshed, with hierarchies determining what information flows in and out of the family system.

Alliances are subsystems formed among emotionally close members within a system. When the alliance is covert, it is known as a coalition. **Coalitions** are composed of one or more individuals in the system who align themselves against another person or subsystem. Hierarchical subsystems often dictate limitations on these interactions and behaviors. In healthy systems, the hierarchy of power rests with the parental subsystem. In dysfunctional systems, the parental hierarchy may be undefined or split. One parent may refuse to set limits, for example, whereas another uses hostility to demand obedience.

ASSESSMENT OF CLIENT SYSTEM FUNCTIONING

The functioning of a client system is best understood through its communication patterns, processes, and dynamics. A family system's repetitive interactional patterns help maintain balance and create a **state of equilibrium**. Assessing the **repetitive interactional patterns** is critical for understanding how the system functions and remains stable. Interactions that promote healthy boundaries are clear and flexible.

A **functional family system** is dynamic, differentiated, and flexible. In a healthy functioning family, hierarchical subsystems implement appropriate boundaries, rules, and conduct. Functional families have high degrees of emotional differentiation among their members. Hierarchies are established to protect family members and subsystems or the system as a whole. In dysfunctional interactions, hierarchies use their power to control, dominate, and/or pit family members against one another.

Assessing the client system functioning seeks to **conceptualize boundaries, hierarchies, and subsystems**, including how the system manages conflict, solves problems, and allows for individuation and emotional closeness. Therapists also consider the client's **resources** within the family unit, extended family, and community. **Genograms** can be constructed to assess intergenerational patterns of communication and behavior. Therapists assess socioeconomic and cultural influences on the client's conception of the problem, available economic resources, community connectedness, gender roles, and views on mental health treatment.

GENOGRAMS

A genogram is a visual representation of an individual's family that includes information not only regarding the members of the family, but also the status of those members and their relationships to one another. Genograms are useful in a variety of fields, including therapy, counseling, and social work. The process of creating a genogram provides value to the client by allowing them to visualize family dynamics from a macro level and step outside of those dynamics to see how their family unit functions as whole. It is also useful to the person working with the client as it allows them to better understand the client as a product of their family's structure and dynamics. Genograms can identify points of tension within the client's current family structure, or within the client's past and can be a starting point for conversation and investigation regarding any of the client's current struggles, barriers, and strengths.

GENOGRAM STRUCTURE AND SYMBOLS

Genograms rely on standardized symbols and structure to represent members of the family, their role and placement in the client's life, and their dynamics with other family members. The basic symbols and notations of genograms are outlined below. There is additional notation beyond what is included here that is sometimes used, but the particular symbols and linking methods that are used vary by convention.

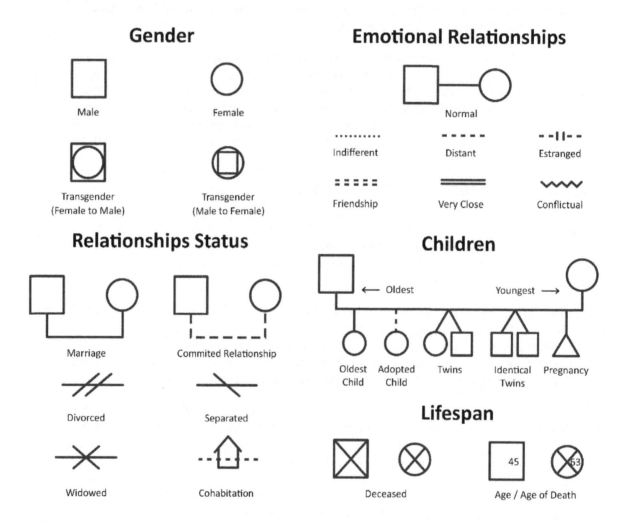

CONTEXTUAL UNDERSTANDING OF THE CLIENT SYSTEM

A **contextual understanding** of the client system is paramount to understanding the system's influence on the client's strengths, limitations, abilities, motivation, and resources. Acculturation, or the fluid process of cultural adaptation, plays a significant role in determining the client's values, identity, attitudes, and behavior—and how well those aspects are integrated with the mainstream culture.

Differences in intergenerational **acculturation** can upend hierarchal subsystems in families with children who are well integrated into the mainstream culture. **Power differentials** created by acculturation not only exist within families but also within communities. Viewing each client through an intersectional lens considers all aspects of the client's multidimensional identity (e.g., age, gender, sexual orientation, religion). **Intersectionality** considers the multitude of diverse components and contextual factors, and it offers a clearer picture of the dynamic influences of power, privilege, and oppression.

Disparities (i.e., between-group differences) in **age** and **SES** contribute to help-seeking behaviors, attitudes toward counseling, use of behavioral health services, and the quality of care received. A low SES is associated with emotional, social, and behavioral difficulties among adolescents and higher rates of depression, anxiety, and substance misuse among adults.

ASSESSING THE CLIENT'S PREVIOUS ATTEMPTS TO RESOLVE THE PRESENTING ISSUES

Therapists assess the client's previous attempt to resolve the presenting issues by identifying the family's/system's problem solving skills, contextual factors, and interactional patterns. Family therapists view presenting issues as they exist within the family system rather than with the individual client. Therapists provide family assessments by joining with the family and establishing a therapeutic alliance. In doing so, the therapist becomes a part of the family and can better identify, clarify, interpret, and understand interactional patterns influencing and maintaining the presenting problem. Therapists seek to define the presenting issues, assess their severity across time, determine past efforts to resolve issues, and assess the client's motivation to change.

By investigating the system's previous attempts at resolving the issue(s), the therapist can determine failed approaches, identify possible barriers, and confront previous obstacles. Once the inner workings of the family are understood, the therapist identifies any misunderstandings or miscommunications that influenced the previous problem-solving attempts. When necessary, families are presented with psychoeducation regarding the presenting issue. Therapy techniques used to assess the family's problem-solving skills include Socratic questioning, genograms, role-playing, assigning tasks, developing communication contracts, and reframing.

IDENTIFYING MEMBERS OF THE CLIENT, COMMUNITY, AND PROFESSIONAL SYSTEMS

Identifying and connecting the client with members in their community and professional systems increases the likelihood that the client will engage with these members and remain actively engaged in the process of problem resolution. Identifying resources across multiple systems allows for a strengths-based approach rather than a deficit-based understanding of the problem. Members or entities that make up a client's community and professional systems include, but are not limited to, the following:

- Coaches
- Teachers
- School counselors
- In-home service clinicians
- Case managers and coordinators
- Peer support specialists for severe mental disorders
- Peer mentors for students in grades K–12
- Recreational centers
- 12-step recovery programs
- Vocational rehabilitation professionals
- Community mental health professionals
- Culturally responsive community support programs
- Community-based psychosocial rehabilitation centers
- Religious and/or spiritual mentors and leaders
- Employee assistance programs
- Online resources and courses
- Student support services on college campuses
- Sociocultural enrichment centers on college campuses

ASSESSING ELEMENTS OF FUNCTIONING THAT IMPACT THE CLIENT'S SYSTEM

Biopsychosocial assessments are used to help therapists develop a holistic conceptualization of multiple factors in the client's system. A comprehensive framework is necessary to help determine the client or family system's risk and protective factors. The therapist can then begin to understand circumstances that promote or hinder the family system's functioning. The existence or absence of each element can also be viewed systemically, with the potential for each interdependent element to affect another. A nonexhaustive list of each element includes the following:

Element	Protective Factors	Risk Factors
SES	Higher instances of optimism and overall sense of well-being. Increased educational and work opportunities. Greater access to quality health care. Greater access to environmental green spaces. Social connectedness. Problem-solving and conflict resolution skills. Affordable childcare.	Fewer educational and work opportunities. Exposure to community violence. Greater instances of behavioral health disorders. Intergenerational transmission of poverty. Exposure to environmental toxins. Disparities in social support. Marital and family conflict. Racism and discrimination among racial and ethnic minority populations in low-SES communities. Unaffordable childcare.

44

Element	Protective Factors	Risk Factors
Emotional	Emotional regulation. Internal locus of control. Families with infants who have an easygoing temperament. Flexible family unit. Parental involvement.	Emotional dysregulation. External locus of control. Families with infants who have a fussy temperament. Rigid boundaries. Lack of parental involvement. Trauma and abuse. History or experience of interpersonal violence.
Physical	The absence of serious medical conditions. Developmental milestones are reached appropriately. Sleep and appetite are within normal limits. Engaging in physical exercise.	One or more health conditions. Drug and alcohol misuse. Developmental delays. Poor sleep hygiene. Poor appetite. Physical inactivity.
Spiritual	Meaning and purpose in life (i.e., existential well-being). Inner peace and acceptance. Enhanced family functioning. Positive spiritual role models. Practices that are open and affirming. Belief in moral order.	Religion and/or spiritual practices that foster and perpetuate family dysfunction. Spiritual abuse within or outside of the family system. Feelings of shame and guilt that are connected to religious or spiritual practice. Religious or spiritual leaders that control or manipulate others. Oppressive spiritual practices disaffirming one's sexual orientation, gender, and personal identity.
Mental	The absence of mental disorders among family members. No intentions to harm oneself or others. Orientation to person, space, and time. Has a full-range and appropriate affect.	History of mental disorders among family members. Suicidal ideation. Homicidal ideation. Audiovisual hallucinations. Affect is flat, sad, fearful, etc. Disorientation to person, space, and/or time.

Assessing for Symptoms of Substance Abuse

SCREENING AND ASSESSMENT

QUESTIONS ASKED IN A CLINICAL INTERVIEW

12 questions to ask a client in a clinical interview as a means of screening for drug/alcohol abuse include the following:

- **Question 1**: Find out the client's motivation for getting a mental health referral.
- **Question 2**: Obtain historical background about the beginning and severity of the client's drug and alcohol use. Discuss changes or deterioration in the client's behavior from the alcohol and drug use.
- **Question 3**: Determine the longest length of time that the client has stayed sober. Delve into the reasons why this period of sobriety ended.
- **Question 4**: Ask about the intoxication level that the client reaches when drinking or using drugs. Are there blackouts? Violent incidents? Is it harder to get a high now than when the client first started using drugs?
- **Question 5**: Find out the arrest record of the client. Pay particular attention to impaired driving (DUI) and domestic violence charges resulting from chemical abuse.
- **Question 6**: Find out about military service where drug or alcohol use was part of the client's service time.
- **Question 7**: Discuss addictive cycles of abuse found in the client's family. Note psychological disorders in family members and dysfunctional family relationships.
- **Question 8**: Find out the psychiatric history of the client.
- **Question 9**: Ask the client about his or her educational and work experience, including any drug or alcohol activities at school or in the workplace.
- **Question 10**: Get the medical and substance use history of the client. Note chronic pain treated with OxyContin or other pain relievers, which subsequently led to addiction.
- **Question 11**: Ask about prior drug and alcohol abuse treatment programs in which the client participated. Is the client a recidivist? If so, use a different treatment technique.
- **Question 12**: Discuss drug and/or alcohol levels revealed by the client's latest toxicology screen.

The answers gleaned in the clinical interview should correspond with other data collected from various sources. If there is a discrepancy, determine the truth of the situation.

MAST AND DAST ASSESSMENT TOOLS

The **Michigan Alcohol Screening Test (MAST)** was developed in 1971. The original assessment consisted of 25 yes or no questions with a complex grading system in which each question carried different weight when scoring. In the most recently revised version of this screening tool, the client must answer yes or no to 22 questions, which are then scored with a 0 or 1 based on the answer. Clients who score 0-2 have no alcohol problem. Clients who score 3-5 are early to middle problem drinkers. Clients who score 6 or more are problem drinkers. This test is accurate with a 0.05 level of confidence, according to the National Council on Alcoholism and Drug Dependence. Some research indicates that the 6-point cut-off for labeling an alcoholic should be raised to 10 points.

The **Drug Abuse Screening Test (DAST)** is the non-alcoholic counterpart to the MAST. If either the MAST or DAST is positive for addiction, then use the **Addiction Severity Index (ASI)** to determine in what areas the drug use has been the most invasive. The areas assessed include medical, legal, familial, social, employment, psychological, and psychiatric. The ASI test is longer, covering 180 items.

SASSI

The **Substance Abuse Subtle Screening Inventory (SASSI-4)** was first developed in 1988 to help identify covert abusers. Multiple revisions have occurred since. Typically, abusers hide their drug problems with lies, subterfuge, and defensive responses because they are:

- Unwilling to accept responsibility
- Hesitant to confront bad feelings and pain
- Afraid of the consequences (incarceration or rehabilitation programs)
- Conflicted (have mixed feelings) about quitting use of the chemical

The SASSI-4 is used to determine the truth, produce profiles useful for treatment planning, and understand the client. It can be administered as a one-page paper and pencil test, a computerized test with automated scoring, or an audio tape test. SASSI-4 takes 15 minutes to complete and 5 minutes to score. The adult version has an overall accuracy of 93%. The Adolescent SASSI-A3 has an overall accuracy of 94%. They both contain face-valid and subtle items, which do not tackle drug abuse in a directly apparent way.

Assessing for Symptoms of Compulsive Behaviors

SYMPTOMS OF BEHAVIORAL ADDICTIONS

Behavioral addictions (BAs) involve patterns of repeated behaviors that persist despite adverse consequences and impaired functioning. Addictive behaviors are reinforced by the activation of the mesolimbic dopaminergic system, or the brain's pleasure and reward circuitry. **Gambling disorder** is the only BA recognized in the DSM-5. The DSM-IV classified gambling disorder as an impulse-control disorder, which was reclassified in the DSM-5 as a "substance-related and addictive disorder." **Internet gaming disorder** is recognized in the DSM-5 but currently lacks empirical evidence to classify it as a mental disorder.

The DSM-5 stopped short of pathologizing BAs, including shopping, sexual activities, and internet use as disorders; however, there are shared symptoms among all BAs. BA symptoms include the following:

- Compulsive patterns of behavior.
- Preoccupation with the behavior.
- Lying to pursue the behavior.
- Using the behavior to change negative feelings.
- Bouts of craving and strong urges.
- Feelings of euphoria or highs.
- Difficulty stopping the behavior despite adverse outcomes.
- The person is irritable, irrational, and defensive when unable to pursue the BA.
- Impairment over multiple domains of functioning (e.g., social, occupational).

CLINICAL PRESENTATION AND ASSESSMENT OF THE EFFECTS OF BA

The experiences of people with BAs are similar to those with substance use disorders (SUDs) in that (1) there is a cyclical pattern of tension, arousal, gratification, and relief, (2) the motivation to engage in pleasure-seeking behaviors is eventually replaced by the motivation to avoid displeasure, and (3) symptoms of psychological withdrawal are experienced when attempting to cut down or stop the behavior.

In addition to assessing specific patterns of behavior, therapists also gather information on the

intensity, frequency, and duration of the addictive behavior, as well as the degree to which functional impairment occurs across multiple domains of functioning (e.g., emotional, social).

Other assessment elements include cultural influences, the age and role (i.e., parent, child) of the individual with the BA, how subsystems and family boundaries are constructed, and the interactional patterns used to preserve homeostasis. Therapists must also be mindful that family dynamics can appear different in various stages of the family member's BA.

There are several **comorbid and coexisting conditions associated with BAs,** including mood disorders, eating disorders, post-traumatic stress disorder (PTSD), substance misuse, suicidality, attention-deficit hyperactivity disorder, child abuse and neglect (current and by history for adults), exploitation of others, financial issues, legal issues, chronic health conditions, certain personality disorders, emotional dysregulation, and a lack of empathy.

PARAPHILIC BEHAVIOR

Paraphilic behaviors are characterized by deviant and harmful sexual interests, fantasies, or practices. The sexual urges or behaviors are recurrent and intense. Clinically significant sexual behaviors and interests are categorized in the DSM-5 as behaviors that fall outside the realm of "genital stimulation or preparatory fondling with phenotypically normal, physically mature, consenting human partners" (normophiliac).

To meet diagnostic criteria for paraphilic disorders, the DSM-5 requires that abnormal sexual interests, fantasies, or urges persist for at least 6 months, followed by acting on those interests and impulses. Qualifying behaviors must cause (1) significant personal distress and functional impairment or (2) physical injury, psychological distress, or impairment of oneself or another person. This may include death, injury, humiliation, or exploitation.

CLASSIFICATIONS OF PARAPHILIAS

The DSM-5 includes eight classifications of paraphilias. Accordingly, sexual arousal occurs in the presence of the following:

- **Frotteurism:** Rubbing or touching one's genitals against or in front of a nonconsenting person
- **Exhibitionism:** Exposing one's genitals or performing sexual behaviors in the presence of an unsuspecting person
- **Voyeurism:** Watching an unsuspecting person who is nude, partially nude, or engaging in sexual behaviors
- **Fetishism:** Using nonhuman objects or specific body parts or functions that are typically not associated with eroticism
- **Sexual masochism:** Wanting to be physically harmed, bound, or humiliated
- **Sexual sadism:** Being physically hurt, bound, or humiliated
- **Transvestism:** Dressing in the clothing of the opposite sex
- **Pedophilia:** Engaging in sexual activities with a prepubescent child

EFFECTS OF PARAPHILIC BEHAVIORS ON CLIENT FUNCTIONING

The various **manifestations and effects of paraphilias** are complex. Research suggests that many paraphilic behaviors result from instances of childhood sexual abuse, early exposure to pornography, and parental maltreatment. It is theorized that individuals engage in paraphilic fantasies of revenge, control, and hostility to combat feelings of rejection, fear, and distrust.

Many clients who engage in paraphilic behaviors have difficulty forming and maintaining healthy relationships with others. As a result, clients often experience strained family and couple relationships. Psychological distress associated with those manifestations may also cause impairments in social, occupational, and other areas of functioning. These effects can be compounded by **co-occurring disorders**, including obsessive-compulsive disorder, substance misuse, personality disorders, PTSD, mood disorders, and anxiety disorders.

When certain paraphilic urges/impulses are acted upon such as pedophilia, voyeurism, and exhibitionism, they are considered sex crimes that carry **legal penalties**. When a client's paraphilic behaviors result in incarceration, families are often challenged emotionally and financially. When appropriate, therapists connect families with sociocultural community supports (e.g., job training, educational training) to improve socioeconomic outcomes. It is essential that therapists continue to assess functional impairments in the presence of a trusting therapist–client relationship. In doing so, therapists continue to uphold the ethical principles of beneficence (i.e., working for the betterment of the individual and society) and the duty to promote respect for human dignity.

SEXUAL BEHAVIORS AND DISORDERS INVOLVING THE INTERNET AND TECHNOLOGY

Sexual behaviors using the **internet and other forms of technology** are vast. Sex-related behaviors can be **interactive** (e.g., cybersex) or **receptive** (e.g., viewing online pornography). Some methods involve sexually arousing material created or viewed on social media websites, with sexually explicit internet material gaining much attention due to its negative influence on adolescent attitudes toward sex, including dissatisfaction with in-person sexual experiences, issues with body image, social development, self-esteem, and early experiences with sexual behavior. **Social media websites** also provide teens with the medium for exploring one's sexual orientation and sexual identity. Studies suggest that **adolescent internet pornography** consumption is associated with higher instances of aggression and permissive attitudes toward sexual behaviors.

Although not recognized as a disorder in the DSM-5, **problematic internet use** is described as behavior that is excessive, compulsive, dysfunctional, and reinforced by the reward centers of the brain. The lure of the internet as a vehicle for experiencing sexual behaviors continues to be on the rise due to material that is **omnipresent, free, and anonymous.** Functional impairment occurs with the compulsive use of online sexual material at much higher rates than noncompulsive use. In addition, **compulsive use** is associated with higher rates of depression, anxiety, substance use, and suicidality. The functional impairment that results may occur across multiple domains (e.g., occupational, educational, social).

Copyright © Mometrix Media. You have been licensed one copy of this document for personal use only. Any other reproduction or redistribution is strictly prohibited. All rights reserved. This content is provided for test preparation purposes only and does not imply an endorsement by Mometrix of any particular political, scientific, or religious point of view.

Assessing Appropriateness for Telehealth

ASSESSING THE IMPACT OF THE USE OF TECHNOLOGY

With technological advances and the subsequent rise in internet use, assessing how clients incorporate technology into their daily lives is necessary for determining relevant psychosocial influences. To understand the impact of technology, therapists assess for the client's ability to access and afford technology, the nature and frequency of use, and the client's digital literacy.

Therapists also assess the client's strengths (e.g., the ability to communicate with friends, family and colleagues), weaknesses (e.g., discomfort with navigating the internet), risk factors (e.g., problematic internet use), and needs (e.g., removing barriers to access therapists, health-care information, online recovery meetings) in the context of their current technological ecosystem.

One method for determining the effects of technology is to use developmental and age-appropriate lines of inquiry. For example, when assessing children and adolescents, therapists obtain information on the amount of allowable screen time, adult supervision of use, discussions on appropriate internet safety, gaming, texting, use of social media, access to streaming services, sex-related online behavior, and cyberbullying. Assessment questions for adults could include online communication patterns with family members, physical symptoms resulting from excessive use (e.g., eye strain, insomnia, tendinitis), and functional impairment resulting from overuse.

EVALUATING A CLIENT'S APPROPRIATENESS FOR TELEHEALTH

Therapists must abide by **legal and ethical mandates** for telehealth, including the use of Health Insurance Portability and Accountability Act of 1996 (HIPAA)-compliant platforms and encrypted systems for storing client data. In addition, potential risk factors, benefits, and limitations specific to telehealth must be determined and reviewed with clients on an ongoing basis. **Telehealth risk factors** include the possibility of technology failure, therapeutic relationship challenges, and the possibility of a confidentiality or security breach.

Therapists use encryption and **two-factor authentication** by selecting words, symbols, or codes to secure data on communication devices. Steps taken to protect client confidentiality and well-being include verification of the client's identity, location, and safety at the beginning of each therapy session. Policies and procedures are also developed to ensure client safety during emergencies or crises. Considerations consist of keeping a record of emergency numbers specific to the client's location, strategies for handling client emergencies, and policies for addressing technology failure or disconnection.

When evaluating a client for telehealth services, therapists consider each client's cognitive, mental health, and emotional needs, and any barriers that would interfere with participation, including access to an uninterrupted and confidential setting, comfort level with technology, and access to broadband internet services for videoconferencing. Therapists use telehealth assessments to identify specific client barriers, including age, management of chronic suicidality, insurance coverage for telehealth services, and accessing services during vacation or when traveling across state lines.

Client Strengths, Resources, and Coping Skills

ASSESSING STRENGTHS, RESOURCES, AND COPING SKILLS AVAILABLE TO THE CLIENT

A **strengths-based assessment** is a collaborative process used to determine a **client's positive characteristics, resources, and coping skills**. The purpose of a strengths-based approach is to enhance the client's self-determination, autonomy, social connectedness, and resiliency. Strengths-based assessments are ongoing and holistic. A fluid assessment helps the client **identify strengths** during a specific point in time, with the overarching goal of matching the client's unique set of resources, assets, and coping skills with specific circumstances and experiences. Identifying positive **core attributes**, such as humor, positive reframing, and acceptance, is also helpful for mitigating problematic aspects of stressful situations.

Strengths-based assessments are person-centered and geared toward identifying strengths across

multiple systems and contexts. For example, potential strengths within the client's **family system** include loyalty, problem-solving ability, motivation to change, and shared values. In the context of the client's **community and social networks**, strengths could consist of positive interpersonal relationships, connections with community leaders, occupational opportunities,

and financial resources. Therapists help clients **identify social and emotional resources**, which could include self-awareness, emotional regulation, self-efficacy, social engagement, and access to supportive community resources. An ongoing assessment of client strengths helps build resiliency and foster hope.

Psychological Testing and Assessment Tools

PSYCHOLOGICAL TESTING THAT SHAPES THE THERAPEUTIC APPROACH

Psychological testing can be conducted in various stages of therapy to obtain a more accurate clinical picture, finalize a diagnosis, identify client strengths and weaknesses, or determine specific treatment needs. **Informal and formal assessment** measures are used at various service intervals to determine a client's level of functioning across multiple domains (e.g., educational, social, vocational). Informal assessments are unstructured and subjective. Examples of informal assessments include the clinical interview, behavioral observations, and rating scales. Behavioral assessments are beneficial for substantiating childhood psychiatric disorders, which require behaviors to be present in two or more settings (e.g., home, school, peer gatherings). Behavioral assessments are effective for measuring behavior across settings and a client's response to treatment.

Formal assessments, which include standardized assessments, help measure cognitive functioning and personality. Standardized assessments are norm based, meaning specific traits or abilities are measured against a comparison group. Scoring results are generally reported as a rank or percentile. Examples of standardized cognitive assessments include the Cognitive Abilities Test (for students in grades K–12) and the Woodcock-Johnson III (for ages 2–90). Personality assessments are used to determine personality traits and styles or to predict behavioral reactions in certain situations. Examples include self-report inventories (e.g., the Minnesota Multiphasic Personality Inventory [MMPI]) or projective tests (e.g., the Rorschach inkblot test).

ASSESSMENT TOOLS

Therapists use a variety of tests and assessments to help substantiate a diagnosis, direct treatment, and measure a client's attributes or capabilities. **Psychological assessments** combine clinical interviews, behavioral observations, health record reviews, and standardized psychological tests to understand how the client thinks, feels, and behaves. A general overview of the multiscale, disorder-specific psychological and personality assessment instruments includes the following:

- **The Minnesota Multiphasic Personality Inventory (MMPI):** This is a self-report measure of psychological maladjustment. Since its inception, there have been multiple updates and revisions. The adult version currently in use is the MMPI-2. The MMPI-2 consists of 567 true/false measures and more than 120 scales. There are 9 validity scales (e.g., defensiveness, lying, faking bad), multiple clinical scales, including scales measuring mental disorders (e.g., depression, schizophrenia) and scales measuring personality characteristics and traits (e.g., somatization, anger).
- **Millon Clinical Multiaxial Inventory-IV:** This is a self-report personality assessment used to measure personality traits and clinical psychopathology. There are 25 scales designed to measure 10 clinical syndromes (e.g., generalized anxiety, bipolar disorder)—3 of which are classified as severe clinical syndromes (i.e., schizophrenic spectrum, major depression, delusional). Assessment measures also include 15 personality patterns (e.g., histrionic, schizoid)—3 of which have severe personality pathology (i.e., borderline, paranoid, schizotypal). Finally, there are three modifying indices (i.e., disclosure, desirability, and debasement), and two random response indices (i.e., invalidity, inconsistency).
- **Rorschach inkblot test:** This test is a projective psychological assessment in which the examiner asks the subject to describe 10 bilaterally symmetrical inkblots. The test assesses personality traits, emotional responses, and cognitive functioning.

MARITAL SATISFACTION INVENTORY

The **Marital Satisfaction Inventory, revised** is composed of 150 true/false items for couples and families. Couples without children are given an inventory with 129 true/false items. It is designed to assist with communication, reconciliation, and perceptual relationship differences. The Marital Satisfaction Inventory, revised measures several elements of marital interaction contributing to marital and/or family discord, including expressions of feelings, problem-solving strategies, time spent together, sexual satisfaction, and dissatisfaction with children. This inventory is helpful for traditional and nontraditional couples because items use the terms "partner" and "relationship."

FAMILY ADAPTABILITY AND COHESION SCALE IV

The **Family Adaptability and Cohesion Scale IV** is a 62-item questionnaire completed independently by all family members older than age 12. It uses a Likert scale to assess levels of family cohesion. There are measurement scales assessing balanced cohesion and unbalanced cohesion, the latter determined by levels of enmeshment and disengagement. There are also measures for balanced flexibility and unbalanced flexibility, the latter determined by levels of rigidity and chaos. Communication and satisfaction scales are also provided.

PREPARE/ENRICH INVENTORY

The **PREPARE/ENRICH inventory** is a comprehensive standardized assessment of couple strengths and growth areas. The inventory is based on David Olson's Circumplex Model of Marriage and Family Systems. This model focuses on areas of marital cohesion, flexibility, and communication. In the year 2000, five versions of the PREPARE/ENRICH inventory were launched, including PREPARE (for premarital couples), PREPARE—CC (for cohabiting couples), and PREPARE—MC (for married couples with children). In 2009, the latest version of PREPARE/ENRICH, known as the customized version, was introduced, which retained several elements of previous versions.

The customized version of PREPARE/ENRICH is an online inventory adapted for a wide variety of couple dimensions, including the relationship stage (i.e., engaged, married, or dating) and relationship structure (e.g., ages, children in the home, previous marriages). The customized version uses the same 10 core scales included in the original PREPARE/ENRICH inventory, and it has new measures for cultural and ethnic issues, faith-based factors (e.g., interfaith), age of children (when applicable), and parenting situations (when applicable).

MEASUREMENT SCALES

The PREPARE/ENRICH customized version includes the following measurement scales:

- Ten **core scales of a couple's relationship**, including idealistic distortion, communication, conflict resolution, partner style and habits, financial management, leisure activities, affection and sexuality, family and friends, relationship roles, and spiritual beliefs.
- Four **relationship dynamics:** Assertiveness (i.e., how well each partner's needs are identified and expressed), self-confidence (i.e., positive feelings about oneself), avoidance (i.e., lacking the initiative to address issues in the relationship), and partner dominance (i.e., the level of control one partner has over the other).
- The **SCOPE personality profile** measures personality types classified as social, change, organized, pleasing, and emotionally steady.
- Five **premarital and married couple categories** include vitalized, harmonious, conventional, conflicted, and devitalized.
- The **couple and family map** is used to assess areas of the Circumplex Model, including cohesion/closeness and flexibility in the couple's relationship and their families of origin.

Diagnosis

DIAGNOSTIC AND STATISTICAL MANUAL (DSM)

Published by the American Psychiatric Association, the **Diagnostic and Statistical Manual (DSM)** is used to aid clinicians in diagnosing and classifying mental disorders. Its current edition, the DSM-5-TR, was released in 2022. The DSM-5-TR contains updated diagnostic descriptions and criteria generated from the systematic review of scientific literature accumulated over the past decade. Numerous changes exist, including new ICD-10-CM codes for suicidal behavior, nonsuicidal self-injury, and substance intoxication and withdrawal. Suicidal behavior and nonsuicidal self-injury can now be flagged without requiring a mental disorder diagnosis.

INTERNATIONAL CLASSIFICATION OF DISEASES (ICD)

The current version of the **International Classification of Diseases (ICD)** is the ICD-10th Edition, Clinical Modification (ICD-10-CM). The World Health Organization maintains the ICD. In the United States, the ICD is monitored by the National Center for Health Statistics and the Centers for Medicare & Medicaid Services. ICD codes are used to substantiate medical necessity and bill insurance companies for reimbursement; identify medical conditions used in mortality statistics, including the cause of death listed on death certificates; help with the worldwide standardization of record keeping and data collection; and to track and report medical conditions.

DEVELOPING A RELATIONAL DIAGNOSIS

MFTs attend to the client's presenting problem as it exists within various systems. It is important to determine if a relational issue exists in the context of a specific relationship or if it is symptomatic of an underlying mental disorder. Common mental disorders treated by MFTs include mood disorders, anxiety disorders, sexual disorders, eating disorders, and PTSD. Some disorders, such as **sexual disorders,** can only be diagnosed if the dysfunction is not exclusively caused by significant relationship distress, either currently or in the person's history. Therapists use assessment instruments (e.g., the Marital Satisfaction Inventory or the Dyadic Adjustment Scale) to evaluate the overall health of a couple's relationship.

The DSM-5 addresses relational issues in the domain **"other relational conditions or problems,"** which includes relational factors that may affect the client's diagnosis, prognosis, and treatment. Intimate adult partner relationships and parent–caregiver relationships, particularly those involving maltreatment or neglect, can significantly influence the client's clinical presentation. The following broad relational categories are included in the DSM:

- Problems related to family upbringing
- Other problems related to the primary support group
- Child maltreatment and neglect problems
- Adult maltreatment and neglect problems
- Adult abuse of a nonpartner

Relational distress is associated with **functional impairment** across cognitive, emotional, and/or behavioral domains. Problematic thoughts include constantly assigning negative attributions to another's behavior or intentions. Emotional consequences include chronic apathy, sadness, or resentment toward one's partner, whereas behavioral consequences include withdrawal and conflict.

Psychopathology

RECIPROCAL INFLUENCE OF PSYCHIATRIC DISORDERS

The reciprocal influence of psychiatric disorders within the client system occurs as a manifestation of **circular interactions** between the client and the client system. The etiology and maintenance of psychiatric disorders are considered in the context of mutually interdependent, nonsequential, interactional factors and systemic behavioral patterns. This approach is in contrast to a linear cause-and-effect analysis of the presenting issues and mental disorders. The reciprocal influence of psychopathology is based on the assumption that behavior A influences behavior B and behavior B influences behavior A. This circular dynamic persists and is maintained by relational dynamics within the client system.

The reciprocal influence of psychiatric disorders acknowledges **multiple causes and effects** within the client system. Systemic reciprocity is based on the theory that parts of a client system engage with one another to maintain homeostasis or balance. **Homeostasis** ensures that parts of a system will interact with others through spoken and unspoken family roles, rules, and expectations. The give and take of behavioral patterns help a family maintain homeostasis. This also holds true when examining individuals within the context of their communities, influenced by cultural expectations, norms, values, and developmental transitions.

CHILD, ADOLESCENT, AND ADULT PSYCHOPATHOLOGY

Child, adolescent, and adult psychopathology is best understood from a **developmental, physical, and sociocultural perspective.** Life-span developmental psychopathology emphasizes the lifelong influences of cognitive, affective, contextual, and systemic factors. From an early age, infants and children experience age-related developmental milestones. A comparative examination of normative events, such as physical and cognitive functioning, is one method for distinguishing psychopathology from healthy development. However, this method alone is insufficient because psychopathology results from the complex and dynamic interaction of multiple factors (e.g., social, cultural) in many areas of a client's life (e.g., school, home, and work).

From a diagnostic perspective, **children younger than age 12** are at an increased risk for separation anxiety disorder and attention-deficit hyperactivity disorder.

Among adolescent populations, there is a shift away from externalized disorders. Adolescents are more likely than children to experience internalized disorders, including depression, panic disorder, and agoraphobia. Adolescents are also more vulnerable to SUD. **Adults** with mental health disorders are more likely to have experienced psychopathology in childhood or adolescence. The clinical manifestations of mental disorders in adulthood are generally mediated by biopsychosocial conditions, including, but not limited to, psychosocial stressors, experiences of trauma, intelligence, the family environment, and SES.

PSYCHOPATHOLOGY IN AGING POPULATIONS

Psychopathology among the aging (i.e., individuals >60) is associated with age-related decreases in mental, social, cognitive, and physical functioning. **Mental disorders** common among the aging include depressive disorders, mood disorders, anxiety, and cognitive impairment. In the United States, white men older than age 65 have the highest rates of **suicide.** Increased episodes of depression and suicidality are associated with loneliness and social isolation among older populations. Depressive symptoms are found to lead to—as well as result from—impairments in other areas in functioning.

Among the aging population, **social and emotional support** has a mediating effect on depression. Individuals older than age 60 who experience social support are more likely to report that their lives have purpose and meaning. Social and emotional support is also associated with improved cognitive functioning and a decreased risk of chronic mental and physical health disorders. Mortality rates are also mitigated by social and emotional support.

Stressors occurring in older age can exacerbate the onset of psychopathology. These stressors include the death of a spouse, retirement, loss of independence, financial issues, and chronic health issues. The comorbid occurrence of **mental and physical health conditions** is also common. For example, older adults with heart conditions are more likely to experience depressive disorders. Similarly, cognitive disorders often co-occur with mental disorders.

Impact of Physical and Medical Conditions on the Client System

AUTISM SPECTRUM DISORDER (ASD)

Autism spectrum disorder (ASD) is classified as a neurodevelopmental disorder in the DSM-5-TR, which characterizes ASD by "persistent difficulties in the social use of verbal and nonverbal communication as manifested by all of the following:

- Deficits in using communication for social purposes
- Impairment of the ability to change communication to match context
- Difficulties with following rules for conversation (taking turns, use of verbal/nonverbal signs to regulate interaction)
- Difficulties understanding what is not explicitly stated."

These difficulties must persist across multiple settings and contexts and result in functional impairment in communication, social interactions, and academic accomplishments. For children with ASD, behaviors such as inflexible adherence to routines and habits, fixated interests, and sensory processing difficulties can be challenging to the family system. In addition, the tendency for individuals with ASD to depend on family members well into adulthood can result in **caregiver stress, increased sense of burden,** and **increased rates of marital dissatisfaction.** The theoretical assumption of family systems theory is that mental disorders such as ASD are contextually bound and are predisposed and perpetuated by family members.

RECIPROCAL INFLUENCE OF BIOLOGICAL FACTORS AND MEDICAL CONDITIONS

The reciprocal influence of biopsychosocial factors is based on the assumption that an individual's health reflects the interplay between multiple systems of functioning. Factors such as biological, social, and other contextual elements are believed to influence a person over time. Biological systems, such as the immune, cardiovascular, and neural systems, affect the development and maintenance of physical and mental health conditions.

Medical conditions resulting from **biological disorders** include genetically inherited disorders. Genetic disorders consist of congenital disabilities, developmental deficits, chronic disease, and sensory difficulties. Examples of genetically inherited conditions include some cancers, muscular dystrophy, high cholesterol, congenital heart disease, hearing loss, learning disabilities, and Huntington's disease.

Dysfunctional behaviors within the client system, including highly conflictual subsystems, can result in biological stress responses. Over time, relational conflict and stress can lead to higher allostatic loads—the cumulative effects of chronic stressors. When the body cannot accommodate these stressors' chronic demands, physiological regulatory systems adapt and change. One adaptation method involves the elevation of stress hormones and biochemical interactions, which can result in higher rates of mental and physical conditions.

BIDIRECTIONAL RELATIONSHIP BETWEEN PHYSICAL AND MENTAL HEALTH SYMPTOMS

There is a **bidirectional relationship** between physical and mental health symptoms. For individuals presenting with behavioral, psychological, and physical symptoms, completing a thorough medical evaluation is essential for ruling out the influence of medical conditions on mental disorders and vice versa. Chronic medical conditions, including diabetes, thyroid problems, heart disease, and cancer, increase the likelihood of a person developing a mental disorder. Therefore, effective client care is contingent upon understanding the underlying causes of a client's psychological and physical symptoms.

A holistic approach enables counselors to use integrative and culturally sensitive assessment strategies to detect and treat behavioral health conditions. **Interdisciplinary collaboration** helps to ensure that mental disorders are considered in the context of coexisting substance use, medical problems, environmental conditions, and cultural values and beliefs.

To substantiate a **DSM diagnosis,** counselors must ensure that the symptoms are not otherwise caused by medical issues or substance misuse. To aid in this process, counselors obtain an updated list of the client's prescribed medications, including all vitamins and supplements. In addition, comprehensive care involves acquiring an accurate history of factors affecting medical conditions, including the dynamic influence of the following elements: biological (e.g., neurochemistry, physiological responses), social (e.g., family, friends), psychological (e.g., thoughts, feelings), spiritual factors (e.g., beliefs and values), environmental factors (e.g., poverty, interpersonal relationships), and behaviors (e.g., coping skills, impulsivity, substance use).

Indicators for Further Psychiatric Evaluation

NEED FOR PSYCHIATRIC EVALUATION

A psychiatric evaluation is performed by a medical doctor and is used to diagnose mental disorders, rule out any medical etiology responsible for the client's symptoms, and determine which medication to prescribe when necessary. Counselors provide an integrative, holistic assessment when working with clients exhibiting psychological, behavioral, and physical symptoms. A referral for a psychiatric evaluation may be warranted for clients with severe symptomology and acute levels of distress. Clients may also require a psychiatric evaluation if they have not made progress on their treatment plan goals or if they have moved to a higher level of care. Indications that a client may require a psychiatric evaluation include the following:

- Paranoia
- Anhedonia
- Hallucinations
- Suicidal ideation
- Severe mood swings
- Sleep or appetite disturbances
- Unexplained memory loss

As with other mental health professionals, a psychiatrist will evaluate the client's behaviors, symptoms, and level of functioning across the following domains: biological, psychological, social, spiritual, cultural, and emotional. Psychiatric evaluations also include reviewing the client's treatment history, including any previous diagnoses, medications, and treatment compliance. Psychiatrists assess for any past or present experiences of trauma and may also order outside tests (e.g., lab work, specialized testing). In addition, psychiatrists determine the influence of life circumstances and the client's unique strengths and vulnerabilities.

NEED FOR PSYCHOEDUCATIONAL EVALUATION

Individuals between the ages of 3 and 21 exhibiting certain behaviors, psychological features, and/or physical symptoms that interfere with learning may be eligible for additional classroom interventions to enhance academic performance. A psychologist will conduct psychoeducational testing to determine if students meet eligibility requirements. Psychoeducational testing and evaluations help identify any social, emotional, behavioral, cognitive, or psychological factors that may interfere with a student's learning. These symptoms may include, but are not limited to, the following:

- Disruptive classroom behaviors
- Inability to stay seated
- Argumentative with authority
- Angry outbursts
- Difficulty retaining information
- Slow processing speed
- Impulsivity
- Developmental delays
- Difficulty reading social cues
- Mood changes
- Anxiety
- Social withdrawal

- Anhedonia
- Sadness
- Distractibility
- Suicidal ideation
- Nonsuicidal self-injury
- Prolonged emotional distress
- Poor vision
- Hearing difficulties

Psychoeducational testing also helps identify specific learning disorders, including dyslexia, dysgraphia, dyscalculia, auditory processing disorder, language processing disorder, visual perceptual/visual motor deficit, and other health impairments. A complete psychoeducational assessment generally includes a clinical interview, questionnaires, standardized testing, observations, and a review of academic performance.

NEED FOR A PSYCHOLOGICAL EVALUATION

A **psychological evaluation** is primarily performed and interpreted by a doctoral-level psychologist and is used to identify the etiology of behavioral, psychological, emotional, social, and physical symptomatology. Components of a psychological evaluation include culturally sensitive psychological tests and assessment measures. The terms "psychological assessment" and "psychological evaluation" are often used interchangeably. The distinction between the two is that the evaluation represents the end product or conclusion of the decision-making process.

Psychological testing comprises standardized assessment instruments and other formal measures (e.g., questionnaires, checklists) used to appraise psychological traits, intelligence, and cognitive functioning. Psychologists generally perform a battery of tests because one test alone is insufficient in recommending a course of treatment. Examples of commonly used psychological tests include the Rorschach inkblot, Thematic Apperception Test, Wechsler Adult Intelligence Scale-Revised, Woodcock-Johnson III Tests of Cognitive Disabilities, and MMPI.

A psychological assessment is a problem-solving process that measures and integrates relevant aspects of a person's history and presenting issues, including behaviors, psychological features, or physical symptoms, to help provide the clarity essential for determining underlying causes of functional impairment. Examples of symptoms that may indicate the need for a psychological evaluation include social withdrawal, thinking and processing difficulties, rapid shifts in emotions and reactions, paranoia, a decrease in sleep and appetite, unexplained weight loss not attributed to physiologic/medical conditions, and somatic complaints.

Grief

IMPACT OF GRIEF ON THE INDIVIDUAL

Grief is an emotional response to loss that begins at the time a loss is anticipated and continues on an individual timetable. While there are identifiable stages of grief, it is not an orderly and predictable process. It involves overcoming anger, disbelief, guilt, and a myriad of related emotions. The grieving individual may move back and forth between stages or experience several emotions at any given time. Each person's grief response is unique to their own coping patterns, stress levels, age, gender, belief system, and previous experiences with loss.

KUBLER-ROSS'S FIVE STAGES OF GRIEF

Kubler-Ross taught the medical community that the dying person and their family welcome open, honest discussion of the dying process. She believed that there were certain stages that people go through while experiencing grief. The stages may not occur in order; they may occur out of order, some may be skipped, and some may occur more than once. **Kubler Ross's stages of grief** include the following:

- **Denial**: The person denies the loss and tries to pretend it isn't true. During this time, the person may seek a second opinion or alternative therapies (in the case of a terminal diagnosis) or act as though the loss never occurred. They may use denial until they are better able to emotionally cope with the reality of the loss or changes that need to be made.
- **Anger**: The person is angry about the situation and may focus that rage on anyone or anything.
- **Bargaining**: The person attempts to make deals with a higher power to secure a better outcome to their situation.
- **Depression**: The person anticipates the loss and the changes it will bring with a sense of sadness and grief.
- **Acceptance**: The person accepts the loss and is ready to face it. They may begin to withdraw from interests and family.

> **Review Video: The Five Stages of Grief**
> Visit mometrix.com/academy and enter code: 648794

ANTICIPATORY GRIEF

Anticipatory grief is the mental, social, and somatic reactions of an individual as they prepare themselves for a perceived future loss. The individual experiences a process of intellectual, emotional, and behavioral responses in order to modify their self-concept, based on their perception of what the potential loss will mean in their life. This process often takes place ahead of the actual loss, from the time the loss is first perceived until it is resolved as a reality for the individual. This process can also blend with past loss experiences. It is associated with the individual's perception of how life will be affected by the particular diagnosis as well as the impending death. Acknowledging this anticipatory grief allows family members to begin looking toward a changed future. Suppressing this anticipatory process may inhibit relationships with the ill individual and contribute to a more difficult grieving process at a later time. However, appropriate anticipatory grieving does not take the place of grief during the actual time of death.

DISENFRANCHISED GRIEF

Disenfranchised grief occurs when the loss being experienced cannot be openly acknowledged, publicly mourned, or socially supported. Society and culture are partly responsible for an individual's response to a loss. There is a social context to grief. If a person incurring the loss will be putting himself or herself at risk by expressing grief, disenfranchised grief occurs. The risk for disenfranchised grief is greatest among those whose relationship with the thing they lost was not known or regarded as significant. This is also the situation found among bereaved persons who are not recognized by society as capable of grief, such as young children, or needing to mourn, such as an ex-spouse or secret lover.

GRIEF VS. DEPRESSION

Normal grief is self-limiting to the loss itself. Emotional responses will vary and may include open expressions of anger. The individual may experience difficulty sleeping or vivid dreams, a lack of energy, and weight loss. Crying is evident and provides some relief of extreme emotions. The individual remains socially responsive and seeks reassurance from others.

By contrast, **depression** is marked by extensive periods of sadness and preoccupation often extending beyond two months. It is not limited to the single event. There is an absence of pleasure or anger and isolation from previous social support systems. The individual can experience extreme lethargy, weight loss, insomnia, or hypersomnia. Crying is absent or persistent and provides no relief of emotions. Professional intervention is often required to relieve depression.

RISK FACTORS AND INDICATORS OF GRIEF

Grief and loss across the life span occur as the result of a variety of risk factors and indicators, including the following:

- **Sudden unemployment:** The impact of the sudden loss of a job or occupation can be extensive, even if the period of unemployment is brief. Sudden unemployment can affect areas of one's social, financial, psychological, and physical well-being. Grief responses can be complicated by a person's negative cognitive appraisal of the job loss and the degree of investment and attachment tied to their former position. Symptoms of complicated grief that accompany sudden unemployment include social withdrawal, deep sadness, an inability to focus on anything else, resentment toward oneself, lacking a sense of purpose, and an inability to accept the circumstances related to sudden unemployment.

- **Runaway children:** For some children, grief-related hopelessness and resentment can lead to running away to escape or avoid the painful circumstances surrounding loss. Children who run away are more likely to have experienced childhood traumatic grief, a condition resulting from chronic and severe loss, characterized by physiological arousal responses, including fight (e.g., anger, aggression, irritability), freeze (e.g., withdrawal, constriction), or flight (e.g., running away, escape). Most children who run away do so to escape abusive home environments, many of which are affected by drug and alcohol misuse, divorce or separations, parental rejection, or death and loss.

- **Chronic illness:** Chronic illness, such as autoimmune disorders, certain cancers, heart disease, and stroke, present unique issues due to their complex causes, multiple risk factors, and functional impairment. The ongoing, generally incurable, and often unpredictable nature of chronic illness can be accompanied with depressive symptoms and complex grief. Individuals with chronic illness experience multiple difficult losses. Emotional indicators of grief include irritability, resentment, anxiety, hopelessness, and social disengagement. Complicated grief is associated with mourning the loss of normalcy, freedom, and personal relationships.

- **Sexual potency:** Sexual potency is the ability for a male to perform sexual intercourse. Erectile dysfunction is associated with certain medications (e.g., antidepressants, blood pressure medication) and chronic medical conditions, some of which include cardiovascular disease, testosterone deficiency, Parkinson's disease, multiple sclerosis, prostate cancer, and diabetes. The loss associated with chronic illness, coupled with an inability to perform during sexual intercourse, can lead to complicated grief. Men can also experience sexual impotency as the result of loss, depression, anxiety, or trauma. Research indicates that 70% of men older than age 70 experience erectile dysfunction, which can compound grief and loss associated with aging and chronic illness. Loss of sexual potency can interfere with emotional connectedness, leading to feelings of loneliness and dissatisfaction.

Impact of Occupational Issues on Individuals and Families

MILITARY PERSONNEL AND THOSE WITH PROLONGED DEPLOYMENTS

Occupational issues affecting military personnel can present various challenges to individuals and their families. Nearly 25% of active-duty military personnel show indicators of a **mental health disorder,** many of whom are diagnosed with PTSD, generalized anxiety disorder, major depressive disorder, and SUD. Conflicts and combat methods resulting in traumatic brain injury (TBI) can further complicate mental health conditions. TBIs are caused by head or bodily injuries and can result in memory difficulties, mental confusion, fatigue, headaches, vision problems, and mood lability.

Research studies show that **prolonged deployment** is one of military personnel's most challenging occupational issues. Longitudinal studies of veteran populations indicate that **combat exposure** is closely associated with negative health outcomes. Soldiers with combat exposure have higher rates of suicide, divorce, substance use, and chronic pain. Military spouses are at risk for depression and anxiety with emotional distress attributed to multiple moves, sudden and prolonged deployment, increased household responsibilities, and financial issues (primarily among junior enlisted soldiers).

During prolonged deployment, **children** in distress can exhibit a host of emotional and behavioral problems, including externalized behaviors (e.g., aggression, defiance), higher levels of anxiety, declining grades, and difficulty sleeping. These risks are more pronounced in families with young children and when the at-home parent endures multiple personal stressors. Several studies show symptom improvement once military personnel return home and are reintegrated with their families. However, reintegration difficulties are more pronounced among military personnel diagnosed with PTSD. Upon return to their families, individuals diagnosed with PTSD have higher rates of family violence and increased emotional and behavioral symptoms among their children.

FIRST RESPONDERS AND MEDICAL PROVIDERS

First responders include individuals trained to provide immediate assistance in the event of medical emergencies, natural disasters, accidents involving hazardous waste, terrorism, fires, and related emergencies. Workers include law enforcement, medical professionals, firefighters, emergency medical technicians, and those with related training. Occupational issues unique to first responders and medical providers include the cumulative effects of work-related stressors, such as chronic exposure to trauma, shift work, and limited downtime.

Research suggests that first responders experience various psychological and physical effects—particularly shift workers—including sleep disruption, headaches, weight gain, and mental distress. These symptoms are compounded by a work culture emphasizing strength and self-reliance while discouraging help-seeking behaviors. Behavioral health issues affecting first responders include, but are not limited to, PTSD, suicidality, depression, and SUD. Children are susceptible to secondary, or vicarious, trauma stemming from caregivers who are emotionally, mentally, and physically affected by job-related stressors. Children and families experience increased anxiety when sensing uncertainty, danger, and distress from the adults in the home.

Other Issues Affecting the Client System

EASTERN AND WESTERN PHILOSOPHIES/RELIGIONS

The primary elements of Eastern and Western philosophies/religions include the following:

Western	Eastern
European origins	Asian origins
Individualism: Emphasis on "I"	Collectivism: Emphasis on "we"
Practical in nature	Spiritual in nature
Logic and reason applied to existential matters	Interpretation applied to existential matters
Rooted in Judeo-Christianity	Rooted in Confucianism, Mahāyāna Buddhism, and Taoism
Linear or goal-oriented development and improvement	Cyclic or never-ending development and improvement
External success and achievement held in high esteem	Inner improvement and self-development held in high esteem

The **main difference** between Western and Eastern philosophies and religions is that Westerners emphasize individual rights (i.e., independence), and Easterners value social responsibility or connectedness (i.e., interdependence). These orientations can impact the client's system in the ways in which decisions are made and the values that are nurtured. For example, Easterners value cooperation, respect for authority, and conformity, whereas Westerners place a higher value on competition, the right to push back against authority, and the pursuit of uniqueness. Easterners value obedience to parents, the maintenance of gender roles and duties, and the wisdom of elderly advice. Western families are more accepting of gender equality, shared roles and responsibilities, and seeking outside information to help make decisions.

ISSUES RELATED TO CHILD CUSTODY

The **impact of child custody** on a client's system is based on multiple factors. Children from families with **conflictual divorces** are at increased risk for emotional, behavioral, social, and academic difficulties. Younger children have more trouble understanding divorce and may worry that it could somehow be their fault. Teens from conflictual homes may become angry and blame one parent for a divorce, mainly if the divorce was unexpected. Adolescents from conflictual divorced families are more likely to engage in substance misuse and early sexual activity than their peers residing in intact homes.

Conflictual divorces tend to lead to **conflictual child custody arrangements.** Children who have had difficulty adjusting to divorce are now faced with additional changes resulting from shared custody, including changing schools or moving to a new home. Parents may encounter financial problems, and the newly single parents may feel overwhelmed and unavailable. Parents and children are significantly impacted by custody battles characterized by anger and bitterness, particularly when children are placed in the middle. Children with one parent who uses a child to meet their emotional needs are more likely to experience depression, anxiety, and mental distress. The emotional and psychological adjustment of all household members and the quality of the parent–child relationship are also significant predictors of mental well-being.

INFIDELITY

IMPACT ON INTIMATE RELATIONSHIPS

In the United States, nearly 20% of married partners and 30–40% of unmarried partners admit to engaging in infidelity. However, statistics vary depending on how infidelity is defined and measured. In its strictest sense, **infidelity** (i.e., cheating, having an affair) is defined as any betrayal of trust resulting from an action involving someone outside of the committed relationship without the primary partner's consent. By this measure, infidelity includes kissing, flirting, sexual intercourse, use of pornography, or romantically connecting with someone outside of the committed union (i.e., an emotional affair).

Technological advancements have contributed to computer-mediated acts of infidelity, such as sexting, exchanging explicit photos, or interactions using live webcam formats. Studies show that **online and in-person episodes of infidelity** are moderately predicted by indicators including relationship satisfaction, sexual satisfaction, permissive attitudes toward sex, and the length of the relationship. Measures of sexual desire and relationship factors were found to be the strongest predictors of infidelity.

Infidelity can have lasting effects on the **client's family system**. For the noninvolved partner, there are feelings of anxiety, depression, grief, loss, acute stress, and resentment. When infidelity is exposed, the overall emotional distress of one or more partners can be exacerbated by negative cognitive appraisal (i.e., personal perception), whereas a stable sense of self-worth serves as a protective factor. Severe emotional distress can lead to suicidal ideations among both partners.

IMPACT ON CHILDREN AND FAMILIES

Infidelity among intimate partner dyads can have lasting effects on the emotional and mental well-being of all members of the family system. These consequences can harm children, especially those exposed to intimate partner conflict, violence, and/or family disruption. The intergenerational consequences of infidelity are profound, particularly when one or both parents experience significant psychological distress. Children and teens negatively affected by parental infidelity experience a full range of emotions, including resentment, sadness, grief, anxiety, shame, and uncertainty.

Younger children who discover parental infidelity tend to feel abandoned, neglected, or unloved. These emotions often manifest in behavioral problems, including withdrawal, defiance, and angry outbursts. **Adolescents** with age-appropriate cognitive abilities report feeling betrayed and hold negative views toward marriage or commitment. Teens may blame the transgressing parent or resent the betrayed party for not preventing the infidelity in the first place. These unilateral parental loyalties can create a dysfunctional parentified subsystem extending throughout adulthood. Adolescents may also react to infidelity by acting out sexually and often continue to have difficulties with intimate relationships as adults.

Social Stratification, Social Privilege, Social Oppression, and Sociopolitical Climate

- **Social stratification** refers to the hierarchal emergence of separate classes of people based on unequal distributions of power, resources, rights, privileges, and responsibilities. Social stratification is based on a person's intersectional identity. Intersectionality consists of multiple dimensions of social identities including race, ethnicity, sexual orientation, gender identity, age, gender, abilities, and other contextual factors.
- **Social privilege** refers to unmerited power based on status. Social privilege allows individuals access to resources, rights, and opportunities based on class distinction.
- **Social oppression** is the inverse of social privilege. Oppression is experienced by those in nondominant social groups on individual, systemic, and institutional levels. It operates through discrimination and racism and is designed to immobilize those who are not in power.
- **Sociopolitical climate** refers to the current state of society as it relates to political factors, including, but not limited to, legislation used to oppress minority populations, landmark political decisions and court rulings, human rights policies, historical events, and other contextual dimensions of a client's experience.

IMPACT

The **dynamic influence** of social stratification, social privilege, social oppression, and the sociopolitical climate is rooted in laws, rules, and policies that provide advantages for some and disadvantages for others. Those elements affect clients on an individual, institutional, systemic, and interpersonal level. **Discrimination** is reflected in denied housing, health care, employment, and educational opportunities. Individuals from marginalized communities are more likely to experience depression, PTSD, and SUD than individuals from privileged communities.

Prolonged exposure to discrimination and racism can result in **allostatic overload** (i.e., toxic stress). Allostatic overload, caused by an overactive hypothalamic-pituitary-adrenal system, changes brain development, influences learning, and leads to poorer behavioral health across the life span. The effects of allostatic overload place individuals at higher lifetime risk for substance misuse, depression, diabetes, obesity, suicide, heart disease, cancer, and stroke.

Mental health conditions are affected by social oppression. Current trends indicate that black men are diagnosed with schizophrenia at a rate four times that of their white male counterparts. Black boys have significantly higher suspension rates and are more likely to be diagnosed with an emotional or behavioral disorder than their white young male counterparts. Untreated and mistreated mental disorders early in life are associated with higher incarceration rates among black males. Incarceration rates for black males in every age group are substantially higher than any other racial and ethnic population.

Resources

COMMUNITY SYSTEMS

Community schools ensure that all children and community members have equitable access to resources and opportunities to support academic and career success. An overarching goal of community schools is to address systemic barriers that limit opportunities in low-income neighborhoods and communities of color.

Community Schools Programs are year-round public schools that offer students and families **comprehensive** educational, social, recreational, and family activities. Partnerships with schools provide opportunities for exposure to the arts, mentor programs, summer camps, job training, and adult education. During the summer months, most community schools remain open and provide free and reduced-price breakfast and lunch for eligible persons. Additional services include early childhood enrichment programs, counseling, access to primary health and dental care, and help with preparing for citizenship exams.

Human service agencies are social assistance programs delivered to a broad range of individuals of all ages and stages of development. The goal of a human service agency is to improve the health and well-being of those served. There are a wide variety of agencies included under the human service umbrella. Examples of human service professionals include, but are not limited to, the following:

- Medical personnel
- Mental health professionals
- Case managers
- Substance abuse counselors
- Child welfare specialists
- Veterans service workers
- Crisis intervention counselors
- Hospice counselors
- Public health educators
- Community outreach professionals
- Corrections officers
- Family court advocates
- School counselors
- School-based community centers
- Probation officers

CLIENT'S USE OF OUTSIDE RESOURCES

The client's use of **outside resources** is connected to improved therapeutic outcomes. Therapists build and maintain a therapeutic alliance by providing opportunities for clients to reach their highest potential. A **strengths-based approach** to counseling fosters this relationship by encouraging the client to use outside resources to educate the therapist on their unique personal, cultural, psychological, and social factors. Capitalizing on the client's strengths, the therapist partners with the client and fosters the belief that the client is independently capable of change.

Clients often bring to sessions meaningful information obtained through online assessments, educational materials, and attendance in support groups. Through **direct support and guidance**, the client becomes more empowered and less reliant on the therapist for change. Online assessments, questionnaires, checklists, and screenings provide more clarity on the presenting problem and complex issues. Support groups targeting treatment issues can serve as adjunctive counseling services. Self-help, counseling, and psychoeducational groups also produce educational materials and offer additional assistance with social skills. Finally, access to and using numerous resources can expeditiously help the client meet treatment plan goals and assist with ongoing postdischarge improvement.

IMPACT OF ECONOMIC STRESSORS

The conditions in which people live, work, and age influence a client's presenting problem and treatment. Socially and economically marginalized populations are more likely to experience **poorer health outcomes** due to disparities in access to care, use of care, and the quality of care received. In addition, **socioeconomic inequities** in communities of color are directly impacted by systemic racism, poor environmental conditions, and the limited availability of support systems and resources.

Research consistently shows that **mental distress** is associated with unemployment, economic hardship, and financial uncertainty. Suicide rates have been shown to increase at rates consistent with unemployment, with one study noting a 1% increase in suicide rates correlated to a 1% increase in unemployment. Poverty affects mental conditions directly, and mental conditions are adversely affected by poverty. **Children and families** are also adversely affected by crime rates, food insecurity, substance use, and unsuitable housing, contributing to increased mental disorders and childhood emotional and behavioral disorders. Extreme poverty denies the ability of those affected to adequately care for themselves, resulting in impairment in emotional, cognitive, social, and psychological levels of functioning.

Medications

PROVIDING REFERENCE MATERIALS

Therapists provide clients, parents, and guardians with reference materials on medication for the following reasons:

- To assist the client with medication compliance
- To reduce health disparities among socially marginalized groups
- To avoid medication errors leading to emotional and physical pain, patient dissatisfaction, medical mistrust, overdose, and/or death
- To provide accurate information and dispel any myths and misconceptions related to medication for treating mental disorders

During the initial interview, it is essential for therapists to obtain information on the client's current medications, including over-the-counter medicines, any allergies to medications, and recreational drug use. At this time, therapists assess the client's health literacy, which is the degree to which the client understands and uses health-related information. Therapists can then provide and review medication literature matching each client's individualized needs. Health literacy is associated with higher medication compliance and reduced behavioral health disparities among socially marginalized groups.

It is helpful for therapists to request medication updates and work to address barriers to compliance when applicable. Therapists must also provide and verbally review reference materials that are culturally and linguistically appropriate. Clients are given the opportunity to ask questions, and the therapist works to dispel any myths or misconceptions about medication and the treatment of behavioral health disorders.

ADVERSE EFFECTS OF NONPRESCRIPTION SUBSTANCES

The adverse effects of nonprescription substances may include, but are not limited to, the following:

Acetaminophen	NSAIDs	Codeine	Antihistamines
Black, tarry stools	Blurred vision and dizziness	Blurred vision and dizziness	Blurred vision and dizziness
Headaches	Headaches	Headaches	Headaches
Abdominal tenderness and lower back pain	Diarrhea and/or constipation	Diarrhea and/or Constipation	Confusion (mainly with the elderly)
Skin rashes, blisters, and related allergic reactions	Skin rashes, blisters, and related allergic reactions	Excessive sweating	Breast tenderness
Blood in stools or urine	Stomach ulcers	Difficulty breathing (rare)	Drowsiness and fatigue
Unusual weakness	Strokes	Seizures	Dry mouth
Sore throat	Heart failure	Heart throbbing	Sore throat
Yellow eyes or jaundice skin	Jaundice	Drop in blood pressure	
Fatigue	Fatigue	Euphoria	Difficulty urinating
Lower back pain	Lower back pain	Insomnia	Joint pain

71

ADVERSE EFFECTS OF NONPRESCRIPTION HERBALS

Nonprescription herbals are supplements that the **FDA does not regulate** in the same way that prescription drugs and over-the-counter drugs are, which may create additional risks for consumers. St. John's wort is an herbal supplement used to treat mild to moderate depression. The primary risk factors are damage to the liver and kidneys.

Adverse reactions commonly associated with **St. John's wort** include:

- Diarrhea
- Insomnia
- Dizziness
- Confusion
- Skin reactions
- Dry mouth

Kava is an herbal supplement used for anxiety. Adverse reactions commonly associated with kava include:

- Fatigue
- Restlessness
- Stomachache
- Tremors
- Alopecia (with long-term use)
- Hearing loss

Ginger is an herbal supplement used to treat nausea, migraines, diabetes, joint pain, weight loss, and menstrual cramps. Adverse reactions commonly associated with ginger include:

- Heartburn
- Diarrhea
- Mouth irritation
- Stomachache
- Skin irritation

Designing and Conducting Treatment

Safety Plan

A **safety plan** is a documented list of actions that an individual can take to help keep them safe in the presence of known or possible danger. Safety plans are implemented for those at risk for suicide, domestic violence, child abuse, or elder abuse. Although safety plans are best created and implemented preemptively, effective safety plans can also be made during or after a crisis, depending on the client's level of distress. When a client is actively experiencing a crisis, therapists assess the client's functional impairment, emotional distress, and risk for harm. Therapists then help the client identify coping skills and resources that can be used to eliminate or mitigate threats to the client, child, or loved one.

Effective safety plans are brief, easy to read, in the client's own words, the result of a collaborative effort between the client and therapist, and reviewed frequently. Crisis plans include, but are not limited to, the following components:

- Warning signs that a person's safety is in danger.
- Identification of individual(s) in the client's life who can assist during a crisis (e.g., family members, neighbors, professionals, friends) and their contact information.
- Coping skills and strategies that have worked in the past, as well as any current skills and strengths identified with the client.
- Immediate steps to take when in crisis. For example, family members of clients actively experiencing suicidality may be instructed to remove lethal means from their environment. Clients who are victims of domestic violence or elder abuse may be encouraged to have a prepacked overnight bag with essentials, thus enabling the client to leave a dangerous situation quickly.

Family Theory and Family Therapy

GOALS OF FAMILY THERAPY

Family therapy is a therapeutic modality theorizing that a client's psychiatric symptoms are a result of **pathology within the client's family unit**. This dysfunction is due to problems within the system, usually arising from conflict between marital partners. Psychiatric problems result from these behaviors. This conflict is expressed by:

- **Triangulation**, which manifests itself by the attempt of using another family member to stabilize the emotional process
- **Scapegoating**, which occurs when blaming is used to shift focus to another family member

The **goals** of family therapy are:

- To allow family members to recognize and **communicate their feelings**
- To determine the **reasons for problems** between marital partners and to **resolve** them
- To assist parents in **working together** and to strengthen their **parental authority**
- To help define and clarify **family expectations and roles**
- To learn more and different **positive techniques for interacting**
- To achieve **positive homeostasis** within the family
  - Homeostasis means remaining the same, or maintaining a functional balance. Homeostasis can occur to maintain a dysfunctional status as well.
- To enhance the family's **adaptability**
  - Adaptability is maintaining a balanced, positive stability in the family. A prerequisite for balanced stability, and a basic goal of family therapy, is to help the client family develop strategies for dealing with life's inevitable changes. Morphogenesis is the medical term often applied to a family's ability to react functionally and appropriately to changes.

THEORETICAL APPROACHES TO FAMILY THERAPY

Four theoretical approaches to family therapy are **strategic**, **behavioral**, **psychodynamic**, and **object relations** theories:

- A **strategic approach** to family therapy was proposed by Jay Haley. Haley tried to map out a different strategic plan for each type of psychological issue addressed. With this approach, there is a special treatment strategy for each malady.
- A **behavioral approach** uses traditional behavior-modification techniques to address issues. This approach relies heavily on reinforcement strategies. B.F. Skinner is perhaps the most famous behaviorist. This approach relies on conditioning and often desensitizing as well.
- The **psychodynamic approach** attempts to create understanding and insight on the part of the client. Strategies may be diverse, but in all of them the therapist acts as an emotional guide, leading the client to a better understanding of mental and emotional mechanisms. One common example is Gestalt therapy.
- **Object relations theory** asserts that the ego develops attachment relationships with external and internal objects. A person's early relationships to objects (which can include people) may result in frustration or rejection, which forms the basis of personality.

STRATEGIC FAMILY THERAPY

Strategic family therapy (Haley, 1976) is based on the following concepts:

- This therapy seeks to learn what **function** the symptom serves in the family (i.e., what payoff is there for the system in allowing the symptom to continue?).
- **Focuses**: Problem-focused behavioral change, emphasis of parental power and hierarchical family relationships, and the role of symptoms as an attribute of the family's organization.
- Helplessness, incompetence, and illness all provide **power positions** within the family. The child uses symptoms to change the behavior of parents.

Jay Haley tried to develop a strategy for each issue faced by a client. Problems are isolated and treated in different ways. A family plagued by alcoholism might require a different treatment strategy than a family undermined by sexual infidelity. Haley was unusual in that he held degrees in the arts and communication rather than in psychology. Haley's strategies involved the use of directives (direct instructions). After outlining a problem, Haley would tell the family members exactly what to do. If John would bang his head against the wall when he was made to do his homework, Haley might tell a parent to work with him and to be there while he did his homework.

VIRGINIA SATIR AND THE ESALEN INSTITUTE'S EXPERIENTIAL FAMILY THERAPY

Virginia Satir and the Esalen Institute's experiential family therapy draws on sociology, ego concepts, and communication theory to form **role theory concepts**. Satir examined the roles that constrain relationships and interactions in families. This perspective seeks to increase intimacy in the family and improve the self-esteem of family members by using awareness and the communication of feelings. Emphasis is on individual growth in order to change family members and deal with developmental delays. Particular importance is given to marital partners and on changing verbal and nonverbal communication patterns that lower self-esteem.

SATIR'S COMMUNICATION IMPEDIMENTS

Satir described four issues that impede communication between family members under stress. Placating, blaming, being overly reasonable, and being irrelevant are the **four issues which blocked family communication**, according to Virginia Satir:

- **Placating** is the role played by some people in reaction to threat or stress in the family. The placating person reacts to internal stresses by trying to please others, often in irrational ways. A mother might try to placate her disobedient and rude child by offering food, candy, or other presents on the condition that he stop a certain behavior.
- **Blaming** is the act of pointing outwards when an issue creates stress. The blamer thinks, "I'm very angry, but it's your fault. If I've wrecked the car, it's because you made me upset when I left home this morning."
- **Irrelevance** is a behavior wherein a person displaces the potential problem and substitutes another unrelated activity. A mother who engages in too much social drinking frequently discusses her split ends whenever the topic of alcoholism is brought up by her spouse.
- Being overly reasonable, also known as being a **responsible analyzer** is when a person keeps his or her emotions in check and functions with the precision and monotony of a machine.

MURRAY BOWEN'S FAMILY SYSTEMS THEORY

Bowen's family systems theory focuses on the following concepts:

- The role of **thinking versus feeling/reactivity** in relationship/family systems.
- Role of **emotional triangles**: The three-person system or triangle is viewed as the smallest stable relationship system and forms when a two-person system experiences tension.
- **Generationally repeating family issues**: Parents transmit emotional problems to a child. (Example: The parents fear something is wrong with a child and treat the child as if something is wrong, interpreting the child's behavior as confirmation.)
- **Undifferentiated family ego mass**: This refers to a family's lack of separateness. There is a fixed cluster of egos of individual family members as if all have a common ego boundary.
- **Emotional cutoff**: A way of managing emotional issues with family members (cutting off emotional contact).
- Consideration of thoughts and feelings of **each individual family member** as well as seeking to understand the family network.

> **Review Video: Bowen Family Systems**
> Visit mometrix.com/academy and enter code: 591496

FAMILY SYSTEM THEORY ASSUMPTIONS ABOUT HUMAN BEHAVIOR

Family systems theory makes several basic assumptions:

- Change in one part of the family system brings about change in other parts of the system.
- The family provides the following to its members: unity, individuation, security, comfort, nurturance, warmth, affection, and reciprocal need satisfaction.
- Where family pathology is present, the individual is socially and individually disadvantaged.
- Behavioral problems are a reflection of communication problems in the family system.
- Treatment focuses on the family unity; changing family interactions is the key to behavioral change.

MOTIVATIONS FOR CHANGE AND MEANS THROUGH WHICH CHANGE OCCURS

The **motivations for change** according to Bowen's family systems theory are as follows:

- **Disequilibrium** of the normal family homeostasis is the primary motivation for change according to this perspective.
- The family system is made up of three subsystems: the marital relationship, the parent-child relationship, and the sibling relationship. **Dysfunction** that occurs in any of these subsystems will likely cause dysfunction in the others.

The **means for change** in the family systems theory approach is the family as an interactional system.

CONTRIBUTIONS TO FAMILY SYSTEMS THEORY

The **psychodynamic theory** emphasizes multi-generational family history. Earlier family relations and patterns determine current ones. Distorted relations in childhood lead to patterns of miscommunication and behavioral problems. Interpersonal and intrapersonal conflict beneath apparent family unity results in psychopathology. Social role functioning is influenced by heredity and environment.

Don Jackson, a major contributor to family therapy, focuses on **power relationships**. He developed a theory of double-bind communication in families. Double-bind communication occurs when two conflicting messages communicated simultaneously create or maintain a no-win pathological symptom.

ASSESSMENT AND TREATMENT PLANNING IN THE FAMILY SYSTEMS THEORY

Assessment in family systems theory includes the following:

- Acknowledgement of **dysfunction** in the family system
- **Family hierarchy**: Who is in charge? Who has responsibility? Who has authority? Who has power?
- Evaluation of **boundaries** (around subsystems, between family and larger environment): Are they permeable or impermeable? Flexible or rigid?
- How does the **symptom** function in the family system?

Treatment planning is as follows:

- The therapist creates a mutually satisfactory contract with the family to establish service boundaries.
- Bowenian family therapy's goal is the differentiation of the individual from the strong influence of the family.

SAL MINUCHIN'S STRUCTURAL FAMILY THERAPY

Sal Minuchin's structural family therapy seeks to strengthen boundaries when family subsystems are enmeshed, or seeks to increase flexibility when these systems are overly rigid. Minuchin emphasizes that the family structure should be hierarchical and that the parents should be at the top of the hierarchy.

Joining, enactment, boundary making, and mimesis are four techniques used by Salvador Minuchin in structural family therapy:

- **Joining** is the therapist's attempt at greeting and bonding with members of the family. Bonding is important when obtaining cooperation and input.
- Minuchin often had his clients enact the various scenarios which led to disagreements and conflicts within families. The **enactment** of an unhealthy family dynamic would allow the therapist to better understand the behavior and allow the family members to gain insight.
- **Boundary making** is important to structural family therapies administered by Salvador Minuchin, because many family conflicts arise from confusion about each person's role. Minuchin believed that family harmony was best achieved when people were free to be themselves yet knew that they must not invade the areas of other family members.
- **Mimesis** is a process in which the therapist mimics the positive and negative behavior patterns of different family members.

THERAPEUTIC METHODS EMPLOYED BY CARL WHITAKER

Carl Whitaker, known as the dean of family therapy, developed **experiential symbolic family therapy**. Whitaker would freely interact with other family members and often played the part of family members who were important to the dynamic. He felt that experience, not information and education, had the power to change family dynamics.

Whitaker believed that in family therapy, theory was also less important than experience and that co-therapists were a great aid to successful counseling. Co-therapists freed one of the counselors to participate more fully in the counseling sessions. One counselor might direct the flow of activity while the other participated in role playing. The "psychotherapy of the absurd" is a Whitaker innovation which was influenced by the "theatre of the absurd," a popular existential art form at the time. In this context, the absurd is the unreasonable exaggeration of an idea, to the point of underscoring the underlying meaninglessness of much of human interaction. A person who repeated a neurotic or destructive behavior, for example, was being absurd. The **psychotherapy of the absurd**, as Whitaker saw it, was a method for bringing out repeated and meaningless absurdities. A person pushing against an immovable brick wall, for example, might eventually understand the psychological analogy to some problem behavior.

THEORIES OF CAUSALITY

Multiple theories of causality exist in the interpretation of family dynamics, which are then applied to the selection of therapeutic interventions. While linear causality (the concept that one cause equals one effect) uses a direct line of reasoning and is commonly used in individual counseling, **circular/reciprocal causality** is often used in family therapy and refers to the dynamic interactions between family members. Think of a situation in which one member of a family (a father, perhaps) has a severe emotional problem accompanied by violent and angry outbursts. The father periodically assaults his teenage son. Reciprocal or circular causality would apply in this family situation, since the father's angry behavior resonates throughout the family, causing different problems for each person. The spouse might feel inadequate to protect her son and sink into a depression. The other children would suffer, too, from anxiety and fear that the same treatment would befall them. Owing to circular causality, a single cause can have many effects.

PARADOXICAL INTERVENTION STRATEGIES

Paradoxical intervention strategies involve the use of the client's disruptive behavior as a treatment itself, requiring the client to put the behavior in the spotlight to then motivate change. This technique tries to accomplish the opposite of what it suggests on the surface. Interventions include the following:

- **Restraining** is advising that a negative behavior not be changed or be changed only slightly or slowly. This can be effectively used in the context of couples therapy when a couple is struggling with intimacy issues. The therapist may challenge the couple to refrain from sexual intimacy for a period of time, thus removing certain stressors from that dynamic, possibly resulting in a positive intimate experience that occurs naturally and spontaneously.
- **Positioning** is characterizing a negative behavior in an even more negative light through the use of exaggeration. "David, do you feel you are not terrifying your family enough with your reckless driving or that you ought to drive faster in order to make them worry more about your wellbeing? Perhaps that way you will know that they care about you," says the therapist using positioning as a technique. It is important that this technique be used only with great care, as it can be harmful to clients with a negative self-image. It is generally used in situations where the client is behaving in a certain negative way in order to seek affirmation or attention.
- **Prescribing the symptom** is another paradoxical technique used by therapists to obtain an enlightened reaction from a client. A therapist using this technique directs the client to activate the negative behavior in terms that are absurd and clearly objectionable. 'John, I want you to go out to that sidewalk overpass above the freeway and yell as loud as you can at the cars passing below you. Do it for at least four hours." The therapist prescribes this activity to cure his client's dangerous tendency toward road rage.
- **Relabeling** is recasting a negative behavior in a positive light in order to get an emotional response from the client. "Perhaps your wife yells at you when you drink because she finds this behavior attractive and wants your attention," the therapist might say. The therapist might even support that obviously illogical and paradoxical argument by pointing out invented statistics, which support the ridiculous assertion.

EXTINCTION, TIME OUT, AND THOUGHT STOPPING

Behavior modification is a term used in facilities like schools and jails to bring behavior into line with societal or family rules:

- **Extinction** is the process of causing a behavior to disappear by providing little or no reinforcement. It is different from punishment, which is negative reinforcement rather than no reinforcement at all. Very often, a student will be removed from the general population and made to sit alone in a quiet room. In schools, this goes by various names, but is often called in-school suspension (ISS). It is hoped that, through lack of reinforcement and response from outside, the offensive behavior will become extinct.
- **Time out** is another extinction technique, generally applied to very young children. A disobedient child will be isolated for a specified, usually short time whenever he or she misbehaves. The method's operant mechanism assumes that we are all social animals and require the reinforcement of the outside world. Deprived of this, we adapt by altering our behavior.
- **Thought stopping** is a learned response which requires the participation and cooperation of the client to change a negative behavior. When it is successful, the client actively forbids negative thoughts from entering his or her mind.

SPECIFIC FAMILY THERAPY INTERVENTIONS

FAMILY THERAPY INTERVENTIONS USED WITH OCD

Family therapy interventions used to treat individuals with **obsessive-compulsive disorder (OCD)** include therapy oriented to develop expression of thoughts and impulses in a manner that is appropriate. This approach assumes that family members often:

- Attempt to avoid situations that trigger OCD responses
- Constantly reassure the individual (which often enables the obsession)

Family therapy to address these issues involves:

- Remaining neutral and not reinforcing through encouragement
- Avoiding attempts to reason logically with individual

FAMILY THERAPY INTERVENTIONS FOR PANIC DISORDERS

Family dynamics and therapy interventions for **panic disorders** include:

- Individuals with agoraphobia may require the presence of family members to be constantly in close proximity, resulting in marital stress and over-reliance on the children.
- Altered role performance of the afflicted member results in family and social situations that increase the responsibility of other family members.
- The family must be educated about the source and treatment of the disorder.
- The goal of family therapy is to reorganize responsibilities to support family change.

FUNCTIONAL FAMILY THERAPY FOR ADOLESCENTS WITH ANTISOCIAL BEHAVIOR

Functional family therapy (FFT) is designed for adolescents (11–17 years of age) with **antisocial behavior**. FFT uses the principles of family systems theory and cognitive-behavioral therapy and provides intervention and prevention services. While the therapy has changed somewhat over the past 30 years, current FTT usually includes three phases:

1. **Engagement/motivation**: The therapist works with the family to identify maladaptive beliefs to increase expectations for change, reduce negativity and blaming, and increase respect for differences. Goals are to reduce dropout rates and establish alliances.
2. **Behavior change**: The therapist guides the parents in using behavioral interventions to improve family functioning, parenting, and conflict management. Goals are to prevent delinquent behavior and build better communication and interpersonal skills.
3. **Generalization**: The family learns to use new skills to influence the systems in which they are involved, such as school, church, or the juvenile justice system. Community resources are mobilized to prevent relapses.

MULTISYSTEMIC THERAPY FOR ADOLESCENTS WITH ANTISOCIAL BEHAVIOR

Multisystemic therapy (MST) is a **family-focused program** designed for adolescents (11–17 years of age) with antisocial and delinquent behaviors. The primary goal is **collaboration** with the family to develop strategies for dealing with the child's behavioral problems. Services are delivered in the family's natural environment rather than at a clinic or office with frequent home visits, usually totaling 40–60 hours over the course of treatment. Sessions are daily initially and then decrease in frequency. A variety of different therapies may be used, including family therapy, parent training, and individual therapy. Therapists use different approaches but adhere to basic principles, including focusing on the strength of the systems, delivering appropriate treatment for developmental level, and improving family functioning. The goals of therapy are to improve family relations and parenting skills, to engage the child in activities with nondelinquent peers, and to improve the child's grades and participation in activities, such as sports.

THERAPEUTIC METHODS FOR COUNSELING AN ADOLESCENT WITH BEHAVIORAL PROBLEMS

When an **adolescent's behavior** is a problem, some parents have him or her sign an agreement to perform in a specified manner. The agreement may state that a reward will be provided to the adolescent so long as the contract is upheld. The therapist can help parents and children write an effective contract. Another time-honored method of behavior conditioning is the withholding of leisure activity until chores are done. In a family therapy session, the therapist might advise stating the case like this: "Your television has a parental guide lock which will not be turned on unless you can demonstrate that all your homework is complete."

ROLE OF THE THERAPIST

The role of the therapist in family therapy is to interact in the here and now with the family in relation to current problems. The therapist is a consultant to the family. Some aspects of the therapist's role differ according to school of thought:

- **Structural**: The therapist actively challenges dysfunctional interaction.
- **Strategic and Systemic**: The therapist is very active.
- **Milan School**: Male/female clinicians are co-therapists; a team observes from behind a one-way mirror and consults and directs the co-therapists with the clients.
- **Psychodynamic**: The therapist facilitates self-reflection and understanding of multi-generational dynamics and conflicts.
- **Satir**: The therapist models caring, acceptance, love, compassion, nurturance in order to help clients face fears and increase openness.

KEY CONCEPTS OF FAMILY THERAPY

Key **concepts of family therapy** include the following:

Behavior modeling	The manner in which a child bases his or her own behavior on the behavior of his or her parents and other people. In other words, a child will usually learn to identify acceptable behaviors by mimicking the behavior of others. Some children may have more difficulty with behavior modeling than others.
Boundaries	The means of organization through which system parts can be differentiated both from their environment and from each other. They protect and improve the differentiation and integrity of the family, subsystems, and individual family members.
Collaborative therapy	Therapy in which a different therapist sees each spouse or member of the family.
Complementary family interaction	A type of family relationship in which members present opposite behaviors that supply needs or lacks in the other family member.
Complementarity of needs	Circular support system of a family, in which reciprocity is found in meeting needs; can be adaptive or maladaptive.
Double-bind communication	Communication in which two contradictory messages are conveyed concurrently, leading to a no-win situation.
Family of origin	The family into which one is born.
Family of procreation	The family which one forms with a mate and one's own children.
Enmeshment	Obscuring of boundaries in which differentiation of family subsystems and individual autonomy are lost. Similar to Bowen's "undifferentiated family ego mass." Characterized by "mind reading" (partners speak for each other, complete each other's sentences).
Heritage	The set of customs, traditions, physical characteristics, and other cultural artifacts that a person inherits from his or her ancestors.
Homeostasis	A state of systemic balance (of relationships, alliances, power, authority).
Identified patient	The "symptom bearer" in the family.
Multiple family therapy	Therapy in which three or more families form a group with one or more clinicians to discuss common problems. Group support is given and problems are universalized.
Scapegoating	Unconscious, irrational election of one family member for a negative, demeaned, or outsider role.

FAMILY MAPPING

A **family map** is a visual depiction of a family's relational connections and patterns. Structural family therapists and Bowenian family therapists use family mapping as a primary assessment technique. Family maps are created for **two purposes:** (1) to identify how the family dynamics are maintaining the problem and (2) to target appropriate therapeutic interventions used to restructure or reorganize the family.

The family map uses graphic depictions to capture interactions among and between family alliances, coalitions, affiliations, and other subsystems. Structural family therapists place symbols on the family map representing familial involvement, underinvolvement, overinvolvement, and conflict. Hierarchies and systems of power are also noted. Families are active participants in developing the family map, which allows the therapist to assess the various ways in which the family members describe their relationships and how they respond to one another in real time. **Family behavior loop mapping** is a form of mapping that uses a behavioral chain to show the step-by-step actions, sequence of events, and patterns that take place to perpetuate family issues. This method helps underscore the contributions of all family members, rather than the family member with the identified problem.

Facilitating Change

FACILITATING CHANGE THROUGH RESTRUCTURING AND REORGANIZATION

The therapist's role in facilitating change is to place the family in a state of disequilibrium. Structural family therapists obtain enough information during the assessment phase to create a relational and systemic hypothesis. Next, the therapist determines and challenges aspects of the family's adaptive functioning or state of equilibrium. Various techniques are used to create the disequilibrium required for the process of restructuring and reorganization. Therapists collaborate with the family by **joining** and shifting family members' perspectives. Therapists use **tracking**, which involves monitoring and clarifying content. **Mimesis** is also used to mimic or reflect the family's communication style, mannerisms, and interactions.

Once the therapist is accommodated into the family system, restructuring communication and dysfunctional interactions can begin. **Enactment** is a restructuring technique that allows the family to act out rather than describe interactions. Therapists use **reframing, shifting boundaries, and unbalancing** to reorganize dysfunctional subsystems. **Psychoeducation** around family dynamics and **assigning tasks** can be done to place the family in a state of disequilibrium. The therapist may use their position within the family to **escalate stress, recreate communication channels,** and **manipulate the physical space** occupied by family members.

HOMEOSTASIS

Homeostasis describes the process that family members use to maintain balance and order. Families maintain homeostasis by monitoring behaviors, adjusting interactional patterns, and promoting cognitive and emotional expressions that maintain balance. Homeostasis is not fixed; instead, it is the result of complex feedback systems that families use to recalibrate or self-correct. Families attempt to maintain homeostasis by explicitly or implicitly **scapegoating** the family member whose problems caused the family to enter therapy. Therapists help families understand that problems do not occur in isolation.

The goal of family therapy is to understand the family's stabilizing forces, recognize elements of the system that contribute to the client's presenting problem, and help illustrate what will happen when the family system changes. Once there is family buy-in, the therapists construct a **formal contract** with the family. Therapists can use formal contracts to develop treatment plan goals. Therapists collaborate with families to establish treatment goals that explain the family's homeostasis, including a noncritical conceptualization of the family system. Positive connotations are used to reframe dysfunctional interactions, allowing the therapist to identify strengths and enlist commitment toward an agreed upon plan of action.

84

Techniques Used to Alter Client Behavior/Perceptions

Therapists work with clients to change **perceptions and behaviors** using the following family therapy techniques:

- **Metaphor:** Metaphors are figures of speech that illustrate symbolic comparisons and similarities. When the client's metaphors are recognized and understood, the therapist can better understand the client's perceptions of circumstances and events. Therapists use metaphors as an alternative to explaining and interpreting the presenting problem or to help illustrate abstract concepts.
- **Reframing:** Reframing is used to help clients view situations from a more positive vantage point (e.g., parental overinvolvement is reframed as protection and care).
- **Rewriting narratives:** Therapists help clients rewrite narratives as a means for externalizing a problem, allowing for cultural considerations, identifying exceptions, and introducing alternative narratives.
- **Mindfulness:** Mindfulness is used to increase present-moment awareness of thoughts, emotions, and physical sensations. Stress reactions caused by the sympathetic and parasympathetic nervous systems are modulated by mindfulness, which begins to change the client's perspective of threatening events.
- **Paradox:** Strategic therapists use paradoxical interventions to "prescribe" the symptom, which is designed to reduce resistant behavior.

Education for Same-Sex Relationships

EDUCATION AND COUNSELING

Counseling goals for same-sex and heterosexual couples are similar in many respects, with couples generally presenting with the desire to improve communication, restore intimacy, and receive love and support. However, because there are issues unique to same-sex couples, therapists are responsible for educating and applying best practices when selecting counseling interventions and strategies. As **sexual minorities**, many same-sex couples face **additional stressors** from stigma, discrimination, and prejudice. In turn, they may lack emotional, social, familial, and religious support, leading to disparities in behavioral health outcomes.

Same-sex couples experience stressors on an **individual** and on a **relationship level.** On an individual level, **social stressors** include the need to hide one's sexual identity, feelings stemming from social rejection and stigmatization, and internalized homophobia. On a relationship level, couples are tasked with living in a heteronormative society, which includes the chronic demand to make quick environmental appraisals to protect themselves from rejection and discrimination. Minority stress, in the form of chronic cognitive appraisal and image management, can have a deleterious effect on relationship satisfaction and quality of life.

Couple-level stressors include difficulties stemming from gender stereotypes and societal expectations of gender roles at work, among peers, or in their communities. Components of one's intersectional identity must also be considered due to the influence of race, ethnicity, gender identity, age, religion, and cultural background. **Stages of sexual identity development** may vary among each member in a couple, which can lead to conflict over the degree of "openness" each partner desires in various social and institutional settings (e.g., work, family, church, community).

Group Therapy

PURPOSES AND GOALS OF GROUP PRACTICE

Group practice takes a multiple-goal perspective to solving individual and social problems and is based on the recognition that group experiences have many important functions and can be designed to achieve any or all of the following:

- Provide restorative, remedial, or rehabilitative experiences
- Help prevent personal and social distress or breakdown
- Facilitate normal growth and development, especially during stressful times in the life cycle
- Achieve a greater degree of self-fulfillment and personal enhancement
- Help individuals become active, responsible participants in society through group associations

ADVANTAGES OF GROUP WORK

Advantages of group work include the following:

- Members can help and identify with others dealing with similar issues and situations.
- Sometimes people can more easily accept help from peers than from professionals.
- Through consensual validation, members feel less violated and more reassured as they discover that their problems are similar to those of others.
- Groups give opportunities to members to experiment with and test new social identities and roles.
- Group practice is not a replacement for individual treatment. Group work is an essential tool for many therapists and can be the method of choice for some problems.
- Group practice can complement other practice techniques.

> **Review Video: Group Work and its Benefits**
> Visit mometrix.com/academy and enter code: 375134

IMPORTANCE OF RELATIONSHIPS IN GROUP WORK

Establishing meaningful, effective relationships in group work is essential, and its importance cannot be overemphasized. The therapist will form multiple changing relationships with individual group members, with sub-groups, and with the group as a whole. There are multiple other parties who have a stake in members' experiences, such as colleagues of the therapist, agency representatives, relatives, friends, and others. The therapist will relate differentially to all of those individuals.

GROUP THERAPY METHODS
PROCESS GROUPS

Irvin Yalom's "here-and-now" or process groups are characterized by the following:

- Yalom stressed using clients' **immediate reactions** and discussing members' **affective experiences** in the group.
- Process groups have relatively unstructured and spontaneous sessions.
- Process groups emphasize **therapeutic activities**, like imparting information, or instilling hope, universality, and altruism.
- The group can provide a **rehabilitative narrative** of primary family group development, offer socializing techniques, provide behavior models to imitate, offer interpersonal learning, and offer an example of group cohesiveness and catharsis.

MORENO'S PSYCHODRAMA GROUP THERAPY

Moreno's psychodrama group therapy is summarized as follows:

- **Spontaneous drama techniques** contribute to powerful therapy to aid in the release of pent-up feelings and to provide insight and catharsis to help participants develop new and more effective behaviors.
- The five **primary instruments** used are the stage, the client or protagonist, the director or therapist, the staff of therapeutic aides or auxiliary egos, and the audience.
- Psychodrama group therapy can begin with a **warm-up**. The warm-up uses an assortment of techniques such as self-presentations, interviews, interaction in the role of the self and others, soliloquies, role reversals, doubling techniques, auxiliary egos, mirroring, multiple doubles, life rehearsals, and exercises.

BEHAVIORAL GROUP THERAPIES

Behavioral group therapies are characterized by the following:

- The **main goals** are to help group members eliminate maladaptive behaviors and learn new behaviors that are more effective. Behavioral groups are not focused on gaining insight into the past, but rather on current interactions with the environment.
- It is one of the few research-based approaches.
- The therapist utilizes **directive techniques**, provides information, and teaches coping skills and methods of changing behavior.
- The therapist arranges **structured activities**. The primary techniques used include restructuring, systematic desensitization, implosive therapies, assertion training, aversion techniques, operant-conditioning, self-help reinforcement and support, behavioral research, coaching, modeling, feedback, and procedures for challenging and changing conditions.

PROGRAMS, WORKSHOPS, AND SUPPORT GROUPS

Programs, workshops, and support groups provide opportunities for clients to express shared experiences, learn and practice coping skills, and reinforce the knowledge and skills obtained in therapy. Support programs can serve as an adjunct to counseling or as a stand-alone recommendation. Support groups and programs each differ in their structure and focus. Therapists wishing to develop support programs must first conduct a needs assessment and screen potential candidates. Next, therapists decide if the group will be ongoing (open) or have a definite end point (close) and determine the setting and other logistical factors (e.g., length, duration). Examples of support groups include:

- **Parenting programs:** Parenting programs consist of group support with psychoeducation on topics such as parenting practices, developmental skills and milestones, appropriate discipline skills and techniques, and self-care. Information on additional community resources is also provided to help with concrete supports.
- **Grief support:** Grief support groups help individuals understand the grief process, identify coping strategies and support systems, and address spiritual and social concerns.
- **Eating disorder support groups:** Facilitator-led eating disorder programs and support groups are a blend of group cognitive behavioral therapy and nutrition counseling. The goal is to address thoughts and feeling about unhealthy eating and provide support in managing symptoms.
- **Stepparenting groups:** Stepparenting groups emphasize effective communication and problem solving, handling power struggles and split loyalties, and coparenting with exes.

MANDATED GROUP TREATMENT PROGRAMS

Individuals attending **mandated group treatment programs** often do so because of a court order or an employer intervention. Participants with mandated correctional treatment must attend a specific number of sessions in an effort to reduce recidivism rates. Therapists work with offenders to identify and treat any co-occurring mental health issues or SUDs. Common group treatment programs include the following:

- **Anger management programs:** Common experiences of individuals mandated to anger management programs include an inability to adhere requests for de-escalation, angry outbursts during alcohol or substance intoxication, road rage, threatening others, destruction of property, and patterns of aggressive behavior that negatively affects one's employment or personal relationships.
- **Domestic violence treatment programs** are mandated for those who perpetrate intimate partner violence (IPV). Also known as batterer intervention programs, these mandated programs are diversionary and target individuals who are criminally charged with IPV resulting in physical assault, emotional abuse, psychological manipulation, and sexual assault. Many IPV programs use the Duluth Model, which focuses on increasing offender accountability and challenging social conditions that perpetuate masculine power, violence, and sexual entitlement. This is accomplished by coordinating a community response with criminal and civil justice programs, victims, and advocacy groups.
- **Sexual offender programs** are mandated for individuals in prisons and communities who are convicted of sexual conduct with an underage minor. Programs use cognitive–behavioral interventions to reduce harm and decrease recidivism rates. Counselors provide insight-oriented psychotherapy designed to help participants learn to take responsibility for their actions and understand the effect their actions have on others. The overall goal of sexual offender programs is to decrease the person's risk to their community.

Evaluating Ongoing Process and Terminating Treatment

Research in Counseling

RELEVANCE OF RESEARCH TO COUNSELING THERAPY

All counselors today receive training in how to apply theories and methods that have been discovered through **research**. The foundations to applying research to counseling are as follows:

- The counselor learns how to **evaluate** the clinical interventions that have been applied in therapy.
- The counselor **remains objective** in their examination of the data.
- The counselor maintains **ethical procedures** and is **accountable** for their actions. This means that the counselor is careful to document their work.
- The counselor is **competent** in their use of terminology and can make a sound interpretation of the research obtained.
- The counselor and the researcher work for the **client's benefit**. The client must not be harmed. The counselor and the researcher recognize that the client has a choice to determine his or her own actions. The counselor and the researcher are fair and loyal to the client. Both desire to help the client develop steps that will assist in the solution of the problem.

STEPS RESEARCHERS TAKE TO HELP CLIENTS

The researcher takes different steps than the counselor in helping the client:

1. The first research step is to **identify the problem** with a series of questions. These questions are used to formulate a research design.
2. The **research design** will utilize the goals that are essential to the researcher's investigation process.
3. The **treatment or interventions** that will be applied are considered in the choice of measuring instruments to be used. The interventions are implemented so that the researcher can collect data on the various interventions and results of each.
4. The **data is then evaluated** to determine the desired outcome. The data is interpreted in accordance with prescribed criteria.
5. The **conclusions** that are reached are used to help increase the knowledge that the research was used to develop. Counselors may use knowledge gleaned from previous research to help a client with his or her problem.

POSITIVISTIC RESEARCH

Positivism is a scientific method that can be applied in social science research. The researcher uses the method to make predictions about what may happen in the future. The researcher takes care in designing experiments that can be disproved or supported by observations of the conditions that occur. The research is accomplished by comparing groups. The numerical data obtained is taken from random samples of a population. The numerical data is compared to the group findings. **Positivistic research** investigates causality by comparing the group members in one group with another group. The variables that are different in each group are known as variable X or variable Y. Typically, variable X refers to an independent variable. Variable Y is known as the dependent variable that can change with the application or the withdrawal of variable X.

POST-POSITIVISM PARADIGM APPLIED TO SOCIAL SCIENCE RESEARCH

The belief of those researchers who support **post-positivism** is that truth cannot ever be fully revealed. The post-positivist will collect data and perform methodical examinations of the data. These examinations help the researcher to develop a probability about the results. Probability is defined as a prediction, which is founded on hypothesized truths that are generally believed. The post-positivism researcher does not deal in absolutes. Instead, the researcher will apply statistical tests that will support their hypothesized and inconclusive information. They refrain from making an assertion about the absolute truth of an answer to the problem. The researcher will state a number of close approximations to the truth based on quantitative research. The term "quantitative" refers to the quantity or the amount, which is described in numerical terms of measurement. Qualitative research is different, in that it uses narrative forms of data.

LAB RESEARCH VERSUS FIELD RESEARCH

Lab research has a high internal validity value because it is more easily controlled in terms of the cause-and-effect relationships of the variables applied under specific conditions. It also eliminates other explanations that can be attributed to a change in the results. However, lab research has a low external validity, in that generalization to other people, places, or time frames may not be so easy to accomplish. Generalization means that the action can be repeated in other situations.

Field research is more easily accomplished because it is done in a natural setting or environment; the researcher travels to the field of study. Field research demonstrates low internal validity because of the lack of control over external variables. Field research has high external validity because it can be generalized to other situations and settings.

BARRIERS TO RESEARCH EFFORTS

Cost has become an issue in the mental health care system, directly affecting the **research efforts** in this field. This issue has increased the need for counselors to be accountable in their work. Accountability is found in the documentation and data collection methods used by counselors. The National Institute of Mental Health (NIMH) issues funding grants to various research institutions. The research is performed on clients in the daily practice of mental health counselors. The research is concerned with gaining insight into the practicality of the counseling interventions applied in the daily life of the client. Therefore, it is necessary for research courses to be offered in college programs. Research courses may be used to instruct the student in standardized tests and evaluation, experimental research design, descriptive and inferential statistics, and the critique of research designs.

PHILOSOPHICAL FOUNDATIONS OF COUNSELING

The philosophical foundations of counseling are based on various theoretical approaches to human nature, behavior, and interactions:

- **Immanuel Kant** held the assumption that reality is based on subjective observations drawn from a person's objective reality or environmental events. Kant's theories are based on interactionism.
- **Sigmund Freud** found Kant's interactionism offered a starting point for his psychoanalytical work.
- **Gottfried Leibniz** was a philosopher who believed in personology, which states that a person can change when his or her perceptual awareness is changed. Leibniz's **theory of mind** is based on subjective reality—how a person perceives things to be within his or her own mind. Leibniz's **theory of personology** evolved into humanistic psychology, resulting in a counseling model known as **Rogers' person-centered psychotherapy**.
- **John Locke** held a more empiricist viewpoint, believing the human brain absorbs environmental events and sensory inputs from its surroundings in an effort to form meaning and knowledge, so studying only nature and the environment unlocks a person's mental health needs. Locke's empiric theories evolved into behavior therapy and behavioral counseling.

Despite the differences in philosophies, the goal of each of these psychotherapy models is the same. Each works to transform a person's thought patterns to affect the way that person handles emotional responses and behaves.

Evaluating Therapy Progress, Modifying Treatment, and Termination

SEQUENCE OF FAMILY THERAPY

Family therapy is solution-oriented, is brief, and occurs in stages. The general sequence involves the following defined stages:

- **Initial stage:** During the initial stage of treatment, therapists are tasked with using assessment techniques to gather information, determine the context of the presenting problem, and formulate a relational hypothesis. The relational hypothesis is used to assess a family's adaptive functioning (i.e., what is maintaining equilibrium). Therapists construct a transgenerational genogram to identify family members' roles, developmental life cycles, and family dynamics. The assessment determines which members of the client system will participate in treatment. Additional tasks include observing family interactions, identifying alliances among members, and determining the family's communication style.
- **Middle stage:** During the middle stage of treatment, the therapist works with the client system to engage members in therapeutic tasks based on the therapist's theoretical orientation (e.g., structural family therapy, strategic family therapy). The family's subsystems are identified, family dynamics are interpreted, and interventions are targeted to the family members most affected (e.g., couples, adolescents).
- **Termination phase:** This final stage is marked by a review of treatment progress, the reinforcement of new patterns of behavior, and an emphasis on all family members' participation in follow-up. Booster sessions may be scheduled with the family to assess the postdischarge progress.

DETERMINING THE NEED FOR EVALUATION BY OTHER PROFESSIONAL AND COMMUNITY SYSTEMS

MFTs must first adhere to ethical standards when determining the need for an evaluation by other professional and community systems. The code of ethics of the Association of Marital and Family Therapy (AAMFT) provides evaluation guidelines. MFTs adhere to Standard 7.6 by avoiding dual roles regarding forensic evaluations. If a client receiving therapy requests a forensic evaluation, the therapist must refer the client to another professional. MFTs prevent conflicts of interest by adhering to Standard 7.7, which states that MFTs should separate custody evaluations from therapy. Therapists make appropriate referrals to other professionals for custody evaluations. Therapists must also refer clients for an evaluation when therapeutic issues fall outside of their scope of competence.

MFTs may also refer clients for evaluations for many reasons, including, but not limited to, the following:

- To determine the primary clinical diagnosis or differentiate it from other diagnostic categories
- To rule out any medical causes for the client's presenting problems
- To determine eligibility for an individualized educational treatment plan and associated services, which may require an evaluation for psychological testing
- To measure intellectual, emotional, neurological, and psychological functioning
- To determine the need for additional, alternative, or specialized services (e.g., treatment for substance use, residential care)
- To determine the need for a higher level of care (e.g., inpatient hospitalization, crisis stabilization)

PROFESSIONAL AND COMMUNITY COLLABORATION

Collaboration is the interdependent process of connecting clients with appropriate resources designed to achieve a common purpose. Collaborative teams help clients systemically resolve current and emerging treatment issues. Members of collaborative teams include professional and community groups, agencies, individuals, and organizations. Therapists can also engage and collaborate with the client's systems, including families, other professionals, and community contacts.

Collaborative professionals are community members who make up multidisciplinary teams for clients with complex conditions. Clients who are served through larger hospital or community mental health centers benefit from collaborating with internal professional systems, including, but not limited to, the following:

- MFTs
- Psychiatrists
- Therapeutic aids
- In-home treatment providers
- Clinical nurse specialists
- Case managers
- School-based counselors
- Psychologists
- Dieticians
- Crisis stabilization providers

Community members can also serve on multidisciplinary teams, including, but not limited to, the following:

- Individuals from churches and faith communities
- Equine therapists
- Recreational therapists
- Art therapy providers
- Advocacy workers
- Probation/Parole officers
- Hospice workers
- Addiction and recovery support members
- Peer specialists
- Vocational services specialists
- Legal professionals

EVALUATING CLIENT APPROPRIATENESS FOR TELEHEALTH

MFTs are responsible for recognizing the implications of **technology-assisted professional services** provided across multiple platforms. **Cell phones** and other mobile technology, including internet-enabled smartphones, provide convenient access via **texting** but are typically not encrypted, making them less secure modes of communication. Section 6 of the AAMFT Code of Ethics (2015) outlines responsibilities associated with using electronic means with clients. MFTs ensure that technology-assisted therapeutic services **comply with relevant policies and laws** and understand their full impact on client needs.

MFTs inform clients of **the risks and benefits** of using electronic communication and related services. Proper **training** must be received before implementation, and supervision and education must be in place to maintain and enhance relevant skills. MFTs choose electronic platforms aligned with best practices and ensure that clients are physically, mentally, and intellectually eligible to use technology-assisted services. MFTs are professionally responsible for following best practices related to confidentiality and seek opportunities to improve the quality of those services. MFTs understand boundary violations unique to technology-assisted professional services and abide by the do-no-harm ethical principle.

Managing Crisis Situations

Assessment

CRISIS

CHARACTERISTICS

A **crisis** occurs when a person is faced with a highly stressful event and their usual problem solving and coping skills fail to be effective in resolving the situation. This event usually leads to increased levels of **anxiety** and can bring about a **physical and psychological response**. The problem is usually an **acute event** that can be identified. It may have occurred a few weeks or even months before or immediately prior to the crisis and can be an actual event or a potential event. The crisis state usually lasts less than six weeks with the individual then becoming able to utilize problem-solving skills to cope effectively. A person in crisis does not always have a mental disorder. However, during the acute crisis, their social functioning and decision-making abilities may be impaired.

DEVELOPMENTAL TYPE

There are basically two different **types of crises**. These types include developmental or maturational crises and situational crises. A **developmental crisis** can occur during **maturation** when an individual must take on a new life role. This crisis can be a normal part of the developmental process. A youth may need to face crisis and resolve this crisis to be able to move on to the next developmental stage. This may occur during the process of moving from adolescence to adulthood. Examples of situations that could lead to this type of crisis include graduating from school, going away to college, or moving out on their own. These situations would cause the individual to face a maturing event that requires the development of new coping skills.

SITUATIONAL TYPE

The second type of crisis is the **situational crisis**. This type of crisis can occur at any time in life. There is usually an event or problem that occurs, which leads to a **disruption in normal psychological functioning**. These types of events are often unplanned and can occur with or without warning. Some examples that may lead to a situational crisis include the death of a loved one, divorce, unplanned or unwanted pregnancy, onset or change in a physical disease process, job loss, or being the victim of a violent act. Events that affect an entire community can also cause individual and community situation crisis. Terrorist attacks or weather-related disasters are examples of events that can affect an entire community.

CRISIS INTERVENTION

Crisis intervention occurs when the goal of treatment is to return the individual to their **pre-crisis state**. This treatment course usually lasts six weeks or less and is geared toward assisting the individual to create new **coping mechanisms** and **adaptive behaviors**. Social and cultural influences can greatly affect the ability and ways in which individuals deal with and work through a crisis. There may be preconceived ideas and beliefs about asking for and accepting assistance from others. It is very important to consider the age of the individual when assessing the need for particular crisis interventions. The needs of an elderly adult will be different than the needs of a child.

Initial focus should be based on managing the current situation at hand to prevent complications and further feelings of helplessness from the patient. In this manner, the focus becomes solving the current problem and supporting the client emotionally, rather than trying to assess or manage underlying or long-term problems. Work should focus on helping the patient to feel secure and identifying negative or irrational thoughts that could be leading the patient into the crisis situation. By focusing on negative causes, the provider can work with the patient to identify solutions to the current situation. This averts the crisis from escalating into other areas, such as violence or suicide, and diminishes the patient's feelings of helplessness. If available, family members of the patient or other members of the health care team should be called in for support, as crisis interventions can be intense and overwhelming for those involved.

The patient who is having a crisis that includes hallucinations, such as hearing voices or seeing objects or people who are not truly there, may be exhibiting behaviors or hallucinating about subjects that are related to a particular theme for the patient. When managing hallucinations during an early or initial assessment, the actual theme or underlying subject may be assessed during this time. Once this topic is uncovered, management of hallucinations may focus more on dealing with the topic at hand, rather than the specific hallucination. The provider can redirect the patient to discuss the underlying feelings rather than the specific vision, voice, or thoughts the patient is experiencing. The provider may respond by saying, "I don't hear what you are hearing, but I think we should discuss your feelings of grief." If the patient is having hallucinations that are telling him to hurt himself or others, however, the provider may need to manage the situation with a crisis intervention rather than redirecting the patient to discuss underlying issues.

BRIEF CRISIS INTERVENTION THERAPIES

Brief crisis intervention therapies help the client come to terms with a life event or societal change, for example:

- Debriefing after violence in the workplace
- Natural disasters (earthquake, tornado, flood)
- Sexual assault
- Criminal victimization
- Suicidal or homicidal ideation (telephone hot lines)
- Catastrophic illness or injury
- Drastic relationship changes, like divorce

Limited therapy sessions may be conducted because of:

- Insurance limitations
- The client's reluctance to engage in prolonged treatment
- A shortage of qualified mental health workers versus heightened public demand for mental health treatment

SIX-STEP MODEL

Brief crisis intervention therapies often follow a six-step model developed by Gilliland in 1982. The end result of these steps should be that the client feels that the therapist helped and provided a positive experience:

- **Step 1**: Identify and concentrate on the problem at hand.
- **Step 2**: Assess the patient's personal history.
- **Step 3**: Develop a therapeutic bond with the patient.
- **Step 4**: Create a plan that uses an eclectic approach in selecting a wide range of intervention strategies.
- **Step 5**: Work out a solution to the problem at hand.
- **Step 6**: End therapy with an understanding between therapist and patient that the client can return whenever necessary.

USING SOLUTION FOCUSED THERAPY FOR BRIEF CRISIS INTERVENTIONS

Solution Focused Therapy is another alternative that provides a productive atmosphere for the client, where the problem can be solved in a non-judgmental environment. The provider in this situation discusses the pros and cons of that solution.

SHORT-TERM CRISIS INTERVENTION METHODS

Short crisis intervention therapies promoted by Health Management Organizations (HMOs) emphasize the heavy cost of mental health services to the insurance system. HMOs affect how mental health care is delivered because they require traditional long-term treatment models to change. Many **short crisis intervention therapies** incorporate:

- Short meeting times of 25 minutes or less, rather than traditional 60-minute sessions
- Restricted goal setting targeted at reaching short-term objectives, rather than consistent emotional insights
- Focused interviewing regarding the problem at hand
- Concentration on the here and now, rather than a detailed history
- Practical instruction about actions to be taken
- Diagnostic care that pinpoints the problem
- Flexible and varied choices of therapeutic tools to be utilized
- Prompt intervention strategies
- Inclusion of a ventilation practice
- Positive transfer of a therapeutic bond
- Selection of clients appropriate for short term crisis intervention therapies, rather than accepting all clients

EMERGENCY MENTAL HEALTH SERVICES

Psychiatric emergency services are designed to quickly assess and make arrangements for patients suffering acute crises; in many situations, patients may be a danger to themselves or others. Emergency services can provide **long-term benefits** to psychiatric clients by preventing potential complications associated with the emergency, which will keep the client safe in the short term and may prevent future complications that would have otherwise not have been addressed. Additionally, this prevention of future complications may keep the patient from ultimately entering long-term rehabilitation facilities, correctional centers, or inpatient hospitalization for significant periods of time, because of the sufficient treatment. Emergency services may also be a faster method of gaining treatment for the mentally ill client and, while not to be used only to gain faster access to care, they typically require immediate consultation with other disciplines and a fast turnaround when devising a plan of care and treatment. This benefits the client by providing rapid assessment and treatment.

COMPONENTS OF TRIAGE IN PSYCHIATRIC EMERGENCY SITUATIONS

Triage in emergency situations focuses on helping the client in acute mental health crisis to gain access to care and treatment and to prevent further complications or harm. The components of triage in these situations include:

- Assessing the client for immediate danger, whether to himself or to others
- Determining if the client has a previous psychiatric diagnosis and what current symptoms, thoughts, or behaviors he is now experiencing
- Assessing his overall level of cognitive functioning through orientation to self and place, assessing his reasoning abilities, and assessing his capacities for self-care
- Measuring the client's abilities to follow directions and adhere to a treatment regimen
- The presence of other diagnoses or disorders, both psychiatric or physical, in conjunction with the current set of behaviors
- Reviewing the client's access to community resources, financial abilities for immediate treatment, and time constraints that may permit or prohibit immediate treatment
- Determining the presence of family or others who can provide support for the client during the crisis and the treatment period following examination

CRITICAL INCIDENT STRESS MANAGEMENT

Critical incident stress management (CISM) is a procedure to help people cope with stressful events, such as disasters, to reduce the incidence of post-traumatic stress disorder.

- **Defusing sessions** usually occur very early, sometimes during or immediately after a stressful event. These sessions are used to educate actively involved personnel about what to expect over the next few days and to provide guidance about how to handle stress reactions.
- **Debriefing sessions** usually follow in 1–3 days and may be repeated periodically as needed. These sessions may include personnel who were either directly involved or indirectly involved. People are encouraged to express their feelings and emotions about the event. The six phases of debriefing include introduction, fact sharing, discussion of feelings, describing symptoms, teaching, and reentry. Critiquing the event or attempting to place blame is not part of the CISM process.
- **Follow-up** is done at the end of the process, often after only a week, but this time period varies.

RESTRICTIVE MEASURES

IMPORTANT DOCUMENTATION

The use of **restrictive measures** is a last resort in most patient settings. When utilized, these measures are to promote **patient safety**. The most common types of restrictive measures include physical restraints and seclusion. Every patient is entitled to being treated with the greatest personal respect and dignity. When a patient's activity is restricted very careful monitoring is required. Specific documentation on the patient's wellbeing should be performed per the facilities policy and usually includes a description of what occurred and physical monitoring of the patient while in restraints. If restrictive measures have to be utilized, staff members should have attempted and documented any and all other attempts to de-escalate the situation. These restraint techniques should only be utilized during the time that the patient is considered dangerous.

SECLUSION

Seclusion involves separating the patient from others by placing them in an environment where they are unable to leave. The patient is usually placed in this environment against their will in order to protect the patient or others from **harm**. This particular type of restraint is viewed negatively, is associated with negative patient outcomes, and is rarely utilized. A **seclusion room** would have padded walls and no furniture. There would be nothing in this environment that the patient could utilize to injure themselves or someone else. Once a patient has been placed in seclusion, they must be observed continuously.

RESTRAINTS

Restraints are considered to be the most restrictive of all measures and should only be utilized if all other alternative measures have failed. There are two main **types of restraints**:

- **Chemical restraints** involve the use of medications to manage a patient's behavior problem. This type of restraint often inhibits their physical movements and is used only when absolutely necessary to prevent injury. This medication is not utilized on a regular basis.
- **Physical restraints** involve the use of a person physically restraining a patient or the use of a mechanical device to restrict movement. These restraints not only restrict the physical movements in an area, but can also restrict their access to other parts of their own body or nearby equipment. Physical restraints are very difficult for patients to remove on their own.

MONITORING AND OBSERVATION

Monitoring, directly watching patients in psychiatric and mental health care, varies, depending on the type of facility and the patient's condition. It is primarily used to ensure safety. **Monitoring** can include the following:

- **Routine checks** are done at prescribed times (e.g., every 15 minutes), or continuous observation may be necessary.
- **Security personnel** (e.g., in emergency departments) may monitor patients to ensure patient and staff safety.
- **Audio/video monitoring** is sometimes used, but patients and families must be aware that this kind of monitoring is in place. It must not violate privacy, and monitors and audio speakers must not be accessible to nonauthorized individuals. Regulations regarding audio/video recordings may vary from state to state.

Observation is an ongoing process that involves observing the patient's behavior and nonverbal actions (e.g., posture, eye contact, expression, clothing, tone of voice) during communication. Observation helps to determine which issues are important to the patient, the types of questions to ask, the patient's perceptions, and the interpretation of messages.

ASSESSING THE RISK OF VIOLENCE TO THE CLIENT FROM OTHERS

Therapists assess a client's risk of violence and appropriate interventions by evaluating multiple factors. First, it is vital to understand that measures of violence are highly **situation dependent** and subject to change; therefore, methods for determining a client's risk of violence are complex, **dynamic, and multifaceted.** For a client at risk for intimate partner violence (IPV), several evidence-based measures can be used to assess the person's risk of being reassaulted or killed. Common **assessment instruments for IPV victims** include the Danger Assessment Scale and the Domestic Abuse Risk Assessment. These assessments must be paired with a clinical interview to determine the client's unique risk factors, current emotional state, and whether the client is at imminent risk of violence or harm.

Clients with a history of IPV are at high risk, particularly in situations in which the perpetrator has recently been released from jail or has repeatedly violated an emergency protective order. Perpetrators with a history of suicidal ideation, controlling behaviors, psychological manipulation, stalking, and coercion also place victims at higher risk. A client's safety may also be at risk after threatening to leave the abuser or is in the process of leaving. Additional victim vulnerabilities include being female, having shared children, pregnancy, and financial dependence.

ASSESSING THE RISK OF VIOLENCE TO THERAPIST FROM OTHERS

Workplace violence against therapists can take the form of verbal or physical threats, intimidation, coercion, and physical violence. Workplace settings that put a therapist at the highest risk include inpatient psychiatric units, crisis stabilization units, emergency rooms, geriatric patient settings, and clients' residential settings. Perpetrators of workplace violence can be clients, patients, residents, or family members. Conditions that increase a **therapist's risk of violence** include, but are not limited to, the following:

- Working in a facility with poorly lit alleyways
- Working with individuals who have immediate access to weapons
- Engaging with individuals involved with gangs
- Working in communities with high crime rates
- Working in hospital settings for individuals with severe mental illness (e.g., psychosis)
- Transporting patients or clients with violent tendencies
- Engaging with individuals who misuse substances
- Serving clients in emergency settings who are in extreme pain

A safety plan for the therapist involves assessing worksite risks, identifying specific hazards, and monitoring progress. Examples of safety measures include installing metal detectors, adding lighting, and improving patient surveillance systems. Items on a safety plan may also include training on trauma-informed care, ensuring that staff in high-risk situations are accompanied, training staff on de-escalation techniques, providing means of emergency communication, and notifying a supervisor before and after home visits.

ASSESSING THE LEVEL OF IMPAIRMENT IN A CLIENT'S LIFE

A **crisis** is defined as an event or situation that disrupts a person's normal state of balance (i.e., homeostasis), resulting in psychological distress and functional impairment. Crisis events can be developmental or **maturational** (e.g., puberty, moving out), **situational** (e.g., car accident, assault), or **existential** (e.g., questioning one's career, illness). Individuals can also develop a **mental health crisis.** Mental health crisis involves a buildup of intense anxiety, anger, panic, and/or desperation.

They are mainly a culmination of events rather than a singular cause.

Changes in **functional impairment** can occur across cognitive, behavioral, emotional, and interpersonal domains. The severity of the crisis can be determined by conducting a **mental status exam.** Therapists investigate any suicidal or homicidal ideation, precipitating events, client supports, and coping skills. Therapists also evaluate the client's judgment, speech, appearance, and behavior. Clients engaging in substance misuse and those with severe mental disorders (e.g., bipolar disorder, schizophrenia) may need to provide contact information for family members and other collateral persons to determine the severity of the crisis. Whenever possible, a full biopsychosocial assessment must be provided to assess for additional risk and protective factors.

ASSESSING THE CLIENT'S TRAUMA HISTORY

Therapists must **assess a client's trauma history** to determine its relation to the crisis and its impact on any preexisting mental health disorders. Therapists are sensitive to the potential for retraumatization and work to provide a safe therapeutic environment from which to explore these factors. Therapists refrain from rapid-fire questioning or matter-of-fact trauma-related inquiries. Providing self-administered screening checklists, such as the **Trauma History Questionnaire,** is helpful for clients who may be reluctant to report trauma experiences verbally. Complex histories of victimization, abuse, and neglect must be considered in light of potentially coercive psychiatric interventions, including forced seclusion and restraint.

The **Crisis Intervention Trauma Treatment (ACT) model** is a staged crisis intervention model. The overall goal of ACT is to restore a person's homeostasis and prevent any crisis-related psychological trauma. The initial steps of the ACT model include establishing a therapeutic alliance, understanding all facets of the crisis, and exploring the client's current thoughts and behaviors. Therapists refrain from asking clients to provide emotionally overwhelming details of the trauma and instead focus on how the trauma symptoms affect the client's current level of functioning.

Reducing Harm to the Self or Others

INTERVENTION STRATEGIES

Appropriate treatment strategies for individuals thinking of harming themselves or others begins with determining the client's current level of risk. It is critical that the therapist understands the client's intent, plans, and means to help determine if the client or others are at imminent risk.

The client's case conceptualization reflects risk factors, protective factors, any history of dangerousness, maladaptive patterns, and precipitating stressors.

Once all of the assessment variables are considered, the therapist provides interventions matching the client's level of risk and needs. These interventions include, but are not limited to, the following:

Low risk:

- Collaborate on a written safety plan.
- Identify client resources and social supports.
- Assist with coping skills.
- Identify ways to minimize risks.
- Emphasize protective factors.
- Review psychiatric medication when applicable.
- Set a follow-up date for 1 week or less.
- Provide a 24-hour crisis phone number.

Medium risk:

- Apply appropriate low-risk interventions.
- Determine ways to keep their environment safe.
- Reduce access to lethal means and dangerous items.
- Instruct the client to identify multiple family members, friends, and professionals that can be used to help them resolve the crisis.
- Review the client's safety plan with a supervisor or seasoned clinician.
- Set a follow-up appointment in 24–48 hours.

High risk:

- Apply any appropriate low- and medium-risk interventions.
- Follow ethical and legal mandates associated with clients at risk of imminent harm, including the duty to warn others.
- Contact police when unable contact and notify the intended victim.
- Arrange for a higher level of care, including crisis stabilization or inpatient psychiatric hospitalization if the client is deemed as an immediate threat.

Referrals and Collaboration in Crisis Management

REFERRALS/COLLABORATION TO AUGMENT MANAGEMENT OF A CLIENT'S CRISIS

Partnerships with referral sources are essential for providing seamless care to clients in crisis. The nature of the client's crisis determines appropriate referral sources. Clients in crisis may present with critical incidents of severe agitation, intentions to harm themselves or others, psychosis, substance intoxication, and/or substance withdrawal. Therapists working within larger systems of care ensure effective **cross-system collaboration** takes place with each referral source.

Intra-agency referral sources include, but are not limited to:

- Mobile crisis teams
- Case managers
- Peer support specialists
- Psychiatrists
- Substance abuse counselors
- Crisis stabilization professionals

Cross-system referral sources include, but are not limited to:

- Schools and universities
- The criminal justice system
- Child protective services
- Law enforcement
- Community health centers
- Hospitals

Collaboration with appropriate referral sources and care systems is critical for meeting a client's needs during a crisis. Elements of a strong collaborative relationship include, but are not limited to, the following:

- The collection of input from all involved sources
- An appreciation of diverse multidisciplinary perspectives
- A commitment to working as a united front
- The development of an integrated safety plan
- Participation in postevent case reviews

ASSESSING AND RESPONDING TO VICARIOUS TRAUMA (VT)

Vicarious trauma (VT) is the emotional aftermath on the therapist resulting from continuous exposure to a client or clients' traumatic material. Over time, therapists exposed to work-related trauma begin to change their worldview. **Vicarious resilience** is used to describe therapists who respond positively to VT. Therapists responding with vicarious resilience are strengthened by witnessing a client overcome adversity with strength and determination. Therapists can have positive, negative, neutral, or mixed responses to VT, and these responses may vary over time.

Therapists who are **adversely affected by VT** must remain aware of the associated signs and symptoms. Common signs and symptoms of VT include the following:

- Experiencing residual effects of a client's rage, sadness, and fear
- Being preoccupied with a client's experiences outside of the work environment
- Developing decreased satisfaction with one's own work performance
- Growing hopeless, cynical, and pessimistic
- Attempting to detach, distance, or otherwise restrict and numb one's feelings
- Becoming less effective in setting appropriate boundaries (i.e., overextending oneself)

VT generally develops over time, and is primarily associated with empathetic therapists. Ways to address VT include, but are not limited to, the following:

- Participate in frequent supervision.
- Increase symptom self-monitoring.
- Seek appropriate social support.
- Maintain a healthy work/life balance.
- Engage in emotional self-care.
- Participate in relevant training.
- Seek involvement in creative, physical, and/or spiritual practices.

Maintaining Ethical, Legal and Professional Standards

Scope and Standards of Practice

SCOPE OF PRACTICE

The **scope of practice** for MFTs outlines the practices and activities that MFTs are eligible and authorized to perform. The Association of Marriage and Family Therapy Regulatory Boards is the entity that governs these practices and activities. This association of state licensing boards ensures that MFTs receive the required level of training, education, and experience to work within their scope of practice.

MFTs are trained to deliver **individual, couples, family, and group therapy.** Within these modalities, the scope of practice for MFTs includes, but is not limited to, the following:

- Conducting treatment planning
- Providing crisis management
- Diagnosing mental disorders
- Providing psychoeducation and consultation
- Assessing and treating SUDs
- Modifying intrapersonal behaviors and dysfunctional thinking
- Helping families improve parenting skills and parent–child relationships
- Applying evidence-based approaches for treating emotional, behavioral, and relational issues

MFTs are prohibited from practicing outside of their scope of practice as well as their **boundaries of competence.** Per Standard 3.10 of the AAMFT Code of Ethics (2015): "Marriage and family therapists do not diagnose, treat, or advise on problems outside the recognized boundaries of their competencies." MFTs have an ethical obligation to develop and maintain personal competency. They are also responsible for refining skills through education, supervision, and training. MFTs also ensure competence when applying new skills in trained areas of specialization Finally, MFTs practice within their scope of practice and competence to protect clients from potential harm (AAMFT, 2015, Standard 3.6).

Relevant Statues, Case Law, and Regulations

CLINICAL RECORDS, HIPAA, AND PRIVACY

Ethical guidelines and standards for statutes, case law, and regulations include the following:

- **Clinical records:** The Code of Federal Regulations (CFR) was revised in 2020 and offers protection for individuals being served by federally assisted programs providing treatment for substance use disorder (SUD). Regulations for clinical records are reflected in 42 CFR Part 2, which prohibits law enforcement's use of clinical records for criminal prosecution unless court ordered to do so. The records of clients in treatment for SUD are kept confidential unless the client provides authorization, with rare exceptions (e.g., medical emergencies).
- **HIPAA:** HIPAA prevents the inappropriate use or disclosure of a client's protected health information (PHI). HIPAA standards protect client confidentiality by clarifying conditions in which entities (e.g., third-party payers) or persons have the right to access a client's PHI.
- **Privacy:** HIPAA's Privacy Rule provides extra protection for psychotherapy notes. This exception allows mental health therapists to keep private psychotherapy notes separate from the medical record.
  - **Psychotherapy notes** are kept for various reasons, including documenting relevant client conversations, constructing a case conceptualization, examining a hypothesis, and considering options for follow-up care.
  - **Progress notes,** on the other hand, are included in the client's medical record and are exempt from extra protection. Progress notes contain information and summaries related to the client's diagnosis, functional status, treatment modality, medication management, response to treatment, session dates and times, results of clinical assessments, and progress toward treatment goals.

MANDATORY REPORTING, PROFESSIONAL BOUNDARIES, AND MANDATED CLIENTS

Mandatory reporting (AAMFT, 2015, Standards 2.1 and 2.2): MFTs have a legal and ethical obligation as mandated reporters to report any suspected child or elder abuse as outlined in the MFT's state or provincial governing laws. MFTs explain limitations to confidentiality to the client as part of informed consent. Some states require MFTs to report suspected acts of domestic violence, whereas other states may require a report if the violent act was committed in front of a minor. Jurisdiction laws may also differ in language and definitions regarding specific acts requiring reporting, the timeline for reporting, and the type of information that an MFT is obligated to report.

Professional boundaries (AAMFT, 2015, Standards 1.3–1.5): MFTs maintain professional boundaries with clients to maximize therapeutic outcomes and minimize exploitation and harm. MFTs exercise caution when engaging in dual and/or multiple relationships and refrain from engaging in relationships that would impair their professional judgment, negatively impact trust, or exploit clients' dependence. MFTs are prohibited from engaging in sexual intimacy with current and former clients and their family members. MFTs make appropriate efforts to avoid business or personal relationships with clients and their immediate family members.

Mandated clients (AAMFT, 2015, Standard 2.2): MFTs discuss limits to confidentiality when working with clients mandated to treatment.

STARK LAW, ANTIKICKBACK STATUTE, FALSE CLAIMS ACT

Standard 8 (financial integrity) in the AAMFT Code of Ethics (2015) cites that MFTs must not offer or accept payment for referrals, including kickbacks, rebates, pay, or other financial compensation. These ethical standards are aligned with the US Department of Health and Human Services, Office of the Inspector General fraud and abuse laws, including the following:

Stark Law (i.e., the Physician Self-Referral Law) (42 USC § 1395nn): With limited exceptions, the Stark Law prohibits physicians from referring patients to "designated health services" payable by federally funded entities (i.e., Medicaid or Medicare) from which the physician or immediate family member has a financial relationship.

Antikickback Statute (42 USC § 1320a–7b[b]): This statute prohibits "willful payment of 'remuneration' to induce or reward patient referrals or the generation of business involving any item or service payable by the Federal health care programs (e.g., drugs, supplies, or health care services for Medicare or Medicaid patients)." This is a criminal law, with violations including jail terms and financial penalties.

False Claims Act (31 USC §§ 3729–3733): The civil sections of this act protect "the Government from being overcharged or sold shoddy goods or services." The criminal section (18 USC § 287) imposes prison terms, stiff penalties, and fines for submitting false claims.

Legal and Ethical Considerations

THERAPIST'S PROFESSIONAL RESPONSIBILITY AND COMPETENCE

MFTs working with **court-ordered cases** have a professional responsibility to practice within the parameters of their professional competency. Standard 3 of the AAMFT Code of Ethics (2015) addresses professional competence and integrity. This standard specifies that MFTs maintain competence through appropriate training, education, and supervision. MFTs are instructed to develop, apply, and maintain competencies to best meet the needs of their clients. MFTs refrain from practicing when mentally impaired or under the influence of a substance. Additionally, MFTs do not "diagnose, treat, or advise" on problems outside their scope of competence.

MFTs who function as **expert witnesses** or participate in **custody hearings** must ensure that those services also fall within their scope of competence. MFTs avoid conflicts of interest by not providing custody evaluations, determinations of residence, or visitation agreements to minors or adults undergoing such legal proceedings. MFTs providing expert witness testimony avoid misleading judgments, baseless facts, and unfounded opinions and instead strive to be accurate, fair, and objective (AAMFT Code of Ethics, 2015, Standard 7.2).

ELEMENTS OF THE BUSINESS PRACTICE OF THERAPY

MFTs are responsible for following **applicable laws and standards** for appropriate management of client records. Standard 8 of the AAMFT Code of Ethics (2015) outlines the MFT's responsibility for financial arrangements. MFTs ensure confidentiality is maintained when storing, safeguarding, transferring, and disposing of client records. MFTs undergoing practice changes also take steps to protect client records during a move, the closing of one's practice, or an MFT's death. MFTs and their supervisors must adhere to technology-related best practices and conform to relevant laws and policies.

Nonclinical **office and medical records** staff must receive appropriate training on confidentiality, methods for collecting payment, and recorded **financial disclosures**. MFTs are ultimately responsible for explaining financial policies to the client before beginning therapy. Policies for financial disclosures include set fees and services, legal measures for nonpayment, means of collecting payment, and policies related to payment for missed or canceled sessions.

RIGHTS OF CLIENTS WITHIN THE THERAPEUTIC RELATIONSHIP

Standard 1.8 addresses client autonomy in decision making. MFTs respect the rights of clients to **make their own treatment decisions**, including, but not limited to, participation in therapy, selecting or refusing a specific treatment modality (e.g., group therapy), or participation in research studies. MFTs refrain from making personal decisions for clients regarding divorce, separation, or reconciliation.

MFTs take steps to ensure that services to clients are not compromised by the client's participation in **research studies**. MFTs seek advice from impartial professionals to avoid dual or multiple relationships. The ethical provisions of research involve communicating the purpose of the study as well as its frequency, length, and duration. Clients understand that they have a right to withdraw from participation at any time (Standard 5.4).

MFTs inform participants about any conflicts of interest and provide the contact information of an individual knowledgeable about the rights of participants in the event that questions arise. MFTs are careful to ensure that those with mental impairments participate only when their ability to consent is undiminished. In the context of research or clinical services, clients have a right to privacy and confidentiality and understand the possible limitations inherent in each.

ASSISTING THE CLIENT IN MAKING INFORMED DECISIONS

The therapist can assist the client in making informed decisions about the following elements relevant to treatment:

- **Informed consent** MFTs ensure that clients can freely consent to treatment and are informed of all associated treatment processes and procedures. Informed consent also necessitates that the client "has been adequately informed of potential risks and benefits of treatments for which generally recognized standards do not yet exist" (AAMFT Code of Ethics, 2015, Standard 1.2).
- **Third-party payers:** Standard 8 of the AAMFT Code of Ethics (2015) addresses financial arrangements with clients and third-party payers. Before the initial intake session, MFTs explain all fees and applicable charges, legal measures for nonpayment, and the procedures in place if third-party payers deny payment. MFTs are ethically obligated to truthfully represent facts to clients, third-party payers, and supervisees.
- **Collateral systems:** Collateral persons are usually a client's spouse, partner, family member, or friend involved in the client's treatment. MFTs help clients make informed decisions about a collateral person's participation in therapy by determining their purpose and role. Once this determination is made, MFTs explain that collateral persons do not have the same privacy and confidentiality rights as the client; therefore, they do not have access to client records. Clients have the right to revoke collateral participation at any time.
- **Alternative treatments:** Alternative or complementary treatments can be nontraditional or standard medical practices. Examples of alternative treatments include relaxation, meditation, yoga, movement therapy, spiritual healing, and acupuncture. MFTs are responsible for adequately informing clients of the potential risks and benefits of treatments "for which generally recognized standards do not yet exist" (AAMFT, Code of Ethics, 2015, Standard 8.4).

MAINTAINING ACCURATE AND TIMELY RECORDS

Standard 2 of the AAMFT Code of Ethics (2015) provides confidentiality standards applicable to clinical records. Confidentiality standards state that MFTs must make reasonable attempts to provide access to clinical records upon client request. MFTs may disclose confidences only with a written authorization form or waiver, unless the law mandates or otherwise permits. When more than one person is being treated, MFTs require a written authorization form for all involved parties.

Access to client records is limited if the MFT believes that releasing the records may cause serious harm to the client (AAMFT, 2015, Standard 2.2). MFTs must also maintain accurate and timely documentation and take reasonable steps to enforce and protect client confidentiality (AAMFT, 2015, Standard 2.2). MFTs are responsible for storing, protecting, and disposing of records in a manner that upholds confidentiality (AAMFT, 2015, Standard 2.5). MFTs look to their local jurisdictions to determine the time frame required for long-term storage. Additionally, client records may not be withheld as a consequence of nonpayment (AAMFT, 2015, Standard 8.6).

RECORD DISPOSAL

MFTs are responsible for **protecting and disposing of client records** in a manner that maintains confidentiality and adheres to applicable laws (AAMFT, 2015, 2.5). Following termination of services, MFTs adhere to federal and state laws, licensure laws, and policies for disposing of sensitive material. MFTs preparing for practice changes store, transfer, or dispose of records in a manner aligned with confidentiality standards (AAMFT, 2015, Standard 2.6). In doing so, MFTs ensure that the client's overall well-being is also considered. Although the AAMFT Code of Ethics (2015) does not specify a time frame for disposing of records, similar disciplines (e.g., psychology) and some state laws (e.g., California) specify a time frame of 7 years for adults. Best practices encourage therapists to apply discretion before disposing of records that may be needed in future court cases. This includes, but is not limited to, clinical notes on child abuse and neglect, client suicide attempts, violence, or harassment.

MFTs must adhere to the HIPAA Privacy Rule, which states that "appropriate administrative, technical, and physical safeguards to protect the privacy of medical records and other protected health information (PHI) for whatever period such information is maintained by a covered entity, including through disposal" (45 CFR 164.530). Further, paper records containing PHI must be destroyed in a way that renders the documents unreadable or indecipherable, including shredding or burning. Similarly, electronic records containing PHI must be cleared, purged, or destroyed.

Impact of Technology on Practice

EXPECTED CONDUCT OF INTERNET THERAPY

Standard 6 in the AAMFT Code of Ethics (2015) addresses **ethical standards for using electronic means** in therapy, supervision, and related professional services. MFTs are responsible for understanding and explaining **appropriate conduct** when providing internet therapy. Telehealth clients are debriefed before beginning treatment on the risks, benefits, and expectations of internet therapy as part of informed consent. MFTs help clients understand appropriate conduct for using a confidential space by ensuring that it is free from distractions and interruptions. For clients in potentially abusive living arrangements, therapists discuss safety measures and work to determine the appropriateness of telehealth and crisis management services.

When considering a client for telehealth, therapists understand that opportunities may be limited for clients who engage in substance abuse, violence, or self-injury. Clients engaging in **unsafe conduct** may require a more controlled, in-person setting. Clients with a history of psychosis, cognitive impairment, paranoia, or dissociation may not be a good fit for telehealth services. Therapists assess each client's motivation, responsiveness to treatment, support system involvement, and other **protective factors** when evaluating if a client is appropriate for internet therapy.

APPROPRIATE USE OF TECHNOLOGY

Technology-assisted services (TAS) include therapy, supervision, and related professional services. Before starting therapy, MFTs attest to compliance with all applicable laws and regulations for providing TAS (AAMFT, 2015, Standard 6.1). Because many TAS services are limited to in-state practices and jurisdictions, MFTs ensure that all applicable laws regarding location of services and practices are followed (AAMFT, 2015, Standard 6.5).

MFTs determine the appropriateness of TAS for each participant, and they proceed with the use of electronic means that best meet the psychological and professional needs of clients and supervisees. MFTs are transparent about the potential risks and benefits and ensure the security of the communication medium (e.g., phone, internet). Further, supervisors, supervisees, and clients agree to work together to minimize any risks associated with TAS (AAMFT, 2015, Standard 6.2).

It is essential that MFTs obtain appropriate education, training, or supervision for TAS before entering into a supervisory or therapeutic relationship. MFTs obtain an informed consent from clients and supervisees outlining the limitations and protections of confidentiality as it pertains to the chosen electronic medium. This consent must be in writing. MFTs choose electronic platforms and means of documentation in accordance with best practices and legal and regulatory standards (AAMFT, 2015, Standards 6.3–6.4). Finally, MFTs are responsible for choosing current technology that optimizes the quality and safety of services and they continue to be updated on technological advances in professional and clinical contexts (AAMFT, 2015, Standard 6.6).

IMPLICATIONS OF TECHNOLOGY ON THE THERAPEUTIC PROCESS

The implications of technology on the therapeutic process are vast. MFTs working with clients engaging in **sexting, online pornography, and chat rooms** recognize the various effects on the client and client system, including subsequent co-occurring sexual dysfunctions, impaired intimacy, aggression, and distorted beliefs about sex roles and relationships. Sexting involves suggestive text messages and may be coupled with nude or seminude photos. Chat rooms are forums that can be used to exchange similar messages. Adolescents engaging in sexting via text or online chat rooms

112

are more likely to participate in risky sexual activities and are at risk for poorer mental health outcomes.

The use of **social media** also carries a risk of harm. Personal exchanges via social media sites may include communication leading to emotional or physical infidelity among couples. Social media postings can also produce conflictual relationships with families and friends when strongly opposed viewpoints are publicly shared and challenged.

Problematic internet gaming is a BA, with excessive use resulting in thoughts, behaviors, and emotions similar to those found with SUDs. MFTs recognize that internet gaming can expose teens to cyberbullying and online predators, threatening the user's safety and worsening depression and anxiety. Similarly, problematic use of social media, sexting, and chat rooms is linked to symptoms of depression and anxiety, including suicidality, with severe mental disorders associated with exposure to manipulation, trauma, bullying, or public humiliation.

Supervisor-Supervisee Relationship

ETHICAL AND REGULATORY GUIDELINES

Standard 4 of the AAMFT Code of Ethics (2015) outlines the expectations for engaging in supervisor–supervisee relationships. MFT supervisors try to **avoid dual or multiple relationships** with supervisees and understand that those conditions increase the risk of **exploitation**. Supervisors know that their role is influential and avoid instances or extensions of the supervisor–supervisee relationship that would interfere with sound judgment and fair treatment. MFT supervisors do not provide therapy to supervisees because this would impair objectivity (AAMFT, 2015, Standard 4.2). MFTs do not engage in sexual intimacy with supervisees during the duration of the supervisor–supervisee relationship (AAMFT, 2015, Standard 4.3). When accepting payment for supervision, MFTs do not enter into financial agreements through deceptive or exploitative practices (AAMFT, 2015, Standard 4.8).

Supervisors in an **existing relationship** with a supervisee are aware of the influence inherent in their position and take appropriate precautions to avoid exploiting the trust and dependency of the supervisee. Examples of existing relationships include business relationships, friendships, and shared community or church fellowships. This precaution is also extended to family members of a supervisee. MFTs oversee a supervisee's competence and professionalism, disallowing supervisees from performing outside of the scope of their practice and competence (AAMFT, 2015, Standards 4.4–4.5). Finally, supervisees must provide written authorization for the supervisor to disclose confidential information (AAMFT, 2015, Standard 4.7).

AWARENESS OF THE INFLUENCE OF THE THERAPIST'S AND SUPERVISOR'S ISSUES

MFTs and supervisors are ethically responsible for identifying and addressing any issues impacting the treatment of the client and the client system. Standard 3 of the AAMFT Code of Ethics (2015) calls for MFTs to seek appropriate assistance for issues that may be detrimental to work performance and decision making. MFTs and their supervisors are ethically responsible for attending to any personal life situation that may be detrimental to client care (e.g., experiences of trauma, grief, and loss). Life situations become detrimental to client care when those issues result in countertransference.

Standard 7 of the AAMFT Code of Ethics (2015) instructs supervisors to avoid exploiting the trust and dependency of their supervisees. In doing so, MFTs and their supervisors are tasked with exploring dual relationships in the context of clinical supervision and client care. Dual relationships impact the supervisor–supervisee dyad as well as the therapist–client dyad. MFTs acknowledge that an imbalance of power, status, and expertise in supervision may increase the risk of exploitation and dependency. MFTs and supervisors understand that unmet emotional, mental, or spiritual needs may place the dyad among one or both parties in supervision or client care, increasing the risk for countertransference and blocking therapeutic growth for the supervisee or client system.

MFT Practice Test #1

Want to take this practice test in an online interactive format? Check out the bonus page, which includes interactive practice questions and much more: **mometrix.com/bonus948/mft**

1. Therapists who collaborate with clients on developing treatment plan goals based on the client's "best hope" for a successful outcome would most likely adhere to which one of the following theoretical orientations?

    a. Exposure therapy.
    b. Psychoanalytic therapy.
    c. Structural family therapy.
    d. Solution-focused therapy.

2. Which one of the following is TRUE of the MFT's role as a mandated reporter?

    a. The therapist must only report proven cases of elder and child abuse.
    b. The therapist must report all suspected and proven cases of elder and child abuse.
    c. The therapist must decide on a case-by-case basis when reporting suspected elder or child abuse.
    d. The therapist must obtain a third-party assessment to determine if suspected cases of elder or child abuse should be reported.

3. An MFT provides ongoing therapy for a 9-year-old client whose parents have recently divorced. The client's mother calls to request an evaluation for the court to address custody and visitation. Assuming that the therapist has obtained the mother's consent to release information, which action best adheres to the MFT's ethical standards of practice?

    a. The therapist may perform the evaluation only if possessing the required education, training, or supervised experience.
    b. The therapist may perform the evaluation only if also obtaining a consent to release information from the father.
    c. The therapist may only provide the court with information about the minor from the MFT's perspective in his or her role as the treating MFT.
    d. The therapist may only provide the court with information about the minor from the MFT's perspective in his or her role as an expert or fact witness.

4. Which one of the following practices can be used to influence client perceptions through intentional nonjudgmental attention to present-moment awareness of thoughts, sensations, and feelings?

    a. Hypnosis.
    b. Mindfulness.
    c. Sensate focus.
    d. Flow.

5. Which theorist deduced that infants form attachments with primary caregivers who provide touch and tactile comfort?

    a. John Bowlby.
    b. Erik Erikson.
    c. Harry Harlow.
    d. Sigmund Freud.

6. The MFT has an ethical obligation to disclose all of the following financial policies EXCEPT:

    a. the fees for canceled or missed appointments.
    b. the use of collection agencies established for nonpayment.
    c. the appeals process for obtaining denied third-party payments.
    d. the duty to provide reasonable notice to fee changes during treatment.

7. Which one of the following prohibits willful payment of "remuneration" to generate business involving any services payable to federal health-care programs (i.e., Medicare or Medicaid)?

    a. False Claims Act (FCA).
    b. Anti-Kickback Statute (AKS).
    c. Stark Law (i.e., the Physician Self-Referral Law).
    d. Mental Health Parity Compliance Act (MHPCA).

8. Which one of the following is used at the onset of treatment to underscore legal and ethical guidelines and establish client–counselor responsibilities, roles, and expectations?

    a. Safety contracts.
    b. Treatment plans.
    c. Therapeutic contracts.
    d. Confidentiality agreements.

Refer to the following for questions 9 - 10:

> A therapist is aware that his own intersectional identity affords him privileges that are not available to his client. The client has met some of their agreed-upon treatment goals when they begin to discuss an incident involving discrimination. The therapist is internally incensed at the injustice and attuned to his desire to protect the client from harm.

9. Which one of the following terms refers to the therapist's internal emotional experiences?

    a. Implicit bias.
    b. Immediacy.
    c. Microinvalidation.
    d. Countertransference.

10. Which one of the following would best enhance the therapeutic alliance?

    a. Relabeling.
    b. Reframing.
    c. Self-disclosure.
    d. Double-sided reflections.

11. MFTs in a supervisory role must refrain from behavior that would exploit or negatively impact supervisory trust. Avoiding this behavior is best accomplished by establishing which one of the following?

    a. Dual relationships.
    b. Professional boundaries.
    c. Emotional barriers.
    d. Nonabandonment.

12. Military personnel who develop mental health disorders are more likely to have experienced all of the following EXCEPT:

    a. combat exposure.
    b. prolonged deployment.
    c. postdeployment reintegration.
    d. traumatic brain injuries.

13. A newly hired MFT provides individual therapy to a client with depression. During the current session, the client presented as disheveled, emotionally dysregulated, and smelling of alcohol. The MFT has no experience working with substance abusing clients. What is the MFT's BEST course of action?

    a. Discuss the case with a colleague experienced in treating co-occurring disorders.
    b. Refer the client to a therapist experienced in treating co-occurring disorders.
    c. Attend a training on co-occurring disorders.
    d. Develop new skills to treat co-occurring disorders.

14. The primary purpose of the mental status exam (MSE) is to:

    a. offer a subjective account of the client's clinical state.
    b. confirm or refute diagnostic impressions and hypotheses.
    c. deliver insight into the client's risk and protective factors.
    d. provide a snapshot of the client's presentation at a specific point in time.

15. Which one of the following Bowenian concepts manifests as a self-fulfilling prophecy?

    a. The family projection process.
    b. Differentiation of self.
    c. The multigenerational transmission process.
    d. The nuclear family emotional process.

16. The type of termination that involves the therapist referring the client for specialized services to best meet client needs is known as:

    a. forced termination.
    b. premature termination.
    c. client-initiated termination.
    d. therapist-initiated termination.

17. HIPAA's Privacy Rule uniformly applies to all protected personal health information but offers extra protection for which one of the following?

    a. Progress notes.
    b. Case management notes.
    c. Psychotherapy notes.
    d. Medication monitoring notes.

18. Which one of the following processes considers the influences of church and school on adolescents and their families?

    a. Genogram.
    b. Family mapping.
    c. Family sculpting.
    d. Multigenerational transmission.

19. A client previously treated for depression presents for a crisis assessment after an increase in suicidal ideation triggered by the death of her spouse. During the evaluation, the client reports a history of child abuse leading to several out-of-home placements in early childhood. How should the therapist respond FIRST?

    a. Develop a no-suicide contract with the client.
    b. Collect the details of the trauma and process the underlying emotions.
    c. Conduct a mental status exam (MSE) to determine the functional impairment.
    d. Provide the client with information on grief support groups in the community.

20. Social justice principles include all of the following EXCEPT:

    a. access.
    b. participation.
    c. equality.
    d. rights.

21. If the AAMFT Code of Ethics prescribes a standard of professional behavior higher than what is dictated by law, MFTs respond with an understanding that:

    a. both the law and the AAMFT Code of Ethics govern the practice of MFTs, but the standards dictated by law supersede those dictated by the code.
    b. both the law and the AAMFT Code of Ethics govern the practice of MFTs, but the standards dictated by the code supersede those dictated by law.
    c. the AAMFT Code of Ethics exclusively dictates MFTs' professional standards of practice.
    d. laws and regulations exclusively dictate MFTs' professional standards of practice.

22. Per the DSM-5-TR, the diagnosis of autism spectrum disorder must include all of the following EXCEPT:

    a. deficits in social development.
    b. impaired social communication.
    c. restrictive or repetitive patterns of behavior.
    d. fear or anxiety specific to social situations.

23. A 10-year-old client attends a family therapy meeting with her adoptive parents. During the session, it is revealed that one adoptive parent does not provide structure or consistency, whereas the other parent yells and demands obedience. This represents a dysfunctional:

    a. coalition.
    b. hierarchy.
    c. alliance.
    d. feedback loop.

24. The parents of a 27-year-old client diagnosed with substance use disorder frequently bail the client out of jail, and the mother blames her ex-husband, the father, for their daughter's problems. This keeps the family system in a state of equilibrium through the process of:

    a. triangulation.
    b. assimilation.
    c. parentification.
    d. centration.

25. A long-term client has met the treatment plan goals but expresses anger and feelings of abandonment at the therapist's ongoing mentions of termination. After determining an end date and validating the client's feelings, the NEXT BEST course of action would be for the therapist to:

    a. consolidate client gains and offer future booster sessions.
    b. set appropriate boundaries and refer the client to another provider.
    c. suggest an alternative end date and extend the treatment plan goals.
    d. adhere to a determined end date and connect the client to community supports.

26. A mother and her 10-year-old son attend therapy to address the child's anxiety and school avoidance. Each time the therapist asks the child a question, the mother answers for him. Salvador Minuchin would describe this family structure as:

    a. complementary.
    b. enmeshed.
    c. emotionally fused.
    d. symmetrical.

27. Which one of the following statements best describes racism?

    a. Racism is historically supported by established institutional policies and practices.
    b. Racism targets individuals in majority populations, although it is less common.
    c. Racism can be reduced by increasing awareness of implicit bias and covert attitudes about race.
    d. Racism consists of intentional and unintentional actions toward members of a specific social group.

28. The therapist's use of standardized progress monitoring instruments and client feedback for the ongoing evaluation of the therapeutic process, outcomes, and termination is considered a(n):

    a. empirically supported treatment.
    b. evidence-based practice.
    c. family-focused treatment.
    d. strengths-based practice.

29. Which one of the following integrates the Outcome Rating Scale (ORS) and the Session Rating Scale (SRS) into each therapy session?

    a. The Clinical Outcomes in Routine Evaluation measure (CORE-10).
    b. The Partners for Change Outcome Management System (PCOMS).
    c. The Daily Living Activities Scale.
    d. The Substance Abuse Outcomes Module.

30. A therapist is issued a court subpoena to testify and release medical records for a current client. Which one of the following is true of a subpoena?

a. It requires the client's consent to testify in court and release medical records.
b. It does not require the client's consent to testify in court and release medical records.
c. It requires the client's consent to release medical records but mandates the therapist to testify in court.
d. It requires the client's consent to testify in court but mandates the therapist to release medical records.

31. Instances that may constitute insurance fraud include all of the following EXCEPT:

a. billing under another therapist in the same practice while waiting to be placed on the client's insurance panel.
b. billing the insurance company for a previously scheduled missed appointment.
c. allowing copay fees to be waived without informing the client's insurance.
d. providing couples therapy and only billing one spouse's insurance.

32. For treating bipolar disorder, which one of the following methods is regarded as a well-established evidence-based intervention for adolescents and adults?

a. Behavioral family therapy.
b. The Gottman method.
c. Structural family therapy.
d. Family psychoeducation.

33. Of the following, which personality trait is the strongest predictor of suicidality?

a. Introversion.
b. Creative flow.
c. Perfectionism.
d. Religious beliefs.

34. At the beginning of each teletherapy session, therapists must verify all of the following EXCEPT the client's:

a. identity.
b. level of safety.
c. location.
d. payment.

35. In the United States, disparities in suicide rates according to age, occupation, geography, race, and ethnicity are lowest among which one of the following groups?

a. Veterans.
b. Youth and young adults aged 10–24.
c. Non-Hispanic American Indians/Alaska Natives.
d. Individuals residing in rural locations.

36. **A client is extremely distressed over his same-sex attraction and behaviors. He states that he would "do anything" to be heterosexual and be relieved of his "sinful existence." He has heard of conversion therapy and would like the MFT to consider this approach. Which one of the following actions BEST reflects the response and ethical standard that the MFT must follow?**

   a. Provide conversion therapy only after receiving the appropriate education, training, and supervision (Standard 3.1: Maintenance of Competency).
   b. Develop new skills specializing in conversion therapy to protect clients from possible harm (Standard 3.6: Development of New Skills).
   c. Assist the client in obtaining the services that he seeks if unable or unwilling to provide the service (Standard 1.10: Referrals).
   d. Respect the client's right to decide about treatment, and help him understand the consequences of the decision (Standard 1.8: Client Autonomy in Decision Making).

37. **All of the following are true of risk and protective factors EXCEPT:**

   a. they are associated with multiple clinical outcomes.
   b. they are generally fixed and remain unchanged over time.
   c. they are influenced by contextual factors (e.g., family, community).
   d. they are cumulative and work interactively and collectively.

38. **Quantitative research studies are those that are:**

   a. deductive in nature.
   b. conducted in a subject's natural setting.
   c. subjective and process oriented.
   d. tentative in their conclusions.

39. **A crisis event includes all of the following elements EXCEPT:**

   a. psychological distress.
   b. functional impairment.
   c. failed coping mechanisms.
   d. disruption of disequilibrium.

40. **A husband and wife seek counseling to address the husband's job loss and lack of initiative in finding employment. The husband reports that he and his wife do not communicate and that his wife "constantly vents about our troubles" to her mother. This is an example of:**

   a. subjugated narratives.
   b. triangulation.
   c. unbalancing.
   d. covert change.

41. **When compared to verbal communication, nonverbal communication is:**

   a. an inaccurate depiction of feelings.
   b. continuous and linear.
   c. less intentional.
   d. easier to understand and interpret.

42. Multigenerational marriage and family therapists (MFTs) describe family systems as having:

- a. balanced or unbalanced degrees of trust.
- b. differentiated or emotionally fused boundaries.
- c. symmetrical or complementary communication styles.
- d. disengaged or enmeshed subsystems.

43. Family systems theorists view family systems as having:

- a. completely closed or open boundaries.
- b. independent elements and structures.
- c. highly predictable patterns of interactions.
- d. explicit or written-down rules and norms.

44. Which one of the following methods reflects a client-centered, nondirective clinical approach?

- a. Schema therapy.
- b. Strategic family therapy.
- c. Structural family therapy.
- d. Solution-focused brief therapy (SFBT).

45. A 3-year-old in a Head Start program is referred to a school therapist due to chronic truancy, poor hygiene, and peer difficulties. The student is an only child, shows developmental delays, and suffers from chronic asthma. The teacher is concerned that the child may be experiencing abuse at home. All of the following facts place the child at an increased risk for victimization EXCEPT:

- a. the child's age.
- b. the child does not have siblings.
- c. the child shows developmental delays.
- d. the child has chronic asthma.

46. Cybernetics was first applied to family communication by:

- a. Gregory Bateson.
- b. Nathan Ackerman.
- c. Salvador Minuchin.
- d. Carl Whitaker.

47. Which one of the following is a 20-item standardized instrument used to assess the likelihood of lethality resulting from intimate partner violence (IPV)?

- a. The Danger Assessment.
- b. The Hurt, Insult, Threaten, and Scream screening tool.
- c. The Women Abuse Screening Tool.
- d. The Humiliation, Afraid, Rape, Kick questionnaire.

48. An initial short-term treatment plan goal for couples experiencing infidelity would be to:

- a. establish safety and address trauma symptoms.
- b. decrease negative cognitive appraisals and attain forgiveness.
- c. understand the motivating factors and causes of emotional detachment.
- d. manage negative communication and create blame-free narratives.

49. Which one of the following requires that uninsured or out-of-network clients obtain notification of expected charges for certain items and services?

    a. Good Faith Estimate Act.
    b. Balance Billing Act.
    c. No Surprises Act.
    d. Self-Pay Act.

50. The parent of an adolescent client reports that her daughter has been cutting herself with a razor blade. The mother is concerned the client may be suicidal. Which one of the following factors would indicate that the client is likely actively suicidal?

    a. Substance use.
    b. Expressed intent.
    c. Traumatic experiences.
    d. Current psychosocial stressors.

51. Although Jean Piaget and Lev Vygotsky are both known for cognitive development theories, Vygotsky differed from Piaget in that Vygotsky placed greater emphasis on:

    a. attaining equilibrium.
    b. stages of cognitive development.
    c. sociocultural context.
    d. adaptation processes.

52. Which one of the following refers to the procedure by which MFTs explain to clients the potential risks, limitations, and benefits of treatment?

    a. Confidentiality.
    b. Due process.
    c. Informed consent.
    d. Scope of competence.

53. An MFT considers beginning asynchronous technology-based counseling with some of his clients. Upon review, he determines that clients LEAST likely to benefit would be those:

    a. in crises.
    b. with severe social anxiety.
    c. residing in rural settings.
    d. who feel stigma regarding mental health treatment.

54. MFTs preparing to close their clinical practice adhere to applicable laws related to storage, transfer, or disposal of client records in a way that maintains confidentiality and:

    a. protects the well-being of clients.
    b. protects the rights of the therapist.
    c. limits client access.
    d. avoids client abandonment.

55. Which one of the following offers in vivo sessions with child–parent dyads to lessen the adverse effects of out-of-home placement for children?

    a. Functional family therapy.
    b. Imago relationship therapy.
    c. Parent–child interaction therapy.
    d. Trauma-focused CBT.

56. Unless otherwise specified, an MFT may withhold client access to records in which one of the following instances?

   a. The client has refused to follow treatment recommendations.
   b. The client has an outstanding unpaid balance for past therapy services.
   c. Releasing the records would seriously endanger the client.
   d. Releasing the records would expose confidential collateral information.

57. Which one of the following philosophical assumptions underlies family systems theory?

   a. Families operate as closed systems, receiving continuous internal input.
   b. Problems operate within a linear, causal continuum.
   c. The sum of each member's parts is less than their whole.
   d. Family relationships are interrelated and interdependent.

58. The therapeutic relationship is best cultivated by trust, connection, and:

   a. contact.
   b. collaboration.
   c. clarity.
   d. competence.

59. For a diagnosis of a paraphilic disorder, an individual must exhibit arousing fantasies, urges, or behaviors meeting all of the following EXCEPT:

   a. they are intense and persistent.
   b. they cause significant personal distress.
   c. they cause another person's injury or death.
   d. they cause distress related to society's disapproval.

60. Which one of the following is an evidence-based assessment measure for adult mood disorders?

   a. Clinical Global Impression (CGI).
   b. Brief Psychiatric Rating Scale (BPRS).
   c. Patient Health Questionnaire (PHQ-9).
   d. World Health Organization Disability Assessment Scale 2.0 (WHODAS 2.0).

61. For Murray Bowen, forming multiple therapeutic alliances with families involves the therapist acting as a(n):

   a. warm and supportive equal.
   b. emotionally distant and objective coach.
   c. active and respectful "stage manager" and director.
   d. flexible observer and catalyst for interactional processes.

62. Using Albert Roberts' (2005) seven-stage crisis intervention model, once the severity of the crisis is determined, rapport is established, and the major problems are identified, the therapist would then:

   a. use active listening and validate emotions.
   b. conduct a mental status exam.
   c. schedule booster sessions.
   d. develop an action plan.

63. A psychodynamic couples therapist assesses a couple's families of origin and relationship patterns and intervenes by attending to unconscious influences. The therapist then explains to the couple that the rationale for selecting this approach is to:

    a. make the relationship, rather than each individual, the primary focus.
    b. prioritize problem-solving strategies over intrapsychic processes.
    c. join with the couple to map the family structure and hierarchy.
    d. use transference as a means of interpreting underlying issues.

64. An MFT provides therapy services to a 14-year-old residing in a juvenile detention center. The client's parent is upset that her child's educational records were released to the detention center without her permission. The MFT correctly informs the parent that the school's actions were:

    a. legally and ethically sound.
    b. a violation of the Family Educational Rights and Privacy Act of 1974 (FERPA).
    c. a violation of the Health Insurance Portability and Accountability Act of 1996 (HIPAA).
    d. a violation of the Individuals with Disabilities Education Act (IDEA).

65. Which one of the following disorders is classified in the DSM-5-TR as a substance-related and addictive disorder?

    a. Compulsive exercise disorder.
    b. Gambling disorder.
    c. Compulsive buying disorder.
    d. Internet gaming disorder.

66. The therapist's regular use of psychometrically sound progress measures is MOST effective when used during:

    a. the early stages of treatment.
    b. the middle stages of treatment.
    c. the final stages of treatment.
    d. the postdischarge stage of treatment.

67. On a genogram, a transgender female is depicted as:

    a. a square inside a circle.
    b. a circle inside a square.
    c. an upside-down triangle inside a square.
    d. an upside-down triangle inside a circle.

68. A patient preparing for hospital discharge expresses that he would like to appoint a family member to carry out predetermined and agreed-upon alternatives to hospitalization if future crises arise. Which one of the following would legally grant the patient the ability to do so?

    a. A safety plan.
    b. A living will.
    c. A psychiatric advance directive.
    d. A conservatorship agreement.

69. Bowenian therapists believe that maintaining multiple therapeutic alliances within the family system involves viewing three-person systems (i.e., triangles) as interactions in which the therapist:

    a. purposely creates and participates.
    b. uses triangles to restructure and reorganize subsystems.
    c. remains emotionally uninvolved.
    d. uses family members as equal participants in interactional meaning making.

70. Enactments involve the therapist:

    a. instructing the family members to role-play a typical day.
    b. directing the family members to take turns talking and listening.
    c. encouraging unstructured interactions among the family members.
    d. prompting family members to express their underlying attachment emotions.

71. Which one of the following terms refers to unmerited power and access to societal resources, rights, and opportunities?

    a. Privilege.
    b. Oppression.
    c. Inclusion.
    d. Stratification.

72. In the ABC-X crisis model, the letter C represents which one of the following?

    a. Available resources.
    b. Definition of a stressor.
    c. Experience of a crisis.
    d. Perception of the stressor.

73. Of the following strategies, which step is LEAST appropriate for therapists working with clients at high risk of harm to others?

    a. Arrange for a higher level of care.
    b. Set a follow-up appointment in 24–48 hours.
    c. Validate feelings and honor client autonomy.
    d. Adhere to ethical and legal mandates regarding the duty to warn.

74. According to Gerald Caplan's four phases of a crisis, if an individual cannot resolve a problem by phase 4, they will exhibit which one of the following?

    a. A rise in tension.
    b. Disruption to their daily living.
    c. Personality disorganization.
    d. Use of emergency problem-solving methods.

75. According to the transtheoretical model (also called the stages of change theory), in which stage would the therapist assist the client with consolidating gains and preserving behavior attained in the action stage?

    a. Termination.
    b. Contemplation.
    c. Preparation.
    d. Maintenance.

76. Which action on behalf of the therapist is essential for maintaining the therapeutic alliance?

    a. Self-disclosure.
    b. Negotiation of treatment plan goals.
    c. Unconditional acceptance of client behavior.
    d. Collecting feedback upon termination.

77. Which is true of the AAMFT's Procedures for Handling Ethical Matters?

    a. Anonymous complaints are recognized, and a course of action will be pursued.
    b. Failure to respond to an ethics complaint within 15 days may result in the termination of the MFT's AAMFT membership.
    c. An MFT whose membership is terminated will have his or her name and ethical violation published in *Family Therapy Magazine*.
    d. For the complaint to be forwarded to the judiciary committee, complainants must waive therapist–client confidentiality.

78. A therapist seeks to blend an individual treatment model with a systemic approach. To do so, the therapist would want to recognize the client's:

    a. intrapsychic processes amid interpersonal interactions.
    b. differentiation of self amid the family projection process.
    c. emotional regulation in relation to family homeostasis.
    d. reduction of resistance in relation to balanced family equilibrium.

79. Upon resolution of a crisis, the overall goal of crisis intervention models (e.g., the SAFER-R Intervention Model or the Seven-Stage Crisis Intervention Model) is to:

    a. reduce the client's risk for harm.
    b. reduce the client's need for follow-up care.
    c. return clients to a higher level of care.
    d. return clients to their precrisis mental health baseline.

80. Which one of the following treatment approaches for adolescent substance use disorder uses a developmental-ecological approach anchored in the belief that change unfolds in stages across several systems, contexts, and domains?

    a. Behavioral family therapy.
    b. Multidimensional family therapy.
    c. Systemic motivational therapy.
    d. Multigenerational family therapy.

81. A cognitive therapist provides individual therapy to an adolescent wishing to improve her interpersonal relationships. The client states, "Everyone at school thinks I'm stupid." Which one of the following questions demonstrates the therapist's use of Socratic questioning?

    a. "What conditions of worth are associated with this thought?"
    b. "What evidence is there for that thought?"
    c. "When was this thinking less severe?"
    d. "Where did this thought originate?"

82. Which one of the following assays is based on David Olson's Circumplex Model of Marital and Family Systems?

    a. The Marital Satisfaction Inventory, Revised.
    b. The Family Adaptability and Cohesion Scale IV.
    c. The PREPARE/ENRICH assessment tool.
    d. The Dyadic Adjustment Scale.

83. According to the AAMFT Code of Ethics (2015), an MFT's core values consist of:

    a. rules of practice by which the MFT must follow.
    b. elements distinct from ethical standards.
    c. measurable standards of professionalism and competency.
    d. standards enforceable by the AAMFT Ethics Committee.

84. A 14-year-old client in the foster care system is being treated for substance abuse after drug-related charges led to court-ordered treatment. The client has progressed in therapy, passed all required drug tests, and is ready for discharge. Which one of the following processes would BEST ensure that the client maintains progress?

    a. Eco-mapping.
    b. Progress monitoring.
    c. Measurement-based care.
    d. Cross-system collaboration.

85. Therapists providing conjoint couples therapy for intimate partner violence (IPV) must carefully assess couple dynamics and alleviate the potential for postsession retaliation resulting from sensitive disclosures. For couples being treated for IPV, which one of the following characteristics places them at lower risk for retaliation?

    a. Couples belonging to cultures with patriarchal norms.
    b. Couples with one partner engaging in substance misuse.
    c. Couples engaging in situational violence.
    d. Couples with one partner who is violently resistant.

86. A clinical supervisor in a remote rural setting is in the market for a new vehicle. His supervisee mentions that her brother works at the only dealership in town and could give him a "really great deal." Of the following, which standard in the AAMFT Code of Ethics (2015) would best inform the supervisor's ethical decision-making process?

    a. 4.5: Oversight of Supervisee Professionalism.
    b. 4.6: Existing Relationship with Students or Supervisees.
    c. 4.7: Confidentiality with Supervisees.
    d. 4.8: Payment for Supervision.

87. An MFT provides therapy to a young couple contemplating moving in together after 2 months of dating. They ask the MFT what they should do. Given the information provided, what is the MFT's best response?

a. Inform them of the benefits of moving in together, and advise them to move in with one another.
b. Caution them about the risks of moving in together after such a short courtship, and advise them not to move in together.
c. Explore the couple's individual and joint reasons for wanting to move in together, and empower them to make their own decision.
d. Explore the influence of religion and cultural contexts with the couple to assist them in following their sociocultural dictates.

88. Which one of the following terms refers to a significant change in a therapist's worldview due to ongoing exposure to clients' traumatic material?

a. Vicarious trauma.
b. Secondary trauma.
c. Compassion fatigue.
d. Burnout.

89. Therapists display a nonjudgmental stance by:

a. providing clients with standards for moral living.
b. conveying acceptance of the client's choices.
c. providing therapist-directed moral agency.
d. conveying acceptance of the client's inherent worth.

90. Of the following, which one is credited with developing general systems theory?

a. Jay Haley.
b. Ludwig von Bertalanffy.
c. Ivan Boszormenyi-Nagy.
d. Nathan Ackerman.

91. Complex trauma primarily stems from which one of the following?

a. Catastrophic events.
b. Marginalization and oppression.
c. Overwhelmed coping mechanisms.
d. Early childhood harm or abandonment.

92. An MFT's colleague and friend confides that she was pulled over and charged with a drunk-driving charge over the weekend. The MFT is shocked because her colleague, also an MFT, has never had any prior arrests or concerning conduct. The MFT is unsure if she has a duty to report the charge to the AAMFT ethics committee for professional misconduct. What should the MFT do FIRST?

a. Obtain a signed authorization from the colleague to make a report concerning professional misconduct.
b. Understand the laws in the local jurisdiction for reporting MFT professional misconduct.
c. Make a formal ethics complaint to the AAMFT ethics committee for professional misconduct.
d. Encourage the colleague to review the AAMFT Code of Ethics to determine if she should self-report.

93. Narrative therapy is to externalization as solution-focused therapy is to:

    a. summarization.
    b. projection.
    c. positive connotation.
    d. scaling questions

94. Strategic therapists use paradoxical directives to:

    a. resolve structural problems.
    b. establish clear boundaries.
    c. create disequilibrium.
    d. enable the use of enactment.

95. A recently hired graduate of an accredited MFT program begins work as a therapist at a large community mental health center (CMHC). The MFT has the ethical responsibility for all of the following EXCEPT:

    a. seeking reimbursement from third-party payers contracting with the CMHC.
    b. explaining to clients the confidentiality limitations associated with the CMHC's selected technological platform.
    c. acknowledging limitations of competency in response to the CMHC's supervisory evaluations and agency reviews.
    d. making ethical decisions with sole adherence to the CMHC's policies and practices.

96. A mother fears that her child will suffer from poor self-esteem. To prevent this, the mother provides the child with constant praise. The child is now a teen who has grown dependent on her mother's affirmations. This is an example of:

    a. an emotional cutoff.
    b. prescribing the symptom.
    c. a paradoxical intervention.
    d. the family projection process.

97. An MFT has been treating a client for major depressive disorder for 9 months. The client has not made progress and has declined a psychiatric medication evaluation. Although his symptoms remain unchanged, the client reports that he benefits from the MFT's support. What is the MFT's best course of action?

    a. Work with the client on a termination plan.
    b. Continue to provide supportive therapy.
    c. Explore cultural considerations related to taking medication.
    d. Enlist the assistance of a family member.

98. Cognitive therapy, behavior therapy, and rational-emotive behavior therapy (REBT) share all of the following characteristics EXCEPT?

    a. They are time-limited methods.
    b. They are present-oriented methods.
    c. They make use of homework.
    d. They are unstructured.

99. MFTs using technology-assisted professional services must make clients aware in writing of all of the following EXCEPT:

    a. the MFT's responsibility to refine his or her skills and maintain competencies for using all chosen technology platforms.

    b. the MFT's obligation to electronically store and transfer clients' identifying information in accordance with best practices standards.

    c. the MFT's and client's responsibilities for minimizing risks associated with technology-assisted professional services.

    d. the MFT's obligation to make clients aware of confidentiality limitations and protections associated with the use of technology.

100. A second-grader is referred to a school therapist for impulsivity, distractibility, and hyperactivity. In addition, the child has difficulty with peer relationships and has fallen behind academically. Which one of the following would be most helpful in determining a provisional diagnosis?

    a. Formative assessments.

    b. Rating scales.

    c. Psychological tests.

    d. Forensic assessments.

101. A therapist meets with a couple for the first time since the initial intake. The couple was told to bring their son to today's family therapy session, but they arrive without him. How would a symbolic-experiential family therapist proceed?

    a. Hypothesize aloud that the family intentionally caused their son's absence.

    b. Tell the family to reschedule for a time in which they can arrive with their son.

    c. Help restore healthy boundaries and parental hierarchies without the son.

    d. Identify the family schemata and its influence on treatment compliance.

Refer to the following for questions 102 - 103:

> A 14-year-old client, her mother, and her father attend family therapy to address the client's school truancy. The family is midway through therapy, and the father remains angry and repeatedly blames the client for creating "family drama," while the mother interrupts him to protect her.

102. How would an SFT intervene?

    a. Block the transactional processes and unbalance the dysfunctional subsystems.

    b. Construct a visual map illustrating family hierarchies and systems of power.

    c. Create a diagram showing intergenerational patterns of communication and behavior.

    d. Ask scaling questions to assess the family's level of confidence in their ability to change.

103. The therapist tells the client, "You seem invested in keeping your family together by allowing the focus to remain on you rather than on your parents' relationship." This is an example of a:

    a. paradox.

    b. metaphor.

    c. reframe.

    d. rewritten narrative.

104. An MFT provides family therapy for a child and her parents, who actively struggle with substance misuse. When the MFT attempts to address the influence of substance misuse on the family dynamics, the parents refocus the attention onto their child's behavior. This is an example of:

    a. mimesis.
    b. detouring.
    c. triangulation.
    d. blocking.

105. Unless in an emergency or as dictated by law, supervisor–supervisee confidentiality:

    a. can be disclosed.
    b. cannot be disclosed.
    c. cannot be disclosed except by verbal authorization or waiver.
    d. cannot be disclosed except by written authorization or waiver.

106. John Gottman believes that for couples to heal from infidelity, they must experience all of the following phases EXCEPT:

    a. atonement.
    b. attunement.
    c. acceptance.
    d. attachment.

107. Qualities of an effective treatment plan include goals and objectives written in a manner that is:

    a. client centered.
    b. program focused.
    c. therapist centered.
    d. deficit based.

108. Mary Ainsworth used the "strange situation" experiment to identify infant attachment styles. In her experiment, which attachment style describes infants who showed no signs of distress when their mother left and remained disinterested when she returned?

    a. Secure.
    b. Disorganized/Disoriented.
    c. Insecure avoidant.
    d. Insecure resistant/ambivalent.

109. Research suggests that therapists are LESS likely to use instruments measuring client progress if the process is:

    a. brief.
    b. ongoing.
    c. standardized.
    d. nonburdensome.

110. During a mental status exam, the therapist notes that the client's thought process is nonlinear, contains unnecessary details, and veers off topic, but it eventually returns to the original subject matter. This is known as:

    a. word salad.
    b. tangential thinking.
    c. flight of ideas.
    d. circumstantial thinking.

111. John Gottman believed that the antidote to the number-one predictor of divorce (i.e., contempt) is to:

    a. take time away and practice self-care.
    b. use social supports and cultivate interdependence.
    c. describe inner feelings and foster a culture of admiration and respect.
    d. accept another's perspective and apologize for any wrongdoing.

112. Therapists are most likely to experience countertransference as a manifestation of:

    a. emotional regulation.
    b. objective awareness.
    c. inner conflict.
    d. rigid boundaries.

113. Which one of the following situations would most likely constitute client abandonment?

    a. A therapist refers a client for specialized services due to treatment needs falling outside the therapist's scope of competency.
    b. A therapist has an unplanned leave of absence due to illness and cannot provide alternate arrangements for his clients.
    c. A therapist in private practice terminates therapy with a client due to lack of payment for services rendered.
    d. A therapist immediately terminates client services after the client becomes threatening and violent.

114. A therapist provides emotionally focused therapy for couples (EFT) to a couple experiencing relationship distress. As the couple enters the final stage of treatment, the counselor prepares the couple for planned termination. In this final stage, the couple is now ready to:

    a. help one another with emotional deescalation.
    b. restructure core emotional experiences to develop a secure bond.
    c. facilitate appropriate solutions and consolidate cycles of secure attachment.
    d. understand that distress is cyclical and self-reinforced and it stems from insecure attachment.

115. Therapists must be cognizant of the influence of social and cultural factors on all of the following EXCEPT:

    a. personal space.
    b. nonverbal interactions.
    c. attitudes toward therapy.
    d. verbal and nonverbal congruence.

116. Two parents and their adult children attend family therapy to address stressors believed to be caused by the father's mood swings. How would a strategic family therapist intervene?

a. Provide directives to reduce the father's symptoms and their impact on the family.
b. Align with the father to increase his power within the family.
c. Determine the father's position and role in the hierarchal subsystem.
d. Determine what works best when the father's mood swings become problematic.

117. Which one of the following tools uses three subscales (symptom distress, interpersonal relations, and social role) to measure client progress?

a. The Child Behavior Checklist (CBCL).
b. The Beck Depression Inventory (BDI).
c. The Outcome Questionnaire (OQ-45.2)
d. The Structured Interview of Reported Symptoms (SIRS-2).

118. Of the following, which one is considered a dysfunctional family configuration?

a. Subsystems.
b. Hierarchies.
c. Coalitions.
d. Scapegoats.

119. Which one of the following is NOT explicitly prohibited by the American Association for Marriage and Family Therapy (AAMFT) Code of Ethics (2015)?

a. Sexual intimacy with known family members of current students.
b. Sexual intimacy with known family members of current supervisees.
c. Sexual intimacy with known family members of former students.
d. Sexual intimacy with known family members of former clients.

120. MFTs are ethically responsible for attending to any personal issues, life experiences, and value systems that influence the therapeutic process. These factors may be detrimental to client care if the therapist experiences which one of the following?

a. Countertransference.
b. Sexualized transference.
c. Exploitation.
d. Nonresponse bias.

Refer to the following for questions 121 - 122:

> A 34-year-old female therapist experienced fear, intimidation, and harassment from an ex-boyfriend while in college. The boyfriend's threats culminated in a physical attack, causing her to drop out for a semester and reenroll in another school. She currently provides therapy to a 22-year-old female and has formed a solid therapeutic alliance with the client.

121. Advocates for victims of stalking use an SLII framework to categorize stalking behaviors. The acronym SLII represents all of the following elements of stalking EXCEPT:

a. suspicion.
b. life invasion.
c. intimidation.
d. interference.

122. During today's session, the client presented as irritable and sad, which she attributes to increased instances of her ex-boyfriend showing up unannounced at work and harassing her. What should the therapist do FIRST?

    a. Initiate a referral to another therapist.
    b. Seek consultation and supervision.
    c. Contact the police to report the ex-boyfriend.
    d. Share her previous experience with the client.

123. Outpatient therapists can safeguard themselves from adult clients in a mental health crisis by all of the following EXCEPT:

    a. sitting or positioning themselves between the client and the door.
    b. validating the client's feelings and allowing the client to vent without interruption.
    c. communicating clearly and concisely (e.g., use of the "broken record" technique).
    d. physically escorting the client to an area where others can readily assist.

124. To determine how the family life cycle impacts problem formation, therapists seek to understand how families navigate all of the following EXCEPT:

    a. marriage.
    b. childbearing.
    c. employment.
    d. empty nesting.

125. During an initial intake evaluation, a client asks repetitive questions about the nature of therapy, including how often and how long she must attend and if her information will be "kept secret." The MFT has limited time for the interview and has yet to gather all of the relevant biopsychosocial assessment information. How should the MFT proceed?

    a. Explain to the client about her right to decide on therapy and that she can discontinue at any time.
    b. Explain to the client that today's session is limited to information gathering, but provide her with written material detailing the therapeutic process.
    c. Help ease the client's anxiety by explaining that her questions will naturally be answered during her treatment, but it is premature to do so now.
    d. Answer the client's questions and attend to the client's expectations about the treatment process before continuing the evaluation.

126. Social stratification:

    a. reflects personal effort and merit.
    b. varies from generation to generation.
    c. is sustained by societal beliefs.
    d. reflects individual differences.

127. Which one of the following types of intimate partner violence (IPV) identified by the CDC includes the perpetration of gaslighting and control of a victim's reproductive health?

    a. Physical violence.
    b. Sexual violence.
    c. Stalking or cyberstalking.
    d. Psychological abuse.

128. Critical incident stress management (CISM) begins with an appointed leader whose purpose is to disseminate factual information, reduce chaos, and identify resources in a process known as:

a. defusing.
b. deescalation.
c. critical incident stress debriefing.
d. crisis management briefing.

129. Jude, an teenaged client, is engaged in treatment, making significant progress on her goals, and is ready for termination. Yet each time the family therapist initiates discharge planning, her parents become resistant. Recently, her mother stated, "We've been here before. Jude is all talk and no action. This has been a waste of time." How might a therapist using motivational interviewing (MI) respond?

a. "You sound discouraged. I'm wondering if Jude can tell the family how things will be different this go-around."
b. "Thinking about ending treatment is difficult. It's been my experience that teens like Jude usually do quite well when they say they are ready."
c. "You feel hopeless—like this is familiar territory. You're wondering if your investment in Jude's therapy will pay off."
d. "You've been here before, and you think that it has been a waste of time."

130. Bartering is permissible only if the relationship is not exploitative, the professional relationship is not distorted, and:

a. the client requests it, and a clear written contract is established.
b. the therapist requests it, and a clear written contract is established.
c. the therapist requests it, and the arrangement is documented in the client's chart.
d. the client requests it, and the arrangement is documented in the client's chart.

131. A client with limited English proficiency is reluctant to begin an antidepressant for depression, citing family concerns over the addictive qualities of antidepressant medications. The therapist's best course of action would be to:

a. establish a safety contract with the client.
b. support client autonomy and decision making.
c. invite the client's family members to discuss the benefits of antidepressant medications.
d. provide reference materials to help the client make a well-informed decision.

132. Several months back, a single father with bipolar disorder arrived at an initial assessment with his two adult sons. The sons live with their father and occasionally help with his care. Recently, one of the sons called the MFT to request the father's medical records. The MFT adheres to the AAMFT ethical standards by correctly telling the son that:

a. he cannot access the records unless all family members provide written authorizations permitting him to do so.
b. he cannot access the records unless his father provides a written authorization permitting him to do so.
c. he can access the records because he is an involved collateral contact person.
d. he can access the records unless there are exceptional circumstances indicating that such access could seriously endanger the father.

133. A family therapist who blends an individual treatment model with a systemic approach would likely adhere to which one of the following theoretical orientations?

  a. Strategic.
  b. Behavioral.
  c. Psychodynamic.
  d. Structural.

134. A structural family therapist (SFT) treats a 14-year-old male and his family to address the teen's aggression toward his mother. In today's session, the SFT uses her authority to briefly join with the teen's brother in an effort to alter the family dynamics. This is an example of:

  a. manipulating space.
  b. triangulation.
  c. unbalancing.
  d. reframing.

135. Therapists teaching clients anger management strategies as a part of crisis intervention help clients understand that it is possible to learn appropriate ways to self-regulate—that expressions of anger are not inherited, fixed, or static. This assumption is grounded in which one of the following theories?

  a. Social cognitive theory
  b. Cognitive learning theory.
  c. Behavioral learning theory.
  d. Moral development theory.

136. An MFT receives a gift from a client and is unsure whether or not to accept it. To make that determination, the AAMFT Code of Ethics suggests that the therapist attend to which one of the following?

  a. Client autonomy.
  b. Informed consent.
  c. Cultural norms.
  d. Confidentiality.

137. Therapists who conduct teletherapy continually assess the appropriateness of service delivery by considering all of the following EXCEPT:

  a. the client's risks and benefits.
  b. the therapist's professional needs.
  c. the influence of the client's and therapist's cultural differences.
  d. the most appropriate mediums (e.g., phone, video) for service delivery.

138. An MFT and her supervisor review a list of potential candidates for a large upcoming research study. The supervisor instructs the MFT to review the AAMFT Code of Ethics (2015) and only accept candidates whose agreement to participate is ethically sound. In general, which one of the following would best meet the code's criterion?

  a. Individuals with a history of anxiety.
  b. Individuals on the MFT's current caseload.
  c. Individuals enrolled in a nearby elementary school.
  d. Individuals receiving treatment for cognitive impairment.

139. Which form of cognitive therapy uses sequenced steps, including disputing the activating event and adopting effective behavior?

    a. Behavioral activation.
    b. Cognitive processing theory.
    c. Rational emotive behavior therapy.
    d. Acceptance and commitment therapy.

140. Which one of the following represents one of the primary elements of Eastern philosophies/religions?

    a. There is an emphasis on collectivism rather than individualism.
    b. Logical or practical aspects are favored over the realm of the spirit.
    c. External achievement is valued rather than inner improvement.
    d. They are linear or goal-oriented rather than cyclic or never-ending.

141. A client who has recently become her aging mother's primary caregiver receives solution-focused brief therapy (SFBT). The client reports that her mother constantly complains, leaving the client feeling as if her actions are "never enough." An appropriate short-term treatment goal would be for the client to identify which one of the following?

    a. Times when her mother was likely to complain but did not.
    b. Dysfunctional thoughts activated by her mother's complaints.
    c. An alternative, blame-free narrative surrounding her mother's complaints.
    d. Maladaptive interactional patterns associated with her mother's complaints.

142. Therapists assess the family's previous attempts to resolve the presenting problem to determine all of the following EXCEPT:

    a. protective factors.
    b. interactional patterns.
    c. motivation to change.
    d. appropriateness for therapy.

143. Assessment is to formulation as:

    a. application is to comprehension.
    b. analysis is to synthesis.
    c. knowledge is to evaluation.
    d. creation is to conceptualization.

144. A kindergarten student has been suspended from school multiple times for aggression toward his peers and defiance with authority figures. The school therapist discovers that the child's behavior began shortly after his father's incarceration. According to the human ecology systems theory, which bidirectional system represents the interaction between the child's home and the school?

    a. Microsystem.
    b. Mesosystem.
    c. Ecosystem.
    d. Chronosystem.

145. Family systems theorists understand psychopathology as a manifestation of which one of the following relational dynamics?

a. Behavior A influences behavior B, which in turn influences behavior C.
b. Behavior A influences behavior B, which in turn influences behavior A.
c. Behavior A influences behavior B, which in turn influences behavior B.
d. Behavior A influences behavior B, which in turn influences neither behavior A, B, nor C.

146. Which one of the following treatment needs is best suited for teletherapy?

a. Chronic anxiety.
b. Substance misuse.
c. Nonsuicidal self-injury.
d. Mild cognitive impairment.

147. Researchers have found that the sole use of informal instruments to measure outcomes and processes is frequently associated with which one of the following?

a. Client-initiated termination due to service dissatisfaction.
b. Therapist-initiated termination due to perceived client dissatisfaction.
c. Clients overestimating their progress and the strength of the therapeutic alliance.
d. Therapists overestimating client progress and the strength of the therapeutic alliance.

148. Jean Piaget believed that children learn and develop through all of the following processes EXCEPT:

a. conservation.
b. assimilation.
c. accommodation.
d. adaptation.

149. Of the following, a family systems relational hypothesis would primarily emphasize:

a. attributions of blame.
b. intrapsychic processes.
c. linear communication.
d. rigid boundaries.

150. Virginia Satir believed that individuals whose self-worth and self-value are determined by the attention and approval of family members exhibit the communication style of:

a. the blamer.
b. the placater.
c. the super-reasonable.
d. the irrelevant.

151. Risk factors for medication-related psychiatric side effects (e.g., psychosis, confusion) include all of the following EXCEPT:

a. increased age.
b. the use of multiple medications.
c. no past or present history of a mental disorder.
d. the use of central nervous system-active medications (e.g., tricyclic antidepressants, traditional antipsychotics).

152. A client receives in-patient services for an eating disorder and attends weekly family sessions with her mother and father. Rather than hear a secondhand account of events, the therapist asks the parents to reenact the last meal that they shared as a family. This intervention is designed for all of the following EXCEPT:

   a. decentralizing the therapist.
   b. identifying circular interactional patterns.
   c. understanding overlearned behaviors.
   d. reducing emotional reactivity.

153. Safety plans differ from no-harm contracts in that safety plans:

   a. include signed promises indicating that the client will refrain from self-harm.
   b. include a prioritized list of coping strategies and resources to lessen imminent risk.
   c. do not offer legal protection in the same way as no-harm contracts.
   d. do not include provisions for clients with limited decision-making capacity.

154. Peer specialists who partner with adult clients with severe mental illness and co-occurring disorders are found to reduce crisis-related incidents through the provision of:

   a. clinical services to enhance the client's interpersonal relationships.
   b. supportive services to assist members of the client's social network.
   c. strengths-based services to help promote and sustain recovery.
   d. volunteer services to foster self-empowerment and skill building.

155. During an initial interview, the client nervously scans the therapist's office, sits with his arms crossed, and avoids eye contact. He later explains that he would rather have a gay therapist. What would be the therapist's BEST response?

   a. "Perhaps if we list the general qualities that you're looking for in a therapist, we can go from there."
   b. "I understand that you would like a gay therapist. Here is a list of openly gay therapists in the area."
   c. "Why don't we get to know one another and see if you are feeling the same after a couple of sessions. How does that sound?"
   d. "Having a gay therapist is important to you. Can you help me understand more about that?"

156. Successful termination is characterized by all of the following therapist-directed actions EXCEPT:

   a. discussing termination at the initial intake as part of informed consent.
   b. processing termination less frequently as the time grows nearer.
   c. selecting measurable criteria marking the end of therapy.
   d. reviewing therapeutic gains and the end of the relationship.

157. Which one of the following theories explains that elder abuse originates from caregivers whose jobs are low in pay, lack prestige, and are necessary for survival?

   a. Social exchange theory.
   b. Stratification theory.
   c. Symbolic interactionism theory.
   d. Political economic theory.

158. Crisis interventions differ from traditional psychotherapy in that crisis interventions:

    a.   are time limited.
    b.   focus on past and current life events.
    c.   address chronic maladaptive patterns of behavior.
    d.   are developed after obtaining a detailed client history.

159. All of the following circumstances may necessitate referring a client for a psychiatric evaluation EXCEPT:

    a.   treatment for severe symptoms causing functional impairment.
    b.   addressing symptoms that have not responded to psychotherapy.
    c.   ruling out any medical etiology responsible for the client's symptoms.
    d.   addressing developmental life cycles and the impact on the client system.

160. A family systems therapist's hypothesis:

    a.   offers a final determination on the degree of family dysfunction.
    b.   reflects a complex, finite understanding of the family system.
    c.   is created using a deficit-based formulation model.
    d.   facilitates change within a family system.

161. Which one of the following treatment methods emphasizes relational ethics, including fairness, trust, and loyalty?

    a.   Narrative therapy.
    b.   Contextual therapy.
    c.   SFBT.
    d.   Existential therapy.

162. For first-generation immigrants, intergenerational differences in acculturation have the potential to:

    a.   generate positive feedback loops.
    b.   disrupt hierarchical subsystems.
    c.   produce covert coalitions.
    d.   upend sibling subsystems.

163. Which is true of the toxic stress response?

    a.   It causes lifelong, irreversible damage.
    b.   It is an acute, time-limited response ending in recovery and rest.
    c.   It involves continuous activation of the parasympathetic nervous system.
    d.   It remains activated even when apparent harm is absent.

164. A child and adolescent family therapist seeks to engage teens in treatment and keep them actively involved. Which one of the following interventions would best enable the therapist to do this?

    a.   Identifying school and community supports.
    b.   Locating appropriate employment opportunities.
    c.   Establishing a behavioral contract rewarding teens' therapy attendance.
    d.   Allowing teens to determine the length and duration of their treatment.

165. Therapists meet with client collateral contacts for all of the following reasons EXCEPT:

    a. to provide concurrent psychotherapy.
    b. to better ensure postdischarge progress.
    c. to help modify the client's treatment plan.
    d. to assist with identifying community supports.

166. Which one of the following statements is true of marital and family research findings?

    a. Same-sex couples who experience discrimination have higher instances of adverse behavioral health outcomes.
    b. Children with same-sex parents experience poorer academic achievement and social adjustment than children with heterosexual parents.
    c. Divorce rates are highest among Hispanic and Asian couples than among non-Hispanic and African-American couples.
    d. Cohabitating couples report higher levels of relationship satisfaction than married couples.

167. A young adult client with substance use disorder and his family attend therapy as part of the client's aftercare. The client is 30 days sober and is beginning to feel hopeful about recovery. The parents direct their comments to the therapist when speaking and describe in detail the shame and embarrassment that the client has caused them. Guided by the principles of recovery, the therapist should:

    a. empower the client to continue with his self-directed recovery.
    b. encourage the client to take responsibility for his actions and to make appropriate amends.
    c. instruct the family to enact transactional patterns of communication.
    d. collaborate with the parents to create relapse-prevention strategies for the client.

168. Which one of the following is found to enhance relapse prevention by helping clients acknowledge present-moment internal experiences without judging them as good or bad?

    a. Transcendence.
    b. Emotion regulation.
    c. Mindfulness.
    d. Differential association.

169. A mother is observed playing with her young child. When the mother excitedly says, "I love you," the child eagerly runs to hug the mother, but the mother rejects the child's affection. This is an example of:

    a. a double bind.
    b. need complementarity.
    c. a conflictual cocoon.
    d. parentification.

170. A therapist has developed a successful working relationship with a family but notices during the current session that the daughter is uncharacteristically quiet and rolls her eyes when the therapist is speaking. This is an example of:

    a. an emotional cutoff.
    b. a therapeutic rupture.
    c. triangulation.
    d. unbalancing.

171. Who is credited with conceptualizing the "use of self of the therapist" into a model promoting four meta goals: raise self-esteem, enhance decision-making skills, increase responsibility, and foster congruence?

    a. Virginia Satir.
    b. Jay Haley.
    c. Salvador Minuchin.
    d. Murray Bowen.

172. A Spanish-speaking client with depressive symptoms attends an initial intake assessment with an interpreter. The therapist aims to build rapport and obtain baseline data for ongoing progress monitoring. Which one of the following would be LEAST effective for the therapist?

    a. Scaling questions.
    b. Mental status exams.
    c. Standardized instruments.
    d. Unstructured clinical interviews.

173. A client presents to an emergency clinic due to nightmares, feelings of inadequacy, worrying, and difficulty sleeping. These symptoms began after an unexpected job loss. The client is likely experiencing a(n):

    a. existential crisis.
    b. situational crisis.
    c. maturational crisis.
    d. adventitious crisis.

174. Which one of the following is a form of elder abuse and NOT a form of child abuse?

    a. Neglect.
    b. Sexual abuse.
    c. Financial exploitation.
    d. Psychological (i.e., emotional) abuse.

175. Measurement-based care is MOST effective when used to:

    a. obtain baseline measures at intake and assess client progress at termination.
    b. provide progress measures to third-party payers at various service intervals.
    c. create a dialogue with the client regarding progress and the therapeutic process.
    d. document the efficacy of the therapist's treatment approach.

176. A transgender male is placed on a 72-hour hold after seeking an emergency psychiatric assessment for psychosis and suicidal ideation. The counselor assigned to follow-up care learns that the client was repeatedly misgendered while receiving inpatient services. Of the following, which is the BEST action for the therapist to take?

    a. Assess the client for gender identity disorder.
    b. Assess the client for gender dysphoria.
    c. Advocate for correct pronoun usage among hospital health providers.
    d. Help the client learn assertive responses when encountering transphobia.

177. A husband and wife seek counseling to assist with their ongoing trust issues. The therapist learns that the wife was placed in foster care at age 3 and experienced several moves before being placed with her grandmother. Which approach would best address the couple's presenting problem?

    a. SFBT.
    b. Narrative therapy.
    c. Emotion-focused therapy.
    d. Strategic family therapy.

178. An MFT provides individual therapy to the mother of a 7-year-old child in foster care. The mother has made therapeutic gains and is compliant with her treatment for depression. The MFT is asked to provide court testimony regarding the child's reunification with the mother. The MFT has an ethical responsibility to give testimony on:

    a. the mother's parental fitness.
    b. the mother's treatment for depression.
    c. whether or not the child should be reunited with the mother.
    d. whether or not the child should be reunited with both parents.

179. The *Diagnostic and Statistical Manual of Mental Disorders*, Fifth Edition, Text Revision (DSM-5-TR) updates address the impact of social determinants on the diagnosis of mental disorders, with specific changes reflecting the influence of:

    a. biomedical factors.
    b. the family life cycle.
    c. racial discrimination.
    d. developmental trauma.

180. Which one of the following terms refers to the notion that in open family systems, multiple methods and strategies have the potential to evoke the same outcome?

    a. Equanimity.
    b. Equability.
    c. Equifinality.
    d. Equipotentiality.

Answer Key and Explanations for Test #1

1. D: Solution-focused therapy can be used to collaborate with clients on developing treatment plan goals based on the client's "best hope." Scaling questions would allow the client and therapist to create mutually shared treatment plan goals. Scaling questions use a Likert scale to rate a client's confidence or motivation regarding their "best hope" for treatment. Exposure therapy is used to treat phobias and certain forms of anxiety. Rating scales are used to measure anxiety during an exposure, but these scales do not represent the client's best hope for successful outcomes. Therapists adhering to psychoanalytic theory are less likely to collaborate with the client on mutually determined treatment plan goals because the therapist is regarded as the expert. SFTs are less likely to collaborate with clients on treatment plan goals than solution-focused therapists because the therapist is viewed as the initial catalysts for change.

2. B: Although local and state laws slightly differ, all 50 states require therapists to report all suspected and proven cases of child abuse. Therapists are responsible for reviewing specific situations with clients in which confidential disclosures may be legally required. The MFT must review the limits of confidentiality at the onset of therapy (AAMFT, 2015, Standard 2.1).

3. C: In this scenario, the mother is requesting an evaluation for custody and visitation. Standard 7.7 of the AAMFT Code of Ethics states that MFTs must "avoid conflicts of interest in treating minors or adults involved in custody or visitation actions by not performing evaluations for custody, residence, or visitation of the minor." MFTs who treat minors may provide the court or the professional performing the evaluation with information about the minor from the MFT's perspective in his or her role as the client's therapist as long as the MFT obtains appropriate authorizations and consents to release such information. Standards that include "required education, training, or supervisory experience" are applied to issues of competency rather than prerequisites for performing a custody evaluation. A signed consent obtained from the father still makes this a conflict of interest. Additionally, Standard 7.2 states that MFTs may provide expert or fact witness testimony in legal proceedings as long as it is accurate and unbiased. Court testimony differs from a custody evaluation.

4. B: Mindfulness can be used to influence client perceptions through intentional nonjudgmental attention to present-moment awareness of thoughts, sensations, and feelings. Mindfulness helps clients concentrate on and monitor their surroundings and has been found to be effective with PTSD and anxiety due to a modulation of the sympathetic and parasympathetic nervous systems. Hypnosis can also influence perceptions but differs from mindfulness in that mindfulness helps shift a person's relationship to an experience, whereas hypnosis focuses on changing the actual experience. Sensate focus is a form of behavioral modification and relaxation used to treat sexual dysfunctions (e.g., erectile dysfunction, difficulty with arousal and orgasm). Flow is described as a deep state of being fully immersed in an activity, a creative endeavor, or daily tasks to the point at which a person might lose track of time or feel as if they are "in the zone."

5. C: Harry Harlow experimented with rhesus monkeys and found that monkeys preferred a cloth surrogate mother over a wire mesh mother who provided food. Harlow determined that attachment develops when primary caregivers provide touch and tactile comfort. John Bowlby's theory of attachment is based on the premise that infants form a safe and secure bond with primary caregivers who are actively engaged in enjoyable interactions with them. Erik Erikson believed that attachment forms between 0 and 18 months of age. During this time, infants develop trust or mistrust, which is based on the caregiver's ability to consistently respond to the infant's physical

145

and psychological needs. Sigmund Freud believed that attachment results from the mother's ability to meet the child's basic physiological needs (e.g., hunger) and oral stimulation.

6. C: The MFT has an ethical obligation before the client's onset of treatment to disclose all of the aforementioned financial policies except the process for obtaining denied third-party payments. Instead, Standard 8.2 of the AAMFT Code of Ethics (2015) states that before entering into a therapeutic relationship, MFTs must disclose the fees charged for canceled or missed appointments and the use of collection agencies for nonpayment and they must provide reasonable notice of any additional charges or fee changes.

7. B: The Anti-Kickback Statute prohibits "willful payment of remuneration to induce or reward patient referrals or the generation of business involving any item or service payable by the federal health-care programs (e.g., drugs, supplies, or health-care services for Medicare or Medicaid patients)." The civil False Claims Act (FCA) "protects the government from being overcharged or sold shoddy goods or services." The criminal FCA imposes prison terms, stiff penalties, and fines for submitting false claims. The Stark Law (i.e., the Physician Self-Referral Law) prohibits physicians from referring patients to designated health services payable by federally funded entities (i.e., Medicaid or Medicare) from which a physician or immediate family member has a financial relationship.

8. C: Therapeutic contracts are used at the onset of treatment to underscore legal and ethical guidelines as well as client–counselor responsibilities, roles, and expectations. Therapists use formal therapeutic contracts as transparent, documented agreements to minimize risks and challenges and to promote the ethical principles of autonomy and beneficence. Safety contracts are verbal or signed contracts provided to suicidal clients. The use of safety contracts alone lacks empirical evidence supporting their efficacy. Treatment plans include documented goals and objectives that the client uses to provide direction and focus with the goal of resolving or minimizing the effects of the presenting problem. Confidentiality agreements are used to describe actions that therapists must take to uphold privacy and exceptions to doing so.

9. D: Countertransference describes the therapist's internal emotional experience. Countertransference occurs when the therapist internally reacts to the client and can be expressed or unexpressed. Implicit bias is also an internal process, but it operates differently than countertransference. Implicit biases are negative associations or stereotypes that a person has toward a specific social group that are "hidden" or unconscious. Immediacy is a behavioral response rather than an internal process and is expressed in the present moment. Therapists use the skill of immediacy to discuss issues specific to the therapeutic process. Microinvalidations also describe behaviors. Microinvalidations describe comments or actions that negate or nullify the experiences of an individual belonging to a targeted social group. Microinvalidations are rooted in negative stereotypes of socially marginalized groups.

10. C: The therapist would use self-disclosure to best enhance the therapeutic relationship. The therapist is aware of his privileged status in relation to his client, which suggests that he is mindful of his own biases. The fact that the client has met some of the agreed-upon treatment goals signifies the likelihood of a therapeutic alliance. The therapist is attuned to his internal emotional state and shared feelings of injustice. Carefully timed self-disclosures can be used to convey genuineness and authenticity. This may involve the therapist sharing emotions evoked in that moment and adopting an openness to addressing the influence of race on the therapeutic relationship. Relabeling is a strategic family therapy technique in which the therapist alters the meaning of an experience by altering the language used to describe it. Similarly, reframing rephrases a problem or situation by presenting it in a positive light. For the issue of discrimination, relabeling and reframing would

146

discourage a discourse on race rather than encourage or elicit a discussion. Double-sided reflections are used in motivational interviewing (MI) to help the client elicit change talk, which is not indicated for the client's experience of discrimination.

11. B: MFTs serving as supervisors refrain from exploiting the trust and dependency of their supervisees by establishing professional boundaries. Dual relationships occur within the supervisor–supervisee relationship because of an imbalance of power and status. Although not all dual relationships are unethical, establishing professional boundaries is the best way to refrain from behavior that would exploit or negatively impact supervisory trust. Supervisors have a responsibility to "not engage in sexual intimacy with students or supervisees during the evaluative or training relationship between the therapist and student or supervisees" (AAMFT, 2015, Standard 4.3). Nonabandonment is an ethical standard applicable to clients in treatment. MFTs make reasonable arrangements for the continuation of clients' care so as not to abandon or neglect them.

12. C: Researchers suggest that military personnel with indicators of a mental health disorder, such as post-traumatic stress disorder (PTSD), are more likely to experience combat exposure, prolonged deployment, and/or traumatic brain injuries. The intensity of combat exposure and the duration of deployment are associated with greater instances of mental disorders. Postdeployment reintegration is not directly associated with mental health difficulties unless the postdeployed veteran has a previous mental health history or actively engages in substance misuse. Prolonged deployment is difficult for military personnel's younger children and families when the at-home parent endures multiple personal stressors. However, for many families, symptoms improve once military personnel return home and are reintegrated with their families.

13. A: The MFT's best course of action is to discuss the case with an experienced colleague. This scenario addresses practicing within the boundaries of the therapist's scope of practice. The AAMFT Code of Ethics (2015) states that MFTs "do not diagnose, treat, or advise on problems outside the recognized boundaries of their competencies" (Standard 3.10) and that MFTs do so "to protect clients from potential harm" (Standard 3.6). Compliance with this standard would also include documenting the conversation with the colleague. Standard 3.1 of the code instructs MFTs to "maintain their competence in marriage and family therapy through education, training, and/or supervised experience." The Clinical Assessment and Diagnosis domain of AAMFT's MFT Core Competencies (2004) states that MFTs must "understand the clinical needs of persons with comorbid disorders," with substance abuse and mental health cited as examples. Referring the client to an experienced therapist would not be the best course of action because MFTs must maintain this competency through "education, training, and/or supervised experience." Attending a training or developing new skills on co-occurring disorders would not be the best course of action. In seeking to protect the client from potential harm, the counselor must address the client's immediate needs and refrain from rupturing the counselor–client therapeutic alliance.

14. D: The main purpose of the mental status exam (MSE) is to provide a snapshot of the client's presentation at a specific point in time. An MSE is an objective measure of the client's level of functioning at a particular point in time and can be conducted during an assessment or on an ongoing basis. The MSE itself is not designed to confirm or refute diagnostic impressions and hypotheses, nor does it provide significant insight into the client's risk and protective factors. The MSE is generally divided into the following categories: appearance, emotional state, cognitive functioning, thoughts, and judgment.

15. A: The family projection process is one of Murray Bowen's eight interlocking concepts that manifest as a self-fulfilling prophecy. There are three steps in the family projection process: (1) a parent focuses their anxiety onto a child and believes that the child has a problem, (2) the child

147

behaves in a manner that confirms their belief, and (3) the parent now treats the child as if something is wrong with the child. This is also known as scanning, diagnosing, and treating. Differentiation of self refers to the ability of a family member to connect with other members and remain independent in their thinking and feeling. The multigenerational transmission process describes how families pass along generational means for relating to one another, especially regarding emotional attachment and the level of emotional intensity expressed. The nuclear family emotional process describes patterns of family relationships that control where problems develop (e.g., spousal conflict, emotional distance, impairment of a child).

16. D: The type of termination that involves the therapist referring the client for specialized services to best meet client needs is known as therapist-initiated termination. Additional circumstances that may lead to therapist-initiated termination include progress toward treatment goals, reduction of symptoms, and confidence that the client can implement learned strategies to apply after discharge. Forced termination occurs when clients end therapy before making treatment progress. This is common when therapy is disjointed (e.g., services are provided by multiple clinicians) or when a client resists planned termination in an effort to avoid emotionally charged endings. Premature termination is the same as forced termination. Client-initiated termination occurs when clients feel that they have adequately met treatment goals, have not engaged with the clinician, or are not motivated to change.

17. C: HIPAA's Privacy Rule provides extra protection for psychotherapy notes (i.e., the therapist's private notes). The purpose of psychotherapy notes varies, with most being used for documenting relevant client conversations, constructing a case conceptualization, examining a hypothesis, and/or considering options for follow-up care. Psychotherapy notes are not part of the clinical record, and the client does not have the right to access them. Progress notes, on the other hand, are part of the client record and are exempt from extra protection. Progress notes contain information and summaries, including, but not limited to, session start and stop times, the treatment modality, selected techniques and interventions, response to treatment, and progress toward treatment plan goals. Case management and medication monitoring notes are also part of the client record and do not have extra protection.

18. B: A family map considers the influence of church and school in an adolescent's life. SFTs use mapping to identify intrafamilial dynamics as well as interpersonal life stressors. Family stressors may also be embedded in work, recreation, health care, friends, and the court system. A genogram is a graphic depiction of a family that represents multigenerational influences and relationships, including births, deaths, marriages, divorces, and other relevant medical, occupational, and historical events in the life of a family. Virginia Satir is credited with developing family sculpting—a process by which the therapist or a family member physically positions other members according to space, attitude, or interactional patterns. The goal of family sculpting is to capture the positioner's perception of the family. The multigenerational transmission process is a Bowenian concept used to explain how family systems tend to pass down anxiety-provoking symptoms resisting correction and change.

19. C: The therapist should respond first by conducting a mental status exam (MSE) to determine functional impairment. Conducting an MSE would enable the therapist to determine the client's cognitive, emotional, behavioral, and interpersonal functioning. It would also allow for further investigation of the severity of the client's suicidal ideation, precipitating events, client supports, and coping skills. Researchers have determined that developing a no-suicide contract with clients is often ineffective. Instead, it is recommended that safety plans are developed detailing actions that clients can take to mitigate suicide risk. Conducting details of the trauma and processing underlying emotions are generally inadvisable. Instead, the therapist should focus on how the trauma symptoms affect the client's current level of functioning. Although it would be an appropriate intervention, providing the client with information on grief support groups in the community should not be the therapist's first response.

20. C: Social justice principles include access, participation, and rights, but not equality. Instead, social justice is rooted in the principle of equity. Equity refers to the delivery of tools and resources specific to the needs of each individual within a social group. The purpose of promoting equity is to end oppression and injustice inflicted by those with societal power (i.e., privilege). Social justice principles also include access to resources helpful in overcoming systemic obstacles, the participation of smaller societal groups to engage in decision making that affects the society at large, and the right to exist in a society free from marginalization and oppression.

21. B: The AAMFT Code of Ethics provides guidelines for ethical decision making, indicating that both law and ethics govern clinical practice. Professional conduct must be evaluated using the AAMFT Code of Ethics and applicable laws and regulations. If the code proposes a higher standard than what is provided by law, the MFT adheres to the code. When the code guidelines supersede the law, the MFT must take appropriate steps to resolve the conflict. The code supports all legal mandates for reporting alleged unethical conduct.

22. D: Per the DSM-5-TR, a diagnosis of autism spectrum disorder does not include fear or anxiety specific to social situations, which *is* common with social anxiety disorder. The DSM-5-TR requires the following symptoms to diagnose autism spectrum disorder: deficits in social development, impaired social communication, and restrictive or repetitive behaviors.

23. B: This represents a dysfunctional hierarchy. Healthy hierarchical subsystems operate with clear boundaries, whereas dysfunctional hierarchies have boundaries that are split or undefined. The adoptive parents represent a split hierarchy. Coalitions are composed of one or more family members who covertly align themselves against a third family member or subsystem. Alliances contain emotionally close family members within a subsystem and are generally open, as opposed to coalitions, which are hidden. Feedback loops are interactions and behaviors that help the family maintain balance or equilibrium; they are not inherently dysfunctional in that they are a function of circular causality.

24. B: The parents' behaviors keep the family in a state of equilibrium through the process of assimilation. The purpose of assimilation is to maintain the status quo. The parents are engaged in the process of enabling. Enabling is designed to reduce the problem; however, the secondary effect of enabling prevents the client from experiencing consequences, thus maintaining the problem and the family system's homeostasis. Triangulation occurs when a third person is used to reduce anxiety and conflict. Parentification is the role reversal that often occurs in families with addicted parents in which the child acts as a parent to themselves and/or their siblings. Piaget used the term centration to describe a child's transition from eccentric thinking toward a reality that considers multiple aspects of a problem or situation.

25. A: The therapist's next best action would be to consolidate client gains and offer future booster sessions. The termination phase of treatment can create anxiety, anger, and feelings of abandonment, particularly for long-term clients; therefore, this phase should begin as early as possible. Termination tasks include processing feelings about ending treatment and reflecting on therapeutic growth. Because this is a planned termination, reflection on therapeutic gains and offering follow-up booster sessions are integral steps to the process. Setting appropriate boundaries is not the best action because it pathologizes feelings associated with termination, and

Mometrix

referring the client to another provider is inappropriate for a client who has met the treatment goals. Suggesting an alternative end date and extending treatment plan goals do not appear clinically indicated, especially because the client has met the goals and is in the final stages of therapy. Connecting the client with community support is helpful for clients who doubt their ability to apply skills learned in treatment, but it would not necessarily alleviate feelings of anger and abandonment related to termination.

26. B: Salvador Minuchin would describe this family structure as enmeshed. Minuchin is credited with developing structural family therapy, which asserts that boundaries among family members (subsystems) are either disengaged (i.e., rigid or isolated) or enmeshed (i.e., overly dependent or close). The goal in working with families is to develop appropriate boundaries among subsystems. Communication interaction family therapists view family communication patterns as complementary or symmetrical. Multigenerational or extended family systems theorists describe family systems as having either emotionally fused or differentiated boundaries.

27. A: Racism is historically supported by established institutional policies and practices. Institutional racism is a form of racism that is supported by institutional policies and practices that use power to oppress racial and ethnic minority populations. Racism cannot target majority populations because racism uses positions of power to discriminate and oppress those in minority social positions. "Reverse racism" is a myth because racism does not exist without unmerited power. Racism cannot be reduced by increasing awareness of implicit bias and covert attitudes about race because racism is a behavior. Privilege involves covert attitudes and beliefs. Unlike microaggressions, racism is intentional, involving direct actions toward members of a specific social group.

28. B: The therapist's use of standardized progress monitoring for the ongoing evaluation of the therapeutic process, outcomes, and termination is considered an evidence-based practice (EBP). EBPs are designed to maximize the therapists' effectiveness and decision-making process through adherence to scientifically based, peer-reviewed research on treatment delivery. EBPs use the therapist's and client's collaborative efforts to monitor the client's progress and alter treatment when necessary. Although often conflated, empirically supported treatment (EST) is similar to EBP but is not identical. EST is research driven, but rather than guide treatment, ESTs are applied to a specific disorder. For example, CBT is an EST for anxiety and depressive disorders. Although monitoring progress, outcomes, and termination is best when treatment is family focused, not all related practices apply to families. Similarly, a strengths-based approach to treatment is useful and may be incorporated into EBP but is not necessarily an essential element of the practice.

29. B: The Partners for Change Outcome Management System (PCOMS) integrates the Outcome Rating Scale (ORS) and the Session Rating Scale (SRS) into each therapy session. PCOMS is an evidence-based client-directed approach to measuring outcomes and the associated predictors of therapeutic effectiveness. The ORS measures client progress and perceived treatment benefits. The SRS includes items assessing the client's perception of the therapeutic alliance. With PCOMS, clients can view an online graph displaying the trajectory of their progress, which is incorporated into each session to assist with fine-tuning treatment goals and relational expectations. The CORE outcome measure (CORE-10) is a brief questionnaire that measures overall psychological distress; it can be used as a screening instrument as well as a measure of client progress. The Daily Living Activities Scale is a 20-item rating scale used to measure the client's level of functioning across several domains. The Substance Abuse Outcomes Module is a 22-item, evidence-based measure for adult multidiagnostic substance abuse.

150

30. A: A subpoena requires the client's consent to testify and provide medical records. Subpoenas in and of themselves do not require the therapist to disclose confidential information or release HIPAA-protected medical records. Standard 2.2 of the AAMFT Code of Ethics (2015) addresses confidentiality and circumstances requiring client authorization stating, "Marriage and family therapists do not disclose client confidences except by written authorization or waiver, or where mandated or permitted by law." Mandated reporting for MFTs refers to the requirement to report child or elder abuse and neglect.

31. D: Insurance companies require MFTs to bill one spouse's insurance for couples therapy. It is customary for the MFT to classify an individual who serves as the identified client. This is often the individual who carries a mental health diagnosis. It would be considered fraud if the MFT billed both spouses for the same services. Instances that may be considered fraudulent include billing under another therapist in the same practice while awaiting to be placed on the client's insurance panel, billing the insurance company for a previously scheduled missed appointment, and regularly waiving copay fees without informing the client's insurance.

32. D: For treating bipolar disorder, family psychoeducation is regarded as a well-established evidence-based intervention for adolescents and adults. The family-focused therapy approach uses a psychoeducation module that provides information to clients and families on bipolar disorder, problem-solving skills, coping skills, emotional regulation, and relapse prevention. Behavioral family therapy is a well-established evidence-based practice (EBP) for disruptive behaviors in children, for treating depression, and substance use. The Gottman method helps treat couples experiencing relationship distress, behavioral problems in children and adolescents, and substance abuse.

33. C: Of the answer choices, perfectionism is the strongest predictor of suicidality. Individuals with this personality trait seek personal flawlessness, react negatively to mistakes, experience self-doubt, and hold unrealistic standards for themselves. Researchers have found that perfectionists equate distress with personal failure, making them less likely to disclose suicidal thoughts. Creative flow is a protective factor against suicidality. Studies show that extroversion, rather than introversion, correlates with higher rates of suicidality. Religious beliefs are also a protective factor against suicidality.

34. D: At the beginning of each teletherapy session, therapists must verify the client's identity, level of safety, and location. These are steps taken to protect the client's confidentiality and ensure their well-being. Therapists are not required to verify the client's payment method prior to each teletherapy session.

35. B: In the United States, disparities in suicide rates are lowest among youth and young adults ages 10–24. Although many causes and circumstances can lead to suicide, there are disproportionately affected populations. According to the CDC (2022), youth and young adults aged 10–24 account for 14% of all suicides, compared to individuals aged 35–64, who account for 47%. Veterans have an adjusted suicide rate that is 52% higher than nonveterans. Non-Hispanic American Indian/Alaska Natives account make up 36% of all suicides, which is the highest rate among all races and ethnicities. Individuals residing in rural locations experience far greater rates of suicide than their urban counterparts. The rate of suicide is 10.9 per 100,000 in large metropolitan settings, compared to 20.5 per 100,000 in nonmetro locations.

36. D: The appropriate response is to "respect the rights of clients to make decisions and help them to understand the consequences of these decisions" (AAMFT, 2015, Standard 1.8). Also known as reparative therapy, conversion therapy is a religious-based practice that attempts to change a person's sexual orientation to match heterosexual norms. Aversive therapy and other psychologically damaging techniques are used to help individuals "recover" from the "disorder" of homosexuality. No scientific evidence supports its efficacy, and multiple studies cite that these interventions cause harm. Providing conversion therapy with any conditions, including expanding the MFT's scope of practice or developing new skills, is unethical. Standard 3.6 of the AAMFT Code of Ethics (2015) states: "When developing new skills in specialty areas, marriage and family therapists take steps to ensure the competence of their work and to protect clients from possible harm." If the MFT is unable or unwilling to provide the service because it would harm the client, a referral to someone offering that service would also be unethical. Respecting the client's autonomy does not exempt the MFT from helping the client understand the harmful consequences of their decision, making this the MFT's best response.

37. B: Risk and protective factors are not permanently fixed nor do they remain unchanged over time. Mental and behavioral health outcomes are influenced by an individual's risk and protective factors, with risk factors increasing the likelihood of specific outcomes and protective factors reducing that same likelihood. Risk and protective factors such as poverty, education, or community safety are not fixed and can change over time, whereas others, such as genetic disposition, remain unchanged. When viewed collectively or individually, risk and protective factors affect multiple clinical outcomes. For example, protective factors such as positive parenting skills can decrease the chances of a person developing a substance use disorder or depressive disorder. In addition, protective and risk factors are influenced by contextual factors in relationships, community settings, and the laws affecting certain members of society. Protective and risk factors are cumulative and work interactively and collectively to help develop or prevent outcomes.

38. A: Quantitative research studies are those that are deductive in nature. Qualitative studies, on the other hand, are inductive, subjective, process oriented, and tentative in their conclusions. The deductive nature of quantitative studies begins with a hypothesis, and quantitative data are collected to test an existing theory. Conversely, qualitative data use inductive reasoning by moving from observations to generalizations. Both forms of data are helpful in providing outcome measures.

39. D: Elements of a crisis include disruption of equilibrium (i.e., homeostasis) rather than disequilibrium. The Assessment, Crisis Intervention, Trauma Treatment (ACT) model is one example of a process that aims to restore homeostasis and prevent further functional impairment. A person's or system's normal state of balance is disrupted during a crisis. Elements of a crisis also include psychological distress, functional impairment, and events resulting in failed coping mechanisms.

40. B: This is an example of triangulation. Triangulation occurs when there is tension and conflict within a subsystem. A third person (i.e., the mother-in-law) is brought into the subsystem to reduce anxiety and to stabilize the subsystem. Members of subsystems and triangles often engage in fluctuating patterns of communication based on the degree of tension and communication among the participants. A subjugated narrative is a concept used in narrative therapy to describe a person's narrative that is suppressed by dominant stories, which are defined by one's cultural beliefs, values, and norms. Unbalancing is a structural family therapy technique used by the therapist to briefly join with another subgroup or family member to change the relationship dynamics. Strategic family therapists use covert change when providing hints, suggestions, or indirect messages to encourage change in a family (e.g., positively reinforcing certain behaviors).

41. C: Nonverbal communication is less intentional than verbal communication. Verbal communication is more distinct, continuous, and linear, with sentence structures reflecting a clear beginning, middle, and end; whereas nonverbal communication constantly fluctuates and generally depends on context. Nonverbal communication is a more accurate depiction of feelings and more difficult to understand and interpret

42. B: Multigenerational marriage and family therapists (MFTs) view family systems as containing differentiated or emotionally fused boundaries. Credited with developing MFT, Murray Bowen used the term "differentiated boundaries" when describing the ability for family members to function autonomously and remain emotionally connected. Conversely, emotionally fused boundaries are those in which family members have an unhealthy level of responsibility for other members' emotional well-being. Developed by Ivan Boszormenyi-Nagy, contextual family therapy views families as those with balanced or unbalanced degrees of trust, loyalty, and mutual understanding. Communication interaction family therapists (e.g., Virginia Satir, Jay Haley) view communication as either symmetrical (i.e., equal) or complementary (i.e., unequal). Symmetrical communication can become competitive, whereas complementary communication may manifest in dominant/submissive interactions. Structural family therapy, developed by Salvador Minuchin, suggests that boundaries among subsystems are either disengaged (i.e., rigid or isolated) or enmeshed (i.e., overly dependent or close).

43. C: Family systems theorists view family systems as having highly predictable patterns of interactions. Characteristics of family systems also include a combination of open and closed boundaries, interdependent elements and structures, and rules and norms that are rarely explicit or written down.

44. D: Solution-focused brief therapy (SFBT) uses a client-centered, nondirective clinical approach. A therapist using SFBT functions as a coach and meets the client in the here and now. SFBT focuses on client strengths and empowering clients to be their own agents of change. Schema therapy is based on assumptions and techniques from many therapies, including CBT, attachment theory, and object relations theory. Therapists using schema therapy assume a directive role when helping clients identify core beliefs and attachment patterns. Therapists using strategic family therapy offer a directive approach and assume the role of expert. Structural family therapists (SFTs) play an active role in facilitating changes within the family's existing structure.

45. B: Risk factors for victimization include children from families with many dependent children, rather than those who do not have siblings. Additional factors that place a child at an increased risk for victimization are younger children, children with developmental delays, and children with chronic physical illness.

46. A: Gregory Bateson was the first to apply cybernetics to family communication. Cybernetics is a mathematical concept used to explain the tendency for systems to work as a whole to maintain balance or equilibrium. Positive and negative feedback loops maintain this process. Nathan Ackerman is credited with integrating psychoanalytic theory and systems theory. Salvador Minuchin developed structural family therapy. Carl Whitaker is known for developing symbolic-experiential family therapy.

47. A: The Danger Assessment, a 20-item standardized instrument, is designed to assess the likelihood of lethality resulting from intimate partner violence (IPV). The Danger Assessment also assesses for near-lethal consequences of IPV and provides four levels of danger, including variable, increased, severe, and extreme. The Hurt, Insult, Threaten, and Scream screening tool is a four-item tool used to assess the frequency of IPV. The Women Abuse Screening Tool is a seven-item instrument used to assess IPV's physical and emotional symptoms. The Humiliation, Afraid, Rape,

Kick questionnaire is a four-item assessment, with questions surrounding humiliation, fear, rape, and physical violence.

48. A: An initial short-term treatment plan goal for a couple experiencing infidelity would be to establish safety and address trauma symptoms. Processing difficult emotions and traumatic symptoms is a critical foundation for couples experiencing infidelity. Decreasing negative cognitive appraisals and attaining forgiveness are appropriate long-term goals. Once a safe and trusting counseling environment is established, therapists can work with clients on understanding motivating factors and causes of emotional detachment, managing negative communication, and creating blame-free narratives.

49. C: On January 1, 2022, as part of Section 2799B-6 of the Public Health Service Act, the No Surprises Act was passed, which dictated that clients who are uninsured or out of network must obtain notification of the expected charges for certain items at the time of service. This also applies to some emergency services. In this law, MFTs are identified as health-care providers who must comply with the mandate to provide good faith estimates (GFEs) to clients who are out of network, uninsured, or self-paying. Providers and facilities must also provide GFEs to clients who do not intend to submit an insurance claim. Providers must notify clients in writing and verbally that the GFE will be provided upon scheduling or by request. The No Surprises Act was passed in response to balance billing, which occurs when providers bill the client for expenses that were not covered by insurance.

50. B: The client's expressed intent would best assist the therapist in determining the likelihood that the client is actively suicidal. Cutting is a form of nonsuicidal self-injury (NSSI). Although suicidality and NSSI look similar, there are some distinctions. Clients with NSSI engage in behaviors to regulate or cope with overwhelming emotions. With suicidality, a person no longer wishes to relieve emotional pain and feel better but to simply cease feeling. Clients who engage in NSSI and those who express suicidal ideation have greater instances of substance use, traumatic experiences, and psychosocial stressors.

51. C: Vygotsky differed from Piaget in his cognitive development theory in that he placed greater emphasis on sociocultural context. Whereas Piaget was a constructivist, Vygotsky was a social constructivist who used the term "zone of emotional proximal development" to describe how a child's learning relies on its surrounding system to develop socially and emotionally. Piaget, rather than Vygotsky, placed greater emphasis on the stages of cognitive development, attaining equilibrium, and the adaptation process.

52. C: Informed consent is the process by which the therapist reviews the "potential risks and benefits of treatments for which generally recognized standards do not yet exist" (AAMFT, 2015, Standard 1.2). Confidentiality is a part of informed consent; however, it is not a term used to describe the process of reviewing treatment information with the client. In general, due process refers to procedures identifying ethical violations, including an MFT's impaired decision making and/or professional judgment. Much like confidentiality, scope of competence may be a part of informed consent, but it does not describe the process. MFTs must work within their scope of competence, which includes applicable education, training, and supervision as prerequisites for diagnosing, treating, or advising clients.

53. A: Clients least likely to benefit from asynchronous technology-based counseling are those in crises. Asynchronous counseling is a technology-based service that uses delayed communication exchanges, including email, self-guided online modules, and chat-based exchanges. Clients in crisis are least likely to benefit from delayed communication. MFTs are responsible for determining appropriate clients for technologically assisted services by considering the "professional, intellectual, emotional, and physical needs" of the client (AAMFT, 2015, Standard 6.1). Clients who are more likely to benefit from technology-based counseling are those who may be experiencing social anxiety, those residing in distant and/or rural settings, and those who would not ordinarily access services due to feeling stigma regarding mental health treatment.

54. A: Standard 2.6 of the AAMFT Code of Ethics (2015) states that MFTs preparing to close their practice adhere to applicable laws related to the storage, transfer, or disposal of client records; maintain confidentiality; and safeguard the welfare of their clients. Ethical standards outlined in the code are designed to protect the rights of clients and research participants rather than the MFT, including clients' rights to access their own records. MFTs avoid client abandonment when preparing for practice changes, but this does not directly apply to storing, transferring, or disposing of client records.

55. C: Parent–child interaction therapy (PCIT) offers sessions in a real-life environment, with child–parent dyads to lessen the adverse effects of out-of-home placement for children. PCIT is an evidence-based therapy for children between the ages of 2 and 7, with attachment and learning theory as its foundational basis. PCIT uses in vivo sessions with children and parents held with the therapist observing sessions, providing coaching through a one-way mirror, and communicating with parents or caregivers through wireless earphones. Functional family therapy is an evidence-based model targeting at-risk youth ages 11–18 currently involved in the juvenile justice program or referred by schools and mental health facilities. Imago relationship therapy is used with couples who have experienced childhood trauma. Trauma-focused CBT helps clients create a trauma narrative and recognize and mitigate associated cognitive bias and avoidance behaviors.

56. C: Unless otherwise specified, an MFT may withhold access to records if releasing the records would seriously endanger the client. This condition is outlined in Standard 2.3 of the AAMFT Code of Ethics (2015), which explains that MFTs must provide "reasonable access" to client records unless there is "compelling evidence" that access would "cause serious harm to the client." Other conditions, such as the client not following treatment recommendations, would not permit the records to be withheld. Standard 8.6 of the code states that client records may not be withheld for nonpayment of services. Concerning the exposure of confidential collateral information, withholding records would not be justified because confidentiality protects the client's information. Collateral support persons do not have protected confidentiality rights.

57. D: The philosophical underpinnings of family systems theory purport that family relationships are interrelated and interdependent. Families are understood as connected units and interact in ways to form a whole. Thus, family systems theory claims that families should be viewed holistically—not as separate components, but as connected, interrelated, and interdependent with external inputs and open systems of operation. Family systems theory assumes that problems have circular rather than linear causality. Circular causality suggests that the client system manifests circular interactions, which operate from mutually interdependent, nonsequential, interactional factors, and systemic behavioral patterns. Family systems theorists believe that the whole family is greater than the sum of each member.

58. B: The therapeutic relationship is best cultivated by trust, connection, and collaboration. Collaboration toward agreed-upon treatment plan goals is essential for forming and maintaining a therapeutic alliance. A trusting therapeutic relationship is associated with successful treatment outcomes. Trust and the belief that the therapist's methods are efficacious may be attained through contact, clarity, and competence; however, collaboration is essential.

59. D: For a diagnosis of a paraphilic disorder, an individual must exhibit arousing fantasies, urges, or behaviors that are not merely due to distress related to society's disapproval. The DSM-5-TR criteria for paraphilic disorder include fantasies, urges, or behaviors that are, in part, intense and persistent, cause significant personal distress, and include another person's injury or death. The DSM-5-TR distinguishes between substantial personal distress and distress related to society's disapproval. To diagnose a paraphilic disorder, the fantasies, urges, or behaviors must cause significant distress or impairment or another person's injury or death.

60. C: The Patient Health Questionnaire (PHQ-9) is an evidence-based assessment measure for adult mood disorders. The PHQ-9 is a brief questionnaire used to assess mood-related symptoms, including anhedonia, sleep disturbance, lethargy, appetite changes, concentration and focus, suicidality, restlessness, and changes in energy levels. The Clinical Global Impression (CGI) assessment tool measures observed symptom severity associated with mental illness, global improvement, and therapeutic response to psychotropic drug treatment. The Brief Psychiatric Rating Scale (BPRS) measures psychosis in individuals who may have schizophrenia or other psychotic disorders. The BPRS is used as an outcome measure for moderate to severe psychosis. The World Health Organization Disability Assessment Scale 2.0 measures functional impairment in cognition, self-care, social interaction, and activity participation. It also measures functional work or school impairment.

61. B: For Murray Bowen, forming multiple therapeutic alliances with couples and families involves the therapist acting as an emotionally distant and objective coach. Bowen believed that alliances with couples and families are formed when the therapist becomes a nonanxious and emotionally detached presence. Virginia Satir viewed the therapist as a warm and supportive equal. Salvador Minuchin believed that the therapist's role was akin to an active and respectful "stage manager" and director. Nathan Ackerman asserted that the therapeutic alliance is grounded in the therapist becoming a flexible observer and catalyst for interactional processes.

62. A: When using Albert Roberts' (2000) seven-stage crisis intervention model, once the severity of the crisis is determined, rapport is established, and the major problems are identified, the therapist would then use active listening and validate emotions. Roberts' model includes the following seven phases: (1) conduct a crisis assessment to determine the severity of the crisis (e.g., MSE, risk assessment), (2) establish a therapeutic relationship, (3) identify crisis precipitants and the main crisis-related problems, (4) encourage exploration of emotions using active listening and validation techniques, (5) explore alternatives and coping skills, (6) formulate a plan of action, and (7) plan for follow-up and booster sessions.

63. A: The therapist explains that the rationale for selecting this approach is to make the relationship, rather than each individual, the primary focus. Psychodynamic therapists work to uncover unconscious contributions to relationship problems, which calls for the therapist to interpret relationship patterns. Cognitive-behavioral couples therapy prioritizes problem solving over intrapsychic processes. SFTs join with couples to map the family structure and hierarchy. Psychodynamic therapists use countertransference rather than transference to interpret underlying issues.

64. A: The school is acting in a legally and ethically sound manner. Student educational records are protected under the Family Educational Rights and Privacy Act (FERPA) and are generally released with a parent's written consent. However, some exceptions exist, including allowing records to be disclosed without parental consent to state and local authorities within a juvenile justice system. FERPA, also known as the Buckley Amendment, protects the privacy of educational records by giving parents the right to access and, if necessary, amend their child's academic records. HIPAA

156

does not protect school records; instead, it pertains to protected information within a health-care system. IDEA provides free and appropriate public education to those with qualifying disabilities and ensures that students are identified and assessed in a nondiscriminatory fashion.

65. B: Gambling disorder is classified in the DSM-5-TR as a substance-related and addictive disorder. Gambling disorder is the only behavioral disorder with a DSM classification. There is still debate over the inclusion of other compulsive behaviors, including exercise, shopping (i.e., buying), and internet gaming. Internet gaming disorder currently lacks empirical evidence to classify it as a mental disorder.

66. A: Progress monitoring is most effective when applied during the early stages of treatment. Studies show that those who do not do well early on in treatment are at higher risk for premature termination and poorer treatment outcomes. In addition, regular use of client-directed feedback and standardized instruments has been shown to enhance the therapeutic alliance, help create appropriate treatment plan goals, and enhance engagement in the therapeutic process.

67. A: On a genogram, a transgender female is depicted as a square inside a circle. Transgender females are individuals who are born male and identify as female. A circle inside a square represents a transgender male. An upside-down triangle inside a square represents a gay male, whereas an upside-down triangle inside a circle represents a lesbian female.

68. C: A psychiatric advance directive (PAD) is a legally binding document that allows patients to appoint a surrogate decision maker to carry out predetermined alternatives to hospitalization and offer additional instructions for future crises. A PAD is established when a client has increased decision-making capacity, which would coincide with the patient's discharge. Facilitated PADs outline client preferences and the ability to consent to or refuse treatment in the event of an incapacitating crisis. A safety plan is a documented list of actions that an individual can take to help keep them safe in the presence of known or possible danger. Safety plans are implemented for those at risk for suicide, domestic violence, child abuse, or elder abuse and are not legally binding. A living will is legally binding but is limited to end-of-life decisions and care if a person becomes seriously ill. Finally, a conservatorship is a legally binding agreement detailing actions that a court-appointed person (the conservator) can make on behalf of another (the ward). Conservatorships are designed for individuals with severe mental illness who frequently refuse treatment after multiple risky events and behaviors (e.g., suicide attempts).

69. C: Bowenian therapists believe that maintaining multiple therapeutic alliances within the family system involves viewing three-person systems (i.e., triangles) as interactions in which the therapist remains emotionally uninvolved. Bowenians believed that the therapist's role is that of a coach and emphasized the need for the therapist to remain objective and emotionally differentiated. As active participants in family interactions, SFTs emphasize the purposeful creation and participation in triangles and support using triangles to restructure and reorganize subsystems. Narrative and other social constructivists stress the importance of collaboration and respect in the alliance by viewing each member as an equal participant in interactional meaning making.

70. C: SFTs use enactments to assess families by encouraging unstructured interactions among family members. When used as an assessment tool, enactments involve the therapist encouraging and observing unstructured interactions. During the observation, the therapist intervenes only to encourage members to continue interacting. The rationale is to force family members to communicate so the therapist can more accurately determine where the breakdown exists. This is in opposition to other forms of family systems assessments. Role-playing is a common practice in couple enrichment programs. Taking turns talking and listening is a method commonly used by behavioral family therapists. Emotionally focused couples therapy encourages the use of directed dialogue to reflect underlying attachment emotions.

71. A: Privilege is a term that describes unmerited power and access to societal resources, rights, and opportunities. Oppression is the inverse of privilege and is experienced by those in nondominant social groups. Discrimination and racism are forms of oppression designed to immobilize those who are not in power. Inclusion refers to empowering and involving individuals or groups of people in a way that conveys recognition of their value and worth. Stratification, or social stratification, refers to the hierarchal organization of separate classes of people based on unequal distributions of power, resources, rights, and opportunities.

72. D: In the ABC-X crisis model, the letter C represents the perception of the stressor. Developed by Reuben Hill, the ABC-X crisis model is used to determine if a family's problem will result in a crisis. The ABC-X crisis model (i.e., the ABC-X stress model) consists of A, the family's set of available resources; B, the family's definition of a stressor; C, the perception of the stressor; and X, the crisis itself.

73. C: Of the strategies listed, validating feelings and honoring autonomy is the least appropriate choice for therapists working with clients at high risk of harm to others because this is an intervention for clients at low risk. Although all of the listed strategies are essential when conducting a risk assessment and developing a safety plan, clients at high risk require interventions to provide immediate assistance to those at imminent risk of harm to themselves and others. Suicidal and homicidal assessments determine appropriate interventions for clients who are at low, medium, or high risk. Appropriate strategies for medium- and high-risk clients include arranging for a higher level of care (e.g., crisis stabilization, hospitalization), setting a follow-up appointment in 24–48 hours, and adhering to the ethical and legal duty to warn mandates.

74. C: According to Gerald Caplan's four phases of a crisis, if a problem is not resolved by phase 4, the individual will exhibit personality disorganization. In addition, the fourth and final phase of a crisis includes depression, despair, and confusion. The four phases of a crisis include (1) a rise in tension associated with the precipitating event, (2) disruption to daily living; failed problem-solving exacerbates distress, (3) use of emergency problem solving methods; trial-and-error use of novel coping skills, and (4) personality disorganization.

75. D: The client is in the maintenance stage of change. James Prochaska and Carlo DiClemente developed the transtheoretical stages of change mode, in which each stage is marked by the degree to which the client has progressed in decision making and purposeful steps toward change. The stages of change include precontemplation, contemplation, preparation, action, and maintenance. Although some models include termination as the final stage, others do not. The termination stage is marked by a client's absolute certainty that he or she will not experience a relapse of the condition (e.g., substance misuse) or problem. The contemplation stage is marked by individuals intentionally deciding to change a behavior or address a problem. The preparation stage is characterized by a readiness to change, and it is followed by the action stage.

76. B: The action on behalf of the therapist essential for maintaining the therapeutic alliance is the negotiation of treatment plan goals. Components of a therapeutic alliance include the client–therapist bond, the collaborative nature of the relationship, and an agreement on the tasks and goals of therapy. The maintenance of the therapeutic alliance involves a shift in power from the therapist assuming an expert role to shared power in codeveloping and negotiating treatment tasks and considerations. Self-disclosure in and of itself may not be therapeutic and can often weaken the alliance when it is not authentic or congruent. Therapists show clients unconditional positive regard when assuming a nonjudgmental stance and showing acceptance of each client; however, this is not the same as unconditional acceptance of client behavior. To maintain the therapeutic alliance, feedback on the nature of the relationship and client progress must be elicited on an ongoing basis rather than upon termination alone.

77. C: The AAMFT Procedures for Handling Ethical Matters states that once a final decision for termination of membership is made, terminated members will have their names and ethical violations published in *Family Therapy Magazine.* The chief executive officer will also publicize the terminated members' earned degrees, their location, and the proven violation of the section of the Code of Ethics. The AAMFT Procedures for Handling Ethical Matters also states that anonymous complaints will not be recognized as a basis for action. Once a complaint against a member is lodged, the AAMFT must respond in 30 days to alleviate the risk of membership termination. When a complaint is filed, a preliminary review is begun; at this time, the complainants waive therapist–client confidentiality and allow the AAMFT to use the information if ethical charges are made.

78. A: A therapist seeking to provide therapy reflecting an individual treatment model with a systemic approach would want to recognize the client's intrapsychic processes amid interpersonal interactions. Nathan Ackerman was the first to integrate psychoanalytic principles with systems theory. Murray Bowen included differentiation of self and family projection processes as two of his eight emphasized family therapy concepts. These concepts are strictly related to family systems and do not include an individual treatment model. Differentiation of self refers to how well a person distinguishes themselves from their families, with low differentiation describing those who are emotionally dependent and high differentiation referring to those with a higher degree of emotional self-sufficiency. Bowen used the family projection process to describe how parents transfer fears or worries onto a child, create the narrative that confirms this fear, and respond by treating their child accordingly. The therapist would not seek to establish congruence between a person's emotional regulation and the family's homeostasis. A client's ability to achieve emotional regulation may or may not affect the family's homeostasis. Similarly, balancing the family's equilibrium may not necessarily be achieved by reducing the client's resistance.

79. D: Upon resolution of a crisis, the overall goal of crisis intervention models (e.g., the SAFER-R Intervention Model or the Seven-Stage Crisis Intervention Model) is to return clients to their precrisis mental health baseline. In doing so, the therapist aims to arrest any crisis-related psychological trauma. Reducing the client's risk for harm often aligns with returning clients to their precrisis mental health baseline; however, for clients at high risk, reducing the risk to moderate may be insufficient. Reducing the client's need for follow-up care is incorrect because crisis interventions include follow-up care, which is generally outlined in the client's action plan. Returning clients to a higher level of care is incorrect because higher levels of care indicate a higher level of risk and need for placement in a more restrictive environment.

80. B: Multidimensional family therapy is a treatment approach for adolescent substance use disorder that uses a developmental-ecological approach anchored in the belief that change unfolds in phases across several systems, contexts, and domains. Multidimensional family therapy uses recovery-oriented principles and addresses four treatment domains: adolescents, parents, family members, and members of the teen's community. There are three stages: building the foundation, activating the change, and sealing the change. Behavioral family therapy is based on the premise that addictive behaviors occur through social learning and conditioning within families and peer groups; it is an adaptation of behavioral couples therapy applied to individuals living with a family member experiencing substance use disorder. Systemic motivational therapy combines components of systemic family therapy with motivational interviewing (MI) and emphasizes the construction and use of mini experiments addressing substance use existing within the family system. Finally, multigenerational family therapy looks at families through generational patterns of behavior.

81. B: The therapist's use of Socratic questioning is reflected in the question "What evidence is there for that thought?" Socratic questioning uses sound logic and reason to help challenge cognitive distortions. The client learns to recognize automatic thoughts associated with her distortions as she engages in the process of cognitive restructuring. Person-centered therapists explore conditions of worth, whereas solution-focused therapists focus on identifying a time when the thinking was less severe. Asking the client where the thought originated can be loosely tied to psychoanalytic therapy, which emphasizes the importance of early childhood thoughts and emotions.

82. C: The PREPARE/ENRICH assessment tool is based on David Olson's Circumplex Model of Marital and Family Systems. The PREPARE/ENRICH inventory is a standardized assessment tool measuring marital cohesion, flexibility, and communication. There are additional versions of the assessment for premarital couples, cohabiting couples, and couples who are married with children. The Marital Satisfaction Inventory, Revised, assesses marital problems contributing to marital or family discord, including expressions of feelings, problem-solving strategies, time spent together, sexual satisfaction, and dissatisfaction with children. The Family Adaptability and Cohesion Scale IV assesses measures of cohesion determined by levels of enmeshment and disengagement. The Dyadic Adjustment Scale measures the relationship dyad's perception of cohesion, overall satisfaction, and emotional expression.

83. B: According to the AAMFT Code of Ethics (2015), an MFT's core values consist of elements distinct from ethical standards. Core values are aspirational and "inform all the varieties of practice and service in which marriage and family therapists engage." Ethical standards, on the other hand, are "rules of practice upon which the marriage and family therapist is obliged and judged." Standards of ethical practice include measurable standards of professionalism and competency (e.g., job appraisals, supervisory evaluations). Standards of practice are enforceable by the AAMFT board of directors. For example, membership may be terminated when there are violations of professional misconduct (e.g., felony convictions) or if an MFT continues to practice when impaired.

84. D: Cross-system collaboration would best ensure that the client maintains progress. Cross-system collaboration is conducted with youth involved with multiple systems to ensure that effective communication occurs across systems of care through partnerships with institutions, including child welfare, juvenile justice, behavioral health services, and educational systems. Eco-mapping is the process of constructing a graphic representation of all ecological systems in the client's life. Various lines and arrows depict strong or stressful influences of the client's primary systems. Progress monitoring is regularly assessing a client's progress at each session and is used to guide treatment. Progress monitoring would enable the therapist to determine that the client is progressing in treatment. The therapist would not use progress monitoring after discharge Measurement-based care (MBC) is the process of using clinical data to drive clinical care. Progress monitoring is a form of MBC.

85. C: Couples engaging in situational violence place them at a lower risk for retaliation. There is emerging empirical evidence indicating that conjoint couples therapy may be appropriate for couples engaged in situational violence because the violence is reciprocal (i.e., both partners are violent), not associated with control or coercion, and less severe. Situational violence results from mutual anger and frustration rather than the desire for power and dominance. Couples at higher risk for postsession violent retaliation include those belonging to cultures with patriarchal norms

160

and those in which one partner engages in substance misuse or is violently resistant. The topology of IPV includes situational violence, intimate terrorism, and violent resistance. Intimate terrorism is the most severe and involves incidents of coercive and controlling violence, which is overwhelmingly perpetrated by males. Violent resistance is used to describe self-defense in the face of intimate terrorism.

86. B: Standard 4.6 (Existing Relationship with Students or Supervisees) would best inform the supervisee's ethical decision-making process. MFTs must "make every effort to avoid conditions and multiple relationships with supervisees that could impair professional judgment or increase the risk of exploitation" (AAMFT, 2015). MFT supervisors have an ethical obligation to avoid exploiting the trust and dependency of supervisees. It being the only car dealership in town does not exempt the supervisor because there are likely other employees with whom the supervisor could conduct professional business. In addition to exploiting his position of power, the potential for blurred boundaries could be further compounded by the supervisor's disclosure of credit history upon making a purchase. Standard 4.5 (Oversight of Supervisee Professionalism) applies to the ethical obligation of the supervisor to ensure the supervisee provides professional services. Standard 4.7 (Confidentiality with Supervisees) refers to disclosure of the supervisee's confidences. Suppose the supervisor took the supervisee up on their offer. In that case, they could do so without mentioning that a supervisor–supervisee relationship exists and still be committing an ethical violation. Standard 4.8 (Payment for Supervision) states that clinical supervisors do not enter into financial agreements through "deceptive or exploitative practices" or "exert undue influence over supervisees when establishing supervision fees."

87. C: Standard 1.8 of the AAMFT Code of Ethics (2015) addresses client autonomy in decision making, stating, "Marriage and family therapists respect the rights of clients to make decisions and help them to understand the consequences of these decisions," applying to instances such as "cohabitation, marriage, divorce, separation, reconciliation, custody, and visitation." The first part of the standard is to help the couple understand the consequences of their decision. This is expressed with the therapist first exploring the couple's individual and joint reasons for wanting to cohabitate. The second part of the standard states that the therapist clearly advises the clients to make their own decisions regarding cohabitation, which is reflected in the therapist empowering the couple to do so. Exploring the influences of religion and culture is not the best response because these issues may be insignificant to the couple and/or they may not wish to align their themselves with those sociocultural dictates.

88. A: Vicarious trauma refers to a significant change in a therapist's worldview due to ongoing exposure to a client's traumatic material. Secondary trauma describes a sudden reaction to learning of another person's traumatic experience. Secondary trauma is similar to vicarious trauma but differs in that vicarious trauma involves a therapist's change in attitude or worldview. Vicarious trauma can lead to compassion fatigue, which is a therapist's preoccupation with clients experiencing the effects of trauma. With compassion fatigue, providers become overwhelmed with ongoing exposure to their clients' trauma and psychological difficulties. Burnout is the result of chronic work stress and frustration. Although burnout can overlap or result in compassion fatigue, it can occur in any profession. Like compassion fatigue, burnout includes symptoms of exhaustion and frustration; however, burnout differs from compassion fatigue in that burnout usually results from being overworked or having excessive work responsibilities.

89. D: Therapists take a nonjudgmental counseling stance by conveying acceptance of the client's inherent worth. A nonjudgmental stance is closely related to unconditional positive regard—a core counseling attribute helpful in establishing a therapeutic alliance. Therapists take a nonjudgmental stance by accepting each client's inherent worth and dignity. Therapists who present a

161

nonjudgmental stance do so by supporting the client in making autonomous decisions. A nonjudgmental stance does not involve the therapist imposing standards for moral living, nor does the therapist convey acceptance of the client's choices. Instead, taking a nonjudgmental stance is designed to provide client-directed moral agency.

90. B: Ludwig von Bertalanffy is credited with developing general systems theory, which served as a precursor for family systems theory. Bertalanffy was a biologist who recognized that open systems are maintained by their input and mutual interaction, paving the way for the acknowledgment of cybernetics, which, when applied to family systems theory, describes circular causality or feedback loops. Jay Haley is one of many family systems theorists who worked together at the Mental Research Institute in Palo Alto, California, to develop communication interaction family therapy. Ivan Boszormenyi-Nagy is a Hungarian psychiatrist known for his contributions to contextual family therapy. Nathan Ackerman is known for integrating psychoanalytic principles with family systems theory.

91. D: Complex trauma primarily stems from early childhood harm or abandonment by caretakers or persons of significance in a child's life. Complex trauma is pervasive and disruptive to growth and development, and it is responsible for insecure attachment and a host of mental and physical disorders. Catastrophic events or critical instances (e.g., mass shooting, earthquakes) are another category of trauma-related crises. Historical trauma includes instances of marginalization, oppression, and discrimination. Overwhelmed coping mechanisms are a component of most crisis-related sequelae.

92. B: The first thing that the MFT should do is to understand the local jurisdiction's laws regarding professional misconduct. The code states that MFTs must "comply with applicable laws regarding the reporting of unethical conduct" (AAMFT, 2015, Standard 1.6). Standard 3.12 states that MFTs may be in violation of the code if they are convicted of any felony or a misdemeanor related to their qualifications or functions. The colleague was charged with a crime but has not been convicted. Additionally, the MFT noted that she has never displayed concerning behavior, making it unclear whether the colleague's conduct was related to her qualifications or functions. Obtaining authorization to make a report is not applicable because confidentiality does not apply to the colleague; however, confidentiality may be a consideration if the incident were to concern a client. Making a formal complaint to the AAMFT ethics committee would be premature. The MFT should first determine whether she is responsible for reporting the incident. The process of ethical decision making may involve encouraging the colleague to self-report, but this would not be the first step in that process because it does not absolve the MFT of her ethical obligation.

93. D: Narrative therapy is to externalization as solution-focused therapy is to scaling questions. Narrative therapy uses the therapeutic technique of externalization, whereas solution-focused therapy uses the therapeutic technique of scaling questions. Externalization is used to help family systems redefine the problem as something external rather than as a permanent part of the family system. Solution-focused therapists use scaling questions when asking clients to rate any number of areas (e.g., problems, goals, priorities) along a continuum (e.g., a 1–10 Likert scale). Summarization is a person-centered concept that therapists use to tie together specific themes or recap what has been discussed. Projection occurs when unacceptable and unwanted thoughts, impulses, fears, or desires are attributed to others. Psychoanalytic therapists consider projection a defense mechanism. Positive connotation is used in the Milan model of family therapy in which the therapist only points out commendable aspects of the family members' behaviors, which often serves as a precursor for a paradoxical prescription (i.e., prescribing the problem).

94. C: Strategic therapists use paradoxical directives to create disequilibrium. Paradoxical directives involve prescribing the symptom. When families resist change, the family system remains balanced (i.e., in a state of homeostasis). When encouraging the family to increase undesirable behaviors, family members can choose to comply or resist, which allows the symptoms to be viewed as involuntary rather than voluntary. Structural therapy involves resolving structural problems, establishing clear boundaries, and using enactment.

95. D: The MFT is not solely responsible for making ethical decisions congruent with the community mental health center (CMHC)'s policies and practices. Instead, the MFT has a responsibility to make ethical decisions that are congruent with the AAMFT Code of Ethics (2015), which states that MFTs must make ethical decisions following governing laws and ethics and must remain accountable to the code when "acting as members or employees of an organization." If the code conflicts with the CMHC's policies and practices, the MFT must seek resolution of the conflict in a way that allows the "fullest adherence" to the code. MFTs are ethically responsible for seeking reimbursement from third-party payers contracting with the CMHC. The CMHC's administrative staff will likely assist with this endeavor, but this does not exempt the MFT from submitting appropriate and truthful documentation for reimbursed services (AAMFT, 2015, Standard 8.4). MFTs are responsible for making financial arrangements with third-party payers in every work setting. MFTs are responsible to clients for disclosing the confidentiality limitations associated with the CMHC's selected technological platform. This must be done in writing and include the protections offered by the CMHC's technology (AAMFT, 2015, Standard 6.3). MFTs are responsible for acknowledging their limitations of competency in all professional and nonprofessional settings in which the MFT is affiliated, including, but not limited to, responses to the CMHC's supervisory evaluations and agency reviews.

96. D: This is an example of the family projection process—a Bowenian family therapy concept involving three steps: (1) a parent fears something is wrong with their child and theorizes what the problem may be (i.e., "scanning"), (2) the parent then interprets the child's theorized behaviors as true and evidence of psychopathology (i.e., "diagnosing"), and (3) the parent responds by "fixing" the behavior through overcompensation (i.e., "treating"), which often exacerbates the condition. Emotional cutoff is a Bowenian family therapy concept that explains how families become emotionally disengaged from one another due to unresolved conflict. Prescribing the symptom is a strategic family therapy technique that involves the therapist asking family members to engage in problematic behavior to push past resistance and engage members in the change process. Prescribing the symptom is one example of a paradoxical intervention. Other examples of paradoxical interventions include restraining, positioning, and relabeling.

97. A: After treating the client for 9 months, the MFT's best course of action is to work with the client on a termination plan. Standard 1.9 states that MFTs can continue with the client–counselor relationship "only so long as it is reasonably clear that clients are benefiting from the relationship" (AAMFT, 2015). The best indicators of this measure are the client's treatment plan, progress reviews, and documentation on the efficacy of the treatment interventions. The client is not following the treatment recommendation (i.e., attend a psychiatric evaluation). It is important to note that the MFT did not recommend nor require that the client take medication—only that a psychiatrist evaluate him. The client stating that he feels supported would not constitute a reasonably clear benefit. Exploring cultural considerations and enlisting the assistance of a family member may be beneficial early in treatment but would not be the best option for a client who has been in therapy for 9 months.

98. D: Therapists who practice cognitive therapy, behavior therapy, and rational-emotive behavior therapy (REBT) use a structured rather than an unstructured approach. These are all time-limited, present-oriented methods, and they all use homework.

99. A: The MFT is not obligated to make clients aware in writing of being well trained and competent in all technology-assisted professional services. Standard 6.6 of the AAMFT Code of Ethics (2015) states that MFTs ensure that they are "well trained and competent in the use of all chosen technology-assisted professional services," but this information is not required in writing. Standard 6.4 of the AAMFT Code of Ethics (2015) states that MFTs must ensure clients and supervisees in writing that all documentation containing identifying information is "electronically stored and/or transferred," following best practice guidelines. MFTs must inform the client in writing of the therapist's and client's responsibilities for minimizing risks associated with technology-assisted professional services as part of the consent to treat (AAMFT, 2015, Standard 6.2). MFTs must make clients aware of confidentiality limitations and protections associated with the use of technology (AAMFT, 2015, Standard 6.3).

100. B: Rating scales would be most helpful in determining a provisional diagnosis. Attention-deficit hyperactivity disorder (ADHD) would likely serve as the provisional diagnosis. There are no formal tests required to confirm an ADHD diagnosis. Therapists use informal testing measures such as behavioral observations, clinical interviews, and rating scales to assist in formulating an ADHD diagnosis. ADHD rating scales include the Vanderbilt Assessment Scale, the Behavior Assessment System for Children, the Child Behavior Checklist/Teacher Report Form, and the Conners Rating Scale. Because ADHD requires behaviors to be present in two or more settings (e.g., home, school, or peer gatherings), informal assessment data from each setting are beneficial. Teachers use formative assessments to assess learning and guide instruction. Psychological tests assist with determining related symptoms, such as executive functioning and attention, but they are only one component of a psychoeducational evaluation, which combines multiple measures to determine client functioning. A forensic assessment is used to determine criminal responsibility and competency to stand trial.

101. A: A symbolic-experiential family therapist would hypothesize aloud that the family intentionally caused their son's absence. Carl Whitaker is credited with developing symbolic-experiential family therapy, which is based on the premise that family members who are symptom bearers are representative of the entire family's communication patterns and disfunction. Whitaker believed in contracting with families to have all members present for therapy appointments. When this was not honored, Whitaker took an active and provocative role with the family by engaging in a battle for structure, exemplified in the therapist's hypothesis that the family intentionally caused the son's absence. Rather than rescheduling with the family, Whitaker would refuse to discuss problems with the family members and instead focus on their resistance to include the son. Strategic family therapists would focus on restoring healthy boundaries and examining hierarchies in a family system. Cognitive family therapists emphasize identifying a family's schemata or core beliefs, and they actively work to restructure beliefs to change dysfunctional behaviors.

102. A: An SFT would intervene by blocking the transactional processes and unbalancing the dysfunctional subsystems. The family is midway through therapy. Constructing a visual map illustrating hierarchies and systems of power is associated with establishing a structural family hypothesis and diagnosis. A genogram is a diagram showing interactional communication and behavior patterns and is associated with Bowenian family therapy. Asking scaling questions is related to SFBT.

103. C: This is an example of a reframe. Reframing is used to help clients view situations from a more positive vantage point. The use of reframing helps break up resistant (i.e., overlearned) patterns of communication. Strategic therapists use paradoxical interventions to "prescribe" the symptom, which is designed to reduce resistant behavior. A paradoxical directive would be to encourage the client and father to have as many arguments as possible between sessions. Metaphors are figures of speech that illustrate symbolic comparisons and similarities. Therapists use metaphors to help illustrate abstract concepts or better explain patterns of behavior. Therapists help clients rewrite narratives to externalize the problem and introduce alternative narratives.

104. B: The parents refocusing the attention onto their child's behavior is an example of detouring. Detouring is a structural family therapy concept used to describe a family system that functions by refocusing attention onto a family member in an effort to avoid focusing on more significant issues. Mimesis involves coping or mirroring the family's communication style and is used by structural family therapists (SFTs) to help join with a family. Triangulation occurs when two family members bring another person into their conflict. This differs from detouring in that, with detouring, families avoid conflict by focusing elsewhere. With triangulation, another person is drawn into the conflict. SFTs use blocking to force family members to implement new patterns of relating to one another.

105. D: Regarding supervisor–supervisee confidentiality, the AAMFT Code of Ethics (2015) states, in part: "Marriage and family therapists do not disclose supervisee confidences except by written authorization or waiver, or when mandated or permitted by law… Verbal authorization will not be sufficient except in emergency situations, unless prohibited by law" (Standard 4.7).

106. C: Gottman believed that there are three phases that couples must engage in to heal from infidelity: atonement, attunement, and attachment. During atonement (i.e., phase 1), couples work toward honest communication, an admission of remorse, and a shared desire to move forward in their relationship. Attunement (i.e., phase 2) is characterized by rebuilding trust and a willingness on behalf of the unfaithful partner to make the relationship a priority. In the final phase, attachment, the couple feels strong enough to begin restoring emotional and physical intimacy. Acceptance is not associated with Gottman's three phases for healing infidelity.

107. A: Qualities of an effective treatment plan include goals and objectives written in a client-centered manner. Effective treatment plans are also culturally relevant, strengths based, and reflect the client's current motivation and capacity to change. Client-centered treatment plans include collaborative goals and objectives in the client's language and reflect the client's current needs. Program-focused treatment plans do not reflect individualized client-centered goals and objectives. Therapist-centered treatment plans are not collaborative because they are created without the client's or collateral support person's input. Strengths-based rather than deficit-based goals and objectives are written in positive terms (i.e., an action that the client will take).

108. C: Infants who displayed insecure-avoidant attachment showed no signs of distress when the mother left, interacted with the stranger during the mother's absence, and remained disinterested when the mother returned. Adults with insecure-avoidant attachment fear abandonment and approach intimate relationships with hesitancy. Infants with secure attachment expressed initial distress upon separation from their mother, resisted the stranger's attempts to comfort them, and became friendly with the stranger when the mother returned. Adults with secure attachments can form safe, trusting, and intimate relationships with others. Researchers Mary Main and Judith Solomon later added disorganized/disoriented as an attachment style. Infants with this attachment style appear fearful and avoidant. Children with disorganized and disoriented attachment are often the victims of childhood and abuse and have difficulty with intimate relationships. Infants who display insecure resistant/ambivalent attachment exhibit intense levels of distress when their mother leaves and respond fearfully to the stranger. When the mother returns, the infant rejects the mother's attempts to console them. Adults with insecure resistant/ambivalent attachment tend to be anxious, uncertain, and emotionally needy.

109. C: Research suggests that therapists are less likely to use instruments measuring client progress if the process is standardized. There are several reasons why therapists are less likely to use standardized instruments to measure client progress, including their cost, the time that they take to administer, the therapist's doubts regarding their efficacy (i.e., the belief that clinical judgment is superior to standardized measures), and the associated training requirements. Instead, therapists prefer measurement tools that are brief, nonburdensome, and ongoing.

110. D: Clients who exhibit circumstantial thinking speak in a nonlinear fashion, provide unnecessary details, and veer off topic, but they eventually return to the original subject matter. Difficulties with thought processes is often associated with psychosis, schizophrenia, bipolar I disorder, or a medical condition. Word salad is characterized by nonsensical, meaningless words and phrases strung together with no clear beginning or end. Tangential thinking is the process of expressing several connected, but off-topic, thoughts. Unlike circumstantial thinking, individuals with tangential thinking do not return to the original subject. Flight of ideas is similar to tangential thinking; however, flight of ideas includes thoughts that are disjointed and veer off topic but are more difficult to follow.

111. C: John Gottman believed that the antidote for the number-one predictor of divorce (i.e., contempt) is for partners to become attuned to their inner feelings and foster a culture of appreciation and respect by letting one's partner know what they have done right. Gottman believed contempt to be the number-one predictor of divorce. Contempt is characterized by a one-up position of superiority, and it communicates condemnation of another person's sense of self. Gottman used the term "four horsemen" to describe the negative communication interactions that increase a couple's chances of divorce. The four horsemen are contempt, criticism, defensiveness, and stonewalling, and there is an antidote for each. The antidote for stonewalling is to take time away and practice self-care. Gottman did not include using social support and cultivating interdependence as an antidote. Accepting another's perspective and apologizing for any wrongdoing is the antidote for defensiveness. The antidote for criticism is to complain without blame by using "I" statements.

112. C: Therapists are most likely to experience countertransference as a manifestation of inner conflicts. Countertransference is the therapist's internal emotional response to a client's specific qualities, exchanges, or responses that are projected onto the therapist in the form of transference. The therapist's emotional responses are based on inner conflicts, liabilities, and unmet needs and can be conscious or unconscious. Countertransference may include emotional dysregulation and subjective awareness or perceptions of the client or the therapist–client exchange. Rigid boundaries are less likely to result in countertransference. In some cases, the therapist's awareness of the need for rigid boundaries may be therapeutic and appropriate in response to emotionally laden interactions. This need is not tied to countertransference.

113. B: When a therapist has an unplanned leave of absence due to illness and cannot provide alternate arrangements for his clients, this would most likely constitute client abandonment. Therapists must provide arrangements for clients during interruptions such as training, vacations, or illness to prevent client abandonment or neglect. These arrangements are reviewed and provided preemptively during informed consent. Therapists are ethically mandated to terminate and refer clients who are outside of their scope of competency. It is appropriate for therapists in private practice and other settings to terminate therapy with a client due to a lack of payment for

166

services rendered. Financial agreements are part of the informed consent process and must be agreed upon before the start of treatment. Terminating client services after the client became threatening and violent is appropriate and would generally not constitute abandonment.

114. C: A couple in the final stage of emotionally focused therapy for couples (EFT) is now ready to facilitate appropriate solutions and consolidate cycles of secure attachment. EFT is an evidence-based practice (EBP) for couples experiencing relationship distress. EFT is presented in three stages: deescalation, bonding, and consolidation of change. In the deescalation stage, the therapist, rather than the couple, assists with emotional deescalation to avoid the cycle of emotional distress. The second stage is characterized by restructuring core emotional experiences to develop a secure bond. The second stage is also marked by couples developing an understanding that distress is cyclical, self-reinforced, and stems from insecure attachment.

115. D: Therapists must be cognizant of the influence of social and cultural factors on personal space, nonverbal interactions, and attitudes toward therapy. An individual's verbal and nonverbal congruence do not vary from culture to culture; however, therapists must be aware of underlying cultural norms associated with both forms of communication to appropriately assign meaning to incongruent communication. Social and cultural factors are influenced by personal space in that cultural norms dictate acceptable degrees of physical separation between individuals in various roles and relationships. Nonverbal interactions are influenced by social and cultural factors, with some nonverbal interactions signifying respect in some cultures and disrespect in others. Attitudes toward therapy are influenced by social and cultural factors, particularly for those in nondominant racial and ethnic groups, in which negative attitudes toward mental health treatment are often the result of inequitable access to health care and the poorer quality of care received.

116. A: A strategic family therapist would respond by providing directives to reduce the father's symptoms and their impact on the family. What sets strategic family therapy apart is the emphasis on reducing client symptoms to change the family dynamics. Structural family therapists (SFTs) focus on changing the family's structure rather than the father's symptoms. SFTs would use the technique of unbalancing to align with the father and increase his power within the family. SFTs would also determine the father's position and role in the hierarchal subsystem. A solution-focused brief therapy (SFBT) therapist would determine what works best when the father's moods become problematic.

117. C: The Outcome Questionnaire (OQ-45.2) uses three subscales (symptom distress, interpersonal relations, and social role) to measure client progress. The OQ-45.2 is a formal instrument designed to measure client progress on an ongoing basis and after termination. The Beck Depression Inventory (BDI) measures behavioral symptoms and attitudes associated with depression using somatic and affective subscales. The BDI is helpful for periodically measuring symptom severity in clients diagnosed with depression. The Child Behavior Checklist has 11 subscales used to identify emotional and behavioral problems in children and adolescents. The Structured Interview of Reported Symptoms is a 172-item assessment used to detect the deliberate feigning of self-reported mental disorders.

118. C: Coalitions are an example of a family configuration that is considered dysfunctional. Coalitions occur when two or more family members form a covert alliance used to team up against another family member. Coalitions can be temporary or long lasting and are often formed across generational boundaries. SFTs identify several forms of family configurations, including coalitions, subsystems, and hierarchies. Subsystems consist of two or more family members (e.g., parents, children). Hierarchies are composed of subsystems that are arranged based on the power that each subsystem or family member holds. Subsystems and hierarchies can be functional or dysfunctional.

In functional families, there are clear boundaries between hierarchies and subsystems. Coalitions are always dysfunctional. Scapegoats are family members who are consistently blamed for family problems. Scapegoating is dysfunctional; however, it does not represent a family configuration.

119. C. The AAMFT Code of Ethics (2015) explicitly prohibits sexual intimacy with current clients or known members of the client's family system (Standard 1.4), former clients or known members of the former client's family system (Standard 1.5), and students or supervisees during the evaluative or training relationship between the therapist and student or supervisee (Standard 4.3). Because former students and known family members are not in an evaluative or training relationship with the therapist, sexual intimacy is not explicitly prohibited.

120. A: These factors may be detrimental to client care if the therapist experiences countertransference. Personal issues, life experiences, and value systems can contaminate the therapeutic relationship when boundaries become blurred and objectivity is lost. For this reason, MFTs are responsible for attending to any personal life situation that may be detrimental to client care (e.g., experiences of trauma, grief, and loss) and seek assistance when work performance and decision making are affected. Countertransference originates with the therapist and is a reaction to the client's transference; therefore, sexualized transference is incorrect because it originates with the client rather than with the therapist. There is a risk of client exploitation when boundaries become blurred; however, because of the power differential and the therapist's influential position, the therapist would not be in danger of experiencing exploitation. Nonresponse bias is an unrelated research concept that occurs when responders from a sample vary significantly from nonresponders (e.g., those who returned a survey vs. those who did not).

121. A: The Stalking Prevention, Awareness, and Resource Center endorses an SLII stalking framework developed by T.K. Logan (2017). The acronym SLII stands for surveillance, life invasion, intimidation, and interference. Surveillance involves watching and following the victim. Life invasion describes nonconsensual appearances in the victim's life, including sending gifts, initiating contact with a third person, or showing up unannounced. Intimidation consists of in-person or online threats, blackmail, or open verbal attacks. Finally, interference describes interfering in various aspects of the victim's life; damaging property; or assaulting friends, pets, or family members.

122. B: The therapist's first action would be to seek consultation and supervision. The therapist was a victim of stalking while in college. Stalking is a pattern of behavior resulting from unwanted pursuit and attention. Victims of stalking often experience fear, intimidation, harassment, unwanted attention, and harm. Seeking consultation and supervision would help the therapist remain objective. The severity of the therapist's college experience and the fact that there is a solid therapeutic alliance indicate that the therapist is at risk for countertransference. Because the key element for victims of stalking is fear, contacting the police is not presently indicated. The client reports multiple instances occurring at her work, which could be part of a behavioral pattern; however, the client reports feeling irritable and sad rather than fearful. Consultation and supervision could help the therapist discern an appropriate risk assessment for the client. Initiating a referral to another therapist is not the best first choice because the client and therapist have formed a working alliance. Sharing her previous experience is not advisable because there is a risk of overidentification, which could overwhelm the client.

123. D: Outpatient therapists can safeguard themselves from dangerous clients by using appropriate deescalation techniques. Techniques may include encouraging clients to move to an area where others can readily assist; however, physically escorting a client would likely increase the client's agitation and place the therapist at increased risk. Instead, therapists can safeguard themselves by sitting or positioning themselves between the client and the door, validating feelings, allowing the client to vent without interruption, and communicating clearly and concisely (e.g., use the "broken record" technique).

124. C: To determine how the family life cycle impacts problem formation, therapists seek to understand how families navigate marriage, childbearing, and empty nesting. The family's life cycle is developmental and involves such milestones as the birth of a child, children leaving home, and the death of family members. Although employment is not a transitional stage of development, retirement is viewed as part of the family life cycle. The therapist's goal is to ascertain how well families change and adapt during these cycles, which brings insight to the client's problem formation, maintenance, and resolution.

125. D: The MFT should answer questions and attend to the client's expectations about the treatment process before continuing the evaluation. Clients must enter into a therapeutic relationship with a proper understanding of expectations, the nature of therapy, and the limitations of confidentiality at the beginning of therapy (AAMFT, 2015, Standard 2). Although the client has the right to autonomously make treatment decisions, explaining that she can discontinue at any time may be perceived as dismissive and not a complete representation of a proper consent to treatment. Explaining to the client that today's session is limited to information gathering does not address the client's right to informed consent. Providing the client with written material does not ensure that the client understands the process. As part of informed consent, the therapist must allow the client to ask questions regarding confidentiality and the nature of therapy at any given time in treatment.

126. C: Social stratification is sustained by societal beliefs. Social stratification refers to the hierarchal classification of separate groups or classes of people whose ranks are determined by unequal distributions of power, wealth, and success. Societal beliefs dictate who is entitled to power, resources, rights, privileges, and responsibilities. Meritocracy is the belief that social stratification results from hard work and merit and that social rank is determined solely through perseverance. Because several factors determine hierarchal rankings, a meritocratic society is an ideal rather than being attainable. For these reasons, social stratification is not a reflection of personal effort or merit, is transgenerational, and reflects societal rather than individual differences.

127. D: Psychological abuse, formerly designated as psychological aggression, is a form of IPV identified by the CDC and characterized by gaslighting and controlling a victim's reproductive health. The CDC's *Intimate Partner Violence Surveillance: Uniform Definitions and Recommended Data Elements, Version 2.0* (2015) includes updates reflecting how psychological aggression is defined, expanding the definition to include "control of reproductive or sexual health," "gaslighting," and "exploitation of vulnerability." Physical violence encompasses acts that include intentional force (e.g., hitting, biting, coercion, restraining) with the potential to result in various degrees of harm (e.g., death, injury). The CDC breaks down sexual violence into the following five categories: (1) rape or penetration of a victim, (2) a victim forced to penetrate another person, (3) nonphysically pressuring a victim to experience unwanted penetration, (4) unwanted sexual contact, and (5) unwanted sexual experiences with no contact (e.g., made to watch pornography). Stalking or cyberstalking involves unwanted attention or contact, resulting in fear of one's safety, the safety of their property, and/or the safety of their pet.

128. D: Critical incident stress management (CISM) begins with an appointed leader who aims to disseminate factual information, reduce chaos, and identify resources and coping strategies in a process known as crisis management briefing. CISM uses a structured approach in response to traumatic events, including, but not limited to, community-wide violence, natural disasters, a coworker's or client's death, and witnessing mass casualties. Defusing, another component of CISM, is used to address a group of individuals involved in the same crisis. The goals of defusing are to lessen the impact of the incident, enhance recovery, and determine specific group needs. Deescalation is a technique that can be implemented during the critical incident stress debriefing response to help victims with overwhelming emotions. Critical incident stress debriefing, an element of CISM, is used within the first 72 hours of the traumatic event to help victims process the incident and identify group members needing more intensive interventions. Critical incident stress debriefing is not a form of therapy, but a blend of supportive assistance, psychoeducation, and a means to identify victims exhibiting more severe signs of distress.

129. C: A therapist using motivational interviewing (MI) might respond by stating, "You feel hopeless—like this is familiar territory. You're wondering if your investment in Jude's therapy will pay off." This is an example of rolling with resistance. Rolling with resistance is an MI principle that typically manifests as discounting the therapist's expertise, arguing, blaming, or expressing negativity about the possibility of change. The correct response accurately reflects the mother's feelings and reframes the mother's resistance as fear of losing therapeutic gains. The response: "You sound discouraged. I'm wondering if Jude can tell the family how things will be different this go-around" is incorrect because MI advocates against the "righting reflex," which is the tendency for therapists to provide advice or use persuasion when advocating change. The response: "Thinking about ending treatment is difficult. It's been my experience that teens like Jude usually do quite well when they say they are ready" is also incorrect because the therapist assumes an expert role, which MI discourages. Lastly, "You've been here before and think that it has been a waste of time" is incorrect because although it does apply a core principle of MI, which is to express empathy through skillful reflective listening, the therapist simply responded by using the mother's exact words instead of reflecting a deeper understanding.

130. A: Conditions of bartering are included in Standard 8.5 of the AAMFT Code of Ethics (2015), which indicates that bartering is not a common practice; however, it may be ethically sound if it meets all of the following conditions: "(a) the supervisee or client requests it; (b) the relationship is not exploitative; (c) the professional relationship is not distorted; and (d) a clear written contract is established."

131. D: The therapist's best course of action would be to provide reference materials to the client to help him make a well-informed decision. The client has limited English proficiency, and his family believes the myth that antidepressants are addictive. The therapist provides reference materials to the client to assist with health literacy. In 2021, the Centers for Disease Control and Prevention (CDC) redefined health literacy on a personal and organizational level, noting that both entities must take the necessary steps to ensure that individuals understand and use health-related information. Therapists also provide and verbally review reference materials that are culturally and linguistically appropriate. Because there is no known suicidal ideation, a safety contract would not best address the client's current needs. Supporting client autonomy would only occur after the client has received information that is culturally and linguistically appropriate. Inviting the family to discuss the benefits of medication is secondary to improving the client's health literacy, and the conversation should cover the associated benefits and risks of antidepressant medications.

132. B: The MFT adheres to Standard 2.3 of the AAMFT Code of Ethics (2015) by correctly telling the son that he cannot access the records unless the father provides written authorization permitting him to do so. With the limited information provided, the father is likely the identified client because he has an established diagnosis and he depends on his sons for help. Because the father is the primary client, the sons serve in collateral roles. Collateral support persons are usually a client's spouse, partner, family member, or friend involved in the client's treatment. At the outset of therapy, MFTs are responsible for explaining that collaterals do not have the same privacy and confidentiality rights as the client; therefore, collaterals do not have access to client records. Clients can sign an authorization to permit a collateral's access to client records, but authorization would not be required for the sons and the father. The client, not the son, could be limited with access to the records in rare exceptions, including concern on behalf of the MFT that access could cause serious harm to the client.

133. C: A family therapist blending an individual treatment model with a systemic approach would likely adhere to a psychodynamic theoretical orientation. Psychodynamic theory views maladaptive behavior as being the result of intrapersonal and interpersonal conflict. One method for addressing intrapersonal conflict is to explore attachment from an object-relations standpoint. Psychodynamic therapists view interpersonal conflict as an individual's interactions with their family or societal systems. Strategic family therapists emphasize the role of family communication and interactions in determining maladaptive behavior. Behavioral therapists reject the psychodynamic notion that intrapsychic processes underlie psychopathology. Structural family therapists (SFTs) assert that maladaptive behavior results from inflexible communication among family members.

134. C: The structural family therapist (SFT) is using the technique of unbalancing, in which the SFT uses his or her own authority to briefly join with an individual or subgroup with the goal of disrupting the family dynamics. Once the family dynamics are disrupted, the SFT then begins to reorganize the family in a manner that reflects healthy boundaries. SFTs also use the technique of manipulating space, which involves physically rearranging family members from their original seating locations. Bowenian family therapists use triangulation to describe instances in which an additional person enters an established dyadic relationship to stabilize the family system. Reframing, another SFT technique, is used to help clients shift their perspective of the problem so it may be viewed in a more positive light.

135. A: Social cognitive theory is grounded in the assumption that it is possible to learn appropriate ways to self-regulate—that expressions of anger are not inherited, fixed, or static. Anger management strategies grounded in social cognitive theory conceptualize clients as individuals capable of learning appropriate behaviors by developing an awareness of cues and triggers, learning appropriate communication skills, and implementing relaxation to decrease physiological and reactionary responses. Cognitive learning theory posits that learning occurs through mental constructs (e.g., thinking, attending). Behavioral learning theory emphasizes the role of association (i.e., classical conditioning) and reinforcement (i.e., operant conditioning). The role of punishment (i.e., operant conditioning) is also emphasized with behavioral learning theory. Lawrence Kohlberg's theory of moral development is based on the premise that moral development is a staged process beginning in childhood and ending for some in late adolescence or adulthood.

136. C: Standard 3.9 of the AAMFT Code of Ethics (2015) states: "Marriage and family therapists attend to cultural norms when considering whether to accept or give gifts to clients. Marriage and family therapists consider the potential effects that receiving or giving gifts may have on clients and on the integrity and efficacy of the therapeutic relationship." Client autonomy refers to the client's right to make decisions and the therapist's role in exploring the consequences of those decisions. Although the provisions of informed consent vary, it generally requires that the client is capable of understanding information related to the purpose, risks, and benefits of therapy. During informed consent, the MFT may broadly address the boundaries of the professional relationship, but gift giving is not a necessary component of this process. The limits of confidentiality do not include gift giving.

137. B: Therapists conducting teletherapy sessions continually assess the appropriateness of service delivery without consideration of the therapist's professional needs. Teletherapy guidelines suggest that therapists continually assess and examine the client's risks and benefits, the influence of the client's and therapist's cultural differences, and the most appropriate mediums (e.g., phone, video) for service delivery. A therapist's professional and personal needs should not supersede the client's needs. Therapists remain attuned to cultural differences and the impact these differences may have on nonverbal cues and cultural biases, expectations, and norms (e.g., refraining from multitasking during teletherapy video sessions).

138. A: Individuals with a history of anxiety would be candidates whose agreement to participate would be ethically sound. Standard 5.3 of the AAMFT Code of Ethics (2015) requests that MFTs be sensitive to diminished consent when "participants are also receiving clinical services, have impairments which limit understanding and/or communication, or when participants are children."

139. C: Rational emotive behavior therapy (REBT) is based on the assumption that irrational or self-defeating beliefs help the client stay "stuck" and serve as barriers to change. REBT uses the "ABCDE" model to identify irrational thoughts (A = the activating event, B = the belief, C = the consequence, D = disputing the unhealthy belief, and E = the effect of the process). Behavioral activation involves engaging in valued activities to change emotions and is often paired with cognitive restructuring as an evidence-based practice (EBP) for depression. Cognitive processing theory (CPT) is an EBP for PTSD that challenges belief systems related to experiences of trauma. Examples of CPT techniques include psychoeducation, Socratic questioning, and modifying unhealthy, trauma-related beliefs. Acceptance and commitment therapy (ACT) is different from other cognitive theories in that it focuses on accepting all thoughts as they are without trying to change them. ACT is coupled with mindfulness and behavioral strategies to evoke lasting change.

140. A: One of the primary elements of Eastern philosophies/religions is an emphasis on collectivism rather than individualism. Western philosophies/religions emphasize individualism, logical or practical elements, and external achievement, and they are linear or goal oriented; whereas Eastern philosophies/religions are spiritual and value inner improvement, and their goals are never-ending.

141. A: An appropriate short-term treatment goal would be for the client to identify times when her mother would likely complain but did not. One way in which SFBT goals are formulated involves looking for exceptions. The therapist uses a strengths-based approach with the client collaborating on treatment plan goals based on the assumption that no problems can occur at all times. Looking for exceptions involves noticing times when the problems could have happened but did not, with or without the client's intentions. CBT would be associated with dysfunctional thoughts. Narrative therapy uses techniques to help clients develop alternative, blame-free narratives. Identifying maladaptive interactional patterns is a systems-based technique focused on problem solving rather than SFBT's solution building.

142. D: Therapists assess the family's previous attempts to resolve the presenting problem to determine protective factors, interactional patterns, and motivation to change. Therapists determine whether the client is appropriate for therapy during the initial screening process. Assessing protective factors helps the therapist understand the family's resiliency, which is helpful feedback for a family in distress. Finally, therapists assess the families' interactional patterns to determine hierarchies, alliances, coalitions, norms, roles, and tasks unique to the family system.

143. B: Assessment is to formulation as analysis is to synthesis. During the initial intake and throughout the course of therapy, therapists conduct assessments by gathering information from the family and collaborative sources. That information is analyzed and synthesized to help formulate a case conceptualization (i.e., formulation). Rudi Dallos and Ros Draper (2010) propose systemic assessment elements, including problem deconstruction; contextual factors; and the family's beliefs and explanations, problem-maintaining patterns and feedback loops, and emotions and attachments. Elements of formulation include the therapist's consideration of their own beliefs and assumptions, wider contextual factors, collaboration with outside sources and treatment teams, and therapist engagement.

144. B: Urie Bronfenbrenner is known for the human ecology systems theory and the human ecological framework, in which the mesosystem is the bidirectional system representing the interaction between the child's home and school. The ecological systems are interactional and bidirectional, with each system mutually influencing the other. The microsystem is closest to the individual and is composed of systems in a person's immediate surroundings, including the family, school, church, and community. The mesosystem describes the interaction of those systems and their relationship with one another. The kindergartener's behavior at school and his home life represent the mesosystem. An ecosystem refers to settings that are external to a person but have an indirect influence. An example of an ecosystem for a child would be a parent's workplace. A chronosystem describes the patterns of events and changes in a person's life and their influence over time.

145. B: Family systems theorists understand psychopathology as a manifestation of relational dynamics illustrated by the following: Behavior A influences behavior B, which in turn influences behavior A. This best illustrates the circular dynamics inherent in family systems theory. Circular dynamics originate from mutually interdependent systems that begin and end at the same point. Viewing behavior A as influencing behavior B, which in turn influences behavior C represents linear, rather than circular, causation. Viewing psychopathology as behavior A influencing behavior B, which in turn influences behavior B is incorrect because behavior B cannot influence behavior B, nor can it influence behavior A, B, and C because there is no C with circular causation. Circular causality involves a feedback loop comprising a chain of causes and effects that return back to the original cause as either altered or reinforced. Circular causality suggests that the client system is a manifestation of interactions described as mutually interdependent and nonsequential.

146. A: A client with chronic anxiety would be best suited for teletherapy. Although all individuals are different, opportunities may be limited to clients who engage in substance misuse or self-injury and those with cognitive impairment. Clients with chronic anxiety may be a better fit as treatment primarily consists of cognitive-behavioral therapy (CBT). CBT homework assignments can be completed using synchronous (e.g., live video sessions) and asynchronous (e.g., text, email) methods of service delivery.

147. D: Researchers have found that the sole use of informal instruments to measure outcomes and process is correlated with therapists overestimating client progress and the strength of the therapeutic alliance. Research indicates that therapists overestimate the frequency and consistency with which client check-ins are performed. Studies also show that therapists are overconfident when using clinical judgment alone to gauge the therapeutic process and client progress. For these reasons, it is advisable to use formal and informal measures. Client-initiated termination can happen for various reasons, including meeting treatment plan goals, not connecting with the therapist, or being poorly motivated to continue. Although use of informal measures may lead to client dissatisfaction, this outcome is less frequent than the therapist's overestimation of therapeutic gains. Therapist-initiated termination due to client dissatisfaction is less likely because therapists tend to be overconfident in their estimations of success when informally evaluating the therapeutic process and outcomes. Using informal measures alone results in therapists rather than clients overestimating client progress and the strength of the therapeutic alliance.

148. A: Piaget believed that children learn and develop through assimilation, accommodation, and adaption. Conservation is a concrete operation (rather than a process) that is learned between the ages of 7 and 11. Children demonstrate knowledge of conservation when understanding that something has the same quantity even when its appearance changes. Conservation is a task, whereas assimilation, accommodation, and adaptation are all processes that children use to learn and develop. Assimilation is used when applying previously known concepts to new ones. Accommodation happens when children alter previously learned concepts upon receipt of new information. Finally, adaptation is a process that uses assimilation and accommodation to help individuals meet changing circumstances and situations.

149. D: A family systems relational hypothesis would place primary emphasis on rigid boundaries. A family systems hypothesis considers the entire family when making an educated guess about their level of functioning. Assumptions are based on family structures, including interactional patterns involving hierarchies, coalitions, alliances, rules, norms, and tasks. Boundaries within a family structure determine subsystems and can be either enmeshed/diffuse or rigid/disengaged. Rigid boundaries occur when expressing and meeting emotional needs become challenging. Family systems hypotheses are nonpathologizing, which excludes attributions of blame. Hypotheses include inferences based on the interpersonal rather than intrapsychic process. Hypotheses reflect circular rather than linear communication patterns, with linear patterns reflecting a one-way message between the sender and receiver.

150. B: Virginia Satir believed that individuals whose self-worth and self-value are determined by the attention and approval of family members exhibit the communication style of the placater. Satir used communication stances to illustrate how family members interact under stress. The placater is characterized by people pleasing and can become codependent on the identified client within the family structure. Placaters often take the blame to protect other family members from being held accountable. Satir describes the blamer as the family member who lashes out in anger to hide feeling unworthy or unwanted. The super-reasonable family member remains detached and calm. The irrelevant family member uses distraction or silliness to avoid unpleasant emotions. The irrelevant is likely the youngest sibling who will act silly to divert attention away from the problem.

151. C: Risk factors for medication-related psychiatric side effects (e.g., psychosis, confusion) include a past or present history of a mental disorder, increased age, use of multiple medications, and use of central nervous system-active medications (e.g., tricyclic antidepressants, traditional antipsychotics).

152. D: This intervention is not designed to reduce emotional reactivity. The intervention described is an enactment. SFTs use enactments to decentralize the therapist, identify circular interactional patterns, and understand overlearned (i.e., patterned) behaviors. Bowenian therapists use strategies to reduce emotional reactivity. SFTs are more concerned with understanding structural problems, which may require enacting emotionally laden interactions. The therapist can then help families change interactions that keep families stuck in their original structure.

153. B: Compared to no-harm contracts, safety plans differ in that safety plans include a prioritized list of coping strategies and resources to lessen imminent risk. Safety plans consist of a documented list of actions that an individual can take to help keep them safe in the presence of known or possible danger, including suicidality. Effective safety plans are collaborative, brief, easy to read, and written in the client's own words. Studies show that no-harm contracts are ineffective for various reasons, including the tendency for therapists to use no-harm contracts as a replacement for a more in-depth assessment and intervention. Safety plans do not include signed promises indicating that the client will refrain from self-harm. Neither safety plans nor no-harm contracts offer legal protections for the therapist and generally do not include provisions for clients with limited decision-making capacity.

154. C: Peer specialists who partner with adult clients with severe mental illness and co-occurring disorders are found to reduce crisis-related incidents through the provision of strengths-based services to help promote and sustain recovery. Peer support specialists are individuals in recovery who provide strengths-based, person-centered, and trauma-informed care and supportive services. They provide a shared experience in recovery from mental disorders and/or substance use disorders. Although a by-product of peer support is often improved interpersonal relationships, peer support is designed to complement rather than duplicate clinical services. Peer support is provided directly to the client instead of the client's social network. Peer support specialists foster self-empowerment and skill building, but they are not volunteers: Peer support specialists receive certification and training and are paid to provide supportive community-based services.

155. D: The therapist's best response would be: "Having a gay therapist is important to you. Can you help me understand more about that?" The therapist's "best" response considers that it is an initial interview. An overarching goal of the initial interview session is to build a therapeutic alliance. This involves the therapist taking a nonjudgmental stance by showing empathy, unconditional positive regard, and genuineness. Nonjudgmental attitudes are those in which clients feel validated, understood, and free to be their authentic selves. It is also the goal of the therapist to clarify expectations about the nature of counseling. The "best" answer validates the client's concern and seeks to understand the importance of a gay therapist from the client's standpoint. Listing the general qualities of a therapist does not validate the importance of having a gay therapist. Providing the client with a list of referrals is premature because the client may only require reassurance that the therapist can understand the client's life experiences. Asking to check back in after a couple of sessions may be received as dismissive rather than validating the client's immediate request.

156. B: Successful termination is not characterized by processing termination less frequently as the time grows nearer. Instead, termination should be discussed more frequently as the time grows nearer. Adequate time is necessary for clients to process the end of the therapeutic relationship and to have any final discussions on their readiness for termination. Other therapist-initiated actions that characterize successful termination include discussing termination at the initial intake as part of informed consent, selecting measurable criteria marking the end of therapy, and reviewing therapeutic gains and the end of the relationship.

157. B: Stratification theory explains that elder abuse originates from caregivers whose jobs are low in pay, lack prestige, and are necessary for survival. Additionally, affected caregivers with low job satisfaction attempt to control the elder, which, the theory contends, leads to abuse. Social exchange theory posits that each person in a relationship gives and receives items of value, and the exchange benefits both parties. When the elder's dependency on the caretaker creates an imbalanced dynamic, abusive behavior occurs. Symbolic interactionism theory explains that abuse is the result of cultural beliefs and interactions. What is abusive in some cultures (e.g., out-of-home placement) is not in others. Political economic theory asserts that elders lose their position in the family and society through marginalization as they lose their role as an independent provider.

158. A: Crisis interventions vary from traditional psychotherapy in that crisis interventions are time limited. In general, crisis intervention takes place over the course of 6–8 sessions. The primary goals of crisis intervention are to stabilize the client, reduce crisis-related symptoms, and help the client return to a precrisis level of functioning. Clients who exceed those parameters are generally referred for continued care. Crisis interventions focus on current life events, address acute symptoms and patterns of behavior, and are developed after obtaining enough information to determine the client's current level of risk.

159. D: Of the described circumstances, addressing developmental life cycles and their impact on the client system would not necessitate a referral for a psychiatric evaluation. A family's developmental life cycle includes transitional stages (e.g., the birth of a child, children leaving home) that generally occur in all families. Circumstances that may necessitate a psychiatric referral include treating severe symptoms causing functional impairment, addressing symptoms that have not responded to psychotherapy, and ruling out any medical etiology responsible for the client's symptoms.

160. D: A family systems therapist's hypothesis facilitates change within a family system. Family systems therapists do not use hypotheses as a definitive determination of family dysfunction, nor are hypotheses used to offer a complex, finite understanding of the family system. Instead, the primary purpose of the hypothesis is to inspire change, even if the hypothesis is inaccurate. Rather than a deficit-based formulation model, family systems theorists base the hypothesis on patterns of interactions among family members. Hypotheses are also used to posit assumptions based on the family members' attachment, power, or relevant cultural and community influences. From this position, the therapist can begin to engage in circular questioning and continue to reject or refine hypotheses on an ongoing basis.

161. B: Contextual therapy emphasizes the relational ethics of fairness, trust, and loyalty. Ivan Boszormenyi-Nagy is credited with developing contextual therapy, which is based on the assumption that family dysfunction occurs as the result of a lack of accountability and subjective partiality. Narrative therapists work to uncover socially constructed stories that contribute to a family's or individual's subjugated narrative (e.g., stories grounded in cultural beliefs and values). SFBT focuses on the resiliency and strengths of an individual or family as a whole. Finally, existential therapy posits that each individual eventually faces death, suffering, and guilt (i.e., the "tragic triad").

162. B: For first-generation immigrants, intergenerational differences in acculturation have the potential to disrupt hierarchical subsystems. Families with first-generation immigrants tend to experience gaps in acculturation, with children adapting to the mainstream culture at faster rates than their parents, causing a shift within the parental subsystem. Intergenerational differences are likely to produce negative feedback loops as change is rejected and the family system attempts to stay the same. Coalitions, by nature, are covert and tend to be unaffected by family differences in acculturation. Intergenerational differences are more likely to affect hierarchical subsystems than sibling subsystems.

163. D: The toxic stress response remains activated even when apparent harm is absent. Toxic stress is experienced in childhood with multiple causes, including abuse, neglect, poverty, violence, trauma, or food insecurity. Toxic stress is cumulative and is shown to increase a person's lifetime risk for mental and physical health problems. The effects of toxic stress can be prevented or reversed when children become cared for by nurturing, engaging, and stable adults. Toxic stress is chronic and prolonged rather than acute and time limited. Toxic stress does not follow the same trajectory as other stressors, which end with recovery and rest. Instead, the sympathetic nervous system is in overdrive and remains activated, even when the stressor is not present.

164. A: A child and adolescent family therapist would identify school and community supports to help engage teens in treatment and keep them actively involved. School and community supports include, but are not limited to, coaches, teachers, 12-step recovery programs, and/or religious or spiritual leaders. Locating appropriate employment opportunities may benefit some teens, but it would not necessarily lead to engagement and continued involvement in therapy. Behavioral contracts may have some initial benefit in engaging clients in therapy but are less likely to elicit continued involvement. Although allowing teens to control certain aspects of their therapy may reduce dropout rates, the therapist determines the length and duration of treatment based on each client's individual needs.

165. A: Therapists do not provide concurrent psychotherapy to client collaterals. The therapist is responsible for helping the client and the client collateral contacts understand their purposes and roles. Collateral contacts are individuals in the client's life who meet with the client and therapist to better ensure postdischarge progress, help modify the client's treatment plan, and assist with identifying community supports for the client. Collateral support systems can include friends, family, and other significant client support persons who are invested in the client's care.

166. A: Research findings suggest that same-sex couples experiencing discrimination have higher instances of adverse behavioral health outcomes. Researchers have found that the overall health and well-being of children with same-sex parents do not differ from children with opposite-sex parents in cognitive development, academic achievement, social adjustment, and self-esteem. Divorce rates are lowest among Hispanic and Asian couples than non-Hispanic and African-American couples. Cohabitating couples report lower levels of relationship satisfaction than married couples.

167. A: Guided by the principles of recovery, the therapist should empower the client to continue with his self-directed recovery. Inspired by the widely circulated Center for Substance Abuse Treatment's *National Summit on Recovery Conference Report* (2005), a working definition of recovery and recovery principles emerged and was adopted by the Substance Abuse and Mental Health Services Administration. Some of the guiding principles of recovery assert that recovery is self-directed and empowering, emerges from gratitude and hope, exists on a continuum, addresses associated stigma and shame, involves personal recognition for change, and is holistic. The client is in early sobriety and beginning to feel hopeful about recovery. At this stage, shame-based interactions are likely to impede the client's growth, contributing to the therapist's choice of empowering the client with his self-directed recovery. Encouraging the client to take responsibility for his actions and make appropriate amends is not associated with the principles of recovery and may be premature at 30 days of sobriety. Enacting transactional communication patterns is a structural family therapy technique that may help redirect communication from the parents to the client and is less likely to reflect adherence to recovery principles.

168. C: Mindfulness is found to enhance relapse prevention by helping clients acknowledge present-moment internal experiences without judging them as good or bad. The relapse-prevention model is a cognitive-behavioral approach designed to equip clients with the skills required to appropriately identify internal (e.g., thoughts) and external (e.g., triggers, cues) experiences that place them at a greater risk for relapse. Through mindfulness, clients are taught to monitor present-moment emotions and sensations without judging or acting on them, thus improving responses to internal and external triggers. Transcendence is the state of existence that defies or goes beyond normal understanding or limits. Emotion regulation is the ability of an individual to use techniques to monitor or regulate the intensity and duration of an emotional response. Finally, differential association is a theory used to explain how a person's behavior is influenced by their social network, particularly among members whose interactions are prolonged.

169. A: This is an example of a double bind. Gregory Bateson was among the first family therapy theorists; he used the term double bind to explain the confusion that occurs when two contradictory messages are conveyed and one party is unable to escape from the relationship in which it occurs. Bateson asserted that the confusion resulting from the double bind is associated with schizophrenia. Need complementarity is a theory of mate selection among couples; it suggests that each partner is attracted to a person with opposite complementary needs. The conflictual cocoon is a Bowenian concept used to describe repetitive and cyclical patterns of behavior among intimate partners characterized by episodes of closeness, conflict, and distance. The "cocoon" refers to the protection this dynamic offers from spilling over into involvement with the couple's children. Parentification refers to role reversal between a parent and child, in which the child takes on the role of the parent. When this occurs, the parentified child becomes responsible for managing and caring for a parent or sibling.

170. B: This is an example of a therapeutic rupture. Therapeutic ruptures occur as the result of a broken therapeutic alliance, and they happen when there is a communication breakdown. This can manifest in client withdrawal or confrontation. The daughter's response illustrates withdrawal or disengagement from the therapist, which may occur as a means of coping with the daughter's conflicting needs for autonomy and relatedness. Research indicates that repairing therapeutic ruptures enriches the therapeutic alliance. Emotional cutoff refers to families becoming emotionally disengaged from one another in the presence of unresolved conflict. Triangulation occurs when two family members bring another person into their conflict. Unbalancing is a therapeutic intervention involving the therapist briefly joining with a family member or subgroup to disrupt the existing family dynamics.

171. A: Virginia Satir developed the Satir model, which promotes four meta goals: increase self-esteem, enhance decision-making skills, increase responsibility, and foster congruence. Satir believed that these four goals enhance the therapist–client relationship and prepare therapists to embark on a lifelong journey of transformation. This transformation involves therapists initially experiencing congruence within themselves so that it can be recognized in others (e.g., clients). Satir expanded on this notion by identifying the "third level of congruence," which involves inner harmony and a deeper connection with God, life energy, and spirituality. Her model encourages therapist grow and development of "the self of the therapist."

172. C: The use of standardized instruments would be least effective for the therapist in this situation. Although standardized instruments help provide valid and reliable data, their weakness is that they are prone to cultural bias. Hispanic/Latinx clients tend to experience greater degrees of stigma regarding mental health and may not be as forthcoming as their Caucasian counterparts. Hispanic/Latinx clients may also use somatic experiences to describe their emotions. Informal or nonstandardized instruments would help the therapist build rapport and monitor client progress. Examples of informal assessments include scaling questions, mental status exams (MSEs), and unstructured clinical interviews. Scaling questions are informal measures that allow clients to rate various aspects of their treatment, including motivational level, priorities, and progress using a 1–10 Likert scale. MSEs rely on informal methods, such as the therapist's observations, to obtain client measures and can be used through treatment. Unstructured clinical interviews would enable the therapist to build rapport and inquire about the influence of the client's culture on the presenting problem.

173. B: The client is likely experiencing a situational crisis. Situational crises are unexpected and cause a person to experience functional impairment and psychological distress. Existential crises involve a person's anxiety about their life's choices and whether they have accomplished all that they would have liked to in life. Existential crises are related to a person's sense of identity and existence, and their cause is often internal. Maturational or developmental crises are those experienced during transitional life events (e.g., puberty, moving away from home). An adventitious crisis occurs as the result of "events of disaster," including, but not limited to, acts of terrorism, global pandemics, fires, wars, floods, and violent crimes.

174. C: Financial exploitation is a form of elder abuse and not a form of child abuse. There are multiple reasons why victims of elder abuse do not report abuse, one of which is their financial dependency on the caregiver, particularly informal caregivers (e.g., unpaid family members or friends providing protection and care). Forms of elder and child abuse include neglect, sexual abuse, and psychological or emotional abuse.

175. C: Measurement-based care (MBC) is most effective when it is used to create a dialogue with the client regarding progress and the therapeutic process. MBC is an EBP used before or during a clinical encounter to obtain regular feedback and inform treatment. MBC is also used to obtain baseline and termination measures, as well as provide measures to third-party payers. However, the effectiveness of ongoing progress monitoring lies in applying the data in real time to aid client progress. Documenting the efficacy of the therapist's treatment approach is insufficient. Instead, documenting a discussion with a client on the efficacy of a therapist's treatment approach is what is most effective.

176. C: The best action would be for the therapist to advocate for correct pronoun usage among hospital health providers. The therapist must validate emotions associated with being misgendered and take action to educate other health providers. There is potential for transphobic remarks to worsen the client's suicidality, which further necessitates the need for the therapist to advocate for transgender-affirming care. It would not be appropriate to assess for gender identity disorder because the DSM-5 eliminated that diagnosis and replaced it with gender dysphoria, which was maintained in the most recent update to DSM-5-TR. Assessing the client for gender dysphoria is not the best option because the client is seeking services for psychosis and suicidality. Gender dysphoria includes distress related to gender identity that some, but not all, transgender clients experience. Helping the client learn assertive responses when encountering transphobia is incorrect because it places the onus on the client, who likely remains in crisis.

177. C: Emotionally focused therapy (EFT) would best address the couple's presenting problems. EFT works to identify dysfunctional communication patterns and behaviors rooted in childhood attachment. Couples are encouraged to recognize the origins of these difficulties and discover ways to establish safe and secure connections with one another. SFBT is designed to help reinforce what couples are doing well and empower them to implement strategies based on identified strengths and skills. Narrative therapy can be used to help couples identify and rewrite stories rooted in cultural beliefs, norms, and values. Finally, strategic family therapy uses techniques such as reframing and paradoxical interventions to help couples and families solve problems in the present moment.

178. B: The MFT has an ethical responsibility to provide testimony on the mother's treatment for depression. The MFT is likely being called as a fact witness. Fact witnesses are asked to testify to their client's current condition and prognosis. Expert witnesses, on the other hand, have special skills or knowledge and would be called on to provide testimony on custody and reunification. An MFT cannot serve in the joint role of therapist and expert witness. Because the mother was seen for individual therapy, the MFT would not have sufficient evidence to provide testimony on the mother's parental fitness. If parenting was addressed in sessions, the MFT would still be ethically bound to offer testimony that is "accurate, objective, fair, and independent" (AAMFT, 2015, Standard 7.2). The MFT would be challenged to provide unbiased information on the mother's

179

parental fitness and an opinion on reunification, and even less so on the father, who is not the MFT's client.

179. C: The *Diagnostic and Statistical Manual of Mental Disorders*, Fifth Edition, Text Revision (DSM-5-TR) updates address the impact of social determinants on the diagnosis of mental disorders, with specific changes reflecting the influence of racial discrimination. When creating the DSM-5-TR, the American Psychiatric Association obtained input from multiple sources, including practitioners serving on the Ethnoracial Equity and Inclusion Work Group. The end product reflects the influence of social determinants of health, including factors such as education level, health-care access, social support, and socioeconomic status. Social determinants of health are influenced by structures in society that categorize individuals into social strata, with inequitable resources allocated to individuals who are not in power. The resultant oppression and marginalization are associated with an increased risk for early adverse experiences of trauma. Biomedical factors and the family life cycle are not included in the text updates for the DSM-5-TR. In addition, developmental trauma (i.e., multiple childhood traumas) is not currently included in the DSM-5; however, several experts in the field advocate for its inclusion.

180. C: Equifinality is the notion that in open family systems, the use of multiple methods and strategies has the potential to evoke the same outcome. In an open family system, therapists are encouraged to remain flexible with the methods chosen to evoke change because there are many ways to do so. Equanimity is a Buddhist concept used to describe a balanced mental state that remains neutral or nonreactive to all situations and circumstances. Similarly, equability describes a state of mind that is serene or is not easily disturbed. Equipotentiality is used in behavioralism to describe the process by which any two stimuli have the ability to make a paired association.

MFT Practice Test #2

1. Which one of the following statements is true of collateral contacts?

    a. They have a right to confidentiality and can assert privilege.

    b. They must sign an informed consent form to participate in therapy.

    c. They have access to the client's clinical notes.

    d. They serve in various predetermined roles.

2. Leo, a 26-year-old male with alcohol use disorder, attends therapy with his parents. The father demands that Leo "stop with the 'poor me' attitude, move out on his own, and experience some real-life consequences." The father also blames his wife for constantly rescuing Leo and neglecting her role in the marital relationship. Which one of the following options would best illustrate the family's conflictual interactions?

    a. Karpman's drama triangle.

    b. The Johari window.

    c. Maslow's hierarchy.

    d. Walker's cycle of violence.

3. The difference between valid and reliable measurement tools is best described as:

    a. Reliable instruments measure what is intended; valid instruments provide consistent results.

    b. Valid instruments measure what is intended; reliable instruments provide consistent results.

    c. The two terms are interchangeable, with no significant difference in meaning.

    d. Reliable instruments are easily used; valid instruments are accurate.

4. A client with anorexia nervosa and chronic depression presents for a crisis assessment due to a series of failed interpersonal relationships and thoughts of suicide. Which one of the following targeted interventions is specifically designed to treat problems of overcontrol (e.g., perfectionism, self-criticism) and enhance social connectedness?

    a. Acceptance and commitment therapy (ACT).

    b. Solution-focused brief therapy (SFBT).

    c. Radically open dialectical behavior therapy (RO DBT).

    d. Exposure and response prevention (ERP).

5. An individual is MOST likely to be a homicidal threat when:

    a. Intoxicated on a mind/mood-altering substance/medication

    b. Making a direct and specific lethal threat toward another

    c. Coping with delusions/hallucinations of a command nature

    d. There is a prior history of regular violence toward others

6. In exploring childhood abuse, a gestalt therapist would encourage a client to:

    a. Recite memories of abuse to more fully release this unfinished business

    b. Confront past abusers to achieve meaningful catharsis

    c. Become the wounded child to meaningfully address the abuse

    d. Write undelivered letters to past abusers to bring closure

7. Which one of the following individuals would benefit most from using collateral informants during a client's assessment?

    a. Individuals diagnosed with mental health disorders.
    b. Individuals diagnosed with substance use disorders.
    c. Individuals diagnosed with behavioral health disorders.
    d. Individuals diagnosed with neurocognitive disorders.

8. Arnold Lazarus developed a holistic therapeutic approach known as multimodal therapy. It offered seven classifications of a person's personality, as referenced by the following acronym:

    a. FORMS I.D.
    b. CLASSIC I.D.
    c. BASIC I.D.
    d. START I.D.

9. According to the AAMFT Code of Ethics (2015), professional misconduct may include all of the following EXCEPT:

    a. continuing to practice as an MFT while no longer being competent to do so due to a physical impairment.
    b. continuing to practice as an MFT while no longer being competent to do so due to a mental impairment.
    c. continuing to practice as an MFT while no longer being competent to do so due to being subject to an employee performance improvement plan.
    d. continuing to practice as an MFT while no longer being competent to do so due to alcohol or substance abuse.

10. A Milan systemic family therapist works with an adolescent diagnosed with bulimia nervosa and her family. The therapist requests that the parents spend time away from the teen to disrupt patterns of harmful "games" and recreate health boundaries. This technique is known as:

    a. establishing rituals.
    b. paradoxical reframing.
    c. invariant prescription.
    d. pretend techniques (reversals).

11. Which one of the following communication styles reflects an underlying desire to hide feelings of pain and hurt?

    a. Placater.
    b. Blamer.
    c. Distractor.
    d. Computer.

12. Neuro-linguistic programming (NLP) is a therapeutic approach most closely associated with:

    a. John Grinder, Richard Bandler, and Gregory Bateson
    b. Richard Wiseman, Bertram Gawronski, and Susan Fisk
    c. Hans Eysenck, Arthur Jensen, and John Rowan
    d. Edward Tolman, Robert Sternberg, and James Gross

13. The misdiagnosis of schizophrenia in black people suggests the tendency for therapists to engage in which one of the following heuristic biases?

a. Negativity bias.
b. Social desirability bias.
c. Confirmation bias.
d. Decision fatigue.

14. Functional family therapy is carried out in:

a. Three phases
b. Four phases
c. Five phases
d. Via a structured change gradient

15. MFTs seeking to provide supervision through electronic means must comply with relevant laws and ensure that all of the following conditions are met EXCEPT:

a. the means of electronic communication medium is secure.
b. the potential risks and benefits of electronic supervision are reviewed and documented.
c. the supervisor–supervisee contract specific to electronic supervision is board approved.
d. electronic supervision is appropriate for the professional needs of the supervisee.

16. Reality therapy argues that individuals are always striving to meet core needs, and that problems arise primarily when the ways selected are dysfunctional. The core needs as identified in reality therapy include all of the following sets EXCEPT:

a. Power and freedom
b. Wealth and possessions
c. Love and belonging
d. Survival and recreation

17. Critics of general system theory argue that, when working with domestic violence victims, which of the following concepts must be challenged?

a. Blocking.
b. Externalization.
c. Circular causality
d. Emotional neutrality

18. Object relations theory suggests that initial relationships formed during infancy shape relationship expectations in adulthood. Three main object relations include all of the following EXCEPT:

a. attachment
b. frustration
c. disjunction
d. rejection

19. An MFT enrolls a new client in group therapy for generalized anxiety disorder. The closed group met for 8 weeks, upon which time the client reported symptom improvement, and her case was closed. Six months later, the client requests access to her medical records. The MFT is ethically obligated to provide the client access with written authorization from:

    a. the client.
    b. the client and each group member.
    c. the client and verbal authorizations from each group member.
    d. the client and a documented statement of confidentiality from each group member.

20. Therapists who fail to take appropriate preventative measures with high-risk clients who die by suicide may be charged with negligence in all of the following circumstances EXCEPT when the:

    a. appropriate standards of care were not upheld.
    b. duty of care was determined and not provided.
    c. presumed harm to the client was not foreseeable (i.e., proximate causation).
    d. presumed harm to the client would not have occurred "but for" the therapist's actions (i.e., actual causation).

21. The FIRST step in processing any client presentation is to:

    a. Obtain a psychosocial history
    b. Determine presenting symptoms/complaints
    c. Look for medical history and current conditions
    d. Seek collateral contacts for further information

22. The term *collateral reports* in an assessment refers to:

    a. Reports filed with multiple agencies involved in a client's care
    b. Documentation produced to support a DSM diagnosis
    c. Mandated reporting in cases of abuse or neglect
    d. Secondary contacts to augment a first-hand assessment

23. Clinicians adhering to which one of the following evidence-based practices (EBPs) are least likely to encounter termination by design?

    a. Client-centered therapy.
    b. Solution-focused therapy.
    c. Cognitive behavioral therapy.
    d. Mindfulness-based stress reduction.

24. The overarching focus of contextual therapy is:

    a. Boundaries and respect
    b. Fairness and trust
    c. Caring and kindness
    d. Expectations and accountability

25. To evaluate a client's alcohol use disorder, any of the following might be used, EXCEPT:

    a. AUI
    b. BAI
    c. MAST
    d. SASSI

26. The personality assessment tool organized around the five factor model of personality domains is the:
   a. MAPI
   b. MBTI
   c. MMPI
   d. NEO PI-R

27. A 34-year-old female with a history of posttraumatic stress disorder (PTSD) presents for an initial intake complaining of sadness, difficulty sleeping, and poor appetite. The therapist wishes to select a standardized functional rating scale to acquire outcome measures. Which one of the following would provide this measure?
   a. Daily Living Activities (DLA-20) assessment.
   b. Patient Health Questionnaire-2 (PHQ-2).
   c. Mood and Feelings Questionnaire (MFQ).
   d. Primary Care PTSD Screen for DSM-5 (PC-PTSD-5).

Refer to the following for questions 28-29:

> Jada and Ava attend couples therapy due to relationship distress stemming from Jada's recurrent bouts of depression. Ava reports feeling disconnected and says that Jada has rejected her attempts at intimacy. Jada has a history of suicidality and has had several psychiatric hospitalizations. She sees an individual therapist and a psychiatrist. The marriage and family therapist (MFT) obtains a release of information to contact Jada's therapist and learns that Jada is having an affair.

28. Ethically, the therapist must:
   a. disclose knowledge of the affair to the couple.
   b. meet with Jada separately and encourage her to disclose the affair.
   c. keep the information confidential but guide the couple toward disclosure.
   d. adopt a no-secrets policy, permitting clinical judgment to determine disclosure.

29. Ava reports being blindsided upon learning of the affair, and both partners are willing to address this in therapy. The first step in this postdiscovery process would be for the therapist to:
   a. safely manage the couple's emotional reactions.
   b. assess the couple's potential for forgiveness.
   c. determine the circumstances surrounding the affair.
   d. resolve issues of ambivalence concerning separation.

30. Which of the following identifies how narrative therapy unfolds?
   a. Problem narrative identification, re-authoring, and recruiting support
   b. Identifying problem narratives, mitigation, and internalizing
   c. Client teaching, family education, and changing family narratives
   d. Identifying problem sources, pressuring change, and overcoming negativity

31. The earliest that a diagnosis of PTSD can be made would be in:
   a. One month
   b. Two months
   c. Four months
   d. Six months

32. The Health Insurance Portability and Accountability Act of 1996 (HIPAA) includes the foundational rule addressing the storage and transmission of electronic records known as the:

    a. Privacy Rule.
    b. Security Rule.
    c. Confidentiality Rule.
    d. Breach Notification Rule.

33. A cognitive-behavioral therapy, rational emotive behavior therapy (REBT) was developed in the 1950s by:

    a. William Glasser
    b. John B. Watson
    c. Albert Ellis
    d. Aaron T. Beck

34. Exposure and response prevention (ERP) is an evidence-based practice for which one of the following?

    a. Persistent depressive disorder.
    b. Schizophrenia.
    c. Obsessive-compulsive disorder.
    d. Bipolar disorder.

Refer to the following for questions 35-36:

> A therapist conducts a suicide risk assessment with a client diagnosed with major depressive disorder. The client is a tennis pro and has struggled with the "constant demand to be the best." Today, she is in acute distress due to being abruptly fired from her job, leaving her feeling "humiliated and hopeless."

35. Given these variables, which one of the following theories would best predict the client's risk level?

    a. Interpersonal theory of suicide.
    b. Diathesis-stress theory.
    c. Theory of planned behavior.
    d. Differential activation theory.

36. Which one of the following lines of inquiry would best determine if the client is experiencing suicidal ideation?

    a. "Do you think you have the means to end your life?"
    b. "Do you ever have thoughts about not wanting to live?"
    c. "Do you have plans about how you would kill yourself?"
    d. "Do you think you would ever carry out your plan to kill yourself?"

37. In Mary Ainsworth's "strange situation" experiment measuring infant attachment, observations of caregivers and strangers entering and leaving the room were conducted. When the mother left the room, securely attached children initially showed:

    a. significant signs of distress and feared the stranger.
    b. signs of distress and resisted the stranger's attempt to console them.
    c. no signs of distress and interacted with the stranger without difficulty.
    d. no significant signs of distress and did not interact with the stranger.

38. MFTs respect each client's right and responsibility to make personal relationship decisions such as marriage, divorce, or reconciliation, by honoring which one of the following ethical principles?

a. Justice.
b. Autonomy.
c. Beneficence.
d. Nonmaleficence.

39. Which one of the following options is NOT true of an MFT's ethical responsibilities for conducting professional evaluations in legal contexts?

a. MFTs avoid performing custody evaluations on clients seen in therapy.
b. MFTs avoid offering professional opinions on clients seen in therapy.
c. MFTs refrain from performing forensic evaluations on clients seen in therapy unless they are legally mandated to do so.
d. MFTs only provide testimony in legal proceedings if specific competencies are acquired and maintained.

40. Genograms differ from structural family maps in that genograms:

a. incorporate intrafamily dynamics.
b. identify hierarchies and subsystems.
c. allow for constant revision and refinement.
d. include relevant physical and mental health information.

41. Bronfenbrenner's ecological theory asserts that:

a. Minimal behavioral change occurs spontaneously
b. The environment has minimal impact on behavior
c. Human development is reflective of environmental systems
d. Collateral influences have measurable contributions to change

42. The therapeutic modality known as *narrative therapy* was introduced by:

a. Steve de Shazer and Insoo Berg
b. Bill O'Hanlon and Carolyn Attneave
c. Cloe Madanes and Froma Walsh
d. Michael White and David Epston

43. Which of the following alcohol screening tests is designed specifically for use with adolescents?

a. CAGE
b. CRAFFT
c. MAST
d. AUDIT

44. Which one of the following substance abuse recovery programs proclaims to be spiritual but not religious?

a. Rational Recovery.
b. Self-Management and Recovery Training (SMART Recovery).
c. 12-step groups (e.g., Alcoholics Anonymous [AA], Narcotics Anonymous [NA]).
d. The Oxford Group.

45. A therapist provides an initial assessment with a client who discloses that they tested positive for HIV several years ago. Are there sufficient grounds for the therapist to break confidentiality?

    a. Yes, only if multiple sexual partners are unaware of exposure.

    b. No, only if the client promises they will inform all affected sexual partners

    c. Yes, only if an identified 3rd person is unaware of exposure.

    d. No, there are never grounds for the therapist to break confidentiality

46. Emotionally focused therapy (EFT) includes elements of multiple theoretical models, but is MOST firmly rooted in:

    a. Systems theory

    b. Attachment theory

    c. Person-centered theory

    d. Experiential theory

47. In assessing a client, the information that should be obtained is:

    a. Limited to the purpose of the assessment

    b. Unlimited, in the best interests of the client

    c. Limited, unless something of concern arises

    d. Limited to data for reimbursement purposes

48. Which one of the following refers to the congruence between a therapist's words and actions?

    a. Empathy.

    b. Genuineness.

    c. Self-actualization.

    d. Unconditional positive regard.

49. Empirical evidence suggests that standardized outcome measures with the greatest efficacy are:

    a. obtained from a variety of sources.

    b. paired with subjective measures.

    c. diagnostically comprehensive.

    d. used collaboratively.

50. According to Bowen, when *triangulation* is identified, the therapist should:

    a. Align with the most dominant party

    b. Align with the most vulnerable party

    c. Avoid taking sides to facilitate change

    d. Confront both parties to force change

51. An MFT using the McMaster Approach to Families would like to use an instrument to measure a family's structural arrangement (e.g., roles), transactional characteristics (e.g., problem-solving, communication), and affective responsiveness. Which one of the following instruments would best meet the MFT's needs?

    a. The Family Adaptability and Cohesion Scale IV.

    b. The Dyadic Adjustment Scale.

    c. The Family Assessment Device.

    d. The Conflict Tactics Scale.

52. Research on the effectiveness of standardized measures used to produce outcome-driven data suggests all of the following EXCEPT:

a. The use of standardized screening and diagnosis alone improves client treatment outcomes.
b. The use of repeated, validated, and reliable instruments improves client treatment outcomes.
c. The use of standardized measures incorporating client feedback improves client treatment outcomes.
d. The use of standardized measures that track symptoms and overall functioning improves client treatment outcomes.

53. Which one of the following options reflects a collaborative effort between parties to modify maladaptive behaviors through positive reinforcement?

a. Safety plans.
b. Process agreements.
c. Contingency contracts.
d. Therapeutic negotiations.

54. Greg and Danny began seeing a couples counselor after their foster child, Felix, was reunified with his biological mother. The couple had fallen in love with Felix and had hoped to adopt him. Since Felix's reunification with his mother, the couple has been at odds over their decision to foster another child. Greg is ready to try again, while Danny states, "I will never open our home again. It will always end in heartache." This is an example of which one of the following?

a. Minimalization.
b. Personalization.
c. Emotional reasoning.
d. Overgeneralization.

55. General systems theory (or systems theory) is the basis for family systems theory and other systemic perspectives, therapies, and techniques. According to general systems theory, a *system* is BEST defined as:

a. Any objects or entities acting in harmony
b. A biochemically active organism
c. A set of elements existing in interaction
d. Any organized collaboration

56. When delivered as a comprehensive program, which one of the following therapies provides consultation to help prevent therapist burnout?

a. Acceptance and commitment therapy (ACT).
b. Integrated cognitive behavioral therapy (I-CBT).
c. Dialectical behavior therapy (DBT).
d. Rational emotive behavior therapy (REBT).

57. Excluding the interpretation of regulatory standards, MFTs maintain professional competence in the field by engaging in the pursuit of knowledge through all of the following options EXCEPT:

    a. education.

    b. training.

    c. supervised experience.

    d. consultation.

58. Use of the Crisis Assessment Tool (CAT) allows mobile crisis workers to rapidly assess the safety and well-being of children and adolescents. Caregiver participation is critical for assisting the crisis worker with all of the following EXCEPT:

    a. obtaining relevant information for decision making.

    b. identifying immediately actionable steps.

    c. explaining symptom etiology.

    d. examining client needs.

59. From a systemic family therapy perspective, the MOST significant drawback to cognitive-behavioral couples therapy is:

    a. It inadequately deals with past family role models in the relationship

    b. It gives limited attention to the role of emotions in relationships

    c. Its reliance on thought and behavioral change patterns

    d. Its focus on behavioral consequences limits insights into family subsystems

60. An adolescent client describes themselves as being sexually attracted to all people, regardless of gender. What term best describes this adolescent's orientation?

    a. Asexual

    b. Pansexual

    c. Bisexual

    d. Queer

61. The MRI model of therapy centers primarily on issues of:

    a. Social exchange

    b. Cognitive reconstruction

    c. Communication

    d. Behavioral dynamics

62. The term *hermeneutics* refers to:

    a. A feedback loop in systems theory

    b. Establishing mutual understanding

    c. The interpretation of meaning

    d. A positivistic theoretical orientation

63. Which one of the following emergency management techniques refers to actions taken to reduce the damaging effects of unavoidable emergencies?

    a. Prevention.

    b. Protection.

    c. Response.

    d. Mitigation.

64. In 1911, Eugen Bleuler identified the four A's of schizophrenia, which are:

a. Affect, autonomy, associations, and ambivalence
b. Autism, affect, associations, and ambivalence
c. Associations, aggression, autonomy, autism
d. Ambivalence, affect, articulations, and autism

65. An MFT engaging in feedback-informed treatment seeks an instrument designed to obtain client feedback on the following: the effectiveness of the MFT's approach, the degree to which the client feels understood, agreement with treatment goals, and overall client satisfaction. Which one of the following scales would best assist the MFT?

a. The Authenticity Scale (AS).
b. The Session Rating Scale (SRS).
c. The Outcome Rating Scale (ORS).
d. The Brief Psychiatric Rating Scale (BPRS).

66. A therapist at a community-based mental health center provides treatment to a client diagnosed with depression. The client recently requested a copy of her medical record containing protected health information (PHI). In compliance with the Health Insurance Portability and Accountability Act of 1996 (HIPAA), the therapist must provide access to the client's PHI UNLESS:

a. the therapist is reasonably sure that the PHI will be used in criminal, civil, or administrative proceedings.
b. the therapist determines that the records contain PHI that is old, archived, or not readily accessible.
c. the therapist's professional judgment determines that the information may cause the client emotional harm.
d. the therapist's professional judgment determines that the client will not understand the information.

67. The population most often addressed through functional family therapy is:

a. Individual – addressing social relationship issues
b. Family – with problems of discord and contention
c. Marital – with issues of violence or other abuse
d. Adolescent – with serious behavioral problems

68. An MFT provides ongoing services to a 52-year-old female diagnosed with binge eating disorder. The client presents today with her two teenage daughters, who are deeply concerned that the client is in crisis and may need hospitalization. What should the MFT do first?

a. Conduct a comprehensive risk assessment.
b. Refer the client to her primary care provider.
c. Develop a safety plan for the daughters to implement.
d. Ask the daughters to describe the behaviors that they find concerning.

69. Wernicke encephalopathy and Korsakoff syndrome are both due to brain damage caused by:
    a. Alcohol abuse
    b. Vitamin B1 deficiency
    c. Opioid abuse
    d. Malnutrition

70. Existential therapy posits all of the following EXCEPT:
    a. greater freedom comes with greater awareness.
    b. tension exists between freedom and responsibility.
    c. while life tends toward emptiness, purpose and meaning can be created.
    d. meaningful relationships with others precede meaningful relationships with oneself.

71. A condition in which a person with a mental disorder is at risk for self-harm due to their inability to provide food, clothing, and shelter for themselves is known as:
    a. Suicidal ideation
    b. Cognitive disability
    c. Physical dependence
    d. Grave disability

72. The term *family atmosphere* is most commonly associated with:
    a. Crisis intervention
    b. Bowenian family therapy
    c. Freudian therapy
    d. Adlerian family therapy

73. Which is true of homicide rates among youths aged 0–17?
    a. Homicide is the second leading cause of death among youths.
    b. Homicide rates have plateaued over the past 2 decades among all youths.
    c. Homicide rates have decreased over the past 2 decades among females.
    d. Hispanic youths are more likely to die by homicide than their non-Hispanic counterparts.

74. First-order change in a family system, as compared with second-order change, is:
    a. Deeper and more enduring
    b. Neither deep nor enduring
    c. Deep but transient
    d. Not deep but enduring

75. The term *mystification* was introduced by:
    a. R.D. Laing
    b. Virginia Satir
    c. John Bell
    d. Rachel Hare-Mustin

76. Whitaker's "therapy of the absurd" is designed to:
    a. identify self-defeating cognitions.
    b. uncover childhood schemas.
    c. heighten family discord and turmoil.
    d. upend socially constructed gender roles.

77. The term *"double depression"* colloquially refers to:

    a. Persistent depressive disorder superimposed with major depressive disorder
    b. Any depressive disorder superimposed with suicidality
    c. Major depressive disorder superimposed with bipolar depression
    d. Dysthymia superimposed with cyclothymic disorder

78. Perpetrators of elder financial exploitation are either known to the victim (e.g., family, caregivers) or unknown to the victim (i.e., strangers). When comparing both groups, which one of the following statements is true of perpetrators unknown to the victim?

    a. The abuse is longer in duration.
    b. The abuse is less likely to be reported.
    c. The abuse is more likely to co-occur with other forms of abuse.
    d. The abuse results in lower incurred financial loss.

79. When applied to substance use disorder, Prochaska and DiClemente's model of behavioral change involves a series of stages considered to be:

    a. linear.
    b. irreversible.
    c. disordered.
    d. cyclical.

80. The Stark Law prohibits healthcare professionals from profiting off of self-referrals made on behalf of:

    a. all healthcare recipients.
    b. all federal healthcare recipients.
    c. all private-pay healthcare recipients.
    d. all self-pay healthcare recipients.

81. Which one of the following options is put in place to provide continuity of care due to therapist-initiated interruptions?

    a. Termination letters.
    b. Professional wills.
    c. Treatment contracts.
    d. Advance directives.

82. The Columbia Suicide Severity Rating Scale (C-SSRS) considers suicidal behavior as a potentially self-injurious act exclusively committed in conjunction with which one of the following?

    a. A partial desire or intention to die (does not have to be 100%).
    b. A 100% desire or intention to die.
    c. A partial degree of consequential medical injury (does not have to be 100%).
    d. A 100% degree of consequential medical injury.

83. Of the following persons, who is most at risk for death by suicide?

    a. A 30-year-old female with a history of sexual abuse.
    b. A 19-year-old male with a history of depression.
    c. A 32-year-old female with a history of suicide attempts.
    d. A 16-year-old female diagnosed with substance use disorder.

84. Which one of the following skills best reflects a therapist's mastery of the use of self?

a. Empathy.
b. Attunement.
c. Theoretical competence.
d. Self-disclosure.

85. Evidence-based practices for treating schizophrenia include a family psychoeducation model based on the theory that the disorder results from a combination of underlying vulnerabilities and environmental factors. This model is known as the:

a. deficit model.
b. diathesis-stress model.
c. general adaptation model.
d. expressed emotion model.

86. As an element of systems theory, the framework of cybernetics is built around the following three concepts:

a. Experience, learning, and reflexive response
b. Input, processing, and output
c. Structure, form, and function
d. Feedback, recursiveness, and self-regulation

87. Current research on marriage and family therapy outcomes suggests that nearly 65.6% of cases are resolved within:

a. 10 sessions.
b. 20 sessions.
c. 30 sessions.
d. 40 sessions.

88. MFTs honor a client's right to autonomous decision making by providing all of the following EXCEPT:

a. treatment-related information that is culturally and linguistically appropriate.
b. an acknowledgment that the client is free to enter into or remain in treatment unless it is court ordered.
c. recommendations for legal decision making in the context of family relationships.
d. information regarding the MFT's credentials, qualifications, and counseling approach.

89. In motivational interviewing (MI), which one of the following options describes the state of a person who is conflicted over wanting to change and simultaneously not wanting to change?

a. Disequilibrium.
b. Ambivalence.
c. Discrepancy.
d. Decisional imbalance.

90. NSSI occurs in the context of all of the following mental disorders EXCEPT:

a. posttraumatic stress disorder (PTSD).
b. histrionic personality disorder.
c. binge eating disorder.
d. substance use disorder.

91. The Sixteen Personality Factor Questionnaire, Fifth Edition (16PF) can be used to assist counselors in advising individuals on::
   a. Mood problems and impulse tendencies
   b. Career and vocational choices and development
   c. Learning and teamwork styles and limitations
   d. Attitude and behavioral problems

92. Introduced by Henry Stack Sullivan, the term *parataxic distortion* is BEST defined as:
   a. The tendency to blame others for one's own failures
   b. The inability to accurately assess the faults of those we love
   c. The inclination to skew perceptions of others based on fantasy
   d. A need to see others as all good or all bad

93. Experiential couples therapy asserts that beneath states of anger or withdrawal there are other more fundamental emotions, typically:
   a. Hurt and longing
   b. Hate and indifference
   c. Anxiety and depression
   d. Shame and guilt

94. Use of the internet to meet sexual-emotional needs through chat rooms, message boards, and pornography is called:
   a. Technology sex
   b. Internet sex
   c. Computer sex
   d. Cybersex

95. What percentage of individuals with bipolar 1 disorder will experience psychosis during a manic episode?
   a. 10 percent
   b. 20 percent
   c. 40 percent
   d. 50 percent

96. Satir's conjoint family therapy used four *family games* to explore family dynamics and teach the importance of functional roles, rules, and communication. All of the following are conjoint therapy games EXCEPT:
   a. Rescue game
   b. Harmony game
   c. Coalition game
   d. Lethal game

97. Studies by Kurt Lewin identified three distinct styles of group leadership, which include all of the following EXCEPT:
   a. Collaborative leadership style
   b. Democratic leadership style
   c. Autocratic leadership style
   d. Laissez-faire leadership style

98. Limitations to contextual therapy include all of the following EXCEPT:

a. Family member initial unawareness of low trust and lack of fairness
b. Family member opposition to establishing and enforcing boundaries
c. An unwillingness to accept accountability due to past injustices
d. A need for the therapist to be a leader instead of a co-collaborator

99. The term *informed consent* is BEST defined as:

a. The requirement that clients be informed of all treatment risks and benefits.
b. The requirement that clients be provided written information outlining ethical standards of care.
c. The requirement that therapists refrain from providing treatment to minors or those legally incapable of consent.
d. The requirement that therapist obtain verbal consent to record any images, audio, or observations.

100. The term *schism* (referring to a family division into competing groups) was first introduced by:

a. Nathan Ackerman
b. Theodore Lidz
c. Gregory Bateson
d. Milton Erickson

101. Which one of the following theorists used nomothetic research to formulate his theory?

a. Carl Rogers.
b. Gordon Allport.
c. Abraham Maslow.
d. BF Skinner.

102. Emotional affairs include all of the following EXCEPT:

a. an element of secrecy.
b. a compulsive desire or need.
c. a deep emotional connection.
d. implicit or explicit sexual chemistry.

103. When seeing a family, the therapist should identify the primary client as:

a. The entire family
b. The person seen as "the problem" in the family
c. The parents in the family
d. The agreed-upon party or parties

104. A therapist receives a call from the irate father of a 9-year-old client. The father is upset that the therapist reported the family to child protective services, and he is requesting that his son's case be closed. The therapist summarizes the call on an information note and places it in the client's record. The parents later request a copy of the client's record. The HIPAA Privacy Rule indicates that the family has the right to:

   a. receive a copy of the record, including the information note.
   b. receive a copy of the record, excluding the information note and any additional psychotherapy notes.
   c. receive a copy of the record, including the information note, once the child protective services case is closed.
   d. receive a copy of the record, excluding the information note, unless client authorization is obtained.

105. A school-based therapist provides cognitive behavioral therapy to a 10-year-old client diagnosed with generalized anxiety disorder. The therapist would like to maximize outcomes by obtaining collateral support from the client's teacher. Teacher involvement would provide opportunities for all of the following scenarios EXCEPT for:

   a. generalization of learned skills.
   b. reassurance during feared situations.
   c. social reinforcement and rewards.
   d. modeling coping behaviors.

106. An MFT provides individual therapy to a veteran diagnosed with schizophrenia. The client is not progressing in therapy and is noncompliant with his medication. The client's family desires to be involved in his care. Which one of the following treatments would best meet the client and family's needs?

   a. Relationship therapy.
   b. Structural family therapy.
   c. Behavioral family therapy.
   d. Strategic family therapy.

107. Which is true of clients' rights when participating in research studies?

   a. Clients cannot withdraw from participation under any circumstances.
   b. Clients can withdraw from participation at any time.
   c. Clients cannot withdraw from participation after signing a written consent.
   d. Clients can withdraw from participation if determined they did not have the capacity to consent.

108. The American Society of Addiction Medicine criteria for assessment and treatment planning include all of the following dimensions EXCEPT:

   a. acute intoxication and/or withdrawal potential.
   b. treatment compliance.
   c. readiness to change.
   d. emotional, behavioral, and cognitive conditions.

109. Violations of the federal Anti-Kickback Statute include all of the following EXCEPT:

a. accepting remuneration for medically necessary services.
b. offering compensation for reimbursed healthcare services.
c. routinely waiving client copays or deductibles.
d. causing client harm or financial loss to healthcare programs.

110. A 26-year-old male with a lengthy history of bipolar disorder presents for an emergency assessment. He states that, despite multiple hospitalizations, he believes he is not bipolar, which eventually leads to medication noncompliance and symptom exacerbation. The client reports that when he is stressed, he copes by "staying up all night gaming." Of the following, which intervention would be most effective for this client?

a. Stress inoculation therapy.
b. Functional family therapy
c. Cognitive processing therapy.
d. Interpersonal and social rhythm therapy.

111. Therapists using acceptance and commitment therapy seek to help clients change their relationship with problematic beliefs and thoughts by unhooking. This technique is known as:

a. cognitive defusion.
b. forceful disputing.
c. emotional regulation.
d. developing congruence.

112. Research studies show that the presence of a gun in domestically violent situations increases a woman's chances of death by homicide (i.e., femicide) by:

a. 200%.
b. 300%.
c. 400%.
d. 500%.

113. Which one of the following instruments is used each session to measure a client's functional progress along four scales: individual, interpersonal, social, and global (i.e., overall)?

a. ORS.
b. SRS.
c. PHQ-9.
d. BDI.

114. The theory of reciprocal inhibition posits that:

a. Responding to others is not a natural phenomenon
b. There is a lack of desire to respond to another when your needs have already been met
c. Where positive efforts are ignored, relationships are held back
d. Anxiety and relaxation cannot exist simultaneously

115. Internal family systems theory is based on the premise that early experiences of shame and pain manifest into protectors, known as:

a. anima and animus.
b. blamer and placator.
c. topdog and underdog.
d. firefighters and managers.

116. A therapist would like a readily accessible informal means for measuring treatment progress. Which one of the following therapies consists of techniques that would enable the therapist to do so?

a. Gestalt therapy.
b. Solution-focused brief therapy.
c. Person-centered therapy.
d. Narrative therapy.

117. A marriage and family therapist (MFT) provides therapy to an 8-year-old child and her mother. The mother reports that the father, who resides in another state, has a history of physical violence. The father has previously been absent and uninvolved but has recently remarried and is requesting joint custody. The mother asks the therapist for a letter to the court indicating the therapist's professional opinion and recommendations. In compliance with ethical standards, the therapist provides a letter:

a. recommending against joint custody based on the MFT's duty to protect.
b. recommending against joint custody based on applicable empirical evidence.
c. excluding custody recommendations while providing general treatment information (e.g., client diagnoses, attendance, and treatment progress).
d. excluding custody recommendations while providing a professional opinion based on the family's clinical presentation.

118. The primary theoretical foundation for integrative behavioral couples therapy is:

a. Brief/solution-focused
b. Problem-focused
c. Cognitive-behavioral
d. Eclectic

119. A therapist collaborates with clients to create time-sensitive treatment plan goals using the SMART method. SMART goals also reflect all of the following parameters EXCEPT:

a. specific.
b. meaningful.
c. attainable.
d. realistic.

120. Risk factors for suicide contagion among adolescents include exposure to all of the following EXCEPT:

a. a recent suicidal death of a celebrity or a high-profile person.
b. social media posts regarding a peer's death by suicide.
c. schoolwide screenings for suicidal ideation after a student's death by suicide.
d. sensationalized media publications with details of the suicide.

121. A therapist provides emotionally focused therapy (EFT) to a couple struggling with infidelity. The couple is in the final phase of counseling and is discussing termination. The therapist explains that the final stage of therapy is indicated when the couple successfully:

a. reauthors their stories with new and fulfilling meanings.
b. differentiates and detriangulates from their families of origin.
c. integrates and consolidates change based on secure attachments.
d. finds positive connections through a restructured family system.

122. Which one of the following types of therapy uses a humanistic approach with individuals diagnosed with gambling disorder and their spouses?

a. Conjoint intimacy-enhancing therapy.
b. Congruence couples therapy.
c. Hope and forgiveness focused therapy.
d. Cognitive existential couples therapy.

123. According to the American Association for Marriage and Family Therapy (AAMFT) Code of Ethics (2015), a therapist must refrain from providing custody evaluations:

a. on current clients.
b. on current clients unless appropriate consents are obtained.
c. on current clients unless a subpoena dictates otherwise.
d. on current clients unless the testimony can be deemed accurate, objective, and fair.

124. Kitchener's model of ethical justification uses a critical-evaluative level of reasoning, which considers standards of behavior against a prescribed set of criteria (i.e., ethical codes) known as:

a. ethical theory.
b. ethical rules.
c. ethical reasoning.
d. ethical principles.

125. Legislation referred to as the IDEA Act is designed to ensure that:

a. Each special education student is placed in a self-contained classroom
b. 504 accommodations are provided for students with mental impairments
c. Students with disabilities between the ages of 3-21 receive free and appropriate public education and related services.
d. Each public or private school student, regardless of disability, receives education comparable with their peers.

Refer to the following for questions 126-127:

> A therapist receives training in interpersonal therapy (IPT) and plans to provide this evidence-based practice (EBP) to each client on her caseload. To determine the effectiveness of IPT, the therapist uses claims data to evaluate whether IPT was provided for the recommended 16 sessions over the course of 3 months. Based on these data, the therapist concludes that 60% of her clients showed improvement.

126. The therapist's conclusion that 60% of her clients showed improvement fails to consider all of the following confounding variables EXCEPT:

    a. client diagnoses.
    b. the therapeutic alliance.
    c. high implementation costs.
    d. cultural factors.

127. Confounding variables in this study affect which one of the following options?

    a. Internal consistency.
    b. Interrater reliability.
    c. External validity.
    d. Internal validity.

128. According to Jungian analytical psychology, *archetypes* represent:

    a. Bridges that connect various parts of the psyche
    b. Models of people, behaviors, or personalities
    c. Examples of idealized personality traits
    d. Parts of the conscious mind that are rejected or repressed

129. Although both Carl Whitaker and Virginia Satir founded experiential family therapy, there were distinct theoretical differences in their approaches. These differences are best described by which of the following statements:

    a. Whitaker emphasized the use of power and control between family members, while Satir focused more on the need for self-actualization and differentiation.
    b. Whitaker emphasized the influence of non-verbal messages on relationships, while Satir focused more on family structural dynamics and roles.
    c. Whitaker emphasized the need for emotional family cohesion while Satir focused more on improving family communication.
    d. Whitaker emphasized the influence of prior family history on the dynamics of subsequent family behaviors, while Satir focused more on cultural and societal expectations that shape family behaviors.

130. A student under MFT supervision carries a small caseload during his final school semester. While conducting an initial intake on an assigned client, the student reviews informed consent and is ethically obligated to explain which one of the following processes?

    a. Planning for termination.
    b. Providing professional opinions.
    c. Reviewing nondiscrimination policies.
    d. Disclosing professional affiliations.

131. Cognitive-behavioral theorists see the relationship between cognition and behavior as having a(n):

    a. Linear relationship, leading directly from thoughts to behaviors
    b. Bi-directional relationship, where thoughts influence behaviors and vice versa
    c. Independent relationship, with thoughts and behaviors acting separately and producing consequences unique to each other
    d. Linear relationship, leading directly from behaviors to thoughts

132. The purpose of the Outcome Questionnaire-45 (OQ-45.2) includes all of the following EXCEPT:

a. to provide baseline screening measures.
b. to detect areas of immediate concern.
c. to serve as a diagnostic tool.
d. to assist in discharge planning.

133. All of the following are common academic aptitude tests EXCEPT:

a. SAT (Scholastic Aptitude Test)
b. GRE (Graduate Record Examination)
c. EST (Educational Skills Test)
d. ACT (American College Testing)

134. Therapists using text messaging to deliver technology-based services seek to minimize risks incurred through misinterpretation of intent or a lack of professional boundaries by refraining from which one of the following?

a. Accepting friend requests from clients.
b. The use of emojis and common text abbreviations.
c. Responding to clients after business hours.
d. The use of unencrypted platforms.

135. A therapist runs a court-ordered group for perpetrators of child sexual abuse. One participant is difficult to engage and argumentative. The therapist's theoretical orientation is eclectic, with an emphasis on motivational interviewing. To reduce ambivalence, which one of the following responses best captures the spirit of motivational interviewing?

a. "You say that you want to get your probation officer off your back. Group participation would be a step in the right direction."
b. "On the one hand, you say you want to get your probation officer off your back, but on the other hand, you refuse to participate."
c. "Whether you participate or not is up to you; however, it's important that you allow other group members to benefit."
d. "You think that you were unfairly accused and shouldn't have to participate."

136. Which one of the following statements best represents a feminist family theory core tenet?

a. Living in a patriarchal society negatively affects men and women.
b. There is one objective truth and perception of reality.
c. Gender stratification is essential for change.
d. Hegemonic femininity is the basis for gender equity.

137. The MFT Code of Ethics (2015) addresses sexual intimacy with a former client, specifically indicating that:

a. It is never permissible under any circumstances
b. It may be permitted in certain circumstances but is typically unwise
c. Is always permissible provided both parties are fully consenting adults
d. It is dependent on the issues dealt with and the length of the therapy

138. Which one of the following is characterized by intermittent behavioral reinforcement amid a relational power imbalance?

   a. Cognitive dissonance.
   b. Trauma bonding.
   c. Learned helplessness.
   d. Psychological entrapment.

139. Lenore Walker (1979) theorized that intimate partner violence involves the following three phases:

   a. Yelling, physicality, and placating
   b. Tension-building, battering, and honeymoon
   c. Threats, actions, and resolution
   d. Intimidation, violation, and placation

140. If a credible homicidal threat is made, a clinician is obligated to:

   a. Warn the client of possible legal consequences
   b. Contact the police and provide them with the information.
   c. Have the client involuntarily committed
   d. Call the police and warn the intended victim

141. Virginia Satir identified five styles of communication. Which of the following is NOT one of the five styles?

   a. Blamer
   b. Engager
   c. Distractor
   d. Placater

142. The first task in couples counseling regarding infidelity is to:

   a. Reestablish a sense of safety
   b. Clearly assign blame
   c. Minimize the meaning of the affair
   d. Vent intense emotional feelings

143. The bias that occurs when one characteristic of a person influences an evaluator's perception of the subject's other traits is called:

   a. The Hawthorne effect
   b. The placebo effect
   c. Trauma bonding effect
   d. The halo effect

144. All of the following represent *horizontal stressors* in a family EXCEPT:

   a. Birth of a child
   b. Family member failures
   c. Children leaving home
   d. Death of a parent

145. Which one of the following relational tasks in psychoanalytic self-psychology involves the therapist providing praise, affirmations, and a celebration of achievements?

a. Idealizing transference.
b. Mirroring transference.
c. Twinship transference.
d. Reparenting transference.

146. A therapist designs an informal self-administered survey to screen for client drug and alcohol use over the past 30 days. The validity of the therapist's survey would likely be impacted by which one of the following types of bias?

a. Recall bias.
b. Confirmation bias.
c. Social desirability bias.
d. Self-serving bias.

147. In gestalt therapy, one of the five major channels of resistance is referred to as *retroflection*, which refers to:

a. Doing to oneself something we desired to do to someone else, or doing something by ourselves that we would have preferred to have done for us
b. Accepting others' opinions and values without personally reviewing or examining them
c. Assigning aspects of ourselves to others in order to dismiss them from being part of ourselves
d. Lessening or muting boundaries between the self and another

148. The Olson Circumplex Model (Olson, 2000) dimensions of family interactions include all of the following EXCEPT:

a. cohesion.
b. flexibility.
c. differentiation.
d. communication.

149. Which of the following standardized assessment tools is MOST useful for measuring nonverbal intelligence in culturally and neurologically diverse populations?

a. The Stanford-Binet Intelligence Scale (SBIS)
b. The Toni-2 Intelligence Test (TONI-2)
c. The Wechsler Adult Intelligence Scale (WAIS)
d. The Thematic Apperception Test (TAT)

150. A family presents for an initial assessment. The therapist constructs a genogram of the family, including both parents, who are divorced but continue to coparent their adopted 10-year-old son. Which one of the following statements accurately depicts this family's genogram?

a. The parents are connected by a dotted line, and the child is connected by a solid line with two slashes in the middle.
b. The parents are connected by a solid line with two slashes in the middle, and the child is connected by a dotted line.
c. The parents are connected by a solid line with an X in the middle, and the child is connected by a solid line.
d. The parents are connected by a dotted line, and the child is connected by solid and dotted lines.

151. Of the following, which group therapy approach focuses on subjective life experiences, as related to freedom, responsibility, and the awareness of death.

a. Existential groups.
b. Gestalt groups.
c. Psychoanalytic groups.
d. Transactional analysis groups.

152. When attempting to modify a behavior, the most effective pattern of reinforcement is:

a. Continuous or constant reinforcement
b. Partial or intermittent reinforcement
c. Escalating reinforcement
d. Diminishing reinforcement

153. George is a 45-year-old male presenting for an initial assessment with reports of sadness and sleeplessness. He has a history of depression but says his symptoms worsened a little over 1 year ago with the sudden death of his spouse. George reports daily bouts of intense yearning, hopelessness, and the belief that a part of himself has died. In addition, he reports being poorly motivated to reintegrate socially and is barely maintaining employment due to his excessive use of sick days. Which one of the following is the most likely diagnosis for George?

a. Major depressive disorder.
b. Persistent depressive disorder.
c. Prolonged grief disorder.
d. Acute grief disorder.

154. The Gottman method's "sound relationship house" concept illustrates multiple facets of healthy relationships, including all of the following EXCEPT:

a. building love maps.
b. sharing positive life energy.
c. making life dreams come true.
d. turning toward instead of away.

155. All of the following standardized measures can be used as youth suicide screening instruments EXCEPT the:

a. Columbia Suicide Severity Rating Scale (C-SSRS).
b. Ask Suicide-Screening Questions (ASQ).
c. Patient Health Questionnaire-9 (PHQ-9) Modified.
d. Screening to Brief Intervention (S2BI).

156. The primary purpose of the MFT professional code of ethics is to:

a. Identify unethical therapists
b. Prosecute unethical therapists
c. Ensure ethical understandings among therapists
d. Set standards that engender public trusta

157. The primary difference between generalized anxiety disorder and a panic disorder is:

a. One is less troubling to the sufferer than the other
b. One has more recognizable symptoms than the other
c. One is persistent while the other involves a specific fear
d. The terms can be used interchangeably, as they are basically the same

158. The Outcome Questionnaire-45.2 (OQ-45.2) measures treatment progress across all of the following domains EXCEPT:

a. social roles.
b. symptom distress.
c. the therapeutic alliance.
d. interpersonal relations.

159. A couple receives therapy from a therapist specializing in the Gottman Method. The therapist initiates a discussion regarding treatment progress and termination. Which one of the following indicates that the couple is ready to be discharged?

a. A culture of appreciation has replaced criticism.
b. Emotional regulation has replaced emotional reactivity.
c. Internalized stories have become externalized and reauthored.
d. Congruence has replaced incongruence.

160. The original Milan systemic model is guided by all of the following principles EXCEPT:

a. hypothesizing
b. restructuring
c. circularity
d. neutrality.

161. An eating disorder that involves the persistent eating of substances with no nutrition, such as dirt or paint, is known as:

a. Rumination disorder
b. Avoidant food intake disorder
c. Binge-eating disorder
d. Pica

162. The FACES scales were designed to evaluate families for:

a. Anger and conflict
b. Anxiety and conflict
c. Adaptability and cohesion
d. Autonomy and coercion

163. An MFT provides Gestalt therapy to a client who asks about discharge. Upon review of the client's treatment plan, which one of the following accomplishments would help the client and therapist reach this decision?

a. The client has become more fully integrated in mind and body.
b. The client can now challenge maladaptive thinking and make any necessary behavioral changes.
c. The client shows increased insight into unconscious processes and intrapersonal conflicts.
d. The client is free to engage in creativity, love, and connection.

164. In screening clients for group, the therapist has a PRIMARY ethical duty to:

a. Protect all clients from harm by screening for incompatibility
b. Ensure clients will feel at ease and comfortable in the group
c. Find group times that will meet the optimal schedule for the client
d. Ensure group fees are negotiated to the satisfaction of the client

165. To help clients feel validated and supported, EFT family therapists use all of the following tools EXCEPT:

a. slowing the pace.
b. using a soft tone.
c. using simple phrases.
d. adopting positive connotations.

166. A 19-year-old college female receives counseling for substance misuse. She is compliant with therapy, and after exploring the positive and negative aspects of abstinence, she remains undecided. Using a motivational interviewing approach, which stage-appropriate strategies would provide the greatest benefit?

a. Build relapse prevention skills.
b. Continue to assess the client's commitment to change.
c. Offer a menu of choices (e.g., 12-step groups, medication-assisted therapy).
d. Examine the discrepancy between the client's behavior and her values.

167. An MFT has provided services to a client diagnosed with posttraumatic stress disorder (PTSD) for nearly 1 year. At the 6-month mark, the client met her short-term goals, as evidenced by a decrease in having fewer distressing memories and fewer angry outbursts. However, for the past 6 months, the client has not made therapeutic gains. The therapist should:

a. ask the client if she would prefer another provider.
b. contact the client's payer source to reauthorize additional services.
c. seek consultation from a professional who specializes in treating PTSD.
d. refer the client to another provider who specializes in treating PTSD.

168. An MFT provides therapy to an 8-year-old foster child and her foster mother, who has expressed interest in adopting the child. After the termination of parental rights hearing, the foster mother calls the MFT in distress after learning that the judge ordered a continuance to help the biological mother comply with the case plan. The caseworker petitioned the MFT to provide testimony at the next court date and has obtained the appropriate consent to release information. How should the MFT respond?

    a. Provide an expert opinion that is limited to the therapist's scope of competence.
    b. Provide expert testimony to the court based on the client's therapeutic challenges and progress.
    c. Conduct a detailed forensic evaluation, and restrict court testimony to those findings.
    d. Provide information to the court from the perspective of the client's treating therapist.

169. Countertransference refers to a therapist's internal response to a client's clinical presentation and is most commonly associated with:

    a. past experiences.
    b. therapeutic ruptures.
    c. dysfunctional interactions.
    d. sexual attraction.

170. You are the therapist for a family which started to see you to deal with the effects of a major automobile accident. Everyone was injured and the husband sustained a severe head injury in the accident. Post-rehab testing revealed a subsequent IQ of 62 (He had a 107 prior to the accident). Which diagnosis would be the most likely?

    a. Dementia, mild, due to head trauma
    b. Mild neurocognitive disorder due to traumatic brain injury
    c. Borderline intellectual functioning
    d. Intellectual disability, mild, due to head trauma

171. Tasks/learning groups include all of the following EXCEPT:

    a. Problem-solving groups
    b. Education groups
    c. Work groups
    d. Personal growth groups

172. An MFT's aspirational ethical commitment to service, advocacy, and public participation includes all of the following EXCEPT:

    a. providing pro bono services.
    b. providing remuneration for referrals.
    c. developing laws that promote diversity, inclusion, and equity.
    d. encouraging public participation in practitioner regulations.

173. Sexual relationships among colleagues in the workplace are ethically:

    a. Prohibited in all cases
    b. Permitted in all cases
    c. Prohibited between superiors/inferiors
    d. Permitted between equal colleagues

174. There are two kinds of Hamilton scales, which are used to assess:

a. Fears and phobias
b. Anxiety and depression
c. Hallucinations and delusions
d. Stress and coping

175. Incorporating routine outcome monitoring into clinical practice prevents the therapist from overestimating his or her ability to detect treatment failure, or from engaging in which one of the following types of bias?

a. Implicit bias.
b. Cultural bias.
c. Self-assessment bias.
d. Confirmation bias.

176. A 75-year-old male presents for an initial assessment experiencing clinically significant levels of distress that began after his wife's death nearly 3 months ago. Since her death, the client reports feeling isolated and emotionally numb. He also states that he has been depressed all day, every day, for at least 1 month. Using the DSM-5-TR criteria, the clinician assigns which one of the following?

a. Acute stress disorder.
b. Prolonged grief disorder.
c. Persistent depressive disorder.
d. Uncomplicated bereavement.

177. According to Johnson's typology of domestic violence (2008), males perpetrate which form of intimate partner violence (IPV) at much higher rates than females?

a. Situational couple violence.
b. Common dyad violence.
c. Violent resistance.
d. Intimate terrorism.

178. Therapists using technology-assisted services must make clients and supervisees aware in writing of all of the following EXCEPT:

a. the limitations and protections of confidentiality.
b. the associated risks and responsibility for minimizing such risks.
c. compliance with applicable laws safeguarding client information.
d. his or her knowledge, training, and education in compliance with standards of practice.

179. Game analysis in transactional analysis refers to:

a. Analysis of the individual psyche
b. Creation of a life plan
c. Identifying sequences of repeated transactions
d. Analysis of interpersonal transactions

180. Who formulated the ecological systems theory?

a. Urie Bronfenbrenner.
b. Mary Ainsworth.
c. Ludwig von Bertalanffy.
d. Ivan Boszormenyi-Nagy.

Answer Key and Explanations for Test #2

1. D: Collateral contacts serve in various predetermined roles. Identifying the contact's role at the outset of treatment or upon the initial request for a collateral contact's involvement is essential. Collateral contacts are not clients, and, as such, they are not bound by confidentiality and cannot assert privilege; however, the therapist must make every effort to protect clients' privacy. A signed informed consent is not required, but the therapist must document the role of the collateral contact and must provide clear guidelines on how they can best assist the client. It is also helpful to include a signed release of information detailing which information will be exchanged and the method for doing so. The role of the collateral contact includes, but is not limited to, providing emotional support to the client, helping the client understand their diagnoses and medication needs, or aiding in supportive assistance outside of therapy sessions. Collateral contacts do not have access to the client's clinical notes.

2. A: Karpman's drama triangle best illustrates this conflictual interaction, assigning the victim role to Leo, the persecutor role to the father, and the rescuer role to the mother. The persecutor blames the victim for the conflict and tends to be critical, authoritarian, rigid, dominating, and superior. The victim is described as helpless and powerless and believes that change is not possible. The rescuer takes on the "let me help you" stance, which can lead to enabling within codependent relationships. The rescuer cannot allow the victim to experience the consequences of their destructive patterns of behavior. Each role is depicted on the point of an inverted triangle. These roles do not always remain stable, with rescuers turning into victims, victims into martyrs, and so on.

3. B: To be *valid*, an assessment instrument must measure what is intended to be measured – for example, if a client's level of depression is being assessed, a valid instrument will measure meaningful aspects of mood and depression. For an assessment to be *reliable*, it must provide consistent results. An instrument that has not been reliably standardized cannot be relied upon by another professional, using the same instrument and technique. Finally, to be fully valid and reliable, the professional conducting the assessment must have adequate skills and familiarity with the population being served. For example, someone not familiar with issues of amputees may determine a diagnosis of psychosis for a client experiencing "phantom pain" in a missing limb, when the symptoms are well within the norm for this condition.

4. C: Individuals diagnosed with anorexia nervosa and chronic depression exhibit difficulties involving overcontrol, including perfectionism, cognitive rigidity, and self-criticism. Radically open dialectical behavior therapy (RO DBT) differs from DBT, with DBT addressing symptoms involving a lack of control, which presents as emotional dysregulation and poor impulse control. Acceptance and commitment therapy targets symptoms of psychological inflexibility, cognitive fusion, and avoidance of feelings. Solution-focused brief therapy (SFBT) uses a client-centered approach to emphasize client strengths and autonomy. Lastly, exposure and response prevention (ERP) is an evidence-based practice (EBP) for obsessive-compulsive disorder. ERP exposes clients to objects, situations, or images that tend to result in distressing thoughts and emotions. The success of ERP is contingent upon clients facing triggers head-on without using compulsive behaviors, which occur through habituation.

5. B: A client's verbalization of a threat to harm another person should be taken seriously, and therapists must assess the individual's risk continuum. In evaluating risk, relevant *biopsychosocial factors* include a psychiatric disorder (especially mania, schizophrenia with command voices, stimulant intoxication, a Cluster B personality disorder, and/or poor impulse control), family

210

violence and/or disruption (e.g., death, divorce, separation, restraining order), and current or anticipated stressors. Individuals with a history of violent behavior resulting in crime or imprisonment are at an increased risk. Sociological factors include personal isolation, poor social support systems, psychocultural barriers to help-seeking, limited treatment access, and regular exposure to violence are also contributing factors. Determining the client's access to firearms is essential. It is also critical to assess for protective factors and determine if others are at imminent (i.e., immediate) risk of harm.

6. C: In this way, the client avoids abstract discussion and instead promotes direct present-moment experiences that lead to self-awareness. The therapist works to create situations through which the client can explore how and why he presently behaves as he does. Gestalt therapy seeks to help clients develop independence, responsibility, and wholeness. This may include needed reintegration of previously disowned personality. Among other things, therapy promotes: 1) holism; 2) client insight; 3) integration of feelings, thoughts, behaviors, and body; 4) self-acceptance; 5) environmental awareness; and 6) personal accountability. Work is accomplished through observation of moment-to-moment behavior and organizing in a natural environment, and through interpretive dream-work.

7. D: Collateral sources of information are most beneficial when the individual has difficulty communicating, including individuals with neurocognitive disorders (e.g., dementia, delirium). Children and adolescents also benefit from the use of collateral informants. Examples of collateral sources of information include teachers, family members, spouses or partners, and other professionals. Individuals with mental health disorders, substance use disorders, and behavioral health disorders would also benefit from collateral informants, but to a lesser degree than those with limited communication.

8. C: Lazarus' multimodal therapy acronym is defined as follows:

B - Behavior (i.e., habits, actions, reactions)
A - Affective response (i.e., emotions and moods, and reactions to them)
S - Sensation (i.e., taste, touch, smell, sight, hearing, and responses to them)
I - Images (i.e., self-concept, memory, dreams, and other measures of imagination)
C - Cognitions (i.e., analytical thinking, planning, reasoning, ideas, insights, etc.)
I - Interpersonal relationships (i.e., interactions, and their importance)
D - Drugs (i.e., health, nutrition, hygiene, exercise, diet, and neurobiological functions)

Abnormal behavior is generated through such problems as conflicts, unhappy experiences, and social deficiencies. The Multimodal therapy approach expands behavioral psychology to include interactions between sensory, imaging, cognitive, and interpersonal factors. Following the identification of an individual's needs (per the BASIC I.D.), the therapist produces a modality profile and an intervention plan based on an analysis of the interactions among modalities in the client's BASIC I.D. Direction and techniques are arranged in an optimal *firing order*. Then client education proceeds to help the client better understand behavior and the antecedent causes. Continued assessment allows the modality profile to be adjusted as needed.

9. C: Professional misconduct is outlined in standard 3.12 of the AAMFT Code of Ethics (2015). MFTs may violate the Code if they are convicted of a felony or misdemeanor or engage in conduct that is likely to result in a criminal conviction related to an MFT's qualifications or functions. Professional misconduct also includes continuing to practice while no longer being competent due to physical or mental impairment or an impairment resulting from alcohol or substance abuse. The existence of a performance improvement plan may or may not be indicative of an episode of professional misconduct. Other forms of professional misconduct include infractions received by other professional organizations, licensure suspensions or revocations, and failure to comply with an AAMFT ethics investigation.

10. C: The invariant prescription technique is commonly used when an unbalanced alliance (e.g., over-protector or inappropriate confidant) has occurred between one parent and a child with serious problems (e.g., anorexia, psychosis). The technique involves both parents leaving home at times unexpected by the child. Part of the process is that the purpose of the departure must remain a "secret." Over time, this controversial strategy disrupts the inappropriate alliance (i.e., "game") and reconnects the parents, and it usually interrupts much of the troublesome symptomatology in the child as well. Establishing rituals is a Milan systemic therapy technique used to disrupt patterns of interactions. For example, in the odd/even day ritual, one parent is assigned to make all decisions in managing a problem child on odd days and the other on even days. Consultation is permitted, but decisions are made unilaterally. Subtle learning includes: 1) someone must always be in charge of the children (preventing neglect); and 2) both parents must share in decisions and caring (balanced parenting). From this, new family patterns can emerge. Paradoxical reframes, also known as positive connotations, are therapist statements used to help family members view interactional patterns as protective mechanisms used to achieve family harmony. Pretend techniques/reversals are the therapist's directives encouraging the family to act "as if" there were different circumstances or outcomes.

11. B: Virginia Satir identified communication styles or stances that block communication between family members. The blamer finds fault in others and responds in a conflictual manner to hide painful feelings. The placater is a people pleaser whose underlying motive is to hide fearful feelings. The distractor often changes the topic or talks incessantly because of an underlying fear of reality. Finally, the computer communication style operates in a matter-of-fact, systematic manner. The computer appears calm and rational but hides beneath a widespread fear of emotions.

12. A: One of the most rapidly growing fields of applied psychology, neuro-linguistic programming (NLP) is used to evaluate a client's construction of reality. NLP, advanced by John Grinder, Richard Bandler, and Gregory Bateson in the 1970s, is one of the fastest growing fields of applied psychology. Focused on creativity, learning, and change, it seeks to evaluate the construction of reality. "Neuro" refers to processes of the five senses, which produce individual experiences. "Linguistic" refers to the use of language to construct and share experiences. "Programming" refers to methods used to organize inner processes and produce results. In sum, NLP recognizes that the world of experience is not the "real" world, but rather the world as perceived and unconsciously lived as though real – which can result in misperceptions and problems. By way of these inner models, one can exchange problematic feelings, thoughts, beliefs, and habits for those that are more helpful or useful.

13. C: The misdiagnosis of schizophrenia in black people suggests a tendency for therapists to engage in confirmation bias, which is the propensity to seek information that confirms a hypothesis and minimizes information that challenges it. This process involves the use of heuristics, or mental shortcuts, grounded in implicit stereotypes and attitudes. To address racial biases, DSM-5-TR includes culture-related diagnostic issues and the impact of culture and racism on mental disorders, as well as the prevalence of risk factors in specific ethnic groups. Negativity bias occurs when adverse events or feelings tend to be more impactful than positive ones, even when they exist proportionately. For example, a negative remark on a performance evaluation has more impact than multiple positive remarks. Social desirability bias is the tendency to underreport undesirable attributes and overreport desirable ones. Finally, decision fatigue results from a decreased capacity to make sound decisions when overloaded with multiple choices and decision-making demands.

14. C: The five phases of functional family therapy (FFT) include engagement, motivation, relational assessment, behavior change, and generalization. During the engagement period, the therapist seeks to increase the family's responsiveness to therapy, establish a strengths-based approach, and build credibility. The motivation phase is marked by the therapist's efforts to decrease blame, negativity, and hopelessness. Motivational techniques include positive reattribution, which involves: 1) developing positive themes, 2) reframing problems as a family focus rather than individual blaming, and 3) bolstering hope and expectations of change. In phase three, a relational assessment is conducted. A relational assessment is used to help the therapist identify the function or "payoffs" for problematic behaviors, interactional patterns of communication, sources of resistance, individualized family needs, and hierarchies within the family system. The goal of phase four, changing behavior, is accomplished through systematically training the family in communication, problem solving, coping, competent parenting, conflict management, problematic behavior sequencing (blaming, negativity, etc.), the reciprocation of positive behaviors, and with the therapist modeling specific behavioral changes. Lastly, in the final phase of FFT, the goal is to generalize change. This includes utilizing community systems and resources to maintain and enhance the positive changes achieved.

15. C: Standard 6.1 of the AAMFT Code of Ethics (2015) addresses technology-assisted professional services, including, but not limited to, phone and internet. MFTs must determine the appropriateness of technology-assisted supervision; inform the supervisee of the potential risks and benefits; ensure the security of the chosen technology; and obtain related education, training, and experience. MFTs providing clinical supervision must have a board-approved contract, but the board is not required to approve contracts specific to technology-assisted supervision.

16. B: Much like Maslow's needs hierarchy, William Glasser's reality therapy (RT) identifies core human needs that are universal: 1) *power* (includes winning, feeling worthwhile, and overall achievement); 2) *love and belonging* (encompasses loved ones/families and group affiliations); 3) *freedom* (autonomy and personal space); 4) *recreation*; and 5) *survival* (i.e., food, shelter, and sex). A core RT principle is that everyone is working continuously to meet these needs, whether consciously or unconsciously. Problems arise when efforts are not effective. Therefore (after the establishment of a therapeutic relationship), among the first steps in RT is to measure success in meeting these fundamental needs. Key counseling questions are: 1) "What do you want?" 2) "What are you doing to get what you want?" 3) "Is it working?"

17. C: As related to gender and power, *circularity* (sometimes called *circular causality*) suggests that each participant in a dyadic exchange has equal responsibility for the process and outcome, even if it ends in violence or other abuse – clearly a "blame the victim" perspective. The traditional goal for each to feel sided equally was ineffective when the relationship was unequal at the outset. Structural family therapists use blocking to force family members to implement new patterns of relating to one another. As such, blocking would not be challenged by advocates for domestic violence victims. Similarly, externalization is not associated with domestic violence or general system theory. Instead, it refers to a technique used in narrative therapy to redefine the problem as something external rather than a permanent part of the family system. Lastly, emotional neutrality is not associated with general system theory. Instead, Murray Bowen used the term emotional neutrality to describe an individual's capacity to function amid emotional tension. For Bowen, this involves avoiding triangulation and investigating circumstances in a logical and controlled manner.

18. C: These three main object relations are attachment, frustration, and rejection. Attachment refers to the desire of the ego to have stable and comfortable relationships with closely identified objects (people or things of importance). Frustration emerges when: 1) needs are not adequately met; 2) needs are met, but in ways not recognized; 3) identification with frustration (often through childhood background patterning) leads to chronic seeking of something to be frustrated about; or 4) causing frustration in others is used to obscure against personal frustration. Rejection emerges when the self is unconsciously seen as small, weak, and potentially victimized by others, seen as powerful, abusive, and rejecting.

19. B: According to standard 2.3 of the AAMFT Code of Ethics (2015), MFTs provide clients with reasonable access to their records. Additionally, "when providing couple, family, or group treatment, the therapist does not provide access to records without written authorization from each individual competent to execute a waiver." Verbal authorization to obtain records is only acceptable in the event of an emergency.

20. C: Therapists who fail to take appropriate preventative measures with high-risk clients who die by suicide may be charged with negligence unless the presumed harm to the client was not foreseeable (i.e., proximate causation). Experts in the field are assigned to negligence cases and are tasked with determining standards of care by considering whether the actions in question were appropriate and reasonable compared to the actions of other therapists in similar situations. The duty of care is a responsibility determined by the therapeutic relationship, with the duty of care owed to clients seen during the time in which the negligence accusations were made. Proximate causation or actual causation would also validate charges of neglect.

21. B: After obtaining the *presenting problem or chief complaint*, the second step is to find and identify symptoms. In determining how symptoms may support a subsequent DSM diagnosis, it is helpful to consider symptoms from the perspective of *symptom clusters*. Ultimately, everything to be done (selection of assessment tools, aftercare, referral, etc.) must arise out of properly identified symptoms and stressors. There are 10 key symptom categories are: 1) *emotional* concerns (fears, anger, etc.); 2) *compulsive* behaviors (skin picking, overwork, etc.); 3) *impulsive* behaviors (sexual conduct, abuse, etc.); 4) *hyperactivity*; 5) *learning* issues (poor attention, distraction, etc.); 6) *neuromuscular* elements (dysgraphia, encopresis/enuresis, etc.); 7) *cognitive and perceptual* problems (panic, confusion, etc.); 8) *physical* complaints (forgetfulness, cramps, etc.); 9) *sleep* problems (insomnia, nightmares, etc.); and 10) *addictive* problems (drugs, pornography, etc.). The third step involves issues of *duration*: constantly, comes and goes, a week ago, etc. Fourth are issues of *intensity*: strong, disabling, a little, a lot, etc. Combining symptoms (often in clusters or categories) with duration and intensity, from all relevant sources, will ultimately lead to an appropriate diagnosis.

22. D: *Collateral report* sources may vary widely, from past health and/or mental health providers, hospital staff and/or records (drug tests, discharge summaries, etc.), legal records (divorce, arrests, sentencing, etc.), school reports, family members, friends, witnesses, etc. The purpose of collateral reports is to gain a broader understanding of a client's situation, support systems, vulnerabilities, strengths, etc. The consequences of failing to obtain collateral reports can range from benign to extremely serious. For example, a client who denies suicidality may have voiced true intent to many others and/or made obvious detailed plans and preparations of which the interviewer is unaware. A client presenting as psychotic may have an underlying medical condition of which the interviewer has not been apprised. Collateral reports are especially valuable when mental illness or substance use disorder predisposes confusing or evasive interviewing, and to obtain information that will be incomplete due to a client's incapacity to recall or report. Where collateral sources of information are lacking, the integrity and availability of information remains a significant challenge that should continue to be pursued.

23. A: Termination can occur by design or by default. Termination by design, or planned termination, regards the end of therapy as predetermined, resulting from bilateral (i.e., client and therapist) decision making. Termination by default occurs when the decision to end treatment is unilateral, with either the therapist or client choosing to end therapy prematurely or unexpectedly. Client-centered therapy is open ended and nondirective, making it prone to termination by default. Termination by design is associated with brief, or time-limited, treatment, which includes, but is not limited to, solution-focused therapy, cognitive behavioral therapy, and mindfulness-based stress reduction. Solution-focused therapy, or SFBT, is grounded in the present moment and can be conducted as a stand-alone, or adjunct, treatment in as few as 3–5 sessions. Cognitive behavioral therapy focuses on present-time thinking and lasts between 6 and 20 sessions. Mindfulness-based stress reduction is a manualized therapy that can generally be completed in 6 weeks.

24. B: Contextual therapy, as developed by Ivan Boszormenyi-Nagy, emphasizes "therapeutic leverages in mobilizing trust" to bring about greater family wholeness and stability. Based on the psychodynamic model, emphasis is placed on mutual support, trust, fairness, and loyalty. These and other ethical principles are necessary to generate and maintain positive family relationships. Fairness (justice) must always be achieved only through standards of accountability and boundary setting, rather than by blaming, retaliation, or revenge. Not unlike Bowenian Therapy, contextual therapy recognizes that destructive family patterns can often be traced back multiple generations. The goal of relational ethics is balanced through giving and receiving. Family dysfunction arises when a loss of accountability and caring leads to a deterioration of trust. Expressions of disturbance arise when an imbalance in giving and receiving and/or loyalties and ethical conduct emerge among family members. When families are unable to balance entitlement and fulfillment needs (especially as related to caring), negative symptoms are experienced. Perpetuation of these imbalances can extend to future generations, leading to further failure and/or exploitation of others.

25. B: The AUI (*Alcohol Use Inventory*) is a set of 24 scales that measure various features of involvement with the use of alcohol. The MAST (*Michigan Alcohol Screening Test*) is one of the oldest and most accurate alcohol screening tests available, effective in identifying dependent drinkers with up to 98 percent accuracy. The SASSI (*Substance Abuse Subtle Screening Inventory*) evaluates alcohol and other substance use disorders.

26. D: The *NEO Personality Inventory-Revised (NEO PI-R)* is used to assess the Big Five personality domains (and six trait factors in each), from the five-factor model (FFM) of personality: extraversion, agreeableness, conscientiousness, neuroticism, and openness to experience. The NEO PI-R is a 240-item self-administered test, designed for adults and the elderly with at least a sixth-grade reading ability, usually completed in 35-45 minutes. The *Millon Adolescent Personality Inventory (MAPI)* assesses personality, behavioral issues, and expressed concerns of adolescents ages 13-18. This 150-item true/false tool requires a sixth-grade reading capacity and is usually completed in 20-30 minutes. The *Myers-Briggs Type Indicator (MBTI)* is primarily used to assess high school and college students, classifying a person into one of 16 personality types based on four paired tendencies: world view/extraversion or introversion; information gathering/sensing or intuition; decision making/thinking or feeling; and treatment of others/judging or perceiving. It is particularly effective matching students with teaching styles. The *Minnesota Multiphasic Personality Inventory-2 (MMPI-2)* is a broad-based assessment of personality, emotional, and behavioral disorders in adults.

27. A: The Daily Living Activities (DLA-20) assessment would serve as a standardized functional rating scale allowing for the acquisition of outcome measures. The DLA-20 allows the client and therapist to assess functional levels along 20 domains, some of which include health and safety, problem-solving and coping skills, managing time and money, and family and interpersonal relationships. The Patient Health Questionnaire-2 (PHQ-2) is a screening tool used to detect

215

depression and anhedonia, and it serves as the first step in determining the presence of clinical depression. The PHQ-9 should be used to determine probable depressive disorders. The Mood and Feelings Questionnaire (MFQ) is a youth and parent measurement instrument for depression. Finally, the Primary Care PTSD Screen for DSM-5 (PC-PTSD-5) is a diagnostic screening tool for probable PTSD.

28. D: Adopting a no-secrets policy and allowing clinical judgment to determine disclosure best illustrate the therapist's ethical obligation. A no-secrets policy authorizes consent for the therapist to determine whether, when, and to what extent confidential disclosures will occur. This is the best course of action because it is a written statement obtained at the outset of treatment and is included as part of informed consent. Disclosing the affair to the couple is inadvisable due to the potential for rupturing therapeutic alliance(s) and potentially worsening Jada's suicidality and depression. Meeting with Jada separately and encouraging her to disclose the affair is only appropriate once a no-secrets policy is enacted and specific disclosures are stipulated within the policy. For example, some policies specify that each partner will be provided with the opportunity to first disclose, whereas other policies permit clinical judgment to determine disclosures in all circumstances. Keeping the information confidential may or may not be in the couple's best interest, and guiding the discussion toward disclosure is vague.

29. A: The first step in the postdiscovery process would be for the therapist to safely manage the couple's emotional reactions. During the postdiscovery, or trauma, phase, emotions range from anger, hopelessness, grief, and shock to depression. The therapist must first assist the couple with safely managing their emotions before determining the circumstances surrounding the affair, assessing the couple's potential for forgiveness, and resolving ambivalence concerning separation. When discussing the circumstances related to the affair, the therapist's role is to interrupt destructive interrogation patterns and defensiveness by helping the couple communicate respectfully and constructively. To successfully treat couples who experience infidelity, all contact with the affair partner must be terminated.

30. A: Narrative therapy unfolds in three stages: 1) Narrative exploration: personal and family history is reviewed, problem-saturated narratives are identified and told, and problems are separated from persons (e.g., externalize problems as an "affliction" rather than blaming the person, so the client and family can unite in defeating the problem, not the person). 2) Re-authoring: look for unique outcomes (explore past pitfalls/successes and identify how and why they occurred) in order to deconstruct damaging narratives and reconstruct productive ones. In this process, the therapist questions beliefs and assumptions, identifies contradictions and family resistance, and mitigates "totalizing" views (that polarize and create antagonism). Problems are explored through effects (not causes) to avoid blame, destructive elements are identified, problem influences are mapped (who benefits, what feeds/starves the problem), as well as relative influence (where it disrupts and where there is some control)), and ways to overcome (taking charge). Finally, 3) recruit support: the client and family unite as change agents to re-author old narratives and start new narratives about the client. Recruiting support from the client's past, as well as therapist support letters, can all help reinforce new narratives.

31. A: Symptoms of PTSD include recurring intrusive memories, avoidance of places and people associated with the trauma, negative mood and cognition, and alterations in reactivity and arousal. These symptoms must exceed one month for *post-traumatic stress disorder (PTSD)* to be fully diagnosed. While the disorder was first identified in Vietnam-era war veterans, many traumatic events can precipitate the condition. Examples include abductions, physical and sexual assaults, severe auto accidents, and disasters. Nearly 80 percent of individuals diagnosed with PTSD have one or more comorbid disorders. Mental disorders with the highest comorbidity include substance abuse, depressive disorders, and additional anxiety disorders. Early traumas may predispose susceptibility to PTSD later in life. *Prolonged Exposure, EMDR, and CBT* are evidence-based practices for PTSD.

32. B: The Health Insurance Portability and Accountability Act of 1996 (HIPAA) includes the Security Rule, which addresses the storage and transmission of electronic records. The Security Rule applies to data protected by encryption and multifactor authentication. Multifactor authentication uses two or more verifying measures (e.g., password, biometric data, knowledge data) to allow users remote access. Requiring a combination of factors allows for higher security and protection of data stored in the client's electronic health record and information transmitted online (e.g., via email). HIPAA includes two additional rules for a client's electronic data. The Privacy Rule outlines standards for protected health information (PHI) and an individual's right to obtain copies of their PHI. This excludes the therapist's private psychotherapy notes. The Breach Notification Rule mandates entities to notify clients and authorities in the event of compromised security (e.g., data breaches). Notifications must also include efforts made to mitigate further risk.

33. C: Rational emotive behavior therapy (REBT) views emotional consequences as produced by an individual's belief system instead of external causal events. An individual's happiness and growth stem from intrapersonal and interpersonal life. Culture, environment, family, and social group all influence personal choices. REBT therapy helps individuals and family systems to positively change where possible and to develop acceptance where change options are limited. People innately possess the capacity for both rationality and irrationality. Early formative experiences and environment can help shape the tendencies toward each. Because perceptions, emotions, thoughts, and behaviors generally coexist, they become core features of the REBT therapeutic relationship. Whereas all individuals are capable of rational thinking, the REBT therapist views emotional disturbances arising primarily through *self-talk*, which can lead to *cognitive distortions*. Cognitive distortions emerge when events are framed in absolute terms, such as "should," "must," "always," "have to," or "ought." The irrational nature of such absolute thoughts produces emotional and behavioral disequilibrium, and thereby subverts the achievement of important goals and purposes. William Glasser is associated with reality therapy, John B. Watson is associated with behaviorism, and Aaron Beck is known for cognitive therapy.

34. C: Exposure and response prevention (ERP) is a form of CBT and an evidence-based practice for obsessive-compulsive disorder, eating disorders, phobias, and some anxiety disorders. ERP involves exposure to objects, situations, or images that tend to result in distressing thoughts and emotions. For clients with obsessive-compulsive disorder, the success of ERP is contingent upon facing triggers head on without using compulsive behaviors. Change is generated through the behavioral process of habituation. Evidence-based practices for persistent depressive disorder include CBT and interpersonal therapy. Treatment for schizophrenia varies but is generally a combination of medication, social skills development, and assertive community treatment. Finally, evidence-based practices for bipolar disorder vary but generally include psychoeducation, CBT, interpersonal therapy, and peer support.

35. B: The diathesis-stress theory would best predict this client's risk level. This theory is the basis for a model determining risk levels for many behavioral health conditions, including suicidality. The theory is based on the assumption that individual vulnerabilities or predispositions confer increased risk when in the presence of psychosocial stressors. In the scenario, the client's vulnerabilities or predispositions include the diagnosis of depression in the presence of an abrupt firing, which represents an acute stressor. The diathesis-stress model also considers personality characteristics in determining vulnerability. Research suggests that high degrees of socially prescribed perfectionism is a vulnerability for suicidal ideation, which is reflected in the client's constant demand to be the best and feeling humiliated. The interpersonal theory of suicide assumes that suicidality results from the interaction between an individual's desire to die by suicide and their capacity to carry out that desire, thus making a solid case for means restriction (e.g., removal of guns). The theory of planned behavior suggests that the strongest predictor of suicidality is the motivation or desire to carry out that behavior. Lastly, differential activation theory hypothesizes that suicidality results from the repetitive pairings of episodes of distress with thoughts of suicide. These pairings become so reinforced that they remain dormant until the next mood-induced episode, which quickly produces cognitive reactivity.

36. B: The question "Do you ever have thoughts about not wanting to live?" reflects suicidal thinking instead of discerning if the client has a suicide plan, access to methods of suicide, or intention to follow through with suicidal behavior. Thoughts about not wanting to live reflect passive suicidal ideations, whereas thoughts of wanting to commit suicide refer to active suicidal ideations. Therapists need to assess for both of these types of thought because they are each predictors of suicidal behavior. Asking clients if they have the means to die by suicide assesses access. Asking clients how they would kill themselves determines if there is a plan in place, whereas determining the desire to end their life reflects intent. When conducting a suicide assessment, qualitative (i.e., standardized assessment measures) and quantitative measures must be obtained, with qualitative measures consisting of open-ended questions (e.g., "Tell me about your plans to take your life").

37. B: Mary Ainsworth expanded upon John Bowlby's theory of attachment using the "strange situation" experiment to identify attachment styles. Ainsworth's experiment measured infant responses and interactional behaviors at various intervals. Each interval involved a series of steps during which an infant, mother, and stranger are introduced, briefly separated, and then reunified. The experimental observations led to Ainsworth's classification of attachment styles as secure, insecure/ avoidant, and insecure resistant/ambivalent. Securely attached expressed initial distress when separated from their mother and resisted the stranger's attempt to console them. When the mother returned, the child began to explore the surrounding environment and interacted with the stranger. Infants who displayed insecure or ambivalent attachment responded with intense distress upon separation from their mothers. The infant reacted fearfully to the stranger and rejected the mother's attempt to provide comfort. Infants who displayed insecure-avoidant attachment showed no signs of distress when the mother left, interacted with the stranger during the mother's absence, and remained disinterested when the mother returned.

38. B: MFTs respect each client's right and responsibility to make decisions by honoring client autonomy. Specifically, standard 1.8 of the AAMFT Code of Ethics (2015) identifies relationship decisions to include "cohabitation, marriage, divorce, separation, reconciliation, custody, and visitation." Standard 1.8 also states that the MFT's responsibility is to help clients understand the consequences of their relationship decisions. The ethical principle of autonomy involves each client's freedom to choose and control the direction of his or her life. Justice emphasizes fair and equitable treatment. Beneficence involves promoting a client's health and welfare, and nonmaleficence involves the pledge to do no harm.

39. B: Marriage and family therapists (MFTs) do not avoid offering professional opinions on clients seen in therapy. Standard VII in the American Association for Marriage and Family Therapy (AAMFT) Code of Ethics (2015) outlines the responsibilities of MFTs when conducting evaluations in various legal contexts. MFTs providing forensic evaluations cannot offer professional opinions on those whom they have not directly interviewed. Additional provisions of standard VII include the following: MFTs avoid performing custody evaluations on clients seen in therapy, MFTs refrain from performing forensic evaluations on clients seen in therapy unless legally mandated, and MFTs refrain from providing testimony in legal proceedings unless specific competencies are acquired and maintained.

40. D: Genograms differ from structural family maps in that genograms include relevant physical and mental health information. Popularized by Bowenian therapists, genograms are pictorial representations of at least two generations of family members. Therapists use genogram shapes and symbols to represent various family relationships, births, deaths, marriages, divorces, sexual orientations, genders, occupations, and significant historical events. Structural family maps are visual representations of a family but differ from genograms in that they are designed to incorporate intrafamily dynamics. Family maps illustrate the effects of family dynamics on the family's structure and show how hierarchies, subsystems, coalitions, and boundaries are created and maintained. Structural family therapists use family mapping to join with the family, identify relational problems, and guide the therapeutic intervention, thus making it a process that is constantly being revised and refined.

41. C: Client behavior can be at least partly understood by examining the surrounding environment. This has been called the *person-in-environment* (PIE) concept. From this perspective, an individual remains in constant interaction with a variety of environmental systems all the time. Some of the systems will be family, friends, educational systems, the workplace, etc. Involvement with each system is considered to be dynamic, with each influencing the other mutually. From this perspective, changing one or more interactive systems can ultimately change a client's interactions and behaviors. According to *Bronfenbrenner's ecological theory* (also known as *eco-systemic theory*), common environmental system domains include: the *micro-system* (the client's living setting), the *meso-system* (relational context between domains – e.g., a child rejected by his father may have trouble with a teacher), the *exo-system* (connections between a client's own context and the context of someone else in their micro-system setting – a spouse feeling her partner's distress with a workplace issue), the *macro-system* (the context of locale and culture, etc.), and the *chrono-system* (socio-historical events and transitions – e.g., a divorce).

42. D: During the 1980s, White and Epston began to develop narrative therapy, which became widely used in the 1990s and beyond. This collaborative approach views individuals as separate from their problems, and as possessing many of the skills needed to solve their problems. Using thematically linked narratives, "problem-saturated" stories often emerge, which are likely to become "identity stories" or self-defining narratives. These stories can exert a powerfully negative influence. The focus then moves to conversations that help people to co-discover their previously unrecognized possibilities and unseen positive story lines. The result is an empowering "re-authoring" of their lives. Steve de Shazer and Insoo Berg followed by developing solution-focused brief therapy, while Bill O'Hanlon produced solution-oriented or possibility therapy. Carolyn Atteave was an American Indian known for extending family systems theory to the client's external social networks. Lastly, Cloe Madanes is one of the pioneers of strategic family therapy, and Froma Walsh is known for identifying key concepts associated with family resiliency.

43. B: This instrument was designed specifically for use with adolescents, drawing upon situations that are common to this age group. CRAFFT is a mnemonic acronym of first letters of key words in the six screening questions: driving a Car while intoxicated; using alcohol or drugs to Relax, feel better, or fit in; using alcohol or drugs when Alone; Forgetting events that occurred while using alcohol or drugs; requests by Family/Friends to limit use; and getting into Trouble while using alcohol or drugs. CRAFFT is meant to determine whether or not a more extensive conversation is warranted. Screening begins by asking the client three opening questions about alcohol or drug use during the past 12 months. If a "Yes" answer is received to one or more of the three opening questions, the clinician must then ask all six CRAFFT questions. The other instruments are: the

AUDIT (Alcohol Use Disorders Identification Test); the CAGE (also an acronym: needing to Cut down drinking, feeling Annoyed at drinking criticism, feeling Guilty at drinking, and needing a morning Eye-opener drink); and the MAST (Michigan Alcoholism Screening Test).

44. C: Faith-based 12-step programs proclaim to be spiritual but not religious, and encourage participants to find a spiritual solution (i.e., turning one's will and life over to a higher power) to a spiritual malady (i.e., addiction). The premise of Alcoholics Anonymous (AA) is that alcoholism is a progressive disease of the mind, body, and spirit. AA members are encouraged to develop a belief— or become willing to believe—in a higher power or a god of one's own understanding. Rational Recovery is based on rational emotive behavior therapy, which targets irrational thoughts and emphasizes personal control of addictive behaviors. Rational Recovery is offered as a secular alternative to AA by deemphasizing powerlessness from substances, thus having a nonreliance on a higher power. Similarly, SMART Recovery, which stands for Self-Management and Recovery Training, does not include spirituality or religious content as part of its program. Finally, the Oxford Group was a Christian organization that viewed recovery as a moral failure and used evangelical tactics to recruit members, causing AA's cofounder Bill Wilson to retain some of the Oxford Group's spiritual principles when branching off and starting AA.

45. C: As derived from the Tarasoff case, the duty to protect has been rigorously debated regarding other mechanisms of harm, with precedents set on either side of the issue. For example, how to handle a situation where a client is HIV positive and is known to be having unprotected sex with a partner who is unaware of the client's HIV-positive status. Given the deadly nature of the human immunodeficiency virus, it has been determined that a clinician may be warranted in breaching confidentiality if education about the dangers and efforts at counseling have failed to alter the HIV-positive client's behavior. For the therapists to break confidentiality, there must be an identified 3rd party, the 3rd party is unaware of the risk, and the client is unreliable in informing those at risk. In the scenario, the client and therapist were meeting for the first time, which suggests that the client may or may not be reliable in following through with their promise to warn all parties (and may not return for follow-up sessions).

46. B: Created by Les Greenberg and Susan Johnson in the 1980s, emotionally focused therapy (EFT) and emotionally focused family therapy (EFFT) propose that relationships are primarily emotional bonds. The aim of EFT and EFFT is to initiate, remedy, and restore attachment bonds among couples or family members. Emotions can be adaptive, and thus problematic emotions and difficult internalized experiences can be improved through careful management. EFT assists clients to more effectively identify, understand, and manage emotional states and experiences. EFT asserts that people must first enter a place before they can leave it behind. Therefore, clients are first helped to engage a maladaptive emotion (e.g., fear or guilt, etc.) in order to transform it. Because emotions are basic neuroendocrine responses to which we react, EFT aims to create new emotive relationships and thereby supplant negative reactive emotions with positive emotions of attachment. About 70-75 percent of participants experience recovery, and 90 percent show significant improvements that are less susceptible to relapse than by other approaches. Thus, EFT and EFFT are evidence-based treatment modalities.

47. A: A clear understanding should be established between the clinician and client as to the purpose of an assessment, and questioning and information sought should be in harmony with that purpose. The MFT Code of Ethics requires that a client's privacy must be respected. Thus, information should never be elicited out of curiosity or for unrelated secondary purposes (e.g., research). Thus, if an assessment is court ordered to explore safety concerns prior to returning children to the home following allegations of abuse or neglect, the assessment should focus on relevant issues (e.g., parenting practices, stressors, coping skills, substance use/abuse, attendance or completion of court-ordered treatment and support systems, etc.). Where significant risks are associated with an assessment, greater breadth and detail may be in order (e.g., suicidality, domestic violence, child abuse, etc.). Similarly, the need to verify information with secondary sources increases proportionally. In general, single-issue voluntary treatment assessments involve the least risks and thus require greater adherence to the targeted purpose and potentially no collateral contacts (e.g., a depressed adult voluntarily seeking treatment).

48. B: Client-centered therapy asserts that there are three core counseling attributes necessary for client change: empathy, congruence (genuineness), and unconditional positive regard. Genuineness is expressed as an authentic alignment between a therapist's words and actions. It involves responding in the present moment to the client's thoughts, feelings, and vulnerabilities. Empathy refers to putting oneself "in another's shoes." Rogers believed that accurate empathetic understanding stems from the therapist's ability to respond compassionately to the client's subjective experience. Finally, therapists convey unconditional positive regard through acceptance, caring, and belief in each client's inherent sense of worth.

49. D: Empirical evidence suggests that standardized outcome measures with the greatest efficacy are used collaboratively. Standardized outcome measures help clients and therapists develop appropriate treatment goals, determine the strength of the therapeutic alliance, and prevent clients from premature dropout. Routine outcome measures are best when they are simple, immediate, and have a clear purpose. Standardized outcome measures are generally not obtained from various sources unless there are school-related issues (e.g., attention-deficit/hyperactivity disorder); however, outcome measures for children and adolescents are still more effective when used collaboratively. Pairing standardized measures with subjective measures does not improve standardized measures' efficacy. Research shows therapists to be poor predictors of client progress, underscoring the importance of using valid and reliable assessment measures. Finally, diagnostically comprehensive instruments are not more effective than other instruments. Studies indicate that comprehensive assessments are less likely to be integrated into the therapy session due to their time demands.

50. C: While the therapist must attend to process (emotional relationship processes) and structure (interlocking triangles), neutrality must be maintained to draw the involved parties into working on issues rather than deferring to the therapist. This is best facilitated when the therapist avoids taking sides and uses "I" statements of opinion (rather than judgments) to encourage self-reflection, growth in relationships, and de-triangulation. Encouraging new behaviors can help facilitate change, as well as identify relationships and processes needing further attention. Education regarding listening and speaking skills (avoiding interruption and focusing on "I-positioning" instead of confrontation and blaming, etc.) can help family members address needs without overreacting and escalating conflicts. Emphasis should be more on "I feel" than critiques of other family members. Three-generation genograms can identify the roots of emotional fusion (i.e., over anxiety and low differentiation) in longstanding family characteristics and processes. Emotional fusion is best revealed by asking questions of individuals (not groups) that encourage self-reflection, diminish anxiety, and slow down emotional processes. The focus should be to turn from how others are upsetting the individual, to their role in the interpersonal problems.

51. C: The Family Assessment Device is a self-report instrument that is based on the McMaster Model of Family Functioning. It can be used in the initial stages of therapy and to track changes following treatment, with measures for affective involvement and responses, behavioral control, problem solving, family roles, communication, and overall family functioning. The Family Adaptability and Cohesion Scale IV measures a family's level of cohesion as evidenced by degrees of enmeshment and disengagement. The Dyadic Adjustment Scale measures cohesion, satisfaction, and emotional expression among members of an intact relationship dyad (e.g., cohabitating couples, spouses). The Conflict Tactics Scale is a standardized assessment instrument that measures the frequency, severity, and prevalence of violent, conflictual, or harmful behaviors, including assault, aggression, sexual coercion, verbal abuse, and injury.

52. A: Research shows that standardized instruments effectively produce improved treatment outcomes when used collaboratively, repeatedly, and purposefully. Research consistently shows that standardized screening and diagnosis alone are not associated with improved treatment outcomes. Measurement-based care includes the use of standardized means of tracking symptoms and overall functioning. The benefits of measurement-based care include, but are not limited to, the following: (1) developing and enhancing the therapeutic relationship, (2) understanding the client's viewpoint, (3) assessing and directing treatment, (4) determining the level of care, (5) allowing client input to construct realistic and attainable goals, and (6) assisting with quality assurance standards.

53. C: Contingency contracts are generally used with individuals diagnosed with substance misuse and children with behavioral disorders. For example, a 7-year-old diagnosed with oppositional defiant disorder earns the privilege of watching television after completing a chore. Contingency contracts operate using the Premack principle, which posits that high-preference activities reinforce the completion of low-preference activities. Safety plans are reserved for clients who are at risk for suicide. The therapeutic contract includes agreements related to the therapeutic process. Finally, therapeutic negotiation refers to the collaborative nature of the therapeutic alliance.

54. D: This is an example of overgeneralization. Overgeneralization is a cognitive distortion occurring when one event is used to determine an absolute rule or conclusion. This cognitive distortion is characterized by the frequent use of the words "always" or "never." Minimalization occurs when a person diminishes the significance or importance of an event when attempting to make an accurate and objective appraisal. Personalization involves fault-finding and blaming oneself for circumstances beyond one's control. A person uses emotional reasoning when using one's feelings to justify actions, erroneously believing them to be an accurate reflection of reality.

55. C: Systems theory was originally posited by Ludwig von Bertalanffy to describe how organisms worked together, and how they flourish or decease depending on openness to their environment. Margaret Mead and Gregory Bateson extended the theory with the concepts of positive and negative feedback (negative maintains homeostasis and is *morphostatic* (unchanging); positive induces change and is *morphogenic* (change inducing)). Jean Piaget and Noam Chomsky also used systems theory in their structural concepts. Systems changed the exploration of causality from a linear view to a circular view causality (i.e., via interacting loops or repeating cycles). Additional key systems concepts include: 1) where a system's set of elements are in interaction, each element is affected by everything that affects any other element; 2) the system is no stronger than its weakest element; 3) the totality of a system is greater than the sum of its parts; and 4) boundaries are, to varying degrees, permeable as to the amount and type of feedback received.

56. C: Dialectical behavior therapy (DBT) includes consultation as a programmatic component to help prevent therapist burnout. Therapists trained in the delivery of DBT attend 1–2-hour weekly consultations to maintain and enhance their motivation and skills and to provide feedback, validation, and problem solving skills for working with high-risk clients, including individuals diagnosed with borderline personality disorder and those experiencing chronic suicidality. Acceptance and commitment therapy (ACT) focuses on clients' relationships with their beliefs, narratives, and memories and uses diffusion to "unhook" clients from those distressing attachments. Integrated cognitive behavioral therapy (I-CBT) is also used with clients experiencing suicidality and comorbid conditions by targeting underlying thought processes and behaviors. Lastly, rational emotive behavior therapy (REBT) uses forceful disputing against irrational beliefs in order to change emotions and behaviors.

57. D: Standard 3.1 of the AAMFT Code of Ethics (2015) states that MFTs "pursue knowledge of new developments and maintain their competence in marriage and family therapy through education, training, and/or supervised experience." Standard 3.2 states that MFTs "pursue appropriate consultation and training to ensure adequate knowledge of and adherence to applicable laws, ethics, and professional standards." Legal and ethical consultations are offered to members of the AAMFT.

58. C: The Crisis Assessment Tool (CAT) incorporates established principles based on communication theory. Communication theory (i.e., communimetrics) involves providing needs-based decision making across multiple levels of care. Caregiver involvement is critical for addressing immediate needs and for ongoing outcome monitoring. The CAT is based on six principles: (1) obtaining relevant information for decision making and treatment planning; (2) using a four-level rating system to determine immediately actionable steps; (3) accurately rating client needs; (4) incorporating cultural and developmental considerations; (5) rating measures that address what is happening, instead of determining why it is happening, with the CAT measures described as "agnostic as to etiology"; and (6) providing time frames for measures (e.g., 24 hours, 30 days). The CAT is primarily used by mobile assessment workers; it is a descriptive tool that refrains from cause-effect judgments, with the exception of the adjustment to trauma item rating (the John Praed Foundation [n.d.]).

59. D: A cognitive-behaviorist focuses primarily on modifying problem behavioral consequences. Due to this perspective, behaviorists do not treat whole families and they usually involve only those subsystems that are central to the targeted behavior. From a systems perspective, this can be problematic, as many problems manifest in an individual or a couple may stem from larger issues in the family system. Further, where the entire family is not involved, new behaviors may fail to be sustained and reinforced. Even so, behavioral couples therapy has been the most researched approach, and it does assist couples in learning to better discuss problems, resist negative thinking, and decondition anxiety. It is also particularly useful in treating disorders of desire, arousal, and orgasmic disorders. In issues of substance use disorders, it may also help in restructuring dysfunctional interactions that can perpetuate the problem.

60. B: Pansexuality is the sexual attraction to all people/genders whereas bisexuality is the sexual orientation that describes intimate or romantic attraction to more than one gender (but not necessarily all genders). Asexuality (i.e., "ace") describes individuals who lack sexual desire or interest in sexual activity. Asexuality exists on a spectrum, with levels of sexual disinterest that are either complete or partial. Queer is used when referring to a spectrum of identities and orientations that run counter to those traditionally found in a person's cultural mainstream.

61. C: Communication in a family is unavoidable, providing input and output and consisting of *reports* and *commands*. Patterns of commands evolve into family rules and circumscribe all behavior. The therapist assesses for patterns of family dysfunction and patterns of reactions, and then addresses it by improving family communication. Key terms in the MRI model include: 1) *communication*: a tool for power management, from which input and output feedback dysfunction arises and is maintained; 2) *correct behavior*: family behavior is viewed as neither wrong or right, whether individually or as a unit; 3) *circular causality*: communication patterns that result in 4) *feedback loops* (stimulus and response chains) – establishing positive feedback loops is a key intervention; 5) *family homeostasis*: maintained by family rules; 6) *meta-communication*: non-verbal communication; 7) *negative feedback* (preventing change); 8) *relabeling*: reframing client issues and behaviors to stress the positive; and 9) *symmetrical relationships*: similar behaviors between individuals that are founded on commonalities. The MRI Model was developed at the Mental Research Institute in Palo Alto, California, as set up by Don Jackson in 1958 to observe schizophrenics and their families.

62. C: A Greek term for "interpretation" (derived from the name of Hermes, the messenger of the gods), it was originally used to refer to the interpretation of meaning in scriptural texts (more properly, "exegesis"). However, Aristotle introduced the term into the domain of philosophy. It has since been broadened to refer to the interpretation of levels of meaning found in all human experiences. The study of feedback loops in systems theory (whether positive or negative in action) is known as "cybernetics." Cybernetic feedback loops allow systems to be self-correcting and self-sustaining. While hermeneutics can promote greater shared understandings, it is not primarily a communication tool. Psychoanalysis is clearly a positivistic theoretical orientation (i.e., rooted in scientific observation, deduction, and theoretical certitude), while hermeneutics is decidedly not positivistic in nature.

63. D: The Federal Emergency Management Agency has identified the following five mission areas as part of the National Preparedness Goal for communities: prevention, protection, mitigation, response, and recovery. Mitigation refers to actions taken to reduce the damaging effects of unavoidable emergencies, such as loss of life and property. Prevention refers to actions that arrest an emergency or stop it from occurring. Protection involves keeping communities safe against threats and hazards in a manner that allows personal growth, interests, and aspirations to flourish. Lastly, response refers to immediate actions after an emergency or catastrophic event that protects lives, resources, and property to meet a community's basic needs.

64. B: Bleuler's four A's of schizophrenia may be defined as: 1) *autism* – meaning a preoccupation with internal stimuli; 2) *affect* – often inappropriate to external context (e.g., laughing at tragic or distressing things); 3) *associations* – loosened associations (connections) with reality, with illogical or fragmented thought processes; and 4) *ambivalence* – simultaneous, contradictory thinking, filled with uncertainty as to decisions to make or actions to take. Other pathognomonic (disease-indicative) symptoms: 1) delusions – false and culturally inappropriate beliefs; 2) hallucinations, especially hearing voices (auditory hallucinations); and 3) odd or abnormal behavior – acting in bizarre ways, dressing inappropriately, and otherwise behaving strangely. In the acute phase, five areas of disturbance (symptoms) are commonly noted: 1) thought form (illogic); 2) thought content; 3) perception; 4) emotions; and 5) behavior. Thought disturbances may involve: *over-inclusiveness* (irrelevant information interrupting logical thought); *neologisms* (making up words that only mean something to the client); *blocking* (simple speech that halts mid-sentence and resumes tangentially, often due to auditory hallucinations); *clanging* (word choice based on sounds such as rhyme; *echolalia* (echoing words mindlessly); *concreteness* (inability to think abstractly); and *alogia* (e.g., "poverty of speech").

65. B: The Session Rating Scale (SRS) is a four-item self-assessment measure of the therapeutic alliance as determined by the client's rating of the effectiveness of the MFT's approach, the degree to which the client feels understood, the client's level of agreement with treatment goals, and the client's overall satisfaction in the direction of therapy. The Authenticity Scale (AS) measures the concept of congruence as proposed by Carl Rogers. Congruence is believed to shape the client's overall growth and foster an authentic client–counselor relationship. The Outcome Rating Scale (ORS) assesses levels of psychological distress. It is combined with the SRS as part of the Partners for Change Outcome Management System, an evidence-based, client-directed approach to measuring outcomes and associated predictors of therapeutic effectiveness. The SRS and ORS are designed to be used in each session. The Brief Psychiatric Rating Scale (BPRS) measures psychosis in individuals with schizophrenia and related disorders.

66. A: In compliance with the Health Insurance Portability and Accountability Act of 1996 (HIPAA), the client must be provided access to her protected health information (PHI) unless the therapist is reasonably sure that the PHI will be used in criminal, civil, or administrative proceedings. Therapists who are deemed a covered entity must comply with HIPAA unless state laws are more stringent (i.e., the client would be offered more protection). This is further outlined in the Code of Federal Regulations (CFR): 45 CFR 164.524(a)(1)(ii). Therapists must respond to a client's request for PHI within 30 days "regardless of whether the PHI that is the subject of the request is old, archived, and/or not otherwise readily accessible" (45 CFR 164.524[b][2]). On very rare occasions, a client is denied access if the therapist's professional judgment determines that the access is "reasonably likely" to threaten the life of the client or that of another person. Access cannot be denied if the therapist's judgment determines that the information included would be emotionally harmful to the client or if it is information that the client would not understand.

67. D: The most common application of functional family therapy (FFT) is among adolescents with serious behavioral problems. FFT is sometimes used in situations of couple and/or parental abuse in a marriage or family context. Originally developed by James Alexander and colleagues, FFT integrates systems theory with behavioral and cognitive therapy. FFT targets sequential behavioral patterns (e.g., delinquency, drug abuse, acting-out behaviors, etc.) and their associated meanings oriented along two dimensions: relational connection (interdependency in closeness vs. distance) and relational hierarchy (control and influence). Based on the theoretical communication and systemic concept of "equifinality" (Watzlawick et al., 1974), very disparate family relational patterns (e.g., anger and fighting vs. warmth and cooperation) are often used produce the same functional outcomes (power or subservience vs. closeness or distance). FFT endeavors to understand and systematically revise those factors that motivate and reinforce behavior. FFT posits that all individuals develop through a mix of personal capacities and environmental harmonies and diatheses (conditions of dysfunction), which then interact to produce enduring patterns of relational interaction. The optimal goal is to achieve "midpointing" – a relationship balanced between independence and positive emotional linkage.

68. D: The MFT would first ask the daughters to describe the behaviors that they find concerning. This is the first step in determining if the client is at risk for harming herself or others. Asking the daughters to describe the current crisis is relevant because it (1) helps the therapist understand potential variations in the definition of a crisis, (2) allows for the consideration of cultural norms and influences, (3) provides an opportunity for the therapist to observe boundaries and communication, and (4) permits collaboration with the family on treatment goals and interventions, which may or may not involve an outside referral, the development of a safety plan, or a more comprehensive risk assessment.

69. B: Although alcohol use is frequently implicated when these conditions appear, it is not the alcohol itself that causes either condition. Any condition that inhibits absorption of vitamin B1 could be implicated. Vitamin B1 deficiency causes brain damage in the lower areas called the thalamus and hypothalamus. This damage is known as *Wernicke encephalopathy*. Symptoms include confusion and loss of mental activity (can progress to coma and death), loss of muscle coordination (ataxia) often seen in leg tremors, and visual changes such as abnormal eye movements (back and forth movements called nystagmus), double vision, and eyelid drooping. *Korsakoff syndrome* (or *Korsakoff psychosis*) results from permanent damage to areas of the brain involved in creating and retaining memory. Symptoms include severe memory loss, an inability to form new memories, making up stories (confabulation), and seeing or hearing things that are not really there (visual and auditory hallucinations). Without treatment, both conditions will worsen; with treatment, the disorder can be slowed or stopped (but not reversed). Although *delirium tremens* (DTs) can also produce hallucinations and delusions, it will quickly resolve as alcohol withdrawal subsides.

70. D: Existential theory posits that greater freedom comes from greater awareness. Tension exists between freedom and responsibility. Everyone is obligated to direct their own life and to accept responsibility for and consequences of their choices. While life tends toward meaninglessness, emptiness, loneliness, and guilt, meaning and purpose can be created, pursued, and accomplished. Lastly, learning that a relationship with ourselves precedes meaningful relationships with others. Therapeutic tasks to complete also include: 1) developing the trust to search and find answers; 2) overcoming the fear that we'll find no "core" or meaning inside ourselves; 3) finding our sense of self-identity; 4) stop using "doing" to avoid "experiencing"; 5) accepting anxiety as a function of striving, which cannot be avoided if we are to find meaning; 6) facing oneself is frightening, but it is the path to change; 7) death is frightening, but that same fear propels us to grow and thus lifts us; 8) rejecting determinism allows freedom; 9) regaining control lets us shape our lives; and 10) "the question": given past life patterns and the results, are you ready to choose a new pattern?

71. D: To be *gravely disabled*, an individual must have: 1) an enduring *mental disorder* that leaves him/her: 2) presently impaired; 3) unable to provide for food, clothing, and shelter; 4) to an extent that will directly result in physical danger or harm to the person. Severe physical disability does not quality if one can direct care with third-party assistance. Bizarre or eccentric behavior alone does not qualify. Nor is anticipated decompensation sufficient. Common qualifying conditions include chronic organic brain syndromes (Alzheimer's, etc.) and chronic schizophrenia. Frequent symptoms include: 1) *food*: has no food, cannot distinguish between food and non-food, consuming spoiled food, etc.; 2) *clothing*: oblivious to public nudity or exhibitionism, a total lack of hygiene, unable to dress safely for weather; 3) *shelter*: homeless from inability to seek or accept assistance, dangerous home practices (filth, fire hazards, infestations, lack of heat, water, and/or bathing/toilet facilities, hoarding nonsensical items and losing essential items; 4) *finances*: totally unable to comprehend and/or manage simple finances, extremely vulnerable to exploitation; and 5) *health*: cannot understand or follow medical instructions, becomes lost frequently without seeing it as a problem, regularly socially abusive, threatening, or assaultive.

72. D: The term "family atmosphere" refers to the nature of the relationships existing among family members. The focus is on the influence of the family of origin on one's current personality, as revealed by a review of the past to determine its present impact. Interpretation and insight development are fundamental elements of Adlerian group counseling. As a system, each member of a family exerts influence on all other members. As role models, parents help shape all family relationships. The term "family constellation" includes each family system (i.e., parents, children, and extended family), by which alignments and relationships within the family are established and maintained. Key motivations for these alignments and relationships include: 1) birth order (which shapes subsequent behaviors); 2) family goals; and 3) growth of increasing skills that are ultimately needed for independence and achieving success. Family atmosphere is not unique to crisis intervention. Bowenian family therapy uses the term multigenerational transmission process, which occurs when anxiety-provoking symptoms are passed down from generation to generation. Adler initially partnered with Sigmond Freud, but broke away to emphasize the influence of birth order, social interest, and family constellation.

73. C: According to a recent study published in *JAMA Pediatrics* (Wilson et al., 2022), homicide is the number one cause of death among youths aged 0–17. Over the past 2 decades, there has been a steady annual increase in homicide rates among all subpopulations, with significant increases in the years 2019–2020, during which time the number of homicides rose 27.7%. From 2018 to 2020, homicide rates increased 16%, whereas females saw a decline between 1999 and 2020. Black children had the highest increases, followed by Hispanic children. There was a slight overall decrease for white children (0.7%), whereas Asian Pacific Islander children saw an overall decrease of 4.4%. The leading cause of death for children younger than age 10 is child abuse and neglect. For children 11–17, crime and arguments among acquaintances were the most common causes of homicide, with guns being the most common means used in children's deaths.

74. B: Enduring and meaningful family systems changes typically occur through: 1) meaningful learning; 2) significant events (major losses, family structure changes, etc.); 3) substantial change in one or more family members; or 4) through completed positive feedback loops. Changes such as these eventually engage the entire family system. *First order* change consists of minor structural changes, but without completion of positive feedback loops it remains vulnerable to "relapses." *Second-order* change is high level and alters the entire system, such as establishing entirely new transactional patterns, and is thus more enduring. *Calibration* is the baseline from which change is measured. *Wholeness* refers to the interdependent family system, where change in one can produce change in all. The concept of *equifinality* posits that similar results can be achieved in many different ways. *Equipotentiality* posits that a similar event can produce highly diverse outcomes (e.g., incest can produce promiscuity in one and fear of sex in another). *Non-Summativity* posits that because a family is greater than the sum of its parts (Von Bertalanffy) and different from the sum of its parts (Lewin), it should be treated as a unit, not as individual members.

75. A: As a key family therapy researcher in the 1970s, Liang drew upon Marx, who conceived of mystification as a misrepresentation of events (process) or actions (praxis) to serve the interests of one class over or against another. Laing theorized a similar set of events between individuals and particularly family members. Mystification was used to "mask" family issues through conflicting and contradictory narratives. Recognizing this pattern would be crucial to progress in the practice of family therapy. John Bell is known for implementing family therapy with concepts, strategies, and techniques used in group therapy. Virginia Satir is known for communications/humanistic model or human validation process model of family therapy, which emphasizes emotional experiences and enhanced communication. Another important contributor to family therapy in the 1970s was Rachel Hare-Mustin, who wrote an article entitled "Feminist Approach to Family Therapy" in 1978. Her goal was to enhance the strength of women both within the family construct and in society.

76. C: This approach utilizes techniques and interventions (sometimes even rude and confrontational, then playful and cajoling) that intensify longstanding turmoil to the point where issues of the "here and now" are more evident. At times, rather than attempting to eradicate family pathology, it is augmented until it "self-destructs." This way, family self-actualization is achieved, and reasonable responses to absurdities (e.g., sarcasm and manipulation) come out on top. In this process, the therapist retains a "facilitator" role, and the family interaction processes are revealed through the "reflection" of a genuine and non-defensive observer. Narrative therapists believe self-defeating cognitions create family dysfunction, while Whitaker encourages authentic expressions of emotional discomfort and pain. Cognitive-behavioral therapists seek to uncover individuals' childhood schemas about themselves, their future, and their world and how these beliefs affect their present-day perceptions and behaviors. Lastly, feminist theories seek to dismantle or upend socially constructed gender roles within a family.

77. A: Individuals experiencing persistent depressive disorder and major depressive disorder usually go through intermittent periods where symptoms of depression worsen. The BDI-II may be used to measure depression severity, augmented with an assessment of suicide and homicide risks. In about 6 percent of the population, major depressive disorder may clear and leave a lesser depression lasting two years or more, known as persistent depressive disorder or dysthymia. Both cognitive-behavioral (CBT) and interpersonal psychotherapy (IPT) offer effective treatment. CBT helps patients change their thinking and behavior, often targeting overgeneralization, perfectionism, and catastrophizing. IPT helps improve troubled relationships and adaptation to stress. Other issues addressed in IPT include unresolved grief, relational disputes, and poor social and communication skills.

78. D: Compared to perpetrators of elder financial exploitation who are known to the victim, perpetrators who are unknown to the victim commit crimes that result in lower incurred financial loss. Elder abuse consists of sexual abuse, neglect, physical abuse, emotional abuse, and financial exploitation (i.e., the improper or illegal use of a dependent or vulnerable individual's money, property, funds, or valuable assets). Instances of financial exploitation by a stranger are shorter in duration and are more likely to be reported. Exploitation perpetrated by strangers includes telephone scams, mass mailings, internet scams, one-time in-home workers, and financial service providers. Perpetrators known to their victim include family members, relatives, or any individual on whom the victim is dependent. Cases involving known perpetrators are underreported and tend to co-occur with other forms of abuse, including neglect and physical abuse. The financial loss incurred is more significant due to the perpetrators' continued access to funds that often go undetected until the victim's funds are depleted.

79. D: Prochaska and DiClemente's model of behavioral change involves a series of stages considered to be cyclical. Prochaska and DiClemente's (1992) transtheoretical model of the stages of change consists of the following stages: precontemplation, contemplation, preparation, action, and maintenance. Individuals may pass through the stages in a linear fashion; however, it is not unusual for individuals to approach the steps in a cyclical manner. This holds true not only for individuals with substance use disorder, but for any individual faced with a challenging decision or lifestyle change. Individuals in the precontemplation stage lack awareness of behaviors that may require change. The contemplation stage is marked by having an awareness of behaviors requiring change but lacking a concrete plan for doing so. In the preparation or determination stage, clients acknowledge the detrimental consequences of their behavior and actively prepare to make a change. The action stage is characterized by making concrete changes. Finally, in the maintenance stage, individuals take the action steps required to sustain change. The cyclical nature of the stages is exemplified when individuals encounter relapse. Some experts include relapse as an unofficial sixth stage. When relapse occurs, some may restart the process with the precontemplation phase, whereas others may restart the process with the preparation stage. Although the stages are ordered, they are not linear. Additionally, the stages are not described as irreversible because passage through one stage does not indicate that the person will not cycle through that stage again if maintenance is not sustained.

80. B: The Stark Law prohibits healthcare professionals from profiting off of self-referrals made on behalf of all federal healthcare recipients. This law (aka the Physician Self-Referral Law) prohibits physicians and other healthcare providers from referring patients to designated health services payable by federally funded entities (e.g., Medicaid, Medicare). The law also prohibits self-referrals for healthcare services that may benefit an immediate family member, including ownership/investment benefits and compensation agreements. The law was created to protect Medicaid and Medicare recipients from unnecessary medical services. This law is unique in that penalties for violation are severe, even if the prescriber's actions were deemed unintentional.

81. B: Therapists keep professional wills in place to provide instructions for therapist-initiated interruptions that are generally unanticipated, including injury, illness, or death. Professional wills identify colleagues responsible for informing clients of the service interruption and allow for follow-up care to be arranged. A termination letter is an individualized treatment summary that formalizes termination and provides documentation that the professional relationship has come to a close. The termination letter contains a brief treatment summary, the reason for termination, the diagnosis at discharge, progress made toward the client's goals, and beneficial referrals or resources. A treatment contract is a signed form outlining informed consent, client rights and responsibilities, agreed-upon fees, confidentiality, and treatment expectations. Finally, an advance directive is a legal document outlining individuals' preferences for medical care if they cannot make those decisions for themselves.

82. A: The Columbia Suicide Severity Rating Scale (C-SSRS) measures suicidal ideation and suicidal behavior. Suicidal behavior is regarded as a potentially self-injurious act in the presence of at least some desire or intention to die. The C-SSRS helps provide clients and clinicians with agreed-upon definitions for what is considered suicidal thinking and behavior. It is also helpful for tracking suicidality over time. An actual suicide attempt or suicidal behavior is defined as a "potentially self-injurious act committed with at least some wish to die, as a result of the act... (the) intent does not have to be 100%. If there is any intent/desire to die associated with the act, it can be considered an actual suicide attempt." The rating scale further clarifies that medical injury or harm does not need to be incurred for an action to qualify as suicidal behavior but rather the potential for it must be present. For example, a person attempting to kill themselves is unsuccessful because of a malfunctioning firearm. Similarly, intent can be inferred in the absence of an expressed desire to die if the behavior can be clinically inferred as highly lethal (e.g., jumping from a building or a self-inflicted gunshot wound).

83. C: Although several combined factors can cause a person to be more likely to die by suicide, individuals with a history of suicide attempts are at the highest risk. Therapists understand that the most significant risk factor for death by suicide is previous suicide attempts, regardless of an individual's age, gender, diagnosis, or sexual orientation. Additional risk factors for death by suicide include individuals older than age 45; men; individuals with substance use disorders; lesbian, gay, bisexual, transgender, and queer individuals; and individuals who are nonbinary (those whose gender is not exclusively male or female). Risk factors also include experiences of trauma, mental disorders, a family history of suicide, chronic pain, and direct exposure to another person's suicidal behaviors. Regarding racial backgrounds, Native Americans have the highest rates of suicide in the United States.

84. B: Attunement best reflects a therapist's mastery of the use of self. The therapist's use of self involves intentional and conscious responses helpful for addressing countertransference and enhancing the therapeutic process. Attunement describes the emotional synchrony between an infant and a caregiver. In healthy attachment, the caregiver is responsive and deeply understands the infant's inner experiences. Similarly, attuned therapists respond genuinely and congruently in the present moment. The therapist's use of self involves the ability to accurately attune to how the therapist's culture, family, social positionality, spirituality, morals, worldviews, etc. influence the therapeutic process. The therapist's use of self involves differentiating between personal and professional roles and identifying with the client's experiences. Through introspection and attunement, the therapist develops the skills of differentiation and identification. Empathy focuses on the client's underlying feelings, whereas the self of the therapist involves "self-insight, self-access, and self-management" (Aponte & Kissil, 2017). Theoretical competence is not an element of the therapist's use of self. Self-disclosure must be balanced with intentionality and determining the appropriateness of sharing personal information.

85. B: The diathesis-stress model is based on the premise that schizophrenia results from a combination of underlying vulnerabilities and environmental factors. The diathesis-stress model of schizophrenia suggests that the disorder results from a vulnerability or predisposition to the disorder (i.e., diathesis) and environmental or psychosocial stressors, including trauma and urbanicity. Evidence-based practices for treating schizophrenia include family psychoeducation using a diathesis-stress framework to illustrate the impact of problem solving, communication, and crisis intervention on recovery and functioning. The model suggests that caregivers and clients learn effective ways to reduce psychosocial stressors to improve relationships with caregivers and decrease the burden of the illness on the family system. The deficit model is another framework used in treating schizophrenia. This model is based on the theory that myths, misconceptions, or lack of knowledge of schizophrenia negatively impact interactions between clients and caregivers, resulting in worsened symptomatology. General adaptation syndrome describes a person's physiological response (i.e., flight or fight) to stressors. Finally, the expressed emotion model is used to treat schizophrenia. Research on expressed emotion indicates that emotional overinvolvement (e.g., hostility, criticism) is associated with increased relapse rates.

86. D: *Feedback* is information from past experiences/behaviors that allows the system to monitor and regulate itself. *Feedback loops* refer to self-correcting mechanisms for adjustments to keep a system stable (negative feedback), while *positive feedback loops* monitor outcomes of efforts to produce change. *Recursiveness* (the key to *circular causality*) refers to the reciprocal influences between a system and its environment (e.g., no experience is independent of others – e.g., to ignore others, there must be others to ignore, who will then react). The *ripple effect* refers to the influence that change exerts on all other elements in a system and its environment. *Circular causality* emphasizes that if A acts upon B, then B influences A in the exchange as well – as opposed to the old *linear causality*, which suggests one way only. *Open systems* exchange readily with the environment; *closed systems* tend toward isolation – with different *boundaries* allowing for each. *Isomorphism* refers to parallel though separate systems or structures that respond the same (an abuse victim may later abuse in way he or she was once abused).

87. B: Marriage and family therapy is intended to be brief, cost-effective, and solution-focused. According to the AAMFT (n.d.), MFTs "regularly practice short-term therapy, 12 sessions on average. Nearly 65.6% of cases are completed within 20 sessions, 87.9% within 50 sessions."

88. C: MFTs are ethically obligated to honor a client's right to autonomous decision making, which does *not* entitle clients to recommendations for decision making in the context of family relationships. Standard 1.8 of the AAMFT Code of Ethics (2015) states that MFTs honor the rights of clients "to make decisions and help them to understand the consequences of these decisions." Further, therapists communicate that clients "have the responsibility to make decisions regarding relationships such as cohabitation, marriage, divorce, separation, reconciliation, custody, and visitation." A client's right to autonomous decision making also includes the MFT providing information that is culturally and linguistically appropriate; acknowledging that the client is free to enter into or remain in treatment (being free from therapist coercion or manipulation) unless it is court ordered; and providing information regarding the MFT's credentials, qualifications, and counseling approach.

89. B: Ambivalence is used in motivational interviewing (MI) to describe the state of a person who is conflicted over wanting to change and simultaneously not wanting to change. MI therapists explore ambivalence with clients in the contemplation stage of change. Therapists engage clients in weighing the pros and cons of making a decision. Disequilibrium is a family systems concept that refers to a state of imbalance occurring when families are unable to accommodate or assimilate new experiences and challenges. MI therapists help clients develop discrepancies when exploring ambivalence. Developing discrepancy is an MI principle designed to help clients recognize inconsistencies between their current behaviors and their future goals and values. The goal of developing discrepancy is to tip the decisional balance toward change.

90. B: NSSI occurs in the context of posttraumatic stress disorder (PTSD), binge eating disorder, and substance use disorder. NSSI, as well as suicidal behavior, is also associated with depression, particularly depressive episodes marked by hopelessness and perceived burdensomeness. Borderline personality disorder rather than histrionic personality disorder is a comorbid antecedent for NSSI. Researchers have found that although all eating disorders may coexist with NSSI, binge eating and purging occur at higher rates than restrictive eating, as seen with anorexia.

91. B: The *Sixteen Personality Factor Questionnaire, Fifth Edition (16PF)* utilizes factor analysis to measure personality dimensions. The 185-item questionnaire, for ages 16 and older with at least a fifth-grade reading ability, is usually completed in 35-50 minutes. Scales include: 16 bipolar dimensions of personality; 5 global factors; and, 3 validity scales. It is used in vocational and educational advising. There are several other assessment tests. The *Psychological Screening Inventory (PSI)*. A 130-item mental health screening tool for adolescents and adults that can be completed in about 15 minutes, it offers information about the need for further therapy. The *Tell Me a Story Test (TEMAS)* identifies patterns of emotions in children ages 5 to16. Translated into Spanish, it uses normed culture-specific picture cards. The *Tennessee Self-Concept Scale, 2nd Edition (TSCS:2)* gauges feelings of self-worth in those ages 7 to 90. Administered in 10-20 minutes, it includes 15 scores within four subscales: self-concept, supplementary, validity, and summary, plus a scale for feelings about school or work. The adult version requires a third-grade reading ability (for ages 13 and over), while the child format requires a second-grade reading ability (for ages 7-14).

92. C: Introduced by Henry Stack Sullivan, parataxic distortion or transference distortion is a faulty perception based on projected fantasy rather than actual experience (e.g., falling in love and seeing the other as perfect). The fantasy involves past experiences and expectations in response to emotional stress (e.g., new relationship formation, or the cognitive dissonance required to maintain a difficult relationship). Sullivan's additional relationship concepts include: 1) anxiety (encompassing all emotional suffering, such as guilt, shame, etc.): a warning signal, as it can bind an individual into unhealthy relationships and patterns. Recovery involves self-dynamism (developing characteristics that generate approval). 2) security and security operations: refers to any interpersonal attitude (often unconscious) or action used to diminish anxiety and enhance emotional well-being. Healthy security operation (e.g., sublimation – a socially acceptable outlet for distress – or selective inattention – ignoring that which is distressing) sustains an individual's interpersonal competence. Unhealthy security operations may have social costs or even result in psychiatric illness. Such operations are part of the self-system – or, more completely, the self-protecting system.

93. A: Experiential couples therapy (ECT) focuses on two levels of exploration: 1) discovering the hurt and longing that underlies defensive withdrawal or expressions of anger; and 2) assisting participants to understand how these feelings are manifest in their relationship. This process utilizes underlying attachment longings to help participants focus more on their own needs instead of blaming and fault-finding. ECT reframes problems as cycles instead of intents, facilitates new patterns of emotional expression, and thus produces new positive-emotion-linked experiences. Change occurs by: 1) identifying the "triggers" of negative emotional patterns; 2) learning to accept the negative as only one part of the self/relationship; 3) finding the underlying vulnerable feelings and hurts; and, finally, 4) turning to the vulnerable and caring part of the relationship to reduce negativity and find mutuality and genuine care together.

94. D: Cybersex has become a significant systemic disruptor of couples and families. It involves all forms of cyber-technology used for sexual arousal (literature, images, sound files, and videos). This form of Internet usage can produce problematic triangulation in already troubled relationships;

providing a disengaging release, it can leave crucial conflicts unaddressed and unresolved. Cybersex can also lead to transient uncommitted relationships that superficially meet psychosexual needs but blunt and distort the formation or remediation of more significant relationships. Individuals at high risk for cybersex dependence include those with ongoing sexual compulsivity disorders or addictions and those with a history of long-term sexual abuse.

95. D: Bipolar disorder 1 is characterized by alternating symptoms of depression and mania. Symptoms include agitation, grandiosity, insomnia, poor concentration, and hyperactivity. The manic phase consists of elevated mood, increased energy, and wakefulness. Alternately, depressive symptoms consist of sadness, low energy, hypersomnia, and hopelessness. Mood-congruent psychotic features have hallucinations and delusions matching their current mood. For example, a person experiencing a manic episode may experience grandiose delusions. During a depressive mood, a person may experience excessive guilt or the delusion that someone is after them.

96. B: The games reveal interactional "rules" found in some families. The rescue game assigns one person to placate (agree) with all others, one to always blame (disagree, while causing guilt), one to defend the person blamed (a rescuer), and another to respond with irrelevance (i.e., to distract, often by simply changing the subject). The goal is to reveal the turmoil and chaos that result when families lack cohesion and collaboration. The coalition game involves two people assigned to always agree while a third disagrees (or two who disagree and a third agrees), revealing the problems of divisive alliances, impasses, and elements of triangulation. The lethal game involves everyone agreeing with everyone else, regardless of costs or needs. Finally, the growth (or "vitality") game can be used to highlight the benefits of the family working well together. In this game, people speak openly, flexibly agreeing or disagreeing depending on family needs and realities while yet being allowed to remain a part of the system/family. These "games" can be valuable tools for learning and better understanding the barriers and benefits involved in family interaction and communication dynamics.

97. A: Lewin's leadership styles are: 1) *autocratic*: the leader seeks no input or consultation from members of the group, typically resulting in substantial discontent; 2) democratic: all group members are given a voice in decision making, though the group's leader typically still makes the final decision; and 3) laissez-faire: everyone in the group is encouraged to make (and be solely responsible for) their own decisions. Basic group leadership tasks include finding therapeutic material or resources, operationalizing, and sustaining the therapeutic process. Key features of group leaders are reflected in the acronym CHASE: Charming (kind), Honest, Acceptable, Self-disclosing (though limited) and Empathetic. Creation and maintenance of a group requires: 1) adequate preparation in advance; 2) gate-keeping (to ensure milieu is therapeutic); 3) a unifying force; and 4) stability (consistent structure, etc.). Issues for group leaders to guard against among members: 1) chronic tardiness; 2) serial absences; 3) sub-grouping (forming cliques); 4) scapegoating; and 5) time hogs.

98. A: Awareness of damaged trust and injustice at the outset of therapy is not a prerequisite for successful participation in contextual therapy. Indeed, building this awareness is one of the primary therapeutic goals of this approach. However, as awareness of trust and fairness evolves, it is important for the therapist to allow family member goals to evolve and change as well. Contextual therapy requires a meaningful level of personal consciousness and systemic awareness that may be beyond some family members. Similarly, the persistent misuse of power by family members who are intellectually immature and lack insight will blunt the effectiveness of this approach for some families. Other families may resist a collaborative approach and will require more aggressive direction and guidance. In such circumstances, other treatment modalities may be required. Of additional note, some have criticized the emphasis of contextual therapy on fairness and trust, as this narrow focus may obscure many of the other values and positive benefits that are readily produced within families.

99. A: *Informed consent* requires that no agreement to receive any treatment will be deemed valid unless sufficient information has been provided to achieve meaningful consent. The information provided should include the potential risks (both if the treatment is refused and if the treatment is provided), the hoped-for benefits, the associated costs, and the available options. While every remote potential eventuality and outcome cannot always be addressed, the information presented should include that which a "reasonable person" would expect in the presenting circumstances. Simply delivering information, however, is not sufficient to secure genuine informed consent. The client must also be helped to understand the information in language and with examples appropriate to his or her intellectual capacity, primary language and communication skills, and educational background. Where an individual lacks the capacity to consent (e.g., a minor, a developmentally delayed adult, a cognitively impaired frail elder, or someone suffering from mental illness, etc.), informed consent from a legal guardian should be obtained.

100. B: He also introduced the term "skew" in reference to the distortions that a serious personality disorder can introduce into a family. This American psychiatrist's studies of schizophrenia and family interaction patterns and dynamics made significant early contributions to the ultimate emergence of the field of family therapy in the 1960s. Other key contributors include: Nathan Ackerman, author of *The Psychodynamics of Family Life* (1958), who used family process dynamics in the treatment of mental disorders; and, Gregory Bateson, who produced the theory of dysfunctional communication known as the "double bind." His controversial theory posited that veiled contradictory messages from differing levels could produce confusion and even schizophrenic behaviors when devolving upon individuals within a family construct. Milton Erikson is known for hypnosis and inspiring the works of Virginia Satir and Gregory Bateson.

101. D: BF Skinner used nomothetic research methods to develop the theory of operant conditioning. Nomothetic research methods use quantitative data to produce evidence-based results that can then be generalized to larger populations. Skinner conducted experiments with animals and generalized his findings to humans. The nomothetic approach uses the scientific method to confirm the hypothesis about populations that are "interindividual" variations or those existing across people. Alternatively, an idiographic approach aims to make predictions for one person across time. Idiographic research examines "intraindividual" and qualitative data to formulate personality theories of one person over time. Examples include Maslow's hierarchy of needs, Rogers's person-centered theory, and Allport's trait theory.

102. B: Emotional affairs include an element of secrecy, a deep emotional connection, and implicit or explicit sexual chemistry. Sex addictions involve a compulsive desire or need that can manifest in compulsive masturbation, online pornography, and repetitive sexual encounters. This behavior is often driven by obsessive thinking. In recent decades, emotional affairs have increased with advancements in technology and social media. Emotional affairs can be just as destructive to relationships as physical affairs; however, combined affairs (i.e., emotional and physical) tend to have the most significant impact on individuals in long-term committed relationships.

103. A: When multiple clients are involved, it must be agreed upon in advance who the client is, whether it be a child, spouse, or the entire family. In a family with a member who is abusing alcohol and/or substances, it may be tempting to decide that the primary client is the person abusing substances. However, in couples counseling, the client is *the relationship*, and in family counseling the client is the *family system*, as that is what requires remedy and support. Where a substance-abusing member exists, that individual will also need personalized substance abuse counseling

233

outside the family counseling experience. But, when seeing a family, the entire family system remains the client. This does not mean, however, that the entire family will always and only be seen collectively. However, great caution must be exercised, as any display of partiality can substantially blunt counseling effectiveness.

104. A: The HIPAA Privacy Rule indicates that the family has the right to receive a copy of the record, including the information note. The Privacy Rule protects a therapist's psychotherapy notes, which include a healthcare provider's notes "documenting or analyzing the contents of a conversation during a private counseling session or a group, joint, or family counseling session and that are separate from the rest of the patient's medical record" (see Title 45 of the Code of Federal Regulations [CFR] § 164.501). The therapist recorded a summary of the call on an information note placed in the client's record. Thus, the information note is not considered a psychotherapy note. The child protective services case being open or closed does not have any bearing on the parents' right to obtain a copy of their child's records. Because the client is younger than 18, client authorization is not required to release the records.

105. B: Teacher involvement would allow the client to generalize learned skills, provide social reinforcement and rewards, and model coping behaviors. Swan et al. (2016) developed a CARE model to facilitate communication and help collateral contacts (e.g., parents, teachers) provide effective support for school-aged clients with anxiety. The CARE model provides examples of how collaterals "can best support anxious youth by acting as coping models, labeling and validating anxious feelings, rewarding brave behavior, and reducing accommodations" (Swan et al., 2016). Accommodations include excessive reassurance, sending a child home, or avoidance during a feared situation. Although some accommodations may provide short-term aid, they are ineffective long-term solutions. Instead, collateral contacts are encouraged to gradually expose clients to anxiety-provoking situations to promote self-efficacy and aid in the long-term reduction of symptoms.

106. C: Behavioral family therapy is designed for individuals with severe mental illness, including psychosis, schizophrenia, and bipolar disorder. It is a manualized form of therapy with components that include engagement, psychoeducation, role-playing, problem solving, communication, and relapse prevention. Psychoeducation incorporates information on medications, their side effects, and the benefits of medication compliance. Relationship therapy is a general term used to describe couples therapy. Structural family therapy focuses on restructuring families to reflect appropriate boundaries among hierarchies and subsystems. Strategic family therapists join, assess, and restructure families to reduce circular and pervasive patterns of dysfunctional communication.

107. B: The principle of informed consent involves several essential elements. Informed consent requires that clients are made aware of the expected benefits and possible risks, costs, and burdens involved in participation. This includes a discussion of the nature of the proposed treatment, possible alternatives, monitoring for adverse outcomes, follow-up support options, and ensuring a complete understanding of all the information provided. Researchers are ethically obliged to report all results, even if unfavorable. Clients must be provided with the contact information for individuals who can answer questions about the research and explain their rights as research participants. Client confidentiality must be ensured by disguising client identities. Clients who are legally incapable of providing consent include minors or clients with impairments that limit understanding. MFTs must also provide special consideration to participants who also receive clinical services.

108. B: Clinicians conduct biopsychosocial assessments to facilitate identified strengths and needs for each client from the initial stages of treatment through discharge. The American Society of Addiction Medicine criteria are used during comprehensive treatment for mental health and substance-related disorders across all levels of care. There are six criteria dimensions: (1) acute intoxication and/or withdrawal potential, (2) biomedical conditions and complications, (3) emotional, behavioral, or cognitive conditions and complications, (4) readiness to change, (5) relapse, continued use or continued problem potential, and (6) recovery and living environment (Mee-Lee et al., 2013). Each dimension uses a Likert scale to measure severity levels, with 1 representing no to very low risk and 4 being severe or imminent danger.

109. D: The federal government does not need to prove that violations of the Anti-Kickback Statute resulted in client harm or financial loss to healthcare programs. The Anti-Kickback Statute prohibits doctors and related healthcare providers from paying, offering, receiving, or soliciting monetary compensation or remuneration (i.e., anything of monetary value) in exchange for healthcare services. This is a criminal law, with violations for accepting remuneration or compensation, even if the service was medically necessary. Although it is acceptable for providers to waive client copays or deductibles on a case-by-case basis for a client unable to pay, routinely waiving these payments is a violation of the Anti-Kickback Statute. The law is designed to prevent increased costs, unfair competition, and impaired medical decision making.

110. D: Interpersonal and social rhythm therapy (IPSRT) is an evidence-based practice for bipolar disorder. It is based on the notion that symptom exacerbation stems from disrupted bodily systems (e.g., sleep) and social rhythms (e.g., structured routines). IPSRT is built on an "instability model" consisting of three interconnected systems thought to contribute to the recurrence of bipolar disorder: stressful events, medication noncompliance, and disruptions to social rhythms. IPSRT aims to improve coping skills, restore healthy routines, and help clients effectively manage symptoms of bipolar disorder. As such, IPSRT blends psychoeducation, CBT, and interpersonal therapy. One component of IPSRT includes assisting the client with grief or anger over losing their healthy self and moving toward acceptance of a lifelong illness. Stress inoculation therapy is commonly used to treat PTSD. Functional family therapy is an intervention used to treat juvenile delinquency. Cognitive processing therapy is most effective for symptoms of PTSD.

111. A: This technique is known as cognitive defusion. Acceptance and commitment therapy emphasizes a person's relationship with their thoughts and beliefs rather than the beliefs themselves. Diffusion involves helping clients "unhook" from those beliefs, including associated memories and narratives. Clients are encouraged to investigate their relationship with distressing and omnipresent thoughts to which a person feels entangled or attached. Forceful disputing is a rational emotive behavior therapy technique. Emotional regulation is a DBT skill, whereas developing congruence is used in person-centered therapy.

112. D: According to the US Department of Justice's Office on Violence Against Women, the presence of a gun in domestic violence situations increases a woman's chances of death by homicide by 500%. Other methods used in domestic violence homicides include strangulation, throwing someone against the wall, stabbing a person with a kitchen knife, or weaponizing other household items. Children, other family members, and pets in homes with ongoing domestic violence are also at risk. Therefore, therapists must help clients experiencing IPV by creating safety plans to address all elements of a family's risk.

113. A: The Outcomes Rating Scale (ORS) is used each session to measure a client's functional progress along four scales: individual, interpersonal, social, and global (i.e., overall). The ORS is a brief four-question assessment useful for tracking outcomes based on client measures of perceived improvement. Researchers have found that regular feedback leads to improved outcomes, particularly when integrated into each session. The Session Rating Scale (SRS) is also a four-item measure. Scott Miller and the International Center for Clinical Excellence license the ORS and SRS.

The SRS measures the therapeutic alliance by capturing client measures of respect and understanding, relevance of treatment goals and focus, client–counselor fit, and overall alliance. The Patient Health Questionnaire (PHQ-9) is a 9-item questionnaire that measures a client's depressive symptoms within the previous 2 weeks. Finally, the Beck Depression Inventory (BDI) is a 21-item self-report assessment of depressive symptoms.

114. D: The theory of reciprocal inhibition (RI) was developed by Joseph Wolpe in 1958, and was one of many that built on Freud's foundational work. RI is used in the treatment of anxiety and phobia disorders, and more recently in treating post-traumatic stress. RI is applied by producing an anxiety stimulus (or memory) and then pairing it with a relaxation response (e.g., muscle relaxation and feelings of safety and calm). As the individual learns to maintain relaxation, the fear provoked by the stimulus is eventually extinguished. Known as systematic desensitization, the process is foundational to all cognitive-behavioral treatment of anxiety symptoms. It is in ways like this that the protracted processes of psychoanalytic therapy have been channeled into brief psychodynamic therapy (BPT). Other BPT techniques drawn from Freud include dream interpretation, free association, Freudian slips, hypnosis, and projective techniques.

115. D: Internal family systems theory is based on the premise that experiences of shame and pain manifest into protectors known as firefighters and managers. According to this theory, the mind is subdivided into subpersonalities or parts. The "self" represents each person's inner system. Parts of one's personality interact internally, with some becoming more extreme than others. Exiles are parts of the personality that have become isolated from the rest of the system. Exiles have experienced trauma and can become extreme and strong in their desire to be loved and cared for. Firefighters and managers are both protectors. The role of a firefighter is to protect the system from an activated exile, primarily through distraction (e.g., drugs, food, gambling). Managers control day-to-day activities and protect the system from activating exiles. Carl Jung used the terms "anima" and "animus" to describe female (anima) and male (animus) archetypes held in the collective unconscious. Fritz Perls, the founder of Gestalt therapy, used the terms "topdog" and "underdog" to refer to games played to minimize anxiety. Perls noted this was a "self-torture game," with the topdog representing the inner conscious, with its own set of internal standards and morals, and the underdog, which is rooted in shame and guilt. The underdog uses rationalization and justification when unable to meet the demands of the inner conscious.

116. B: Solution-focused brief therapy (SFBT) uses scaling questions to measure treatment progress, motivation to change, and overall satisfaction. Scaling questions are informal, nonstandardized assessment tests used to measure several aspects of a client's treatment. Client perceptions are measured using a 1–10 Likert scale on any number of therapist-selected factors (e.g., goals, problems, priorities). Gestalt therapy approaches assessment in real time and uses observation to detect body language and evaluate problems in the client's physical and environmental context. Person-centered therapy helps clients move from incongruence between personal experiences and awareness to congruence through the use of unconditional positive regard, empathy, nonjudgmental understanding, and genuineness. Lastly, narrative therapy uses assessment strategies to help identify clients' personal stories to externalize problems. Collaborative reauthoring allows clients and therapists to address their treatment progress informally.

117. C: In compliance with ethical standards, the therapist provides a letter excluding custody recommendations while providing general treatment information (e.g., client diagnoses, attendance, treatment progress). This letter is permissible after appropriate consents are obtained. This is the best option; however, the therapist is under no ethical obligation to honor the mother's request for a letter. Standard 7.8 states that MFTs "avoid offering professional opinions about persons they have not directly interviewed. Marriage and family therapists declare the limits of their competencies and information." The therapist has not met nor interviewed the father. The MFT's duty to protect is not applicable because the father has been uninvolved and resides in another state (i.e., the child is not in imminent danger). Although excluding custody recommendations is appropriate, the therapist should not provide a professional opinion based on the family's clinical presentation because she has not met the father.

118. D: The theoretical roots of integrative behavioral couples therapy (IBCT) are eclectic in nature. Practitioners feel this offers them more freedom and flexibility, escaping the limits of a narrow theoretical perspective. Common counseling methods used include Bowen family systems theory, brief/solution-focused therapy, cognitive-behavioral therapy, problem-focused therapy, and narrative therapy styles. The IBCT process involves a non-linear, circular model of assessment, goal setting, interventions, maintenance, and validation. The therapist works with the couple to create a blame-free environment and a common therapeutic goal. IBCT recognizes that each couple is the product of their continual action and reaction within the relationship. Behavioral disorders develop as the couple feels trapped and increasingly polarized. Common manifestations include: 1) distancer-pursuer (one endeavors to move emotionally closer while the other pulls away); 2) submissive controller (one controls the other, secretively the other wants to be controlled, as in many abusive relationships); 3) emotional flooding and stonewalling (one partner's emotions build and flood out, until problems appear unresolvable, causing them to reject criticisms and avoid problem solving.

119. B: SMART is an acronym that stands for specific, measurable, attainable, realistic, and time sensitive. SMART goals provide concrete means for the therapist and client to monitor ongoing progress. Specific goals reflect exactly what to monitor, measurable goals help gauge incremental progress, attainable goals involve how the goal will be accomplished, and realistic goals are reasonable and relevant.

120. C: Risk factors for suicide contagion among adolescents include, but are not limited to, the recent suicidal death of a celebrity or other high-profile person, social media posts regarding a peer's death by suicide, and sensationalized media publications providing unnecessary details about a suicide. Suicide contagion, which is most common among adolescent populations, describes copycat attempts of one or more persons influenced by the suicidality of another. Suicide contagion can occur with exposure to either fictional or nonfictional accounts of suicide. Effective schoolwide mobilization after a suicide must be timely, intentional, and coordinated. Timely action is imperative, given the potential for the rapid spread of misinformation or disinformation via social media. As part of postvention strategies, schoolwide or targeted screenings help identify at-risk students for suicide, dispelling the myth that asking youth about suicidal ideation increases their chances of attempting suicide.

121. C: The final stage of emotionally focused therapy (EFT) is indicated when the couple successfully integrates and consolidates change based on secure attachments. Developed by Sue Johnson, EFT works to identify dysfunctional communication patterns and behaviors rooted in childhood attachment. Couples are encouraged to explore the origins of these patterns and discover meaningful ways to establish safe and secure connections. EFT is presented in three stages: deescalation, bonding, and consolidation of change. In the deescalation stage, the therapist uses deescalation techniques to help couples avoid negative interactions and emotional distress. In the bonding stage, the therapist helps couples understand the role of insecure attachment in emotional distress and elicit new core experiences. The final stage involves facilitating appropriate solutions and consolidating change based on secure attachments. Narrative therapy focuses on reauthoring stories with new and fulfilling meanings, Bowenian therapy is associated with differentiation and detriangulation, and restructuring the family system is used in structural family therapy.

122. B: Congruence couples therapy is an EBP for individuals diagnosed with gambling disorder and their spouses. It is a trauma-informed and humanistic practice that helps couples develop relational and communication skills required for functional alignment in the following domains: intrapersonal, interpersonal, intergenerational, and universal-spiritual. Conjoint intimacy-enhancing therapy targets individuals dealing with cancer experiences by exploring the underlying cancer-related feelings, fears, and concerns necessary to promote mutual understanding and intimacy. Hope and forgiveness focused therapy is a brief intervention that mixes cognitive behavioral and solution-focused techniques to modify irrational beliefs, reduce conflict and resentment, and establish hope and resilience. Cognitive existential couples therapy targets cancer experiences within the couple unit by addressing its effects on sexual functioning, body image, and lifestyle.

123. A: Per the AAMFT Code of Ethics (2015), therapists must refrain from performing custody evaluations on current clients. Section 7.7 states, "Marriage and family therapists avoid conflicts of interest in treating minors or adults involved in custody or visitation actions by not performing evaluations for custody, residence, or visitation of the minor." Therapists may provide information to the clinician performing the custody evaluation from the standpoint of the treating therapist as long as the marriage and family therapist (MFT) obtains appropriate consents to do so. An MFT would not receive a subpoena to provide the court with a custody evaluation on a current client. Ethical standards for providing court testimony differ from those pertaining to custody evaluations. Section 7.2 applies to MFTs serving as a fact or expert witness in legal proceedings, stating, "When offering testimony, as marriage and family therapy experts, they shall strive to be accurate, objective, fair, and independent." For this reason, MFTs do not provide current clients with custody evaluations, nor do they act as a fact or expert witness on their behalf.

124. B: Kitchener defined ethical rules as the standards of behavior against a prescribed set of criteria (i.e., ethical codes). Kitchener's model of ethical justification is grounded in the belief that ethical reasoning must consider each individual's complex circumstances. The model consists of two levels of reasoning: intuitive and critical-evaluative. Also known as ordinary moral sense, the intuitive level of reasoning refers to ethical knowledge that is developed over time. Intuitive reasoning allows therapists to make reflexive, in-the-moment decisions. The critical-evaluative level consists of ethical rules, principles, and theory. Each component in the critical-evaluative levels builds upon the other while simultaneously identifying factual information and relying on intuition. Ethical rules use standards of behavior, such as those found in the AAMFT Code of Ethics, to guide decision making. The next level, ethical principles (i.e., ethical values), involves protecting the health and well-being of all, which includes abiding by the principles of fidelity, autonomy, justice, nonmaleficence, and beneficence. Lastly, ethical theory is used when ethical principles conflict. After identifying the conflicting principles, the therapist determines if the decision is sound enough to be generalized to similar cases (i.e., universality) and whether the decision involves the least amount of avoidable harm (i.e., balancing).

125. C: IDEA has four separate sections. *Part A* outlines and defines terms. *Part B* gives guidelines for individuals 3-21 years of age and provides financial support for state and local schools as needed if they comply with six main principles: 1) zero rejection – all children provided a *free and appropriate public education (FAPE)*; 2) children with known or suspected disabilities receive an evaluation in all relevant areas; 3) preparation of an *individualized education plan (IEP)* to optimize education; 4) education provided in the least restrictive environment; 5) compliance safeguards, and 6) ongoing input from the parent(s) and child. *Part C* offers preemptive services to children from birth through two years of age. *Part D* describes national activities to be undertaken to improve the education of children with disabilities (e.g., grants and transitional services, etc.). Students under IDEA receive education and services based on their qualifying disability rather than educational setting, which ranges from specialized instruction in the general classroom to hospitals and residential treatment. Students qualifying under 504 cannot receive simultaneous special education services. Lastly, FAPE does not apply to students in private schools.

126. C: The relationship between claims data and client improvement fails to consider the following confounders: client diagnoses, the therapeutic alliance, and cultural factors. Confounding variables are third variables that produce distorted associations and conclusions about the effects of one variable on another. Confounders result in inaccurate causal conclusions between the therapist's treatment (e.g., interpersonal therapy [IPT] for 16 sessions over the course of 3 months) and outcomes (e.g., client improvement). Collecting claims data to determine client improvement is a process measure. Process measures determine whether an intervention adheres to the frequency, length, and duration of the EBP. Client diagnoses are confounding variables because IPT is an EBP for depression. The therapist used IPT with each client on her caseload, regardless of their diagnoses. The therapeutic alliance is a confounder because it tends to positively affect client improvement. Disparities among racialized populations serve as confounders, with cultural factors potentially invalidating the study results. Gathering claims data is purported to be a low-cost/low-burden means of data collection (Brown et al., 2014).

127. D: Confounding variables affect internal validity. Internal validity determines if there is a cause-and-effect relationship between the EBP (i.e., the 16 sessions of IPT over the course of 3 months) and client improvement, which is determined by auditing claims data. Confounding factors, such as the therapist's use of IPT with all of the clients rather than only clients with depression, is an unaccounted-for variable likely to affect client improvement measures. Internal consistency (i.e., internal reliability) is used to determine if there is a correlational relationship between items on the same test, but it does not apply to this study. Internal consistency applies to outcome measures (e.g., surveys, questionnaires) rather than process measures. Interrater reliability refers to the degree to which two or more judges, or raters, agree with one another, which also does not apply to this study. External validity is determined by the degree to which a causal relationship can be generalized to other settings or contexts. Because there is not a causal relationship between claims data and client improvement, the external validity cannot be determined.

128. B: Understanding archetypes requires an understanding of the psyche. Jung believed the psyche consists of three elements: the *ego*, the *personal unconscious*, and the *collective unconscious*. The *ego* is the conscious mind, the *personal unconscious* holds memories (including those suppressed), and the *collective unconscious* is a form of psychological inheritance (holding the knowledge and experiences of the species). Archetypes reside in the collective unconscious, and consist of "powerful ideas" (such as ethics and religion) and help define and organize experiences. Jung identified four major archetypes: 1) the *self*: the unification of unconsciousness and consciousness, culminating in *individuation*; 2) the *shadow*: instincts, repressed ideas, weaknesses, desires, and shortcomings, seen in dreams as some dark, wild, or exotic figure; 3) the *anima or animus*: the "true self" (not the *persona mask*) and the main source of communication with the *collective unconscious*, and the *syzygy* (divine couple) in unified wholeness; and 4) the *persona* (Latin for "mask"): our presentation to the world, shielding the ego from negative assaults.

129. C: More specifically, Whitaker felt that optimal self-fulfillment was dependent on the quality of family cohesiveness, whereas Satir felt that quality personal and family experiences depended on good communication skills and practices among family members. Experiential family therapy

239

utilizes techniques to promote communication and interaction, and encourages clients to reduce defensive fears to allow for genuine emotional expression. The result is enhanced communication and greater compassion and nurturing among family members. This approach draws on humanism (a focus on the here and now), gestalt (role playing and emotional confrontation), and psychodrama (sculpting, family drawing). Whitaker theorized that "emotional suppression" was the culprit in most family dysfunction. He saw a tendency in families to repress the expressive and instrumental functions of emotion by: 1) attempting to regulate children's behavior by controlling their feelings; and 2) constraining emotions that promote individuality (resulting in children emotionally estranged from themselves). Thus, his goal was to aid families to recover emotional authenticity, by which to produce more meaningful and honest family attachments.

130. A: The student is under MFT supervision for his final school semester. Because of the MFT's limited time, he is ethically obligated to review planning for termination as part of the informed consent process, which consists of providing clients or prospective clients with information that would help them make an informed decision about participating in therapy, including the associated and potential risks and benefits. Clients have the right to know if their therapy or the therapeutic relationship is time limited. MFTs must ensure that their clients will experience continuity of care if they continue to require treatment. Providing professional opinions is reviewed in standard 7.8 of the AAMFT Code of Ethics (2015) and refers to offering professional opinions on individuals that have not been personally interviewed. This standard pertains to forensic evaluations. Reviewing nondiscrimination policies is not associated with informed consent; however, providing therapy free from discrimination remains an ethical responsibility. Disclosing professional affiliations is included in standard 9.3, which states that MFTs "do not hold themselves out as being partners or associates of a firm if they are not" (AAMFT, 2015).

131. B: Because of this, cognitive-behavioral therapy (CBT) utilizes numerous behavioral interventions that tend to produce a salutatory effect on cognition – e.g., positive activity scheduling and graded task assignments. Similarly, cognitive changes can produce positive behavioral improvements. Therefore, cognitive therapists typically combine cognitive and behavioral interventions in the clinical process. As the most heavily researched form of psychotherapy, CBT has long been proven efficacious for treating a variety of disorders, including depression, anxiety and panic disorders, social phobia, cocaine use order, bulimia nervosa, and other psychophysiological disorders. It is rooted in the works of Ivan Pavlov (behavior therapy), John B. Watson (classical conditioning), Joseph Wolpe (systematic desensitization), Jean Piaget (stages of cognitive development), Aaron Beck and Albert Ellis (cognitive therapy), Donald Meichenbaum (cognitive-behavior therapy), as well as Gerald Patterson, Robert Liberman, and Richard Stuart (behavioral family therapy leaders) and behavioral therapists Frederick Kanfer and Jeanne Phillips.

132. C: The Outcome Questionnaire-45 (OQ-45.2) is designed to provide baseline screening measures, detect areas of immediate concern, and assist in discharge planning. The OQ-45.2 is a 45-item outcome measure that provides a snapshot of a client's current level of functioning. Feedback measures are provided for three domains: social role, symptom distress, and interpersonal relations. Social roles are measured by performance in school, work, family, hobbies, and community activities; symptom distress measures reflect depression, anxiety, and stress; and the interpersonal relations domain measures impairments in interpersonal functioning. The OQ-45 is not a diagnostic tool.

133. C: The EST (Educational Skills Test) is not an academic test of any kind. One of the most commonly used general educational aptitude tests is the WRAT (*Wide Range Achievement Test*), which assesses arithmetic, reading, and spelling. Assessment recording forms can be evidenced based, user led, form led, standardized assessments, or non-standardized assessment tools.

Standardized assessment tools are designed to measure individual function in aptitude, behavior, intelligence, and personality. Achievement tests fall into three broad categories: 1) *General Survey Batteries*: focused on fundamental subjects taught in schools; 2) *Single Subject Tests*: focused on a single subject or content area; and 3) *Diagnostic Batteries*: to determine proficiencies and deficiencies in areas of math, reading, and spelling. These tests help evaluate progress in educational endeavors, helping to determine the quality of education, student learning, and progress made.

134. B: Therapists using text messaging to deliver technology-based services seek to minimize risks incurred through misinterpretation or the blurring of professional and social relationships by refraining from using emojis and common text abbreviations (e.g., LMK [let me know]). There are several benefits and risks associated with technology-based therapies that must be included in the informed consent process. These include expectations for response times, use of social media (e.g., friend requests), and privacy and security measures. Therapists following best practices specific to text messaging have a responsibility to remain professional and avoid casual exchanges that may strongly parallel social interactions.

135. B: The response that best captures the spirit of motivational interviewing is "On the one hand, you say you want to get your probation officer off your back, but on the other hand, you refuse to participate." This response is an example of developing discrepancy and is used to reduce ambivalence. The basic principles of motivational interviewing include expressing empathy, rolling with resistance, developing discrepancy, and supporting autonomy. The therapist's response is designed to evoke change talk by "tipping the decisional balance"; in doing so, the therapist allows the client to make his or her own decision as opposed to advice giving, confrontation, adopting an "expert" stance, or fixing the problem for the client. An example of the "expert" role is telling the client that group participation would be beneficial. The statement "whether you participate or not is up to you" honors autonomy; however, it is followed by advice giving (i.e., "it's important that you allow other group members to benefit"). Finally, the response "You think that you were unfairly accused and shouldn't have to participate" may be an example of empathy and reflection; however, it is not the best response because it does not target ambivalence and it may not be an accurate reflection of the client's thoughts and feelings.

136. A: Feminist family theory asserts that living in a patriarchal society negatively affects men and women. Unlike its predecessors (e.g., structural family therapy, strategic family therapy, experiential family therapy), feminist family theory is based on the premise that reality is a subjective truth cocreated through language. Feminist theory rejects gender stratification (i.e., social rankings with men at higher statuses) and views gender as a social construct perpetuated by hegemonic masculinity (i.e., a practice that normalizes men's dominant social position) and hegemonic femininity (i.e., a practice that normalizes women's social position as inferior). Advocates of feminist theory believe the patriarchy to be just as damaging to men as it is to women, citing that the patriarchy damages men by disconnecting them from their emotions, perpetuating binary stereotypes (e.g., men as breadwinners), and creating and maintaining masculine norms of violence and entitlement.

137. A: The Code also specifies that sexual contact with known members of a client's family systems is prohibited. Additionally, sexual intimacy is prohibited with current clients and known family members. MFTs are also discouraged from engaging in sexual intimacy with current students and supervisees. The Code does not explicitly prohibit sexual intimacy with former students or supervisees; however, therapists are encouraged to explore such a relationship cautiously and inform the potential partner of any risks.

138. B: Trauma bonding is characterized by intermittent behavioral reinforcement amid a relational power imbalance. Trauma bonding describes the deep emotional connection and dependency between a person who has experienced violence and their aggressor. Victims of IPV experience cognitive dissonance when there is a lack of congruency between their choice to stay in the relationship and their experiences of abuse. Dissonance reduction involves subconsciously focusing on experiences of affection and rewards. Learned helplessness occurs in abusive situations when an individual believes the abuse is inescapable and has no end, resulting in resignation and depression. Similarly, psychological entrapment involves patterns of abuse and violence that occur after a victim's failed attempts to escape, upon which the victim engages in justification for staying in the relationship.

139. B: Lenore Walker (1979) theorized that relationships with partners who are abusive are marked by the following cycles: Phase 1) Tension-building (anger, arguing, and blaming); Phase 2) Acute battering incident (verbal assault escalating to the physical); and Phase 3) the Honeymoon (loving contrition) stage (apologizing, promising, caring, gift-giving, etc.). The tension-building phase can last anywhere between a couple of weeks to years. The acute stage is the shortest duration yet most volatile. This phase is marked by explosive violence as tension reaches its breaking point, resulting in severe physical or sexual assault, psychological abuse, and/or forceful restraint. Walker's theory is based on encounters with females in heterosexual relationships. During the acute phase, the woman experiencing violence is in survival mode and often cannot leave due to fear of triggering subsequent attacks. In phase 3, the person experiencing abuse is hopeful that the abuse will discontinue as the aggressor displays acts of loving contrition.

140. D: Therapists may determine that a client at risk to others if they seriously threaten physical violence toward another person. Therapists have both a duty to warn and a duty to protect. The duty to warn involves contacting the intended victim, while the duty to protect applies to releasing confidential information for threats made in the context of a therapist-client relationship. Therapists are duty-bound to notify not only the appropriate authorities and agencies charged to protect the public but also to make a good-faith effort to warn the intended victim(s). If unable to do so, therapists must seek someone who is reasonably believed able to warn the intended victim(s). The duty to warn stems from the 1976 legal case, Tarasoff v. Regents of the University of California, wherein a therapist heard a credible threat and only called law enforcement authorities (failing to notify the intended victim). The murder occurred, and the case was appealed to the California Supreme court, through which the duty to protect an intended victim was established. Counselors may but are not obligated to warn the client of the legal consequences of carrying out a plan. Similarly, the counselor is not obligated to commit the client involuntarily but may do so if it is determined that another person is at imminent risk.

141. B: The five communication styles are: 1) Blamer: using guilt and accusation to cover their own inadequacies and emptiness, they attempt to control by bullying and attacking faults; 2) Irrelevant or Distractor (often the youngest child): wish the problem away and pretend it doesn't exist, hoping others will do the same; 3) Placater: fearing rejection, they strive to please and ultimately becoming enmeshed and dependent; 4) Super-Reasonable (also called "Computers"): afraid of feelings, they use emotional detachment and intellectual rationalization to keep emotions and others at a "safe" distance, to protect their feelings and emotional vulnerabilities. The above four styles are dysfunctional: avoidant, dishonest, manipulative, and/or resistant to change. The fifth style is functional: 5) Leveler (or Congruent): they are open, direct, honest, and genuine. Body posture, facial expression, and vocal tone are all consistent and congruent to the message. Levelers share feelings instead of concealing them. They respond with integrity and unified beliefs, thoughts, and emotions – framing problems realistically, accurately, and openly, with desires and intentions portrayed honestly.

142. A: Assigning blame is a polarizing activity, minimizing the meaning of the affair trivializes the betrayal, and prematurely venting intense emotional feelings (likely already expressed prior to seeing a therapist) before establishing safety can produce raw feelings with no refuge for recovery, etc. Baucom et al. (2006) offer a three-stage counseling model. Key features of Stage 1 include: 1) boundary setting, 2) self-care techniques, 3) time-out and venting techniques ("how to" of both without making things worse), 4) emotional expressiveness skills and discussion of the impact of the affair, and 5) coping with flashbacks (e.g., an unexpected phone number, receipt, etc., that generates fear, and how to cope). Stage 2: Exploring contributing factors (crucial to understanding why the affair occurred and how the partner has responded). Stage 3: Moving on, which involves a summary of the affair, discussion of forgiveness (which does not mean lost accountability), and determining if continuing the relationship is a healthy for them or not.

143. D: The *Hawthorne effect* refers to the process where experimental subjects alter their behavior simply because they are being studied, rather than because of the experimental intervention. The Rosenthal effect (also known as the Pygmalion effect) occurs when someone (e.g., a student) internalizes the expectations of a superior – e.g., high expectations lead to improved performance. In education, it may be known as the "teacher-expectancy effect." The *placebo effect* refers to a perception of change (for better or worse) due to an expected intervention, even when it is not present (e.g., being given a sugar pill instead of medication, and then thinking one feels better). The *trauma bonding effect* consists of strong emotional ties that arise between a victim and his or her physical and/or emotional abuser. A subset of this is the *Stockholm syndrome*, where kidnap victims develop feelings for their kidnappers, or, in reverse, the *Lima syndrome*, where kidnappers develop feelings for those they kidnap, leading to release without advantage, etc. *Demand characteristics* cause a subject to behave in accordance with what he believes an experimenter expects.

144. B: Two categories of experiences, horizontal and vertical stressors, encompass and/or identify the more common challenges that may arise within families. Horizontal stressors are expected or common life events that families encounter as they move through the stages of the family life cycle. Examples include infertility or child bearing, demise of a parent, career changes, menopause, health problems, etc. Vertical stressors are patterns of a relational nature that may be transmitted intergenerationally. Examples include family expectations, hopes, failures, secrets, emotional challenges, taboos, etc. The family cycle of life consists of eight "stages": Stage 1: couples living without children; Stage 2: couples bearing children; Stage 3: families with children of pre-school age; Stage 4: families that include school-aged children; Stage 5: families that have teenagers; Stage 6: families with young adults being launched; Stage 7: families with parents in middle age (from empty nesters to retirement); and Stage 8: family members who are aging (retirement to demise of both partners).

145. B: As part of psychoanalytical self-psychology, Heinz Kohut used therapeutic tasks to promote a "corrective emotional experience" through "self/object" relationships required for a healthy sense of self. Kohut's techniques for facilitating growth are preceded by empathetic attunement, which lays the groundwork for mirroring transference, idealizing transference, and twinship transference. Mirroring transference involves the therapist's use of praise, affirmations, and the celebration of client achievements. Idealizing transference involves therapists representing caregivers as influential, self-assured, safe, and secure. Finally, twinship transference is used to foster a sense of belonging and assist with developing social skills required for interpersonal and intimate relationships.

146. C: The validity of the therapist's survey is likely impacted by social desirability bias. Social desirability is a response bias that results from the survey respondent's desire to present themselves positively. Social desirability biases commonly occur when respondents are asked about sensitive or private experiences, such as drug and alcohol use or sexual behavior. Social desirability biases lead to underreporting, which affects the survey's validity. Recall bias occurs when survey respondents provide answers based on only their most recent experiences—for example, a supervisor providing an annual performance evaluation bases ratings solely on recent job performance. The therapist's survey requested information limited to the past 30 days, making it less likely to be invalidated by recall bias. Researchers are vulnerable to confirmation bias, which is the tendency to accumulate evidence in support of one hypothesis over another. Confirmation bias is affected by a person's preconceived notions, preferences, and opinions, which can result in an inaccurate diagnosis or an ineffective treatment approach. Finally, self-serving biases occur when a person attributes their success to inner qualities and failure to external circumstances—for example, attributing a passing test score to hard work and perseverance while attributing a failing score to an unfair test.

147. A: The other four of the five channels of resistance are: 2) *introjection*: accepting others beliefs and values without review or assimilation to make them congruent with ourselves; 3) *projection*: assigning aspects of ourselves to others in order to dismiss them as being part of ourselves (e.g., blaming others to avoid our own feelings of guilt, etc.); 4) *deflection*: avoiding awareness and/or contact with the environment/others by being vague, using distraction, overusing humor or questions, living vicariously, etc., leading to reduced life experiences and self-awareness; and 5) *confluence*: blurring boundaries between oneself and environment/others in order to fit in, avoid conflict, obtain approval, etc.

148. C: The three dimensions of the Olson Circumplex Model (Olson, 2000) are cohesion, flexibility, and communication. Differentiation is associated with intergenerational or Bowenian family therapy. The Olson Circumplex Model assumes that communication skills (e.g., engagement and openness) are essential for helping families attain functional or "balanced" levels of cohesion and flexibility. Rigidity, the inverse of flexibility, occurs in family systems resistant to change. Too much flexibility leads to chaos. In a balanced family system, a shared understanding of essential boundaries, roles, and rules is required for stability and change. Cohesion refers to the emotional connectedness and closeness among family members. When cohesion is unbalanced, families are either enmeshed or disengaged.

149. B: Many psychometric researchers assert that there is no way to assess intelligence in a culturally free or fair manner. Standardized assessments and those who administer them cannot avoid bias entirely. In many instances, modifications that include language interpretation cannot be compared to the normed population. However, the Test of Nonverbal Intelligence, Version 2 (TONI-2) is specifically designed as a language- and culture-free instrument for measuring abstract problem-solving ability. It may be appropriately used by clients ages five through 85 and has been designed to be as free as possible of linguistic, motoric, and cultural factors. It is, therefore, ideal for use with people who may be non-English speakers, learning disabled, aphasic, deaf, or sufferers of stroke, head injury, or cerebral palsy. Requiring as little as 15 minutes (though not timed), it is administered either individually or to groups of five or fewer participants. Examiners need only modest experience in psychometry, and thus may be teachers, psychologists, psychological associates, educational diagnosticians, or other professionals.

150. B: This family would be depicted with a genogram showing the parents connected by a solid line with two slashes in the middle and the child is connected by a dotted line. Parents who are divorced or separated are both connected by a solid line with two slashes in the middle. Parents who remain married are connected by a solid line, whereas parents who are divorced and remarry are connected by a solid line with an X down the middle. Biological children are connected to their parents by one solid line, whereas foster children are connected by a dotted line.

151. A: Existential groups focus on subjective experiences, as related to freedom, responsibility, and the awareness of death. Existential crises typically concern the meaning of life, aloneness, anxiety, guilt, and awareness of death. Existential vacuum is the emptiness when life seems meaninglessness. Groups serve by calming destructive behaviors, revealing external views, offering diverse perspectives, and allowing new behaviors practice. Additional group approaches include: Gestalt groups focus on the here and now, ensuring participants are fully present and growing. Psychoanalytic groups focus on experiences from the first six years of life, as the roots of conflicts usually lie there, working through repressed material. Psychodrama groups act out problems, experiences, wishes, and fantasies, encountering buried feelings and experiencing new situations. Transactional analysis groups help members learn to make better choices, implement goals, help members with self-critiques, and get them to see behaviors as "life scripts." Behavior therapy groups work to modify behaviors, as opposed to thoughts, unconscious conflicts, or past experiences. Rational emotive behavior therapy groups replace irrational, self-defeating beliefs with rational, self-enhancing ones.

152. B: In most situations, intermittent reinforcement is the strongest reinforcer as it generates episodically renewed hope, leaving the respondent highly engaged. Through response consequences, reinforcement schedules greatly influence operant conditioning. Reinforcement is continuous when it happens every time a behavior occurs; reinforcement is partial or intermittent when it occurs only occasionally. Four types of intermittent reinforcement schedules are: 1) *fixed interval*: repeated at regular intervals (e.g., every 30 seconds); 2) *variable interval*: at irregular intervals (e.g., after two, seven, and four seconds, etc.); 3) *fixed ratio*: at fixed intervals (e.g., every third response); and 4) *variable ratio* (a rate tied to the number of responses, potentially varying in number but not on average ratio). With consequences, effectiveness can be affected by four factors: 1) *satiation* (effectiveness wanes as satisfaction is fulfilled – e.g., no longer hungry, etc.); 2) *immediacy* (rapidity of feedback to the response – quicker is better); 3) *contingency* (consistency in delivery of the consequence over time – ideally, consistent and immediate, unless also intermittent); and 4) *size* (determining if the consequence (positive or negative) is worth the effort).

153. C: George's most likely diagnosis is prolonged grief disorder. First introduced by the American Psychiatric Association in the 2022 Diagnostic and Statistical Manual of Mental Disorders, Fifth Edition, Text Revision (DSM-5-TR), prolonged grief disorder is marked by persistent and intense grief interfering with daily life. Prolonged grief differs from normative grief in that it is persistent, intense, and unrelenting. Symptoms must last at least 1 year to meet the criteria for prolonged grief disorder. In addition, three of the following symptoms must occur within the past month: intense emotional pain, marked disbelief and shock, difficulty reintegrating into society, disruption of one's sense of identity (i.e., believing that a part of the self has also died), avoidance of any reminders of the loved one's death, feeling emotionally numb, and the feeling that life is futile. Individuals with a history of depression are at greater risk for developing prolonged grief disorder. In addition, it differs from other depressive disorders in that the symptoms center around the death of a loved one.

154. B: The Gottman method's sound relationship house concept illustrates nine components of healthy relationships. These components each mark a "floor" in the house and include the following: floor 1, build love maps (a guide to each partner's inner world); floor 2, share fondness and admiration (naming admirable qualities); floor 3, turn toward instead of away (eliciting a

245

response or "bid" for connection); floor 4, the positive perspective (providing a positive approach to problem solving); floor 5, manage conflict (learning how to manage rather than resolve conflicts); floor 6, make life dreams come true (creating space in the relationship to discuss hopes and aspirations); floor 7, create shared meaning (understanding one another's narratives); floor 8, trust (faith in one another); and floor 9, commitment (cherishing a partner for a lifetime). Universal (rather than positive) life energy is associated with Virginia Satir, who believed that all people are universally connected.

155. D: Standardized instruments that serve as youth suicide screenings include the Columbia Suicide Severity Rating Scale (C-SSRS), the Ask Suicide-Screening Questions (ASQ) tool, and the Patient Health Questionnaire-9 (PHQ-9) Modified. The Screening to Brief Intervention (S2BI) instrument screens for youth substance use. The C-SSRS measures suicidal thoughts and behaviors. The ASQ tool, which can be used with youth and adults, is a 20-second screening measure composed of four questions used to detect suicidal ideation. The PHQ-9 can be modified for adolescents and includes a short screener that assesses the severity of suicidality.

156. D: The AAMFT Code of Ethics is designed to assist and guide therapists and ensure clients' well-being to the greatest degree possible. MFTs are responsible for honoring public trust through advocacy, public participation, and commitment to the highest standards of service. Additionally, MFTs have an ethical commitment to 1) life-long continuing education; 2) engage in the process of ethical decision-making if an employer, supervisor, or another professional requests that an MFT engages in behavior violating standards outlined in the AAMFT Code of Ethics; 3) not divert clients seen via an institution to one's own private practice; 4) set fees fairly, and make allowances for those unable to afford services; 5) present one's qualifications accurately; 6) only offer services for which one is qualified; 7) keep a client's needs paramount; 8) responsibly wield influence; 9) refrain from engaging in multiple relationships; 10) avoid personal bias, discrimination, stereotyping, and prejudice; 11) refrain from harassment, exploitation, and sexual activity with students, supervisees, current clients and former clients.

157. C: *Generalized anxiety disorder* involves anxiety (worry) that is present all the time, but without reason for worry. Twice as common among women, the disorder tends to begin in childhood or adolescence. Feelings involve a sense that something bad is about to happen. Symptoms include fatigue, poor concentration, irritability, and muscle tension. *Panic disorder* involves intense attacks of fear about losing control or dying, etc., coupled with various physical symptoms. Symptoms are often physical: tachycardia, angina, trembling, nausea, perspiring, vertigo, etc., as well as confusion, dread, and a need to flee. Attacks often begin abruptly and peak in 10 minutes, lasting from minutes to hours. Attacks are either unexpected or triggered (e.g., by crowds, stress, fear of another attack, etc.), called situation-bound panic attacks. Panic disorder is noted as with or without agoraphobia (most often with). Frequent comorbid conditions include major depression, social and specific phobias, and alcoholism.

158. C: The Outcome Questionnaire-45.2 (OQ-45.2) is a transdiagnostic instrument used to measure, monitor, and deliver feedback on client progress. The questionnaire measures client functioning along three domains: social role, symptom distress, and interpersonal relations. The OQ-45.2 does not provide measures associated with the therapeutic alliance. Clinically significant scores in the social role domain indicate dissatisfaction, discord, or inadequate performance in school, work, family, and community life. High scores on symptom distress reflect depression, anxiety and stress. Interpersonal relations measures impairments in interpersonal functioning, including tension, conflict, and feelings of inadequacy among friends, coworkers, and intimate relationships. Additionally, the OQ-45 is useful for guiding treatment and discharge planning and identifying areas of immediate concern, such as substance misuse, suicidality, and conflict in the work setting.

159. A: A culture of appreciation replacing criticism indicates that the couple is ready to be discharged. The Gottman Method assists couples with understanding dysfunctional communication styles, including criticism, contempt, defensiveness, and stonewalling (the four horsemen). A culture of appreciation is fostered by providing affirmations and validation through small acts of love, affection, or kindness. The goal of EFT is to replace emotional reactivity with emotional regulation. Narrative therapists help couples successfully externalize and reauthor their personal internalized stories. Client-centered therapy seeks congruence between each partner's self-image and ideal self.

160. B: The original Milan systemic model is guided by principles that include hypothesizing, circularity, and neutrality. Salvador Minuchin is associated with restructuring, a process used in structural family therapy to shift patterns of behavior through unbalancing, raising intensity, and reorganization. Mara Palazzoli, Gianfranco Cecchin, Luigi Boscolo, and Giuliana Prata are credited with developing the Milan systemic model. The guiding principle of hypothesizing is unfolded over several sessions, beginning with an idea or theory about the family's presenting problem, refining the hypothesis, sharing the hypothesis with the family, creating an intervention based on the hypothesis, and adopting further revisions when necessary. The Milan system model is based on the works of Gregory Bateson, who originally conceptualized circularity. Hypothesizing and circularity work hand-in-hand as the hypothesis evolves based on progressive alterations which return it to the original cause, culminating in a novel sequence that either alters or confirms the existing hypothesis. Neutrality ensures that the therapist's nonjudgmental disposition does not influence the process.

161. D: Pica is a feeding and eating disorder that involves the consumption of substances with no nutrition. Pica is a common diagnosis among children under six years old, women who are pregnant, and individuals diagnosed with autism spectrum disorder, schizophrenia, and/or intellectual disabilities It is more common among those with iron deficiency, and pagophagia, the craving of ice, is especially common in this population. Rumination disorder involves regurgitating food from the stomach and then chewing again, and usually reswallowing it. It is more common in the population of patients with an intellectual disability and has a high mortality rate (25%). Avoidant/restrictive food intake disorder involves eating too little to grow or gain/maintain a healthy weight without self-image issues. This disorder is most commonly diagnosed in children under six. Binge-eating disorder includes over consuming food and then feeling a loss of control regarding the overconsuming of food. It usually leads to solitary dining and secret eating. There is no resulting behaviors to modify the food intake (like exercise or vomiting).

162. C: The *Family Adaptability and Cohesion Evaluation Scales* (FACES-IV) (2004) were developed by David Olson, Dean Gorall, and Judy Tiesel, and were based on the original 1979 *Circumplex Model of Marital and Family Systems*. The 42 items evaluated are divided into six scales of seven items each. The scales are designed to assess the dimensions of cohesion and flexibility within family and couple systems. As a self-reported questionnaire, the six scales are arranged with two balanced and four unbalanced. The two balanced scores represent a linear progression and thus if the scores are higher, then family functioning is more positive. The scales identify six family types: 1) balanced; 2) rigidly cohesive; 3) midrange; 4) flexibly unbalanced; 5) chaotically unbalanced; and 6) unbalanced. If a family scores high on both balance scales and low on the unbalanced scales, it is considered "balanced" and should be more satisfied and functional than other family systems. Inverse scoring identifies a problematic, dysfunctional family system.

163. A: An MFT using Gestalt therapy would know that the client has met treatment goals and is ready for discharge if he or she has become more fully integrated in mind and body. In addition, Gestalt therapy emphasizes present-moment awareness to promote holism, insight, personal responsibility, self-acceptance, and environmental awareness. Therapists providing cognitive behavioral therapy help clients challenge maladaptive thinking and make necessary behavioral changes. Psychodynamic therapists focus on increased insight into unconscious processes and intrapersonal conflicts, whereas existential therapists help clients engage in creativity, love, and connection.

164. A: The therapist has an ethical duty to understand the principles of group milieu, and ensure that clients brought into the group will benefit through and not detract from or be harmed by the group and its mix of personalities and issues. Other ethical obligations of the therapist include: 1) discussing the standards and limits of confidentiality in a group setting; 2) providing adequate follow up with group members; 3) obtaining a release of information from any client also seeing another therapist before speaking with that clinician about the group member; and 4) approaching any other clinician involved with a group member with a collaborative attitude and an effort to coordinate interventions and treatment goals.

165. D: Adopting positive connotations is not associated with EFT. The use of positive connotations does, however, characterize the Milan model of family therapy. Therapists use positive connotations when reframing client behaviors or traits rather than criticizing or condemning specific family members. EFT is based on the assumption that corrective emotional experiences promote the level of awareness, regulation, and acceptance necessary for therapeutic change. The acronym RISSSC is used to represent the tools of EFT: R (repeat key phrases), I (use images with emotional content), S (use simple and concise summaries), S (slow the pace), S (use a soft tone), C (use client words to validate narratives).

166. D: The most stage-appropriate strategy would be to help the client examine the discrepancy between her behavior and her values. The client is compliant with therapy and has likely participated in the decisional balance activity designed to promote change talk over ambivalence. This is an indication that she is in the contemplation stage of change. Motivational interviewing helps individuals pass through the stages of change, which include precontemplation, contemplation, preparation, action, and maintenance. Building relapse prevention skills is associated with the maintenance stage. An assessment of the client's commitment to change occurs in the precontemplation stage, whereas offering a menu of choices is associated with the preparation stage.

167. D: The therapist should refer the client to another provider who specializes in posttraumatic stress disorder (PTSD). MFTs are bound by the AAMFT Code of Ethics (2015), which states that MFTs "continue therapeutic relationships only so long as it is reasonably clear that clients are benefiting from the relationship" (standard 1.9). The client met her short-term treatment goals but has not made therapeutic gains since then; thus, reasonably clear benefits are observable as outlined in the client's treatment plan. Although the therapist has an ethical duty to engage the client in conversation regarding the need for a referral, the power differential could impair the client's autonomy and her sound decision-making capacity. Consulting with a professional who specializes in PTSD is not the best answer at this late juncture in the client's treatment.

168. D: According to standard 7.7 of the AAMFT Code of Ethics (2015), MFTs must avoid conflicts of interest when providing court testimony regarding clients who are minors and providing information to the court or evaluating clinician from the perspective of the child's treating therapist. Standard 7.6 states that, unless otherwise legally mandated, to avoid dual roles MFTs should "avoid providing therapy to clients for whom the therapist has provided a forensic evaluation and avoid providing evaluations for those who are clients, unless otherwise mandated by legal systems" (AAMFT, 2015). When MFTs conduct forensic interviews and evaluations, standard 7.3 states that MFTs must remain within their scope of competence. Even if limited, an expert opinion or expert testimony provided by an MFT violates the ethical standard for dual relationships because the testimony is likely to be biased. When in the sole role of a forensic evaluator, an MFT seeks to provide fair, accurate, independent, and unbiased testimony.

169. A: Countertransference refers to a therapist's internal response to a client's clinical presentation and is most commonly associated with past experiences. Emotional reactions to a client's presentation or transference are tied to the therapist's former conscious or unconscious experiences. If improperly managed, countertransference has the potential to manifest in therapeutic ruptures, broken alliances, dysfunctional interactions (e.g., inappropriate self-disclosures, boundary violations), and sexual attraction. Additional manifestations of countertransference include the loss of objectivity (i.e., bias), preoccupation with a client, or the dislike of a client who is difficult to explain or who is unreasonable.

170. B: A diagnosis of intellectual disability requires both cognitive impairment (an IQ of 70 or lower) and an onset before the age of 18, in addition to deficits in mental abilities and adaptive functioning. The condition would be identified as a neurocognitive disorder due to traumatic brain injury, given the history. Dementia is no longer used as a DSM-5-TR diagnosis- it has been subsumed under neurocognitive disorder.

171. D: Therapy groups are often called *T-groups*, and include encounter, awareness, self-help, and leaderless groups, as well as consciousness raising, sensitivity training, and personal growth groups. *T-groups* emphasize decision making, problem solving, and feedback, with a goal of improving relationship skills by emphasizing group processes. *Personal growth* and *encounter groups* are usually organized around a set day and time, and encourage personal growth and development by risk taking and self-disclosure, etc. *Guidance groups* focus on the prevention of problems that face specific high-risk populations, usually by improving life skills, motivation, and goal setting. *Counseling groups* are organized around prevention and/or correction needs, and include encounter, organizational development, and sensitivity groups. *Psychotherapy groups* are tertiary prevention groups that endeavor to reeducate, rehabilitate, and enhance participants' overall healthy functioning.

172. B: MFTs have an aspirational ethical commitment to service, advocacy, and public participation as outlined in the AAMFT Code of Ethics (2015). Specifically, MFTs aspire to "devote a portion of their professional activity to services for which there is little or no financial return," which describes pro bono services. Developing laws that promote diversity, inclusion, and equity exemplifies "laws and regulations pertaining to marriage and family therapy that serve the public interest." Additionally, MFTs "encourage public participation in the design and delivery of professional services and in the regulation of practitioners." Providing remuneration (i.e., compensation) for referrals is unethical, per section 8.1.

173. C: Sexual relationships are not ethical where a supervisor-supervisee relationship exists. This remains true even when the superior is supervising a trainee, intern, or student, as well as any other position where one individual is positioned to exercise control or authority over another. Peer relationships can still become problematic, as promotions and work assignment changes can produce a power asymmetry where one did not previously exist. Of further note, clients may sometimes also endeavor to exploit the relationship, or the relationship may otherwise adversely affect the professional environment. If a sexual relationship nevertheless becomes inevitable, preventive steps must be taken to avoid conflicts of interest. This may include a transfer of duties or a transfer from one department to another may be advisable. If, however, repositioning is to avoid encountering a supervisor-supervisee relationship, the move alone may be exploitive by altering the career path of the one transferred or depriving a supervisee of optimal supervision. Thus, supervisors must maintain appropriate boundaries to protect the supervisee, student, or intern, etc.

174. B: The *Hamilton Anxiety Scale* (HAS or HAM-A), also termed the *Hamilton Anxiety Rating Scale* (HARS), was developed to assess anxiety in people already diagnosed with an anxiety disorder. It is particularly useful in measuring improvement over time. Based on 14 items, a proctor is needed to administer this 20-minute instrument. Key limitations include: 1) self-reporting can be easily manipulated, and 2) it lacks utility when used with other psychiatric disorders. While very popular, it is in need of further validation studies. The *Hamilton Depression Scale* (HDS or HAM-D), also termed the *Hamilton Rating Scale for Depression* (HRSD), is a 17- or 21-item scale (depending on format, with 17 items more common) that is completed in 20-30 minutes by a trained rater. While originally designed for use only with a primary diagnosis of depression, it is frequently used to evaluate depressive symptoms with other primary disorders (e.g., schizophrenia and bipolar disorder), though its usefulness in this regard limited. When used with disorders other than primary depression, it should be paired with additional assessment scales. Where indicated, further assessment of depressive symptoms may be made using the *Hamilton Depression Inventory* (HDI).

175. C: Also known as the Dunning–Kruger effect, self-assessment bias is the tendency for a person to overestimate their abilities or knowledge. Numerous studies suggest that therapists are poor predictors of client treatment failure, which the use of progress measures helps reduce or alleviate. Implicit bias is defined as any negative, automatic, and unintentional associations or stereotypes that a person has toward a specific social group. Cultural bias is the tendency for a person to evaluate, judge, or consider certain occurrences, circumstances, or happenings in terms of one's own societal norms, values, or beliefs. Confirmation bias occurs when a person uses novel information to validate preexisting beliefs or notions.

176. D: The clinician most likely assigns the condition of uncomplicated bereavement. Uncomplicated bereavement is listed as a V code in the DSM-5-TR. V codes are used when a mental disorder is unsubstantiated and includes "other conditions that may be a focus of clinical attention." The client does not meet the criteria for acute stress disorder because there are not enough trauma-related symptoms. Although the client exhibits symptoms of prolonged grief disorder, the diagnosis is unsubstantiated because the symptoms must last at least 1 year. Finally, persistent depressive disorder is unsubstantiated because the symptoms must last at least 2 years.

177. D: According to Johnson's typology of domestic violence, intimate terrorism is perpetrated by males at much higher rates than females. Intimate terrorism is a form of intimate partner violence (IPV) characterized by power and control. Johnson asserts that gender-based IPV differs from other patterns of violence. Elements of intimate terrorism include coercion, manipulation, forced isolation, threats, domination, stalking, physical aggression, and sexual violence. Situational couple violence (i.e., common couple violence) is a pattern of IPV that stems from situational stressors. Research suggests that men and women engage in situational couple violence at equal rates and that this form of IPV results in fewer injuries. Violent resistance is a form of IPV perpetrated by women in response to intimate terrorism. Mutual violent control involves intimate terrorism perpetrated by both partners.

178. D: There is no ethical requirement stating that therapists using technology-assisted services must make clients aware in writing of their knowledge, training, and education in compliance with standards of practice. Therapists do have an ethical obligation to ensure that they have received related training and are competent in the use of their chosen digital platform; however, this obligation is not required to be written. Standard VI of the American Association for Marriage and Family Therapy (AAMFT) Code of Ethics (2015) addresses the ethical requirements for providing technology-assisted professional services. Therapists must make clients and supervisees aware in writing of "risks, and of both the therapist's and clients'/supervisees' responsibilities for minimizing such risks" (standard 6.2), limitations and protections of confidentiality (standard 6.3), and compliance with applicable laws safeguarding client information (standard 6.4).

179. C: In transactional analysis (TA), *games* differ from other time-stroke engagements such as *withdrawal* (no *strokes*), *rituals* (social programming), *pastimes* (small talk), *activities* (purpose-focused interactions), and *intimacy* (unconditional strokes). A game is always complementary (reciprocal), ulterior, and predictable in outcome. Games always switch player roles in the end, and involve only parent and child ego states. If an adult ego state emerges in a game, then it is a maneuver, as adult functioning is always conscious and game playing is not fully so. Each game has a payoff, and the way to break it is to eliminate the payoff. *Life positions* influence the ways that games are played. The term *life positions* refers to the four ways an individual may construe relationships: 1) *I'm okay, you're okay* (healthiest position); 2) *I'm okay, you're not okay* (others seen as diminished; usually not healthy); 3) *I'm not okay, you're okay* (sees self as weaker than others; tends to unconsciously accept abuse); 4) *I'm not okay, you're not okay* (a no hope position).

180. A: Urie Bronfenbrenner introduced the concept of ecological systems theory—a developmental theory grounded in the assumption that children are affected by the following environmental systems: the microsystem (e.g., family, school, peers); the mesosystem, which represents the bidirectional interaction of each system (e.g., interactions between a child's family and teachers); the exosystem (e.g., neighbors, parental workplaces); the macrosystem, which represents cultural etiologies (e.g., wealth, poverty, and racialized identities); and the chronosystem, which includes environmental changes over time (e.g., life cycle transitions). Bronfenbrenner was critical of theorists such as Mary Ainsworth, who he believed failed to consider the full range of influences on a child with her strange situation procedure (that measured attachments between mothers and their children), characterizing it as unidirectional and linear. Ludwig von Bertalanffy pioneered general systems theory, which influenced several concepts used in family systems theory (e.g., open systems, circular causality). Ivan Boszormenyi-Nagy is known for his contributions to contextual family therapy, which underscores the significance of trust, loyalty, and understanding among members of a family system.

MFT Practice Test #3

To take this additional MFT practice test, visit our bonus page:
mometrix.com/bonus948/mft

How to Overcome Test Anxiety

Just the thought of taking a test is enough to make most people a little nervous. A test is an important event that can have a long-term impact on your future, so it's important to take it seriously and it's natural to feel anxious about performing well. But just because anxiety is normal, that doesn't mean that it's helpful in test taking, or that you should simply accept it as part of your life. Anxiety can have a variety of effects. These effects can be mild, like making you feel slightly nervous, or severe, like blocking your ability to focus or remember even a simple detail.

If you experience test anxiety—whether severe or mild—it's important to know how to beat it. To discover this, first you need to understand what causes test anxiety.

Causes of Test Anxiety

While we often think of anxiety as an uncontrollable emotional state, it can actually be caused by simple, practical things. One of the most common causes of test anxiety is that a person does not feel adequately prepared for their test. This feeling can be the result of many different issues such as poor study habits or lack of organization, but the most common culprit is time management. Starting to study too late, failing to organize your study time to cover all of the material, or being distracted while you study will mean that you're not well prepared for the test. This may lead to cramming the night before, which will cause you to be physically and mentally exhausted for the test. Poor time management also contributes to feelings of stress, fear, and hopelessness as you realize you are not well prepared but don't know what to do about it.

Other times, test anxiety is not related to your preparation for the test but comes from unresolved fear. This may be a past failure on a test, or poor performance on tests in general. It may come from comparing yourself to others who seem to be performing better or from the stress of living up to expectations. Anxiety may be driven by fears of the future—how failure on this test would affect your educational and career goals. These fears are often completely irrational, but they can still negatively impact your test performance.

Elements of Test Anxiety

As mentioned earlier, test anxiety is considered to be an emotional state, but it has physical and mental components as well. Sometimes you may not even realize that you are suffering from test anxiety until you notice the physical symptoms. These can include trembling hands, rapid heartbeat, sweating, nausea, and tense muscles. Extreme anxiety may lead to fainting or vomiting. Obviously, any of these symptoms can have a negative impact on testing. It is important to recognize them as soon as they begin to occur so that you can address the problem before it damages your performance.

The mental components of test anxiety include trouble focusing and inability to remember learned information. During a test, your mind is on high alert, which can help you recall information and stay focused for an extended period of time. However, anxiety interferes with your mind's natural processes, causing you to blank out, even on the questions you know well. The strain of testing during anxiety makes it difficult to stay focused, especially on a test that may take several hours. Extreme anxiety can take a huge mental toll, making it difficult not only to recall test information but even to understand the test questions or pull your thoughts together.

253

Effects of Test Anxiety

Test anxiety is like a disease—if left untreated, it will get progressively worse. Anxiety leads to poor performance, and this reinforces the feelings of fear and failure, which in turn lead to poor performances on subsequent tests. It can grow from a mild nervousness to a crippling condition. If allowed to progress, test anxiety can have a big impact on your schooling, and consequently on your future.

Test anxiety can spread to other parts of your life. Anxiety on tests can become anxiety in any stressful situation, and blanking on a test can turn into panicking in a job situation. But fortunately, you don't have to let anxiety rule your testing and determine your grades. There are a number of relatively simple steps you can take to move past anxiety and function normally on a test and in the rest of life.

Physical Steps for Beating Test Anxiety

While test anxiety is a serious problem, the good news is that it can be overcome. It doesn't have to control your ability to think and remember information. While it may take time, you can begin taking steps today to beat anxiety.

Just as your first hint that you may be struggling with anxiety comes from the physical symptoms, the first step to treating it is also physical. Rest is crucial for having a clear, strong mind. If you are tired, it is much easier to give in to anxiety. But if you establish good sleep habits, your body and mind will be ready to perform optimally, without the strain of exhaustion. Additionally, sleeping well helps you to retain information better, so you're more likely to recall the answers when you see the test questions.

Getting good sleep means more than going to bed on time. It's important to allow your brain time to relax. Take study breaks from time to time so it doesn't get overworked, and don't study right before bed. Take time to rest your mind before trying to rest your body, or you may find it difficult to fall asleep.

Along with sleep, other aspects of physical health are important in preparing for a test. Good nutrition is vital for good brain function. Sugary foods and drinks may give a burst of energy but this burst is followed by a crash, both physically and emotionally. Instead, fuel your body with protein and vitamin-rich foods.

Also, drink plenty of water. Dehydration can lead to headaches and exhaustion, especially if your brain is already under stress from the rigors of the test. Particularly if your test is a long one, drink water during the breaks. And if possible, take an energy-boosting snack to eat between sections.

Along with sleep and diet, a third important part of physical health is exercise. Maintaining a steady workout schedule is helpful, but even taking 5-minute study breaks to walk can help get your blood pumping faster and clear your head. Exercise also releases endorphins, which contribute to a positive feeling and can help combat test anxiety.

When you nurture your physical health, you are also contributing to your mental health. If your body is healthy, your mind is much more likely to be healthy as well. So take time to rest, nourish your body with healthy food and water, and get moving as much as possible. Taking these physical steps will make you stronger and more able to take the mental steps necessary to overcome test anxiety.

Mental Steps for Beating Test Anxiety

Working on the mental side of test anxiety can be more challenging, but as with the physical side, there are clear steps you can take to overcome it. As mentioned earlier, test anxiety often stems from lack of preparation, so the obvious solution is to prepare for the test. Effective studying may be the most important weapon you have for beating test anxiety, but you can and should employ several other mental tools to combat fear.

First, boost your confidence by reminding yourself of past success—tests or projects that you aced. If you're putting as much effort into preparing for this test as you did for those, there's no reason you should expect to fail here. Work hard to prepare; then trust your preparation.

Second, surround yourself with encouraging people. It can be helpful to find a study group, but be sure that the people you're around will encourage a positive attitude. If you spend time with others who are anxious or cynical, this will only contribute to your own anxiety. Look for others who are motivated to study hard from a desire to succeed, not from a fear of failure.

Third, reward yourself. A test is physically and mentally tiring, even without anxiety, and it can be helpful to have something to look forward to. Plan an activity following the test, regardless of the outcome, such as going to a movie or getting ice cream.

When you are taking the test, if you find yourself beginning to feel anxious, remind yourself that you know the material. Visualize successfully completing the test. Then take a few deep, relaxing breaths and return to it. Work through the questions carefully but with confidence, knowing that you are capable of succeeding.

Developing a healthy mental approach to test taking will also aid in other areas of life. Test anxiety affects more than just the actual test—it can be damaging to your mental health and even contribute to depression. It's important to beat test anxiety before it becomes a problem for more than testing.

Study Strategy

Being prepared for the test is necessary to combat anxiety, but what does being prepared look like? You may study for hours on end and still not feel prepared. What you need is a strategy for test prep. The next few pages outline our recommended steps to help you plan out and conquer the challenge of preparation.

STEP 1: SCOPE OUT THE TEST

Learn everything you can about the format (multiple choice, essay, etc.) and what will be on the test. Gather any study materials, course outlines, or sample exams that may be available. Not only will this help you to prepare, but knowing what to expect can help to alleviate test anxiety.

STEP 2: MAP OUT THE MATERIAL

Look through the textbook or study guide and make note of how many chapters or sections it has. Then divide these over the time you have. For example, if a book has 15 chapters and you have five days to study, you need to cover three chapters each day. Even better, if you have the time, leave an extra day at the end for overall review after you have gone through the material in depth.

If time is limited, you may need to prioritize the material. Look through it and make note of which sections you think you already have a good grasp on, and which need review. While you are studying, skim quickly through the familiar sections and take more time on the challenging parts.

255

Write out your plan so you don't get lost as you go. Having a written plan also helps you feel more in control of the study, so anxiety is less likely to arise from feeling overwhelmed at the amount to cover.

STEP 3: GATHER YOUR TOOLS

Decide what study method works best for you. Do you prefer to highlight in the book as you study and then go back over the highlighted portions? Or do you type out notes of the important information? Or is it helpful to make flashcards that you can carry with you? Assemble the pens, index cards, highlighters, post-it notes, and any other materials you may need so you won't be distracted by getting up to find things while you study.

If you're having a hard time retaining the information or organizing your notes, experiment with different methods. For example, try color-coding by subject with colored pens, highlighters, or post-it notes. If you learn better by hearing, try recording yourself reading your notes so you can listen while in the car, working out, or simply sitting at your desk. Ask a friend to quiz you from your flashcards, or try teaching someone the material to solidify it in your mind.

STEP 4: CREATE YOUR ENVIRONMENT

It's important to avoid distractions while you study. This includes both the obvious distractions like visitors and the subtle distractions like an uncomfortable chair (or a too-comfortable couch that makes you want to fall asleep). Set up the best study environment possible: good lighting and a comfortable work area. If background music helps you focus, you may want to turn it on, but otherwise keep the room quiet. If you are using a computer to take notes, be sure you don't have any other windows open, especially applications like social media, games, or anything else that could distract you. Silence your phone and turn off notifications. Be sure to keep water close by so you stay hydrated while you study (but avoid unhealthy drinks and snacks).

Also, take into account the best time of day to study. Are you freshest first thing in the morning? Try to set aside some time then to work through the material. Is your mind clearer in the afternoon or evening? Schedule your study session then. Another method is to study at the same time of day that you will take the test, so that your brain gets used to working on the material at that time and will be ready to focus at test time.

STEP 5: STUDY!

Once you have done all the study preparation, it's time to settle into the actual studying. Sit down, take a few moments to settle your mind so you can focus, and begin to follow your study plan. Don't give in to distractions or let yourself procrastinate. This is your time to prepare so you'll be ready to fearlessly approach the test. Make the most of the time and stay focused.

Of course, you don't want to burn out. If you study too long you may find that you're not retaining the information very well. Take regular study breaks. For example, taking five minutes out of every hour to walk briskly, breathing deeply and swinging your arms, can help your mind stay fresh.

As you get to the end of each chapter or section, it's a good idea to do a quick review. Remind yourself of what you learned and work on any difficult parts. When you feel that you've mastered the material, move on to the next part. At the end of your study session, briefly skim through your notes again.

But while review is helpful, cramming last minute is NOT. If at all possible, work ahead so that you won't need to fit all your study into the last day. Cramming overloads your brain with more information than it can process and retain, and your tired mind may struggle to recall even previously learned information when it is overwhelmed with last-minute study. Also, the urgent nature of cramming and the stress placed on your brain contribute to anxiety. You'll be more likely to go to the test feeling unprepared and having trouble thinking clearly.

So don't cram, and don't stay up late before the test, even just to review your notes at a leisurely pace. Your brain needs rest more than it needs to go over the information again. In fact, plan to finish your studies by noon or early afternoon the day before the test. Give your brain the rest of the day to relax or focus on other things, and get a good night's sleep. Then you will be fresh for the test and better able to recall what you've studied.

STEP 6: TAKE A PRACTICE TEST

Many courses offer sample tests, either online or in the study materials. This is an excellent resource to check whether you have mastered the material, as well as to prepare for the test format and environment.

Check the test format ahead of time: the number of questions, the type (multiple choice, free response, etc.), and the time limit. Then create a plan for working through them. For example, if you have 30 minutes to take a 60-question test, your limit is 30 seconds per question. Spend less time on the questions you know well so that you can take more time on the difficult ones.

If you have time to take several practice tests, take the first one open book, with no time limit. Work through the questions at your own pace and make sure you fully understand them. Gradually work up to taking a test under test conditions: sit at a desk with all study materials put away and set a timer. Pace yourself to make sure you finish the test with time to spare and go back to check your answers if you have time.

After each test, check your answers. On the questions you missed, be sure you understand why you missed them. Did you misread the question (tests can use tricky wording)? Did you forget the information? Or was it something you hadn't learned? Go back and study any shaky areas that the practice tests reveal.

Taking these tests not only helps with your grade, but also aids in combating test anxiety. If you're already used to the test conditions, you're less likely to worry about it, and working through tests until you're scoring well gives you a confidence boost. Go through the practice tests until you feel comfortable, and then you can go into the test knowing that you're ready for it.

Test Tips

On test day, you should be confident, knowing that you've prepared well and are ready to answer the questions. But aside from preparation, there are several test day strategies you can employ to maximize your performance.

First, as stated before, get a good night's sleep the night before the test (and for several nights before that, if possible). Go into the test with a fresh, alert mind rather than staying up late to study.

Try not to change too much about your normal routine on the day of the test. It's important to eat a nutritious breakfast, but if you normally don't eat breakfast at all, consider eating just a protein bar. If you're a coffee drinker, go ahead and have your normal coffee. Just make sure you time it so that the caffeine doesn't wear off right in the middle of your test. Avoid sugary beverages, and drink enough water to stay hydrated but not so much that you need a restroom break 10 minutes into the test. If your test isn't first thing in the morning, consider going for a walk or doing a light workout before the test to get your blood flowing.

Allow yourself enough time to get ready, and leave for the test with plenty of time to spare so you won't have the anxiety of scrambling to arrive in time. Another reason to be early is to select a good seat. It's helpful to sit away from doors and windows, which can be distracting. Find a good seat, get out your supplies, and settle your mind before the test begins.

When the test begins, start by going over the instructions carefully, even if you already know what to expect. Make sure you avoid any careless mistakes by following the directions.

Then begin working through the questions, pacing yourself as you've practiced. If you're not sure on an answer, don't spend too much time on it, and don't let it shake your confidence. Either skip it and come back later, or eliminate as many wrong answers as possible and guess among the remaining ones. Don't dwell on these questions as you continue—put them out of your mind and focus on what lies ahead.

Be sure to read all of the answer choices, even if you're sure the first one is the right answer. Sometimes you'll find a better one if you keep reading. But don't second-guess yourself if you do immediately know the answer. Your gut instinct is usually right. Don't let test anxiety rob you of the information you know.

If you have time at the end of the test (and if the test format allows), go back and review your answers. Be cautious about changing any, since your first instinct tends to be correct, but make sure you didn't misread any of the questions or accidentally mark the wrong answer choice. Look over any you skipped and make an educated guess.

At the end, leave the test feeling confident. You've done your best, so don't waste time worrying about your performance or wishing you could change anything. Instead, celebrate the successful completion of this test. And finally, use this test to learn how to deal with anxiety even better next time.

> **Review Video: Test Anxiety**
> Visit mometrix.com/academy and enter code: 100340

Important Qualification

Not all anxiety is created equal. If your test anxiety is causing major issues in your life beyond the classroom or testing center, or if you are experiencing troubling physical symptoms related to your anxiety, it may be a sign of a serious physiological or psychological condition. If this sounds like your situation, we strongly encourage you to seek professional help.

Additional Bonus Material

Due to our efforts to try to keep this book to a manageable length, we've created a link that will give you access to all of your additional bonus material:

mometrix.com/bonus948/mft

Made in the USA
Las Vegas, NV
24 February 2024

86248579R00149